THE ANCIENT AMERICAN
CIVILIZATIONS

Friedrich Katz is Morton D. Hull Professor of Latin American History at the University of Chicago and Director of its Center for Mexican Studies. He studied in the United States, Mexico and Austria, and then taught Latin American anthropology and history at the Humboldt University in Berlin for fourteen years. In 1968-9 he was visiting professor at the National University of Mexico, and in 1970-1 at the University of Texas, Austin. He has published several books and a large number of articles on Aztec social organisation, as well as on historical problems of twentieth-century Latin America.

THE
ANCIENT AMERICAN
CIVILIZATIONS

Friedrich Katz

PHOENIX
PRESS

PHOENIX PRESS
5 UPPER SAINT MARTIN'S LANE
LONDON WC2H 9EA

A PHOENIX PRESS PAPERBACK

First published in Great Britain
by Weidenfeld & Nicolson in 1972
This paperback edition published in 2000
by Phoenix Press,
a division of The Orion Publishing Group Ltd,
Orion House, 5 Upper St Martin's Lane,
London WC2H 9EA

First published in Germany in 1969 by
Kinder Verlag under the title of
Vorkolumbische Kulturen

A CIP catalogue record for this book
is available from the British Library.

Printed and bound in Great Britain by
Butler & Tanner Ltd, Frome and London

ISBN 1 84212 430 7

CONTENTS

v

LIST OF MAPS

FOREWORD

In the history of mankind there are few empires known through historical sources about which such contradictory ideas persist as the realms of the Inca and Aztecs that confronted the Spaniards in America.

The Aztec empire has been described on the one hand as a tribal community like that of the north American Iroquois and on the other as a fully integrated, totalitarian state. Existing views on the Inca are even more diverse. Did they represent a state with Utopian leanings or did their empire take the form of a tyranny with unrestricted control over each phase of the life of its subjects?

Such contradictions arise partly from the swift annihilation of these empires by their Spanish conquerors, hardly any of whom understood their structure or organisation. Perhaps to an even greater extent the divergent views that exist about the Inca and the Aztecs can be traced back to the fact that when foreign conquerors came to change the course of the history of America, both peoples had been ruling the territories they had subjugated for barely a century and extremely rapid changes had been taking place.

The essential aim of this book is to describe the structure and evolution of these empires as well as the life and thought of their inhabitants. At the same time, however, we shall attempt to compare the two empires, both of which were founded and destroyed at virtually the same time.

In no sense can it be said that the Aztec and Inca civilisations were created in a vacuum. Their culture was the result of thousands of years of ancient evolution without a knowledge of which the cultural achievement of these peoples would be incomprehensible. Therefore some of their cultural predecessors will be outlined briefly in this volume, though obviously in no sense can this volume be considered a history of the whole range of ancient American cultures.

I should like to express my thanks to Mrs Monika Huchel and to Mrs Ilse Wisniewski for their help in the preparation of this book. I should also like to thank Professor Juan Brom of Mexico, and Professor Eric Wolf of Ann Arbor, who read parts of the manuscript and whose valuable comments were greatly appreciated.

F.K.

CHAPTER 1

ANCIENT AMERICA: THE SOURCES

The sources available for the study of ancient American history present us with a very marked dichotomy. On the one hand there is the documentary evidence of the rise and fall of cultures that is mostly recorded in writing by their conquerors or at least in their own language. On the other we have the sources covering the much longer span of the pre-Columbian era, which are for the most part untapped and for which we must fall back on the undeciphered scripts of Indian peoples who were present in a small area of ancient America for only a limited period of time, and on the evidence of archaeological remains. Because of this dichotomy for a number of years all cultural achievements have been attributed only to those peoples whose existence was proved by the documentary evidence handed down to us by the *Conquistadores*. Any other cultures which might have existed before these records were dismissed either as non-existent or as unimportant. Since the beginning of the century, however, this situation has changed radically.

Extensive archaeological excavations carried out at the end of the nineteenth century and especially in the twentieth, and whose importance is being recognised more and more, have led to a completely new evaluation of knowledge in this field. They have proved that peoples whose identity and language were hitherto shrouded in obscurity did in fact establish cultures and even empires for which there are no documentary sources or any evidence, left either by the *Conquistadores* or by the Indians who were alive at the time.

For knowledge of these cultures we are therefore driven to the evidence furnished by archaeology. More and more remains are coming to light all the time. New methods, evolved during the last few decades and developed continuously, have made it possible to deduce a great deal more from archaeological evidence than hitherto: the radio-carbon method has enabled us to determine far more accurately than ever before the dates of ruins unearthed by excavation and thanks to modern means of transport we can now undertake digs in regions that were previously virtually inaccessible. It has been possible to uncover extensive archaeological sites which have yielded artefacts, buildings, inscriptions and pictograms. The results of this work are of the utmost value, for it has been possible to delimit the geographical distribution of many cultures and to describe them, and to determine methods of agriculture, manual skills and building construction. In some cases it has even been possible to excavate objects that under normal circumstances very rarely survive the passage of time. Because of the lack of moisture in the sandy deserts of Peru, textiles are still in pristine condition after many centuries, so it is possible to make valuable reconstructions.

In recent years archaeological findings have in part been reinforced and corroborated by linguistic studies. The distribution of languages and language-groups, and philological developments, have often substantiated theories based on archaeological evidence but have sometimes called them into question. Clearly conclusions based solely on archaeology must be limited, for archaeology cannot by itself enable us to reconstruct the course of history; it may sometimes suggest what this was, but it can certainly do no more. Even the interpretation of pictorial representations of events is frequently open to doubt; the events may be historically true, but the pictures may equally well be symbolic: 'Art tends to concern itself chiefly with traditional symbolic themes, which probably always display the greatest resistance to changes.'[1] Archaeology is able to provide the framework for the social and economic organisation of a people. However, the events that have taken place within this framework can only be suggested by the findings of archaeology, especially when a culture has evolved very rapidly and become more sophisticated. The significance of archaeological excavation is greatly enhanced if it can be tied up with documentary sources. Should it ever become possible to decipher Indian scripts, especially that of the Maya, which we shall consider later, a completely different picture of the ancient American cultures might emerge. But this applies only to a few of the cultures that have so far become known through archaeology, for no written sources have been discovered for the majority.

The important developments in the field of archaeology during recent decades have also given rise to a host of new problems. Often certain objects will attract archaeologists to concentrate their work exclusively on unearthing them: 'It is becoming something of a problem to maintain a balance between work on monuments and other types of excavations – so to speak – in view of the attraction that temples and palaces have always exerted over archaeologists, who after all have to create individual reputations and still have to fill museums.'[2]

2

In recent years a new type of grave looter has emerged, who adds greatly to the difficulties of the archaeologist's work. In days gone by these looters were mainly concerned with searching for precious metals, but today increasing numbers of people have come to appreciate the commercial value of archaeological objects. Rich tourists in many American countries are offered a wide variety of archaeological finds, both real and fake. On the credit side this trade does result in the preservation of a good many objects that might otherwise have been thrown away without a moment's thought. But since there is no question of there having been any scholarly excavation, the significance of these objects, whose exact provenance is often not known, is minimal. Much valuable material is destroyed by such methods; priceless sources are robbed of their importance while illegally acquired objects remain in private ownership for long periods of time before scholars become aware of them.

Again some archaeological constructions in populated parts of the country have been deliberately destroyed or laid waste in order to make room for new buildings. Recently government decrees have been introduced to control such destruction, but these are not operative everywhere.

In estimating the significance of archaeological sources it is above all necessary to emphasise that only a part of these sources – probably only a fraction – has so far been systematically analysed. Each fresh excavation adds to our knowledge, and we can certainly expect in the next few years many discoveries that will invalidate much that was hitherto regarded as certain and is still accepted as such today.

Written sources for the history of ancient America can be divided into two groups, the first of which covers all inscriptions made before the arrival of the Europeans. Such sources are to be found only in Mesoamerica, a region that comprised considerable parts of present-day Mexico and the present Central American states. Two types of evidence are chiefly found – stone inscriptions and picture-writing. While most of the stone inscriptions have been preserved, most of the codices were burned by the Spanish *conquistadores*. The earliest historical evidence to be deciphered was found in the Mixteca region, and especially in the present Mexican state of Oaxaca. It goes back to the seventh century AD. A great many Mayan and Olmec inscriptions, often dating from an even earlier period, have so far hardly been deciphered at all. For a very long time they were thought to be religious or calendrical formulae inscribed on stone, but more recent research indicates that such inscriptions also contain data of historical importance. Should they some day be deciphered, our whole knowledge of Mesoamerica would almost certainly have to be radically revised. Scholars deciphered the first Indian scripts in the second half of the last century and they have made great strides since the beginning of this century. On the other hand the second group of written sources, those that were composed after the Spanish Conquest, has been known for centuries. These annals are of very diverse origin.

1. Recollections, letters and tales written by the Spanish *conquistadores* themselves. Only they had the opportunity of seeing the full flowering of the Aztec and Inca empires that they had overthrown, but most of them possessed neither the ability nor the desire to record their experiences and impressions. But after their conquests had become renowned throughout the world some of them did give verbal reports to historians or chroniclers, who used them to produce more or less exaggerated accounts of the Conquest. López de Gomara and Oviedo y Valdés were two such writers.[3] There were, however, exceptions, both among the *conquistadores* of Mexico and those of Peru – men who were at pains to set down their experiences in writing – and the most gifted writers and observers were to be found in the ranks of the expeditionary forces in Mexico. The most important of these were Cortés himself and the chronicler Bernal Diaz del Castillo.[4] The Conquest of the Incas as recalled by Pedro Pizarro (cousin of the conqueror of the Inca Empire) pales in comparison with the exactitude and penetration of the observations of Cortés and Diaz del Castillo, as do the descriptions given by two of the *conquistadores*, Miguel de Estete and Francisco de Jerez.[5]

However informative these reports may be, they do have their limitations. This is not only because the *conquistadores* were hardly in a position, with the best will in the world, to understand the mental processes and mode of life of their adversaries, but also because only certain aspects of the conquered territories with which they were immediately in contact were of interest to the occupying forces. These aspects – methods of warfare, wealth and the external impressions created by various cities – are dealt with by the *conquistadores* in great detail. But even these sections must be treated with a certain amount of circumspection: the *conquistadores* were naturally enough concerned to show their deeds in a favourable light, and thus liable to exaggerate the value of the territories they had conquered and to make out that their opponents were stronger than they in fact were. In spite of this no specialist can afford to dispense with these records. No account could make a stronger impression by its graphic description and power of expression than Bernal Diaz del Castillo's description of the first sight the *conquistadores* had of the magnificent capital city of the Aztecs, Tenochtitlan.[6]

2. Comprehensive accounts of the life, social and economic organisation, religion and history of the conquered peoples are contained in the reports made by chroniclers and written down in the early decades

following the Conquest. These chroniclers were, for the most part, members of religious orders who had come to the New World to convert the Indians to the Catholic faith. With this end in view they learned the Indian languages, questioned countless people with information to give and wrote exhaustive reports based on their answers. One of the most distinguished of the chroniclers is undoubtedly the Franciscan priest Bernardino de Sahagun, who gave a detailed account of all aspects of life in the kingdom of the Aztecs in his *General History of New Spain*.[7] Sahagun used methods of investigation that were far in advance of his time and show his scholarly approach. He questioned countless people, compared their statements and recorded them as far as possible exactly as they had been made to him. When studying these reports the present-day reader must bear in mind that the authors were forced to use the terminology of their day and of the society in which they lived.[8] Hence the various Indian leaders became 'barons' or 'counts' and their deities are of course referred to as demons and devils. It is not only the desire to convert the Indians to the Catholic faith that accounts for the number of ecclesiastical chroniclers, but also the fact that the Church, or at any rate certain circles in the hierarchy of the clergy, hoped in those first years after the Conquest to turn the regions dominated by the Aztecs into a sort of Church state, such as the Jesuits founded later in Paraguay.

After these efforts had foundered in Mexico the clergy seem to have given up hope in Peru. There were therefore many more lay reporters here than in New Spain. Pedro Cieza de León is one of the most outstanding writers on Peru.[9] He swept through the country as a soldier after the Conquest, in the first half of the sixteenth century. He wrote a detailed study of the history and social institutions of the country, some of which, at any rate, were still in existence at that date. While Sahagun and Cieza de León display a certain sympathy for the countries on which they reported, other Spanish commentators showed a distinct revulsion. This, reinforced by their unfavourable reporting on the Inca and Aztec cultures, was intended to provide a justification for the Conquest. The accounts of the pre-Columbian development of the country given by Pedro Sarmiento de Gamboa on the instructions of the viceroy of Peru are particularly good examples of this attitude.[10]

Some of these records were published within the lifetime of their authors, while others were made available only to a limited readership. Others have remained hidden and unread in various archives. Some have only been discovered and published in the last few decades and it is possible that further investigation in the archives will bring to light some reports that are not so far known at all.

3. Of a completely different nature from the accounts given by the

5

chroniclers, which cover all aspects of the life of the Indians, are the communications of Spanish officials to their authorities about specific matters, for the most part aspects of the social and economic life of the Indian states. Even after the Conquest, the social order of the Indians survived at first mostly unchanged and they maintained many of their institutions. In order to be able to take over the heritage of the Indian leaders, the Spanish conquerors were obliged to find out exactly how those institutions had once functioned. Officials were therefore dispatched to various regions and instructed to carry out surveys, using questionnaires with which they were provided. The results varied considerably and depended to a large extent on the ability and psychological insight of the officials concerned. Thus some of these accounts are superficial and meaningless, whereas others are highly significant. Among the latter are the descriptions of Oidor Alonso de Zurita,[11] who went way beyond his own field, giving a comprehensive account of the land-tenure systems of the Aztecs. His report was published in the nineteenth century. Various others were never printed and some – like the detailed report on an important mountain province of the empire of the Inca by the Spanish Government official Garci Diez de San Miguel,[12] made a few years after its conquest by the Spaniards – have only recently been discovered in the archives of Mexico, Peru or Spain. It may certainly be assumed that there are many unsuspected reports of this kind still hidden in the archives.

Accounts concerning certain aspects of pre-Spanish administration, such as tribute money or the tax levy by the Chiefs of State, are of particular importance. On the basis of these reports it is possible to make not only a descriptive analysis of the social and economic administration of the great pre-Spanish empire but also a detailed, quantitative one. The American historians Borah and Cook[13] made an analysis of reports of this kind a few years ago, establishing important hypotheses about population figures in the Aztec empire on the eve of the invasion and also attempting to assess the actual numbers of people belonging to the individual social strata. There is no need to emphasise the inestimable value of such an analysis to scholarship.

4. Statements made by the descendants of the former rulers of the great empires, trained by the Spaniards and raised to noble rank, form a special group of sources. These writers naturally strove to emphasise to their new masters the glory and power of their ancestors and at the same time to point out that their position had been in no way inferior to that of the Spanish nobility who were now the rulers.

The most important Indian historians of this type in Mexico are Fernando de Alva Ixtlilxochitl[14] a descendant of the last ruler of Texcoco, and Alvarado Tezozomoc,[15] who was related to the rulers of Tenochtitlan. In Peru, Garcilaso de la Vega,[16] a descendant of the

Inca, is an outstanding example. These men were not only familiar with the history of their people, but were gifted writers and produced works that stood out from the dry and detailed reports of many of the Spanish chroniclers. They undoubtedly give an idealised picture of the pre-Spanish empires. The fate of these historians as writers of history, especially Ixtlilxochitl and Garcilaso de la Vega, follows very much the same pattern. For years their works were praised to the skies, only to be condemned later with equal intensity. Today we can look at these studies more realistically. The large number of new sources found after the nineteenth century that shed light on the life and evolution of the ancient American civilisations makes it possible to subject the work of these Indian historians to really critical examination and we can now extract the core of truth in these works from the exaggerations in which it is embedded, for the benefit of scholarship.

5. After the conquest of the ancient American empires many myths, legends and religious observances were recorded either in picture-writing or in Spanish, in Latin or even in the Indian languages. Sometimes, it is true, these early annals already show signs of European influence, but they are nevertheless exceedingly important both for the reconstruction of the past – especially the myths – and for an understanding of the mentality of the ancient American peoples. The records of Mayan myths and traditions in the books of Chilam Balam de Chumayel[17] are of special significance here. The many picture-writings written by former chroniclers and scribes of the Aztec Court after the Conquest present a rich picture of the traditions and history of the Aztec empire.

6. Indian societies were certainly modified by the Spanish Conquest, but they were not immediately destroyed. The Spaniards tried to take over a number of Indian institutions, such as land-tenure, social organisation and the payment of tribute money. Spanish administrators and judges were specifically directed to adopt these measures. The social and economic organisation of the pre-Spanish empire is amply recorded, particularly in legal and administrative documents, but only a few of these have been published so far. This is partly because insufficient interest was shown in them and partly because it is quite impossible to publish the very large number of laws, minutes and decrees, since hundreds of volumes would be required. For years therefore such sources were hardly taken into account by scholars. It is only recently that these legal and administrative decrees have received close examination. The highly important data obtained in this way have transformed much of the knowledge hitherto available. The research carried out by a whole series of scholars – we shall name here only Borah, Cook,[18] Gibson[19] and Carrasco who researched extensively in Mexican archives, and Murra[20] who did the same in Peru – has made it possible for the

7

first time not only to give subjective descriptions of the social and economic conditions prevailing on the eve of the Conquest but to substantiate these with figures, some of which are definitive statistical analyses.

CHAPTER 2

THE ORIGINS OF THE NATIVE POPULATION OF AMERICA AND OF THE AMERICAN CULTURES

When Columbus landed on American soil on the island of Guanahani on 12 October 1492 and saw its native inhabitants, he called them Indians, for he was convinced that he had reached India. From that moment until the present day the controversy over the origin of the aboriginal inhabitants of the American continent has persisted. Arguments are carried on on two distinct levels, which have little bearing upon each other.[1]

The first type of controversy arose between laymen (generally visionaries) on the one hand and scholars on the other. The second type of argument was waged – and still is – by scholars and concerns the origin of the high cultures of ancient America, rather than the origin of the people. If we start considering the huge number of fantastic theories that have been woven round the origins of the American people down to this day, our first reaction is one of total confusion, for there are dozens of widely varying hypotheses that are both unproven and unprovable.

The reasons for this lively interest in a problem that to the outsider may well appear to be of no particular importance are very varied and cannot be reduced to a common denominator. With some writers it is a case of sheer sensationalism, while others are concerned with theories of race and yet others with religious concepts or problems of nationalism. Serious archaeological research did not begin until the nineteenth century and this fact tended to encourage these fanciful theories. A great deal was written on them before the writers were in a position to exploit fully the resources of the material available. The ideas that follow emerge from an analysis of the most important of these theories.

In 1924 Elliot Smith[2] published a work in which he asserted that all the cultures in the world stemmed from the Egyptians. He put forward the hypothesis that the Egyptians migrated to the continent of America and founded the civilisations of Middle and South America there.

A theory that the inhabitants of America were the descendants of the population of a submerged continent found more favour, though those

9

who support this theory argue among themselves as to the identity of the continent in question. For instance Gladwin, an American, and Le Plongeon, a Frenchman,[3] were firmly convinced that in the Atlantic Ocean there once existed a continent called Atlantis, which had a highly developed civilisation. Basing their argument on Plato's description of the sinking of this mythical continent they imagined that the aboriginal peoples of America were able to save themselves in time and to transfer the civilisation of their lost continent to America. When interest in the theory of Atlantis had been exhausted, other writers seized on a new idea: the ancient American civilisations were no longer said to have come from Atlantis, but from Mu or Lemuria, other mythical continents. Both were imagined to be somewhere in the Pacific and it was presumed that they too had been submerged.[4]

Some authors completely refute these theories and uphold a totally different one: they believe that the native inhabitants of America were not emigrants from mythical and vanished continents, but the descendants of the thirteen lost tribes of Israel mentioned in the Bible.[5] The most distinguished representative of this school of thought was an English nobleman, Lord Kingsborough, who devoted his whole life to demonstrating the truth of this connection. He devoted both his time and his entire fortune to this end. The publication and printing of Indian picture-writing was so costly that Kingsborough was finally unable to pay the debts he had incurred and found himself in the debtors' prison in London, where he died in penury.[6] In comparison with the theories of other visionaries, Kingsborough's obsession did at least have some useful consequences, for the significance of the first publication of important picture-writings for authentic scholarly research into these ancient documents must not be underestimated.

The belief that the Indians derived from the lost tribes of Israel is still part of the official dogma of the Mormon Church in the USA.[7]

None of these beliefs or theories is accepted by scholars nowadays. The existence of lost continents thousands of years ago has been refuted by historians and ridiculed by geologists. As far as the lost tribes of Israel are concerned, there is neither chronological nor cultural evidence of connections of any kind with America. Apart from this, historians have only recently determined where these tribes went to and concluded that they most likely underwent a process of assimilation.

Smith's theory that the ancient American cultures, together with all the other cultures of the world, had their origins in Egypt is equally unacceptable today. Contemporary research into the origins of cultures lying geographically closer to Egypt, for instance in the Middle East and in parts of Europe and Asia, rules out the possibility that they derived from Egypt. It is therefore all the more unlikely to be the case for America, since there were great differences in time, the similarities were negligible, and communications in that period made contact on a large scale impossible.

The second theory, which was also put forward in the nineteenth century and was postulated by the Argentinian anthropologist Fernando Amenghino,[8] contrasted strongly with the above beliefs. After the discovery of a few human remains in Argentina Amenghino maintained that man had originated on the American continent and took his discovery to be a proof of this. He then stretched the theory and stated that human beings outside the American continent must have migrated from America. Amenghino's ideas have scarcely any adherents today. It turned out in fact that the human remains he found were of very recent date.[9] Above all there are two reasons why it is highly improbable that man originated on the American continent: no prehistoric types of man such as Sinanthropos in China or Neanderthal Man in Europe have been discovered in America and there are no anthropoid apes, or remains of such apes, in America.

In contrast to all these more or less fantastic beliefs, however, there are certain ideas that are held by almost all scholars concerned with the origins of the American peoples.[10]

The primitive races of America originated in Asia. This theory is supported by the results of research carried out on the basis of physical anthropology. The peoples of ancient America bear striking physical resemblances to the Mongolian peoples of Asia. Research in physical anthropology is widely supported by geography and archaeology. The Behring Strait between Alaska and Siberia is the most favourable crossing place from the Old to the New World. In good weather it is even possible to see the coast of Alaska from Siberia. Geologists assume, however, that there was a land-bridge joining the two continents during the last Ice Age, which made the crossing easy. Archaeology also supports these geographical premises. The earliest archaeological remains have been found in the north and not in the south of the American continent, and the nearer the Behring Strait the more ancient the remains.

There is not quite the same agreement on the date when the aboriginal Americans migrated into America or on the parts of Asia from which they came as there is on their origin.

For a long time it was assumed that migration from the Old World to the New took place about ten or fifteen thousand years ago. In the territories comprising the present USA, arrow-heads have sometimes been found in close association with remains of bones of animals that are extinct today, such as mammoths. To begin with, some archaeologists thought that these remains must be many tens of thousands of years old, since the corresponding animal species had in fact been extinct in the Old World for several tens of thousands of years. But fresh analyses carried out by the radio-carbon method have proved that they are of much more recent date and that animal species that had become extinct in the Old World survived for a much longer period in the New World. Today it is presumed that these cultures of primitive hunters, named according to the sites where arrow-heads were found (Clovis, Sandia, Folson), go back to up to fifteen thousand years. Within a period of at most five thousand years populations of this cultural level must have spread over the whole of the American continent, for at the southernmost tip of South America, in Patagonia, similar arrow-heads have been found that are ten thousand years old. As far as it is possible to judge from these finds, these people were skilled in hunting large animal species that existed in America, and they had already mastered a fairly advanced technique for working stone, which can be seen above all in the way the arrow-heads are fashioned.

Are we in fact concerned here with the most ancient human species in America? More recent finds, such as those in Tule Springs in the USA and in some territories in South America, give cause to doubt this, for they suggest the existence of far more ancient cultures. Remains of blunt stone implements that reveal a far less developed technique of stone-working than that of the primitive hunters referred to above have come to light. The significance of these finds is hotly contested, but they have at any rate led some scholars to the conclusion that man has existed in America for thirty-five to fifty thousand years.[11] Many believe that further finds may show that he has been in existence there for even longer.

There has been much discussion as to what these migrating peoples brought with them from Asia when they crossed the Behring Strait. Did the more skilled type of stone-working develop on the American mainland or did new groups of immigrants bring their skills with them from Asia? The age of these finds and their similarities with parallel cultures in the Old World have made many experts think that the early hunting tribes already possessed these skills when they infiltrated from Asia. One factor on which almost all scholars are agreed is that it is improbable that there were any farmers among those who crossed the Behring Strait. Agriculture, as we shall see in due course, was developed in areas of America many thousands of miles away from Alaska and with the use of completely different species of plants from those cultivated in the Old World.

The exact country of origin of the various migrating groups from Asia to Latin America is still very much a topic for discussion. Some take Siberia to be the cradle of the most important cultures while others hold the view that the migrants came from Central Asia, or from the southern part of Eastern Asia, infiltrating along the Pacific coast.[12] One thing, however, is certain: the people who came to America from Asia were not members of any one racial group. They came from regions far removed from each other and were from the outset of very different physical appearance. Some anthropologists count up to eight different racial groups among those who infiltrated into America. Linguists have produced similar evidence: Swadesh reckons that there are 110 languages or language groups in the American continent, none of which bears any resemblance to another[13]; other scholars speak of 125 languages with 600 dialects.[14] However the divergences of opinion among scholars concerning the migration from Asia and its attendant problems – the date, its extent and the migrants' country of origin – bear no comparison with the deep-rooted differences that arose concerning later contacts between the Old World and the New. Was contact between the Old World and the New limited to those who crossed the Behring Strait or was there contact across the sea? We have already mentioned fantastic notions about Atlantis and migration from the lands of Egypt; but the theory held by several scholars today, that close relations existed between the kingdoms of the Far East and South-East Asia and the early civilisations of the American continent, is on a totally different level.

The first protagonists of this theory were the representatives of a school of ethnology known as the Vienna School. They started from the conviction that all discoveries made by mankind throughout history have been made once and only once, and have later been made beneficially accessible to all other peoples by a process of diffusion. 'Is it not taxing our credulity too far to try to persuade us that whole series of involved techniques, such as metal casting, the extraction of tin from ore, the making of alloys from copper and tin, the dyeing of gold by chemical means, weaving, ikat and batik, were miraculously discovered twice, once in the Old World and once in America?'[15] asks one of the Vienna School's most illustrious sons, Robert Heine-Geldern. Heine-Geldern and an American archaeologist, Gordon Ekholm, have demonstrated a whole number of technical and stylistic resemblances between the cultures of the Old World and those of the New. They range from the use of pyramids as bases for temples, which can be seen in similar forms in Mesoamerica and in Cambodia, or motifs such as the lotus blossom in India and among the Maya, or resemblances in the motifs adopted in fashioning jade objects to the identity of techniques that we have already mentioned.[16] The accompanying illustrations on page 14 give a few examples.

Other scholars do not accept the theory of diffusion but have demonstrated certain resemblances between the Old and New Worlds. Paul Kirchhoff, for instance, points to striking similarities between the religious sytems in India, China and Central America.[17] Biologists

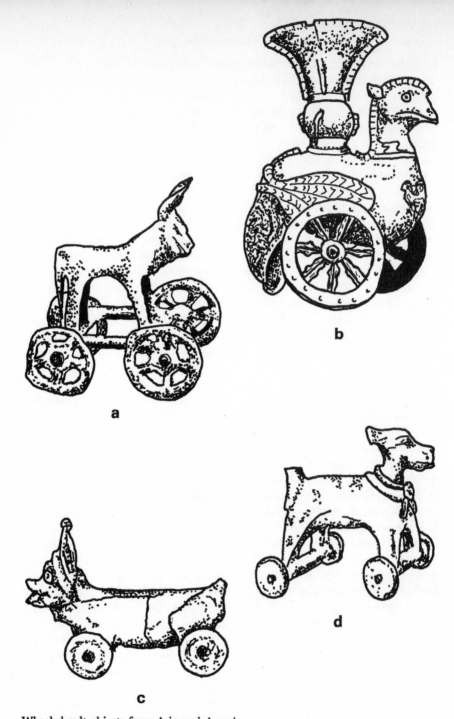

Wheeled cult objects from Asia and America:
a) Phoenicia, b) China, Han Dynasty, c) Panuco, Mexico, d) Tres Zapotes, Veracruz, Mexico.

have demonstrated links between cultivated plants in Asia and America. The American cotton plant, for instance, is defined by a number of biologists as a cross between an American species of wild cotton and another species that is widespread in South-East Asia.[18] The sweet potato indigenous to the uplands of South America is also found in Polynesia and the same can be said for *Lagenaria,* which was known both in the Old World, particularly in Asia, and in pre-Spanish Peru.[19]

Do all these similarities really point to links between the Old World and the New in pre-Columbian times? Robert Heine-Geldern is firmly convinced that they do and has made an attempt to draw up a chronological sequence for such links. In his view the Asiatic emigrants must first have filtered into America from the Far East and from Indonesia between 2000 and 1000 BC. His views are based partly on the great similarities between the pottery of Japan and that of certain parts of present-day Ecuador, which were pointed out by the archaeologists Meggers and Evans. Later influxes must have come, in the next few centuries, from the central and southern provinces of China, in particular from the old coastal provinces of Wu and Yueh. After the conquest of Yueh by the inland province of Chu in 332 BC journeys to South America by the Chinese inhabitants of the coastal areas seem to have ceased. Heine-Geldern presumes that they were followed mainly by representatives of the Bronze Age Dongson culture of Tongking and Annam. These expeditions ended with the destruction of the Dongson culture when Tongking and North Annam were destroyed by the Chinese in the middle of the first century AD. The Chinese crossings to America were then followed by those of the Hindus. Heine-Geldern believes that these were in fact probably Indian merchants and Brahmin and Buddhist missionaries, who had settled in Indochina and Indonesia. These Asiatic-American links continued until about AD 1200, when the Kingdom of Khmer was destroyed.[20]

Heine-Geldern's views have been vehemently attacked by his opponents: if there were in fact such enduring and close links between ancient America and the Old World, how is it that hitherto not a single object of Asiatic provenance has been discovered in America and conversely not a single object of American origin has been found in Asia? How is it that no evidence is to be found in Chinese or Indian sources of such odysseys? How is it that all the elements typical of Old World cultures – the true arch, the wheel, the cart, the plough, the potter's wheel, bellows, glass, iron and stringed instruments – are missing in the New World, and that the most important domestic animals and cultivated plants, such as rice, known in the Old World are not known there?[21]

A number of scholars also doubt whether such far-flung journeys were possible in view of the level of sailing techniques known at that time;

for example, the compass had not been invented. Above all, they cast doubts on the theoretical premises of the diffusionists. Need similarities in the realm of the arts necessarily presuppose contact? At the Congress of Americanists held in Mexico in 1960, the Mexican scholar Alfonso Caso, in a dramatic encounter with Heine-Geldern, showed some motifs in art belonging to cultures that were separated from each other by thousands of years yet exhibited amazing similarities, although logically they could have had no possible relationship with each other.[22] He took this to prove that similarities of style in art do not necessarily signify contact.

Besides, those who oppose the diffusionist theory and reject the suggestion that cultural links existed between the Old and New Worlds emphasise that hitherto, with few exceptions, known links have affected only individual cultural elements and that it is never possible to cite whole systems that take us from a self-contained area in the Old World to a self-contained area in the New World. Lastly, if we suppose that links did in fact exist, the question of whether small groups of missionaries or merchants would have been in a position to introduce a whole civilisation into America keeps on cropping up. Had it been a matter of conquest things would of course have been different; but even those who think that such a link did exist do not assume that there was a conquest, for it is clear that there would have been considerably more evidence if this were the case. Despite this, they contest the validity of such arguments. They feel that logically there could have been cultural elements in the Old World that were not adopted in the New. One culture is never absorbed by another *in toto*. In addition, the seafarers who crossed from the Old World to the New were missionaries and merchants, and not peasants, and would accordingly have introduced agricultural products in limited quantities only. Heine-Geldern affirms that the true arch, which was unknown in America, was also unknown for a long time in parts of Asia. The wheel and the plough were not used in the New World simply because there were no draught animals. Those who think that there was contact between the two worlds can produce small wheeled objects that were made in Mesoamerica: these were at first taken for toys but are now considered to be cult objects. The inhabitants of ancient America, or at least of Central America, were therefore familiar with the principle of the wheel.

Heine-Geldern rejects his opponents' views on ancient sailing techniques and draws attention to the skill with which Indian seamen were able to cross the Indian Ocean. He concludes that it was also possible to cross the Pacific. The case of the seventeen negroes shipwrecked in the sixteenth century who rose to become governors of an Indian kingdom on the coast of Ecuador clearly shows that even small groups could exercise a decisive cultural influence.

The discussion continues unabated and neither side has so far been in a position to dismantle the other's arguments conclusively. At the same time, both sides have produced significant evidence. Gordon Ekholm, one of the most distinguished representatives of the diffusionist school of thought, has produced the best summary of the present state of the controversy: 'We all know that the diffusionist position is still in the experimental stage and that so far no really solid line of reasoning that is beyond all doubt can be used.'[23]

There has been a marked change of emphasis in the nature of the discussion today, for many non-diffusionist scholars do now accept that there was some cultural link between the Old World and the New, though they do not agree with the premises of the diffusionists. They feel that further research will quite possibly reveal that this link was closer and more comprehensive than was previously realised. But they deny that the civilisations of ancient America arose as a result of the influence of the Old World.

The rise of a civilisation presupposes the existence of certain social and economic conditions: agriculture on a scale that enables surplus products to be made, so that a stratum of specialists or a ruling class can be supported, a certain density of population, and so on. Such conditions can of course be introduced from outside when a conquest has taken place or when there has been immigration on a large scale. There is no evidence of this, however, and nor do any of the diffusionists think that this happened. Agriculture on the American continent certainly originated inside America itself and factors such as population density cannot be conjured up from outside. Only when these conditions already exist can outside influences be absorbed and then doubtless determine the direction, rapidity and type of evolution of a civilisation. The rise of a state, on the other hand, must be adapted to its environment. To quote Julian Steward and David Faron:

It is conceivable that the entire technology and, in fact, a preponderance of cultural traits might have been derived from Asia; and yet the social and political forms would have to develop locally as the population increased and evolved new types of interpersonal arrangements . . . That the native upper classes adopted litters, stools, or umbrellas as insignia of status, that certain art motifs found local appeal, that specific religious concepts were found useful is quite understandable. Such traits diffused within the New World, and very likely some may have found their way across the Pacific. But they did not create the basic patterns. They constituted no more than superficial embellishments.[24]

Recently these theories have been decisively reinforced. In a book that appeared in 1965, Robert McC. Adams[25] tried to compare urban development in two regions that had revealed a number of social and economic similarities but which could not have been associated with each other. One of these regions was Mesopotamia between 3900 and 2300 BC and the other was the high Valley of Mexico from the beginning of the Christian era to the Spanish Conquest, up to AD 1519. These two cultures are so far removed from each other, both geographically and chronologically, that any direct connection is out of the question. Adams reveals a striking similarity in urban development, which can only be attributed to similar social and economic conditions:

To sum up, the parallel development of the 'State' in Mesopotamia and Mexico, the parallelism in the forms that their institutions eventually took and also in the processes that led to this show that both instances are characterised by a common core comprising features that appear in a regular fashion. We discover once again that social behaviour does not, generally speaking, conform to laws, but to a limited number of laws, a fact that was perhaps always seen as self-evident in the case of cultural sub-systems (such as relationships) and among 'primitive' peoples (such as hunting-bands). This also applies to some of the most complex and most creative of human societies, not just as an abstract article of faith, but as a positive beginning for a detailed empirical analysis.[26]

While the relationship of Asia to Ancient America continues to be the focal point of the discussion, scholars have been far less receptive to the theories of the Norwegian Thor Heyerdahl.[27] Years ago he formed the view that the inhabitants of Tiahuanaco, a mountainous region of present-day Bolivia, made their way over to Asia on rafts in about the sixth century AD and populated the Polynesian islands. Later they mingled with another group of immigrants from the north-west Pacific: this was the origin of the present-day Polynesians. When his theory was greeted with general scepticism, Heyerdahl sought to prove his point by making his way to Polynesia with a few companions on the kind of raft that had demonstrably existed among the Inca before the Spanish Conquest. The crossing succeeded and Heyerdahl gained important recognition for his endurance in this great physical feat. However, he was still able to convince scholars only to a limited degree. He had demonstrated the possibility of crossing from America to Polynesia but he was unable to dispel doubts about his theories that had been expressed earlier. If the Polynesians really do come from America, why do their chronicles record the exact opposite, naming South-East Asia as their place of origin? Why is their language first and foremost related to South-Asiatic and Malayan languages? Finally, as Trimborn remarked, 'Were the Polynesian Vikings, rather than the Indians, not the sailors who crossed the high seas?'[28]

CHAPTER 3

THE BIRTH OF AGRICULTURE IN AMERICA

In 9000 BC the various cultures on the American continent, which was by then colonised down to its southernmost tip, were in no sense uniform. Its inhabitants spoke many languages, mostly unrelated, and differed considerably in their physical appearance. They were alike in only one respect: none of them had any knowledge of either agriculture or cattle breeding. They lived by hunting, food-gathering and fishing, the nature of which varied depending on the environment. These types of 'hunting' extended from big game hunting on the North American plains – hunting species which, like a certain kind of American elephant and horse, have been extinct for thousands of years – to gathering wild plants and fishing. While the big game hunters always led a nomadic life, those who lived by fishing were settled to a very high degree.[1]

Far-reaching climatic changes seem to have taken place on the American continent in about 7000 BC and these might account for the fact that the big game died out.[2] The big game hunters either turned to gathering plants and small game or died out altogether and were succeeded by other peoples who were already living by these means. These severe climatic changes may have provided the incentive in vast areas of America for seeking new forms of nourishment and there is no doubt that this was largely responsible for the development of agriculture.

For many years students of American civilisations tended to find striking similarities between husbandry as it evolved on the American continent and the developing agriculture of the Old World. Gordon Childe, for instance,[3] speaks of a process that he defines as a neolithic revolution. His view is that husbandry was first practised in two or three places in the Old World and then spread very quickly from there. The advantages of this new method of food production very soon became apparent and in a short time husbandry had replaced hunting. A complete break with the past took place: settled village life developed from nomadic groups and there was a rapid population increase. This process is defined by Childe as revolutionary partly because of the short time in which it took place.

It is not relevant here whether Childe's theory, much debated today, can be fully applied to the Old World. For many years it formed the basis for views held by many scholars concerned with research into the origin and rise of American agriculture, which, they maintained, probably developed in one or at the most two regions.[4] Sharp conflicts raged between those who believed that Middle America was the cradle of agriculture and those who thought that it originated in the Andes region. Because scholars felt that the development of husbandry had been very rapid, they placed its beginnings around 1000 or 2000 BC. Recent digs by archaeologists have, however, forced scholars to discard this date and modify their views. Three entirely new theories have been formulated:

1. It has been established that agriculture existed not in one or even two regions in America, but in at least four very different areas. Indeed MacNeish, one of the most distinguished of these archaeologists, considers it highly probable that it existed in a number of other regions as well.[5] The four areas in which husbandry is considered to have originated are the coast of Peru, southern central Mexico, north-east Mexico and the south-west of what is now the United States. In the first place pumpkins seem to have been cultivated in north-east Mexico, sunflowers in the south-west of the United States and nuts on the coast of Peru. MacNeish assumes that a number of plants were introduced simultaneously in various places. Among these is the Chile pepper, which presumably originated in north-east Mexico, southern central Mexico and Peru. The same can be said for amaranth, which could have originated in southern central Mexico, north-east Mexico and the south-west of the United States. MacNeish is convinced that further excavations will reveal new places of origin for the various plants that were cultivated.

2. Agriculture on the American continent goes back much further than hitherto estimated. Husbandry was already known on the coasts of Peru in 4000 BC.[6] Early archaeological discoveries that show this were treated with scepticism by students of American civilisation when they were made in Peru, but excavations in other parts of the continent have both substantiated the theory and also produced evidence that surpasses the earlier finds. MacNeish, who had worked for many years both in north-east Mexico and in southern central Mexico, reached the astounding conclusion that husbandry had been practised in the region of Tehuacan in southern central Mexico for no less than seven thousand years.[7] A similar date was established for the cultivation of pumpkins in the region of Tamaulipas in north-east Mexico, while amaranth was already being cultivated in the south-west of what is now the United

States in 4000 BC. These archaeological discoveries have refuted all theories that tried to fall back on the Old World for the origins of agriculture in the American continent. Those who support this theory have had to concede that the most important agricultural products of the Old World, for instance, wheat, barley and rice, were completely unknown in the New World. But they still believed that the principle of land tillage had come over from the Old World. But if husbandry is of no more recent date in the New World than in the Old, even this theory is no longer valid.

3. The discovery of husbandry did not result in any significant or rapid modification of the lives of the people who practised it. Indeed it played a very minor role in the production of food for three and a half thousand years after its discovery in southern central Mexico.

The husbandmen of this region were primarily hunters and food-gatherers and at the most only ten per cent of their nourishment was derived from agriculture. Three thousand years were to elapse before agricultural products came to form the staple diet of the inhabitants of this region.[8] Almost four thousand years were to elapse from the beginnings of husbandry on the coasts of Peru to the moment when it played a decisive part in feeding these coast-dwellers.[9] MacNeish therefore rightly points out that when contemplating the New World it is necessary to speak not of a neolithic 'revolution' but of a neolithic 'evolution'.[10]

The differences between agriculture in the New and Old Worlds are not confined to such factors as the pace at which it developed or the products that were cultivated. They are also apparent in significant aspects of methods of cultivation. The combination of agriculture and cattle breeding, so characteristic of the Old World, was entirely unknown in the New. There were no draught animals and, except in Peru where bird dung was used, no animal manure was used. The plough was not known until after the European Conquest. The absence of conditions familiar to the Old World led scholars for some time to regard agriculture in America as 'primitive and inferior'. Undoubtedly there was a smaller range of foodstuffs in the New World than in the Old and, because there were no ploughs, agricultural areas that are today reckoned to be among the richest of the American continent were not used at all in the period before the Spanish invasion. But there is no question of agriculture having been 'primitive': not only were more species of plant cultivated in the New World than in the Old, but the extent of agriculture practised in some areas was so great that on the eve of the Spanish Conquest the population density of the great centres of the ancient American cultures, according to the most recent calculations, equalled the most densely populated areas of Europe. Although a recent estimate of eighty to a hundred million for the population of the American continent at this time is vigorously contested,[11] the figure of three hundred thousand[12] for the capital city of the Aztecs, Tenochtitlan, is confirmed by most scholars. The population density of this city exceeded that of Paris or Madrid at the same period.

It must not be assumed from this, however, that agriculture developed evenly throughout America. Even on the eve of the Conquest considerable areas of northern America and some parts of the west and south were inhabited by hunting and food-gathering tribes.

Husbandry and the crops cultivated were marked by great differences both in method and in extent. In many parts of Central and South America a form of slash and burn agriculture was practised that forced population groups dependent on it to adopt a semi-nomadic way of life and excluded the possibility of any dense settlement. By comparison unusually intensive methods of cultivation were practised in the high Valley of Mexico or in the many valleys of Peru, which did lead to very dense settlement.

Marked differences also prevailed in the importance of individual products and the existence of cattle breeding among the cultural centres of ancient America.

CHAPTER 4

THE GEOGRAPHICAL SETTING OF THE ANCIENT AMERICAN CULTURES

Agriculture was the basis of 'civilisations' to use a term generally employed by historians and ethnologists, though closer definitions of it often differ. Gordon Childe, who coined the term 'urban revolution', tried to define the concept of civilisation more clearly and to characterise it by adducing a number of significant features.[1] Among these he includes a growth in the size of settlements to the point at which they become urban; a central accumulation of capital as the result of tribute money or taxation; an ever-increasing proportion of the population being freed from the labour of direct food production; and public works on a grand scale. From a social point of view the most significant feature was the development of the state, accompanied by ever-increasing class differentiation. Tribal organisation is increasingly replaced by territorial organisation. This is then followed by a series of artistic and intellectual achievements: the invention of writing, progress in the field of exact science, the appearance of naturalistic art and the erection of large public buildings. Childe's definition is in some respects open to question today. Which were primary and which secondary factors? Is it possible to define a society as civilisation if it displays some of these features but not others? Which features are indispensable before it is possible to speak of an 'urban revolution'?

Despite these doubts Childe's definition remains the clearest summary of the features that characterise a nascent civilisation.

The evolution of the societies that displayed these features took place in a limited area of ancient America, in two regions: one in the north, generally designated as Middle America by archaeologists and historians, comprising the greater part of present-day Mexico, Guatemala and Honduras; the other, the central Andean region, stretching over large areas of present-day Peru, Bolivia, Ecuador, Argentina and Chile. An evolution towards civilisation also took place in the area of modern Colombia. The rest of America was populated throughout by hunters and food-gathering tribes or peasant village communities, which in some cases adopted elements at random from most of the neighbouring cultures. This book confines itself essentially to describing the evolution of the two areas of high culture, Middle America and the central Andean region. They differ from one another in a very marked degree, yet have natural phenomena of great diversity in common: in both temperate uplands and tropical lowlands exist in close proximity and they both have great mountain ranges running through them.

The area of Mesoamerica extends from 22° to about 10° latitude.[2] In the east it is bounded by the Atlantic Ocean and in the west by the Pacific Ocean. The northern boundary is formed by the sterile, almost desert-like lands of northern Mexico, which were scarcely suitable for agriculture and are no more so today. Until the Spanish Conquest they were exclusively populated by hunting and food-gathering tribes. A few peasants practising agriculture settled only in north-west Mexico, where fertile areas exist. The southern border of Mesoamerica is less ecological than cultural. It was not so much the degree of evolution, as in the north, as the form of evolution that separated the peoples on either side of the Mesoamerican border.

Along both sea coasts there were plains that are still noted for their tropical heat.[3] In this respect both coasts resemble each other. Shortage of water is an essential feature of the west coast. Rainfall is very low and in those parts where rivers flow into the sea they mostly fall from a great height, so steeply that agricultural work on their banks, even when assisted by large-scale irrigation systems, is hardly practicable. There was, nevertheless, a series of areas on the west coast where these factors did not obtain. Conditions suitable for more intensive agriculture and settlement on a larger scale existed in the region of Soconusco, at the neck of the Isthmus of Tehuantepec (in southern Mexico), and in a few areas at the mouths of rivers further north, possibly owing to a difference in the flow of these rivers into the sea at these points or to better rainfall. Water, in very short supply on the west coast, was over-abundant on the east coast of Mesoamerica. The greater part of this east coast is characterised by intensive rainfall and by the presence of great rivers with vast flows of water. This has resulted in the growth of dense tropical vegetation, which is in parts impenetrable jungle, and in the existence of tropical fauna, all of which constitute no less of an obstacle to human settlement than the arid region of the Pacific lowlands. In contrast to the Pacific coast, which is never more than a narrow strip, the east coast broadens out towards the south into a wide plain, the southern area of which is covered by thick tropical primeval forest. The tropical vegetation can be cleared only with difficulty. The soil is quickly exhausted and weeds invariably become rampant. This region is very sparsely settled today, since the inhabitants are subject to malaria and other tropical diseases. It is presumed that Europeans brought these plagues to America and that the situation was different before the Spanish Conquest. Yet one of the greatest, most remarkable and richest cultures of ancient America, that of the Maya, developed in this tropical primeval forest, rather than in, say, the tropical primeval forests of South America. The reasons for this have not yet been established, but a few hypotheses will be examined later.

In the eastern part of the plain the rainfall lessens and the rich tropical vegetation gives way to one of a poorer type. Rainfall is minimal and there are few rivers. But this region, the northern part of the Yucatan peninsula, does contain underground water caverns, *Cenotes*, which are of greater value to agriculture than the sudden rainstorms of the regions lying further west. Even today this region is densely populated.

Both coastal plains are bounded by two great mountain ranges, in the east the Eastern Sierra Madre and on the west coast, the Western Sierra Madre. The mountains are not easily accessible. The railway that crosses them in the east and joins Mexico to the town of Veracruz on the coast is regarded, even today, as a technical miracle. The traveller is regaled with the sight of vertiginous precipices and steep mountain chains, whose summits are covered by eternal snows. These mountains are not penetrated by any river and for years they constituted a great, if not insurmountable barrier to communication. Between both mountain ranges there lie three high plateaux, themselves separated from each other by mountains. They do not form a flat plain, but a jumble of mountains, valleys and rather larger plains. The most important and most fertile of these high plateaux is the high plateau of Mexico, the Mesa Central, where it is thought that a population of between six and twenty million were living on the eve of the Conquest. It is characterised by exceedingly fertile valleys and plains lying between high mountains. At the centre of this high plateau lies the Valley of Mexico with the capital city of the state, which was ecologically and strategically bound to become the capital. A close network of lakes helped to promote an unusually productive agriculture, which facilitated a greater concentration of population in this region than elsewhere. From the strategic point of view armies could take the field in all directions; on the other hand the height at which the valley lies protected them from their enemies.

In the two more southerly plateaux there were also fertile plains and valleys, the Oaxaca Valley on the south central high plateau and the plain of Guatemala to the south of the high plateau. They were not large and their population density never reached that of the high plateau. A wide variety of climate and vegetation characterises this region. Today, when descending from Mexico City, where the climate is temperate and where the vegetation is largely reminiscent of that of

Europe, the traveller finds an almost bewildering change of scenery further down. Three-quarters of an hour's motor ride away, in the Morelos Valley, cotton is cultivated and a little lower down the first stands of banana appear.

The second great cultural centre of ancient America exists on the west coast of South America, in the region of the Andean mountain chain.[4] It embraces the Inca empire as it was before the European Conquest and extends over several present-day South American states, including parts of the north of Argentina and the north of Chile, the greater part of Bolivia, almost the whole of present-day Peru and also the greater part of present-day Ecuador. The region is bounded by the Pacific Ocean in the west and by the tropical primeval forests of the Amazon basin in the east. The southern limit, as in Mesoamerica, was less ecological than cultural. The cultural realm of the Andes stopped where there were heavy concentrations of Araucanian Indians who had succeeded in halting all attempts at invasion, both by the Inca and later by the Spaniards. The Andean chain of Colombia formed the northern limit. If we look at this region from west to east, superficial similarities with Mesoamerica immediately appear. A narrow coastal plain extends along the west coast, rarely wider than 100 kilometres. Thence, like the Sierra Madre in Middle America, there rises the mountain range of the Western Andes. It bounds a high plateau at whose eastern extremity there is a second precipitous mountain chain. On the other side of the eastern mountain range tropical primeval forest extends for thousands of miles to the east coast of South America, which the peoples of the Andean territories have never reached.

Like the high plateau of Mexico the high plateau of Peru consists of largely infertile lands, interspersed with fertile valleys where there are some important lakes. Lake Titicaca lies at a height of 3,812 metres, is 208 kilometres long and 66 kilometres wide and is the highest stretch of navigable water in the world. As in Mesoamerica climate and vegetation differ widely, zones of tropical heat alternating with cold or temperate zones.

As well as these similarities there exist differences whose significance for both history and social development must not be underestimated. In Mesoamerica as in the Andean region, only a fraction of the land – scarcely two per cent[5] in the Andes and rather more in Mesoamerica – was suitable for agriculture. Then again only part of the agricultural land was sufficiently watered by natural rainfall. In both cases irrigation systems were necessary if large areas of these regions were to be cultivated. In Mexico today, which comprises the greater part of what used to be Mesoamerica, 52·1 per cent of the land can scarcely be cultivated at all without irrigation, while only 6·8 per cent receives sufficient rainfall to guarantee successful agriculture.[6] This is still more true of the lowlands of Peru, which are among the driest areas in the world; it hardly ever rains at all, and it is only by regulating the great rivers that flow down from the uplands that these territories can be made agriculturally useful. This is where the differences begin. In Mesoamerica only small systems that could be undertaken by local groups were necessary for irrigation purposes, with the exception of the Valley of Mexico and a few other areas. On the coast of Peru, on the other hand, the control of the rivers required comprehensive and important public works, which could not be carried out by small groups of men. In contrast to the population on the coast, the peoples of the Peruvian uplands needed hardly any irrigation for their staple foodstuffs. The cultivation of maize, however, required irrigation because of the harsh climate and the relatively long period of growth. Because of the terrain these systems had to be constructed on a large scale and built and maintained over vast stretches of territory. The irrigation systems in Mesoamerica, which were for the most part on a small scale, with the exception, as we have seen, of the Valley of Mexico and the tremendous supraregional irrigation systems of the Andean region, led to a differing social organisation which, without doubt, did have some influence on the further evolution of these regions. The differences did not stop here however. While nature had provided the region of the Andes with less fertile soils than Mesoamerica, it more than compensated the former in other ways. Cattle breeding, so painfully lacking in Mesoamerica, was carried on in the Andean region. Large herds of llama and alpaca had been domesticated in the Andes and played a decisive part in providing food, clothing and, in the case of the llama, above all transport. In this way the poor, agriculturally useless regions of the high plateau of the Andes, the Puna, could still be turned into useful soil. Similarly, there is a series of islands lying along the coast of Peru on which sea birds nest; their droppings are known as guano, which is thought to be one of the most important agricultural fertilisers in the Andean region. A massive improvement in the productivity of the neighbouring countryside resulted from the uses of this fertilising agent.

Further differences become apparent in matters of communication and transport. Communications between upland and lowland areas turned out to be much easier in Peru than in Mesoamerica, as a result of the measured flow of the rivers from the mountain areas. In any case, the existence of animals capable of carrying burdens provided transport facilities in the Andean region. Lastly, in contrast to Mesoamerica important cultures of the Andean region had evolved actually on the coast, so that the sea could provide a direct means of communication. In Mesoamerica only Yucatan, which however played a less important role in the whole complex of Mesoamerican culture than the coast of Peru in that of the Andean region, possessed this sort of advantage.

It is therefore no accident that the spread of isolated cultural achievements, of art styles as a whole and of religious movements in the Andean region evolved differently from those in Mesoamerica, and that finally, on the eve of the Spanish Conquest, the Andean region presented a politically unified and socially and economically integrated whole, none of which can be said for Mesoamerica. These circumstances can be attributed to a number of other factors, but the easier transport facilities certainly contributed not a little to this result.

In Mesoamerica there existed another kind of geographical factor, which was very conducive to centralisation. This was the existence of a clear ecological centre, the high plateau of Mexico, which at the time of the conquest sheltered almost forty per cent of the population of Mesoamerica.[7] Within this high plateau, in the region of the Valley of Mexico, there was a considerable concentration of population. This high valley was destined, strategically, economically and by reason of the density of population and of a certain measure of integration that will be examined later, to become the focal point of the political organisation of significant areas of Mesoamerica. Although it was not here that the greatest cultural achievements took place, it was clearly the region, ever since the rise of the high culture of Mexico, from which the most powerful movements towards political integration emanated and the biggest territorial combinations resulted.

An ecological area of this nature did not exist in Peru. The Valley of Cuzco, which eventually became the centre of the Inca Empire, was not a region that had inspired movements towards political integration long before the Inca, as the Valley of Mexico had. From an economic point of view it also played a different role in the Inca Empire from that of the Valley of Mexico in the state of the Aztecs on the eve of the Spanish Conquest.

A detailed account will be given later of the extent to which these decisive geographical and ecological differences were responsible for the difference in the type of evolution that took place in Mesoamerica and in the Andean region.

What factors account for the rapid and vigorous development of these regions? First we must ask ourselves why cultures originated in precisely these regions. Closely bound up with this question is a second, which may perhaps give rise to still more problems. In the Old World the development of big cities, states and empires, the evolution of sciences such as mathematics, astronomy and above all of writing were dependent on the knowledge of certain techniques. Among these must be included metal tools, the invention of the plough and the wheel, and the use of draught animals for agriculture and transport. In the New World, cities, states, empires and science evolved despite the absence of any knowledge of a large number of the technical achievements of the Old World. The plough remained unknown until the arrival of the Europeans, and agriculture was based on the mattock in all regions of America, although its character differed from one region to another. Metallurgy had been developed, though it served both in Mesoamerica and in the Andean region chiefly for the manufacture of personal ornaments. Only copper, bronze to a limited degree and precious metals were known. Iron was never mined. Draught animals existed only in Peru, where they dragged loads of limited size but were never ridden, so that their usefulness was limited. There were no draught animals in Mexico in any case. The wheel was known in Mesoamerica only as a toy, but was never used. The great states and empires of America came into being and significant scientific discoveries were made by primeval peoples who were still living in the Stone Age. It is therefore not surprising that many scholars denied for many years that the building up of empires or the spontaneous development of writing, of the calendar and mathematics was possible on the American continent. Nevertheless, these achievements can be explained.

The most important premise for the rise of states and empires, for the development of science and technology, is the possibility of ensuring big agricultural surpluses above and beyond the requirements of the peasants for their own nourishment. Such surpluses were not attainable without the plough in the regions that are now the granary of America, such as the plains of North America, or those of Argentina. Not until long after the arrival of the Europeans was agriculture developed in those areas. Yet Mesoamerica and the Andean region, of all the regions of the continent, were pre-eminently suited to the practice of intensive agriculture without the plough. On the one hand this may be attributed to the existence in these areas of the most favourable conditions for agriculture dependent on irrigation. On the other hand the high valleys in Mesoamerica and in the Andean region offered the greatest possibilities for productive agriculture without irrigation. Their soil was much more fertile than the apparently fertile regions of the tropical lowlands, where the soil was soon used up and where rank weeds obstructed all attempts at husbandry.[8]

If we compare the possibilities for achieving surpluses in the Old World and in the New, a further factor must be taken into account: the particular productivity of the basic foodstuffs cultivated in America, above all maize and potatoes, and the relatively small amount of labour required for their cultivation. A family of three cultivating maize in parts of Mesoamerica were able, in only 120 days in a year and without irrigation, to produce twice as much as they needed to live on. A Chinese peasant growing rice needed far more time. This fact offered a built-in possibility of having a surplus that exceeded that of many parts of the Old World and encouraged peasants to undertake other work, ranging from public works to military service, while still bearing their full responsibilities as food producers.

Further factors that increased agricultural productivity in ancient America were the ease with which the cultivated foodstuffs, such as maize, could be stored, and the superlative methods of conservation developed by the Indians. From potatoes, which do not lend themselves to prolonged storage, the inhabitants of the Andean highlands had learned to manufacture a product known as *chuñu*,[9] which will keep for years.

As has already been said, the production of agricultural surpluses was the premise underlying the evolution of cultures in the key areas of the American continent. Nothing would be more mistaken or facile, however, than to draw a comparison that would seek to prove that the most important cultural achievements occurred where agricultural productivity was most highly developed. In that case the reason for the very important achievements made in many areas of science, writing, astronomy and mathematics in the region of the Maya, where agricultural productivity was at its lowest, would be wholly obscure. Although an agricultural surplus is a prerequisite for the evolution of a civilisation, its existence does not presuppose *ab initio* that a civilisation will in fact develop. We can therefore say that agricultural productivity was without doubt an important impetus for the evolution of cultures in the key areas of ancient America, but as an argument for such an eventuality it is not sufficient in itself.

One final factor underlying the development of civilisation was the existence of intensive irrigation. Recently many theories have been postulated about its significance. Most authors agree in considering that irrigation does not only advance agricultural productivity very considerably but also encourages civil, administrative integration and compels an intellectual preoccupation with the forces of nature. However, the basic significance of irrigation in this context is questionable.[10] Was it, as some scholars maintain, the basis for the development of the great ancient civilisations? Or was it only one of the many factors that encouraged their evolution? Was it the main cause for the development of states, or did it develop only after states had already come into being? In the course of this study we shall have another opportunity of examining this highly debatable problem. At all events, it may be said that irrigation played a very important part in a great number of cultures, both in Mesoamerica and in the Andean region.

Above and beyond this, the juxtaposition of various ecological areas in Mesoamerica and in the Andean region has an important bearing on the development of their cultures. This not only led to the development of active trading but also forged strong cultural bonds, helped to increase productivity, enabled one region to adopt another's cultural achievements and facilitated conquest. The variation in regions of high and low productivity and the associated high and low concentrations of population undoubtedly led to the conquest of one region by another and thus led to the development of bigger units.

The effective interrelation of these various factors, none of which can be considered definitive *per se*, might explain the fact that 'cultures', as we call them, or 'urban revolutions' as Gordon Childe prefers to call them, were able to evolve in precisely these limited areas of the American continent.

The cultures of the New World are generally divided by archaeologists and historians into three distinct phases of development. The first is known as pre-classic or formative, the second as classic or florescent and the third as post-classic or historical.[11] In the first phase a number of material and intellectual cultural features may be observed and these come to their full flowering in the next phase. This is followed by a period in which the features of the second phase are replaced by those of the third. This latter is regarded as historical because, in contrast to the preceding eras, a significant number of written records is extant, many of which were made after the Spanish Conquest. These three phases do not tell us much. They can do so only when their content is defined in precise terms. But arguments and differences of opinion arise about the supposed content of these three periods or phases. Are we concerned with three periods characterised by a progressive advance in the control of the forces of nature? Are the periods characterised by a progressive increase in the density of population? Was social organisation radically different, in that in the first period there was rule by village communities, in the second by a priesthood and in the third by a military caste? Are we concerned with progressively increasing territorial units, so that in the first phase we have only village communities, in the second city states and in the third empires? Do similarities exist, moreover, between the characteristic features of these phases in Mesoamerica and in the Andean region? Were the forces motivating the transition from one phase to the next internal or external? All these questions, plus that of the demarcation of the separate phases, constitute problems that are most vehemently discussed and contested. In the analysis of Mesoamerica and of the Andean region that follows, an attempt will be made to elucidate such questions.

CHAPTER 5

THE ADVANCED CIVILISATIONS OF MESOAMERICA

THE BEGINNINGS

The many speculations about the origin of the ancient American cultures and the not inconsiderable number of fantastic theories that have arisen in this connection are most probably attributable to the fact that in America, in contrast to the Old World, civilisations seemed for a very long time to have no precursors. It was not possible, as it was in the Near East, to reconstruct the development of cultures step by step from hunters and food-gathering tribes through neolithic communities.

When French explorers who had come to Mexico in 1860 with the victorious armies of Napoleon III excavated remains of extinct animal species associated with arrow-heads, it was already accepted that human beings had existed for many thousands of years in Mesoamerica.[1] There were doubts, however, about the authenticity of these finds, and even those who regarded them as authentic saw no connection between these original hunting tribes and the later cultures. Meanwhile the French conjectures were corroborated by a large number of fresh excavations. In Tequixquiac[2] for instance, a number of remains of extinct animal species, particularly the mammoth, were found in association with flint and bone instruments. The same is true of Santa Isabel Ixtapan,[3] where similar animal species and arrow-heads were unearthed. Finally in Tepexpan,[4] a human skeleton was dug up close to the remains of these animal species. Despite some irregularities in the excavations, which led to some doubt in the dating of the finds, most scholars today acknowledge that these are the oldest human remains in Mesoamerica.

Tools made of flint and obsidian that have only recently been unearthed in Tlapacoya, in the modern state of Mexico, seem to be very much older. They are presumed to date from 22000 BC. However, these excavations have not yet been completed or fully evaluated.

The presence of human beings many thousands of years before the rise of civilisations in Mesoamerica is indicated by these finds. But was there any sort of link between them? Is it possible to establish a link between Tepexpan man and the inhabitants of the cities of the classic period? The first evidence that the civilisations of Mesoamerica had at least had forerunners was produced only a few decades ago. A group of archaeologists, among whom were Zenia Nutall[5] and in particular Georges C. Vaillant,[6] succeeded in digging up the remains of villages at least three and a half thousand years old. In the localities known today as El Arbolillo, Zacatenco and Copilco refuse heaps were discovered that gave fairly accurate information about the life of these communities. The places in question were villages of a few hundred inhabitants at the most, in which pottery and agriculture were already well advanced. The inhabitants lived, for the most part, by the cultivation of maize, but they also practised hunting and fishing. They had developed a fine monochrome type of pottery. They lived in permanently settled villages, but there is no evidence of any integration into larger units. Burial-grounds have been discovered, some of which were richly furnished, while others were poor in this respect. But they produce no evidence of profound social stratification. Great religious buildings, such as are found in later times, did not exist. But a religion did exist. This is proved not only by the types of burial, but also by the existence of many, indeed thousands of female heads and figures made of clay that have been unearthed all over these sites. The use to which these female figurines were put is not clear. They were found scattered about alongside the dead, as well as in the fields and in houses. Are they effigies of gods? Were they fertility figures, as is sometimes thought? A final answer to these questions cannot yet be given. The village cultures that have been excavated, especially by Vaillant – other similar ones were later found in other parts of Mesoamerica, far into the lowlands – were classified by many scholars as archaic. But Vaillant himself vigorously contested the use of this expression. Although he had found no precursors of these cultures, he was convinced that they could not be the oldest in Mesoamerica. Even though they were the precursors of the advanced civilisations they were far from exhibiting any connection with the earlier hunting tribes. Not only were the two separated by a gap in time of nearly ten thousand years, but perhaps even more important is the fact that the villages already had a fully developed system of agriculture at their disposal. It is therefore necessary to accept that the transition from food-gathering and hunting to agriculture must have been a very gradual process. How and where were the precursors of this development to be found? The answer to this question was not given until after the Second World War, by Richard McNeish. The long-awaited link between hunting cultures and agriculture was first discovered by McNeish during excavations

D

in areas of the northern state of Tamaulipas[7] beyond the boundary of Mesoamerica and later in the Valley of Tehuacan[8] in the middle of the high plateau of Mexico.

The most important results came from Tehuacan. This region is among the most arid in central Mexico. The structure of the mountains is such that rain clouds penetrate only for a short time in the year at the most. As a result remains survived in various caves in this region that in other areas would most probably have been destroyed. Among such remains human excrement is of prime importance, along with remains of animals and plants. Over 750,000 remains were excavated and the work of evaluating their significance has been begun by a group of scholars, led by McNeish, that includes ethnologists, archaeologists, botanists and other experts in the field of natural history.[9] This work of evaluation is not yet anywhere near finished, but McNeish has been able to reach certain conclusions because the human excrement could be minutely examined for the foodstuffs that had been consumed. The cultural evolution postulated by McNeish demonstrates in particular and with unmistakable clarity the slow and gradual transition from hunting to agriculture.

The first phase to be unearthed by McNeish, known as the Ajuerado phase, covers a time in which human beings lived in small groups and lived by gathering wild plants and hunting. The plants included a wild species of maize, for · which scholars had been searching for a long period; remains of it were discovered by McNeish in the Valley of Tehuacan. The people of this phase hunted small game and such big game as were still in existence, the mammoth for example. But McNeish has decided that mammoth hunting was an unusual event and that big game hardly constituted the main part of their diet.

About the year 7200 BC this phase gave place to a new one, which McNeish has designated as the El Riego phase and which lasted about two thousand years. As before, people lived off hunting and food-gathering. But a few changes were noticeable. Gathering played a larger part than hunting, and he presumes that agriculture was born during this period. A number of plants such as the Chile pepper and the avocado pear appear to have been cultivated, but they were an insignificant part of the diet as a whole. During this phase weaving and woodwork developed for the first time. As before, people lived in small groups, though in the spring, when plants were harvested, especially at the time when wild plants were gathered, they may have combined into larger units. What surprised McNeish was that even at this time complex religious customs were developing. He deduced this from the burial-grounds, which displayed a certain degree of complexity.

In the following 2,500 years (the Cocaxtlan phase and the Abejas phase) a very gradual evolution towards the practice of agriculture took place. A number of the most important plants cultivated in Mesoamerica became domesticated during this period, examples being maize, beans and sapots. Nevertheless – and this is perhaps the most surprising discovery that McNeish could have made – at the end of 2,500 years of agricultural development all these plants constituted barely twenty-five per cent of the population's nutriment. That means that seventy-five per cent of foodstuffs still had to be obtained by hunting and gathering. In this period cotton was used for the first time and the first houses began to appear. But as before only stone tools and stone vessels existed. Pottery was still unknown. It did not begin to make its appearance until the Purron phase, which began in the year 2300 BC.

In this period authentic agricultural villages began to develop; we find these in the next phase, beginning about 1500 BC. These villages were similar in structure in many respects to the communities of the Valley of Mexico described above. Compact agricultural villages of this kind occurred at this period in many parts of Mesoamerica and were found beyond the limits of the plateau. Their development in the low-lying territories seems to have differed somewhat, however. While on the plateau permanence was associated with an increasing dependence upon agriculture, on the coast of Mexico conditions differed. Here there were already vestiges of compact and permanent villages long before the practice of agriculture had begun, or the knowledge of pottery was acquired. This is probably due to the fact that on the coast with its rich fishing grounds fishermen were able to gain enough food even without husbandry to enable them to live together in larger communities in one and the same place.

One of the great problems facing all historians, ethnologists and archaeologists concerned with the evolution of advanced civilisations in the New World is that of the development of these village communities into larger units. How did 'specialists' come about, how did a ruling class or the stratifications of a developing society originate? These questions are not easily answered, since research for this period depends exclusively on archaeological sources. These sources, while allowing assumptions to be made, do not permit a final conclusion. It is therefore not surprising that many hypotheses exist. So far it has not been possible finally to confirm any one of them, or to reject most of them.

THE OLMECS

We know that the appearance of new social features is connected with the development of a new art style in widely separated parts of

Mesoamerica. This style is generally known as the Olmec style, because the most important centres in which it is to be found lie in a region of which the inhabitants, at very different periods, were called Olmecs, which means 'the people of the land of the gum trees'. Whether the originators of this style were the progenitors of the inhabitants of this region in historical times cannot in the present stage of research be either proved or disproved.

Aesthetically and artistically it is one of the most important achievements of Mesoamerica.[10] In contrast to the culture of later periods, in which architecture was the most characteristic feature, sculpture forms the basis here. In all centres of Olmec art the main characteristics were heads and figures fashioned in clay, jade and a jade-like stone such as jadeite. Jade was regarded as one of the most valuable raw materials in Mesoamerica. Statues made by the Olmecs are usually a mixture of man and jaguar. They frequently have baby faces with lips drawn back to reveal jaguar's teeth and sometimes, too, they have jaguar's claws. A number of the male figures have something feminine about them, so that many scholars took them to be eunuchs. Two characteristics keep recurring: jaguar-like features and the U-like mark that either represents the mouth or crops up in other parts of the sculpture. The size of these finds varies greatly. In the most important site in the plateau of Mexico, Tlatilco, the finds consist of small, very finely worked heads and figures. Rather further south, in Chacaltzingo, great reliefs carved in stone were found. The largest monuments were not excavated in the plateau area but in the lowlands, in the modern state of Veracruz, in the localities known as La Venta and Tres Zapotes. Was this in fact the centre of Olmec culture?

For years objects in the Olmec style have been found in various parts of Mexico, both on the plateau and in the lowland. No one knows exactly how they should be classified. The confusion was increased by the fact that the provenance of a great many of these objects has never been accurately stated. They had been sold to private collectors and those who had dug them up, either through a lack of any understanding of archaeology or possibly as a precaution – for not unjustifiably they regarded these finds as a significant source of income – refused to divulge any information about where they were found. These archaeological pirates present a serious problem for research even today, because through them important objects disappear, and also because the method of excavation employed is such that any identification of their place of origin or their exact scholarly classification is rendered impossible.

The first decisive breakthrough in research into Olmec culture was made in 1938 when the American archaeologist Stirling began excavations on a big scale in an area not far from the sea coast in the tropical part of the modern state of Veracruz.[11] In the vicinity of what is now La Venta he came upon gigantic objects that clearly exhibit similarities with Olmec finds made on the plateau. Subsequently huge artificial pyramid-like mounds were discovered; these are undoubtedly the precursors of the pyramidal constructions that later became so typical of Mesoamerican cultures. More impressive even than these constructions are the tremendous sculptures that have been found in this region. They are immense human heads hewn in stone with realistic features, weighing up to twenty tons. The faces all have broad flat noses and thick swollen lips. All the heads wear round helmets.

For some time it was believed that these were heads that for some reason or another had been severed from their torsos. But not a single torso has been discovered, with the result that it is now presumed that these are simply sculptures of heads and faces. A relative simplicity of execution is typical of these sculptures and the realism of the facial expression contrasts sharply with later sculptures in the region of the Maya or in central Mexico, where the execution is often overlaid with symbolism. Certain jaguar symbols are noticeable in these sculptures. Jaguar claws appear – either on the helmet or on the ears – and sometimes jaguar teeth as well. Among the small Olmec sculptures the whole human figure is represented. These, too, demonstrate a high degree of realism. The La Venta heads (see figure 2) are among the finest sculptural achievements to be found anywhere in Mesoamerica. While the colossal heads were hewn in stone, the small figures were for the most part carved in jade or a jade-like material.

These sculptures are perhaps the most impressive of the finds in La Venta, but they are by no means the only ones. Large engraved stelae, in some cases with abstract designs, were also discovered. The recurrent jaguar motif is even more pronounced here than in the heads, either in representations of jaguars as such or in a mixture of jaguar and man. This combination in sculpture is of the highest significance. Among the most valuable finds in La Venta are the baby faces with jaguar's teeth. On the same scale as the stelae and the giant heads are the huge sarcophagae and altars, which were also hewn out of stone. They bear engraved designs, partly of a realistic nature and partly symbolic. Here, too, the jaguar motif recurs. Similar finds were also made in further localities of this coastal region: in Tres Zapotes and in San Lorenzo. Giant stone heads and engraved stelae were again found. This whole style is characterised by great simplicity and realism, such as was hardly to be achieved again in Mesoamerica. The Olmec style is regarded as one of the greatest artistic achievements of ancient America. The site at La Venta has been dated by the radio-carbon method to between 800 and 400 BC. Tres Zapotes, the other site where finds were made, is of the same date.

In contrast to La Venta, however, which was abandoned about 400 BC, the settlement at Tres Zapotes continued. Styles developed there that were related to the Olmec style but show a number of new characteristics. In these later periods, which lasted up to the first century AD, signs and mathematical symbols were found; if the Maya Calendar is used, these date the site to 31 BC. This has led to the conclusion that at least in a phase following the Olmec culture, and perhaps even in its early phase, writing and the calendar developed later by the Maya were already known.

If we are to understand Olmec culture we must rely exclusively on archaeology for evidence. It is therefore possible to say without exaggeration that this culture poses many more problems than we are in a position to solve. We must content ourselves largely with varying and indeed contradictory hypotheses, each of which has as much to be said for it as against it. At all events, it may be said with some degree of probability that the rise of Olmec culture was accompanied by a marked degree of social stratification. Evidence for this may be found in widely differing characteristics and phenomena, such as pretentious burial-grounds furnished with rich gifts or a representation in Chacaltzingo of a man kneeling in front of another who is richly clad. This clearly depicts a nobleman and his subordinate. Equally significant is the discovery in Tlatilco of a group of men in jade. In the centre stands a magnificently attired figure round whom are grouped fifteen others who are less well clad and are either standing or reclining. Still plainer is the fact that in the centres of culture a professional hierarchy or priesthood was necessary to maintain these great centres. Besides, Olmec culture had reached such a high stage of development that only professional craftsmen could have fashioned it.

In the lowlands, where the centres of culture were discovered, there must have been a union of larger groups of population. An attempt was made to estimate whether, for example, the population of La Venta, the single great centre of culture, could possibly have produced the sculptures, buildings and monuments that were found there. It was clearly established that the area of La Venta – an island surrounded by a marsh – could have kept only forty-five families with the agricultural practices prevailing at the time.[12] These, again, would have found it impossible to produce the gigantic buildings or even to collect together the necessary stone, for there was no stone in the locality itself. This must have been brought from a distance of almost a hundred kilometres. It is possible to imagine the size of the undertaking and the labour force required only when we reflect that neither draught animals, nor wheels nor carts existed and that everything had to be manhandled and then transported by water. It has been estimated that in order to build La Venta in the course of a few decades, the combined labour force of the whole population of the 'hinterland' of La Venta would have been needed. The population, based on the agricultural system prevailing at that time, has been estimated at about eighteen thousand. These eighteen thousand people would have required the four hundred years during which La Venta functioned as a cultural centre in order to erect these constructions and to maintain the priesthood and the members of the hierarchy inhabiting them, in the time left over to them from the work of husbandry.[13]

Three final conclusions may almost certainly also be drawn. La Venta was abandoned about the year 400 BC, at which time violent destruction in some form or other took place; twenty-four monuments of various kinds were damaged. Another positively established fact is that the Olmec culture was the first in Mesoamerica to spread to both highlands and lowlands and embrace regions that lie thousands of miles apart. Finally, the Olmec culture is considered to be the most ancient of the advanced civilisations of Mesoamerica, although further archaeological finds could still alter this conclusion.

Yet these few established, or for the most part established, facts (in archaeology it is necessary to beware even of the word 'established') cannot resolve even a fraction of the many problems set by Olmec culture. After all, who were the Olmecs and where did they come from? The archaeological sites of Veracruz point to no precursors. It has not been possible, on the basis of excavations undertaken to date on the east coast of Mexico, to gain any impression of the genesis of this culture. The first finds point to a culture that was already highly developed. This fact has led a number of scholars to seek the cradle of Olmec culture outside the coastal area.

At all events they start out from very varied hypotheses. Some believe that its origin is to be found not only outside the area of the east coast of present-day Mexico, but outside America altogether. The suddenness with which the Olmec culture developed is adduced as proof that its original instigators came from outside.[14] Others believed for a time that the place of origin was somewhere in Africa. They point to the pronounced Negroid features of some of the heads found in La Venta and Tres Zapotes and also to the fact that both places would have been accessible from Africa. This hypothesis is hardly tenable today, however. Apart from the Negroid features, which, as has since been established, exist among the Indian population of this region, there are no indications of any similarities with African cultures. Above all, there is no evidence that at that time African navigational skills would have been capable of accomplishing voyages from Africa to America. The majority of those who support an ultra-American origin for the Olmecs favour Asia. They rest their case on the fact that a considerable proportion of Olmec finds – smaller objects at any rate – were found not on the east coast of Mexico, but near the west coast. These scholars presume that small groups landed in this region from South-East Asia and then probably migrated to the east. The adherents of this theory point to a number of stylistic resemblances between the culture of the Olmecs and that of South-East Asia.[15]

The majority of Americanists who believe unreservedly in a Mesoamerican origin for Olmec culture do not share this interpretation. At all events, another dispute has flared up as to whether its origins are to be found on the plateau or in the lowlands. Those who support the theory of a highland origin[16] begin by considering the civilisation of the Old World. They claim that despite all variations observable in their evolution, certain ecological factors were common to both civilisations: soil which was suitable for intensive cultivation, the possibility of irrigation and good means of communication, either by river or sea.[17] These characteristics obtain in Mesoamerica, particularly on the plateau of central Mexico, but not in the lowlands. An important feature was absent here: intensive agriculture, which was impossible because of the nature of the soil. Slash and burn agriculture was practised: a section of forest was burned; the wood ash was used as fertiliser; and then this piece of soil was worked for two or three years. At the end of this period it was all but exhausted and had to lie fallow for at least ten to twelve years. Fresh ground had to be broken. The area that a single family required for sustaining life was therefore far greater than on the plateau; this meant, of course, that the density of population was far less. The population was scattered, and there was virtually no incentive to integrate. In fact neither in South America nor in any other parts of the world where this kind of husbandry was practised did an advanced civilisation develop. Scholars who hold this view are convinced that Olmec culture was initially a product of the plateau, that more intensive cultivation of the soil and agricultural requirements led to class distinctions, to the rise of centres of some size, to the creation of a ruling class who supervised the irrigation systems and concentrated on integrating these densely populated areas. Those who support the theory of a lowland origin, on the other hand, point out that Olmec culture reached its peak in the lowlands rather than on the plateau. Only here did great ceremonial centres come into being. The lowlands must therefore have been not only the place of origin but also the focal point of Olmec culture.[18] Agriculture must have been capable of supporting these centres. They could as well have arisen there despite the fact that incentives were perhaps less pronounced than on the plateau. Those who support the lowland theory argue that intensive agriculture and irrigation are not always indispensable incentives for bringing about centralisation. The region of Veracruz on the coast was one of the great trading centres of Mesoamerica on the eve of the Spanish Conquest. A variety of merchandise was produced here that did not exist on the plateau: feathers, cocoa and cotton, for example. There is still much evidence that the merchants of Tlatelolco, who constituted the greatest trading class of Mesoamerica, originated on the Gulf coast. Why should similar processes not have operated even in Olmec times?

No less controversial are the questions of the political and social basis of Olmec culture, and of its evolution. There are some who see only the rise of a new religion, which was carried to the furthermost corners of Mesoamerica by the zealous work of missionaries. Based on religious conceptions of later cultures, the cult of the jaguar was conceived as being a cult of the rain god or of a fertility god. Most archaeologists concerned with Olmec culture agree with this. At all events, the view is now held that there was peaceful missionary work aimed at effecting peaceful religious penetration of other regions. However, serious doubts have been expressed. While in the key areas of Veracruz hardly any warlike images were found and scarcely any weapons, evidence of this kind increases amongst the more remote Olmec discoveries.[19] In such areas, therefore, the process must have been more violent. Accordingly a few scholars believe that a type of empire must have existed, or at least a forcible integration of fairly extensive areas. La Venta and Tres Zapotes may have been peaceful places of pilgrimage to begin with, but thanks to donations and then also perhaps because reserves of food-stuffs for the population were stored in their temples, so much power fell into the hands of the priesthood that they very soon rose to become overlords of the whole of the surrounding districts, and finally also engaged in military conquest.

The opponents of this theory, while not contradicting it outright, consider that on the one hand the sites of Olmec culture are too far apart for us to conclude that an empire existed, and on the other the ecological basis and the concentration of population were insufficient in the key area for it to constitute the centre of a true empire. What other possibility was there? A third school of thought, led in particular by Michael D. Coe,[20] takes the view that a sort of commercial metropolis existed here, with, as was later the case amongst the Aztec merchants, the inhabitants carrying on their trade by peaceful means as well as by warlike ones. They had settlements in far-flung and distant regions, especially where jade was found, and from there they traded, and possibly also conducted missionary activities. This could explain the military character of the remote Olmec settlements; it also underlines the fact that these settlements really were very far apart. This is also supported by the fact that the merchants of the plateau, and specially those of the commercial city of Tlatelolco, maintained similar colonies on the eve of the Spanish Conquest, some of which were thousands of miles away from the centre.

It is impossible at the present stage of our knowledge either to confirm or to reject any of these theories finally. A number of fresh archaeological discoveries – work is currently in progress – may possibly confirm one or other theory in the near future.

Almost as many problems are posed by the decline of Olmec culture as by its origin, and equally by its evolution and the influence it exercised on the other Mesoamerican cultures.

Archaeological data have proved fairly clearly that La Venta, the most important centre of Olmec culture in the lowlands, was not only abandoned but also probably suffered violent destruction towards the end of the classical flowering of the Olmec culture, in about the year 400 BC. As we have seen, twenty-four monuments were found to have been violently wrecked and destroyed in various ways. How can this be accounted for? Was it conquered by tribes from outside? This is always possible. The expansion far beyond their central territory that the Olmecs managed to achieve could certainly have led to the creation of all sorts of enemies. The wealth of La Venta must also have exercised strong attraction. Apart from this such a conquest could have been aided by the fact that the Olmecs were open to invasion from outside because this central region was thinly populated as a result of the slash and burn type of agriculture that was practised there. It is however equally possible, as many archaeologists think, that internal revolts against the priesthood were responsible for the destruction of the centre. The very delicate balance between population and food supply caused by the narrow margins imposed by this type of agriculture could very easily have brought about this situation. Unfortunately at this stage we can do nothing but conjecture. In any event the destruction and abandonment of La Venta does not appear to have marked the end of Olmec culture, nor even of Olmec influence.

Both in neighbouring Tres Zapotes and in the locality of Izapa on the Pacific coast significant remains of a sort of neo-Olmec culture have been found. This displays its own new characteristics alongside strong Olmec cultural influences. Religious forms, such as the cult of the jaguar, for instance, were further developed here into new art forms. Signs of writing and calendrical data have been found in association with this culture. As has already been said, it is not certain whether writing and the calendar were developed by the carriers of this neo-Olmec culture or by the Olmecs themselves.

In connection with these new finds the decisive question, repeatedly posed by all archaeologists and ethnologists concerned with Mesoamerica, is this: is Olmec culture a sort of mother-culture of all later Mesoamerican cultures? Its influence is discernible in many different parts of Mesoamerica, in the lowlands as well as on the plateau. Nevertheless marked differences do exist. Most archaeologists now take the view that lowland culture, in particular that of the Maya, was definitely influenced by the Olmecs. This is borne out by the calendrical system, and the many hieroglyphs for which prototypes were found amongst the Olmecs. The latest archaeological discoveries do, in fact, contain evidence that the neo-Olmec style of Izapa had a significant influence on the early phases of Maya cultures.

Against this, there is grave doubt as to whether the idea of an Olmec 'mother culture' can be applied to the cultures of the Mesoamerican plateau. The classic cultures of the plateau show marked differences in art styles, in the calendar and in their writing from those of the Olmecs. Be that as it may, the fact remains that the first formulation on the plateau of a class structure, of differences between rich and poor, perhaps also the first signs of a hierarchical priesthood were connected with the Olmecs. If, as Coe assumes, the Olmecs carried out a sort of commercial expansion in widely different parts of Mesoamerica, it cannot be excluded that it was precisely the influence of Olmec merchants that very rapidly led to centralisation on the plateau. How often, though of course under different auspices, has the penetration by European merchants into Asia or, above all, into African territories favoured the introduction of centralised social structures? But these are all hypotheses that cannot so far be resolved in any detail. All we can say is that Olmec culture was the first of a number of advanced civilisations that seem to have arisen, as it were spontaneously, in many different parts of Mesoamerica. Cultures existed that seemed to be continuously connected with each other and also exhibited a number of common features; these unifying factors have given the region the name Mesoamerica.

Nevertheless it is still possible to detect two widely diverging developments: one that unfolded on the plateau of Mesoamerica and another with its centre in the lowlands.

TEOTIHUACAN

In the period of the Olmec civilisation the cultures of the highlands and the lowlands of Mesoamerica had displayed a certain uniformity. This was soon to cease and a process of increasingly pronounced differentiation set in.

The Olmec tradition of scattered ceremonial centres that was introduced into the lowlands and was based exclusively on a foundation of extensive agriculture found its highest expression in the culture of the Maya. On the plateau of Mexico, by contrast, a completely different type of development took place, characterised by a few large cities in a continuous process of expansion, and sustained by intensive agriculture. It is noticeable that in this different type of development intellectual and spiritual achievements can in no way be correlated with the size of the cities, with population density or with the extent to which one state is integrated with another. It was not on the plateau, where such urban developments reached their peak, but in the decentralised lowlands that the greatest intellectual and spiritual achievements took place.

The first significant signs of a central Mexican culture are to be found in the locality of Cuicuilco,[21] south of the modern capital of Mexico City. A great pyramid rises from a field of lava, $22\frac{1}{2}$ metres high and with a circumference of 120 metres. On one side steps lead up to the summit and on the other side there is a ramp. Unlike later pyramids erected in Mesoamerica, the one at Cuicuilco is round. Dressed stone and the skilful proportions that are typical of later constructions of this kind are still lacking. The pyramid of Cuicuilco is of an architectural type and tradition that were to extend to all Mesoamerica in the not too distant future.

The Mexican pyramids discovered by the Europeans served one specific purpose: they acted as the bases for temples or altars erected on their summits. Important religious ceremonies took place there and in the period of the Aztecs mass human sacrifices were made on the pyramids.

These people, living on the eve of the conquest of Mexico, saw the pyramid in their imagination as a reflection of Heaven, which they conceived as a series of gradients. Did these features apply in earlier times as well? Most probably they did, since pre-Aztec pyramids were constructed on similar lines, with temples, altars or at any rate platforms that could have served as supports for temples.

The Mesoamerican pyramids were distinguished by these attributes from those of Egypt, which served exclusively as places of burial. But the differences were not as extensive as they were thought to be for a long time. In recent years magnificent graves have been found in a number of Mesoamerican pyramids, especially in the Maya region. But no pyramids that served exclusively as burial-places have so far been discovered in Mesoamerica.

Cuicuilco was for a long time taken to be a small ceremonial centre similar to Olmec La Venta. These conclusions have been shaken by recent excavations. Three kilometres from Cuicuilco there is another pyramid, smaller than the first. Between the two a great variety of remains of buildings were found, which point to the existence of quite a large settlement, perhaps even a temple city. The construction of large pyramids of this kind required a labour force that a small village community would be unable to raise. Were the inhabitants of Cuicuilco already familiar with intensive agriculture? Was Cuicuilco more than a ceremonial centre? Was there a densely populated locality already in existence? In the present state of our knowledge only conjecture is possible. Further excavations may bring some surprises.

The eruption of the Xitli volcano put a sudden end to the development of Cuicuilco. The area was covered by a thick layer of lava and became uninhabitable. There is some evidence that the volcanic eruption was the last stage in the destruction of Cuicuilco and that the majority of the population had already abandoned the locality.

The focal point of political, economic and cultural life on the plateau of Mexico now shifted to the north-eastern part of the Valley of Mexico, to the lower Valley of Teotihuacan. Here one of the greatest and most important civilisations of pre-Columbian America came into being. There are no written sources concerning the rise and development of Teotihuacan, which was already regarded by the Aztecs as a mythological place. They knew less about it than archaeologists today. Teotihuacan was the traditional burial-place of the gods and the Aztecs believed that giants had dwelt there. This belief may perhaps have been given substance by the fact that the bones of an extinct species of mammoth were found in the vicinity of the city. It is unlikely, though not impossible, that some day written sources giving data on the history of the city will come to light. The inhabitants of Teotihuacan seem to have possessed a form of writing, but so far only a few glyphs have been discovered. If all the inscriptions of the Maya are ever deciphered, some of them might disclose details concerning Teotihuacan, which had close associations with the Maya.

For research into the history of Teotihuacan and the cultural, social and religious organisation of its population we have to rely exclusively on archaeological evidence. Excellent results have been achieved through archaeology. Indeed there are few places on the American continent where excavation and investigation have been carried out so intensively, and on such an international scale.

After an ill-starred dig in 1910, which destroyed more than it brought to light, serious work was begun in 1917 under the leadership of Manuel Gamio, in the middle of the Mexican revolution and while fighting was still in progress. Since then the rate of excavation has steadily gained momentum.[22] Scholars from many different countries have participated with Mexican archaeologists in the work on Teotihuacan. The excavations undertaken were very varied, and monuments, the art of Teotihuacan and its material culture were all included. For instance William T. Sanders[23] undertook detailed examinations of the ecology and agriculture of the Valley of Teotihuacan, while another working party under René Millon[24] explored the boundaries of the city, the number of houses, their size, structure and so on. The introduction of 'computers' to analyse objects excavated in more than four thousand buildings is evidence of the discipline, intensity and scale of the exercise. Thanks to such varied methods of research it was possible to obtain an idea of the scale and structure of the city. It was also possible to reconstruct the daily life of its inhabitants.

It has not been possible, though, for archaeology to tell us who the inhabitants of Teotihuacan were. It was possible to establish only that there was greater continuity with the original inhabitants of the Valley of Mexico than had hitherto been presumed. It is not possible to establish whether the impetus for the development of the city came from the archaic inhabitants of the plateau or from lowland immigrants, nor what their languages were. The city's development was not the result of a consistent evolutionary process – its beginning was marked by a regular population explosion, the interpretation of which has, to date, led to many differences of opinion.[25]

Even in 100 BC, in a phase known to archaeologists as Patlachique, the majority of the inhabitants of Teotihuacan lived in small, probably independent villages on the sides of the valley. On the bed of the valley however there did exist a few villages that were larger than those on the hillsides, though even the largest township did not have a population of more than five thousand. The construction of the first ceremonial buildings may possibly have begun in the Valley of Teotihuacan at that time.

In the first century AD there was a sudden increase in the population. The figure rose to at least thirty thousand and the area of the city extended to seventeen square kilometres. More than half the inhabitants of the Valley of Teotihuacan were already living within the city at that time. At the end of the first century, still during this period of Teotihuacan's development, the construction of the greatest of the city's buildings, known as the Pyramid of the Sun, was undertaken. The name stems from the time of the Aztecs, but it is impossible to establish with any degree of certainty whether it reflected the original purpose of the pyramid. It still rises like a colossus in the middle of the Valley of Teotihuacan, 65 metres high, 220 metres in circumference and a million cubic metres in volume. A broad stairway, interrupted by four platforms, leads to the highest platform, on which presumably a temple once stood, though there are no traces of it left. The pyramid was filled out with dried adobe bricks and its outer walls were held together with mortar and most likely painted with a coat of coloured stucco.

The construction of these pyramids signifies the increasing power of the city's ruling class and it is not surprising that there was a continuous increase in population. Millon estimates that in the second century AD it increased to forty-five thousand, while the city expanded to 22½ square kilometres. Both the increase of population and the construction of monumental buildings at this time testify to the growing might of Teotihuacan. The second largest pyramid of the city was erected during this period; this is the Pyramid of the Moon, which is forty-two metres high. Another example is the Temple of the Feathered Serpent, perhaps from an artistic point of view the most outstanding building in the city. The most important and most striking works of art on this temple are the stone carvings that surround it; feathered serpents alternate with another symbol which, by analogy with those of later times, may be taken to be the Rain God, Tlaloc.

About the year AD 200 the period known to historians and archaeologists as 'classic' began. This name emphasises the fact that in this period Teotihuacan reached the zenith of its development from the point of view of art, architecture, town planning and political domination. This was revealed especially clearly in the organisation of the city. In earlier times building was concentrated on individual major constructions, but there seems to have developed at this time a form of regular town planning. A sort of re-planning then began, reaching its height in AD 500 or 600. Two major axes, one north-south and one east-west, crossed Teotihuacan and divided it into four urban quarters. This division may have a significance that was more than purely geographical. The figure 4 was always sacred in Mesoamerica and many later cities, such as the Aztec city of Tenochtitlan, were also divided into four quarters.

At the point where the axes intersected a building was erected that remains in a good state of preservation even today and which the Spaniards in the sixteenth century called the Citadel. It is a huge complex of buildings rising round the Temple of the Feathered Serpent and surrounded by a wall interrupted by fifteen small pyramids. To the Spaniards this surrounding wall created the impression of a fortress at first sight. The archaeologist Armillas considered that this building was first and foremost civil, rather than military: it was the centre of the temporal and religious life of Teotihuacan. Armillas is of the opinion that the dwellings of the ruling class were here, as well as the administrative buildings.

The temple round which these pyramids rise is unusually well preserved because the carvings of the 'Feathered Serpent' were covered up in the third or fourth century AD, for reasons unknown.

The north-south axis, which the Aztecs called the 'Road of the Dead', was the focal point of the city. All the big cultural and public buildings of Teotihuacan were ranged along this highway, which was forty metres broad and whose entire length of three kilometres was probably covered in white plaster. Near to the pyramids of the Sun and the Moon and the Citadel, all of which have been known for a long time, archaeologists have recently discovered other buildings and plazas. Opposite the Citadel, on the other side of the Road of the Dead, there was a huge plaza, bordered not by temples but by houses, which led many to assume that it had been a market square or administrative centre. In 1965 archaeologists found another great plaza off the southern stretch of the Road of the Dead. It is three hundred and fifty metres square and partly surrounded by pyramidal tumuli, but its significance is still not clear.[26]

The broad and spaciously laid out central road may have gained in importance by contrast with the narrow lanes that contained the city's dwellings. Within the city centre of Teotihuacan all these little streets ran either parallel with or directly across the north-south axis of the city. The dwelling houses were one-storey buildings and had no windows. A door led into a complex group, at the centre of which was a patio surrounded on all sides by dark, windowless apartments. The roofs of the houses were slanting so that rain-water fell into the patio, whence subterranean conduits took it outside the city. The big dwelling house complexes were all of a standard length, of fifty-seven metres or a multiple thereof. They were much too big to have been the dwelling houses of individual families, so it has been assumed that either clans or the clan-like organisations of professional groups lived in them.

In startling contrast to this planned organisation of the city itself, the suburbs, with their conglomeration of dwelling houses, had the appearance of a labyrinth.

In the fifth to the sixth centuries the city's population reached the highest point in its history. The population rose to between eighty-five and a hundred thousand, while the extent of Teotihuacan, perhaps by reason of a closer concentration of the population, shrank to 20·5 kilometres square. At this time Teotihuacan was larger than Rome at the time of the Caesars, even though its population was only one-fifth of that of Rome. The city was by far the largest and most powerful American metropolis of the classic period. The history of the plateau city here reached its zenith and its influence extended many hundreds, indeed thousands, of miles both inside and outside Mesoamerica.

The monumental character of the architecture of Teotihuacan was matched by its art, which was almost exclusively religious in character. Sculpture was primarily devoted to the representation of gods which, in contrast to those of the Olmecs, had fewer human features. The largest sculpture in stone found in Teotihuacan probably represented the Goddess of the Waters and was aptly described by Vaillant as a '. . . sort of monolithic building that symbolises the implacable force of nature'.[27] This austerity and mercilessness are characteristic of the whole of

Teotihuacan art, for the gods represented there were 'remote and terrible in their strength, with masks and features demoniacal and zoomorphic in character.'[28]

Human faces carved in stone bore a completely different character and their significance is not clear. Are they death masks of important personalities? The many terracotta figures, which for the most part are also anthropomorphic, are equally mysterious.

Teotihuacan pottery clearly exhibits two distinct types: rough ware, presumably for household use, and a much finer type intended for export. The latter, to which belong the tripod jars that are so characteristic of Teotihuacan and the finely worked 'thin orange coloured' pottery, was exported to almost the whole of Mesoamerica.

It is consistent with the strictly religious character of Teotihuacan art that the only happy and lifelike subjects represented in the city's art are not scenes of earthly life but of the life beyond the grave. There are frescoes of which, alas, a large number was destroyed through carelessness towards the end of the sixteenth century. Most scholars take the view that the most important frescoes depict the Rain God's paradise. Beside the Rain God there is a landscape, the profusion and richness of which could hardly be surpassed. Rivers, which can also be taken as irrigation channels, flow through green meadows where maize, cocoa, flowers and maguey cactuses are in bloom. Human figures – which have been interpreted as representing the souls of the dead – seem to be leading a very agreeable existence. Some are eating maize, others are bathing in the river, chasing butterflies or playing ball.

On the basis of a certain continuity that extended into the Aztec period it has been possible to identify some of Teotihuacan's gods. Among these were the Fire God, Huehueteotl, and the Rain God, Tlaloc. The significance of the recurrent motif of the feathered serpent is less clear. Can it at this early date be the god Quetzalcoatl, who played such an important role among the later peoples of the Valley of Mexico? Was it a symbol of the forces of nature?

Decline followed hard upon the zenith of Teotihuacan; some consider it to have begun in the sixth century, while others date it to the seventh or eighth centuries. Hardly any new buildings were erected in the city, and the population, while still remaining great, gradually decreased; at this period it was estimated to be about seventy thousand. There are marked signs of decadence in art. There are no more new developments and quality is replaced by quantity. Finally a catastrophe occurred. The city was abandoned, clearly after heavy fighting, in the middle of the sixth century according to some, or in the middle of the eighth century according to others. Traces of burning and destruction have been found.

Archaeology has made it possible to erect, particularly in recent

E

years, this comprehensive and impressive framework for Teotihuacan. It has meant that many hitherto accepted theories have had to be abandoned and a new approach adopted to the problem of Teotihuacan's significance, the form of its cultural diffusion and its social organisation.

For years Teotihuacan was regarded by many scholars as a ceremonial centre inhabited only by a few priests. It was presumed that the population of outlying districts flocked into the city only on great religious occasions. The outward diffusion of Teotihuacan's influence had, in the first place, been only of a religious character. These theories are no longer tenable in view of all the existing evidence concerning the size of the city and the density of its population. But in their place fresh problems have forced themselves upon our attention.

There were few cities of comparable size in ancient America, the only examples being the later Aztec capital city of Tenochtitlan and in Peru Chan Chan and Cuzco. Despite all the differences in their structure, these cities had certain characteristics in common. The population of all three was sustained largely by agriculture, which was carried on intensively in the surrounding countryside. Tenochtitlan, Chan Chan and Cuzco were the capitals of large states, and in them there dwelt an important temporal and religious ruling class. All three cities had developed into great centres of craftsmanship and one of them, Tenochtitlan, was in addition a powerful commercial centre. Did all these features apply to Teotihuacan?

Scholars increasingly take the view that intensive methods of agriculture were probably used in Teotihuacan, which resulted in a tremendous increase in food production. Armillas pointed out that the blue streaks between green fields in the frescoes probably represented irrigation channels.[29] Sanders,[30] who carried out his research in the Valley of Teotihuacan partly with the object of clarifying this question, came to similar conclusions. He adopts the view that intensive agriculture with the aid of irrigation systems, possibly taken over from Cuicuilco, was introduced into the Valley of Teotihuacan about the beginning of our era. Sanders was faced with a difficult problem. How is the age of an irrigation system determined? In parts of the ancient East, where such systems consisted of a series of colossal dams, proof is not too difficult to establish. This was not, however, the case in Teotihuacan. Its irrigation system, which still survives today, is much simpler. Water from a few sources is conducted to the fields by small channels, mostly dug out of the hillsides. How can the age of such a channel be ascertained? It is impossible to reconstruct it absolutely consecutively through the centuries. Sanders takes the view, based on a certain amount of circumstantial evidence, that intensive irrigation of such a kind must have existed. The uncertainties are too numerous for us to discuss them in detail here. Parallels between the structure of agricultural settlement in Teotihuacan in the sixteenth century, in which irrigation demonstrably existed, and the classic period justify the assumption that intensive husbandry was also practised at that time. Do the water conduits discovered in the city not prove that the inhabitants of Teotihuacan possessed the necessary knowledge for the creation of irrigation channels?

The existence of intensive agriculture no doubt aided the concentration of population within the city. Did it have further consequences? Did it cause the rise of Teotihuacan? Did it bring about a powerful reinforcement of the authority of a bureaucracy of water management? It is impossible to answer these questions unequivocally, still less since the irrigation systems of Teotihuacan, unlike those of the ancient East or Peru, required no gigantic constructions organised and continuously administered by a bureaucracy. But it is not impossible that the ruling class of the city made use of the administration of the water supply to strengthen their own position of power. Furthermore, it is possible that the inhabitants of Teotihuacan were already familiar with the very productive Chinampa system of artificial islands in the skein of lakes in Mexico, which was later used by the Aztecs. But no evidence of this has yet been found.

The introduction of intensive agriculture may have been the cause of the rise of Teotihuacan. A second, no less important cause was the development of craftsmanship and trade. Such development was perhaps determined by the ecology of the Mexican plateau. As in the later Aztec period, products of the lowland such as cotton, cocoa and feathers may have proved to be a powerful attraction to the inhabitants of the plateau, who lacked such commodities. But how could the plateau pay for these wares? It was not sufficiently endowed with raw materials. The agricultural products cultivated in Teotihuacan were most of them available in the lowlands as well. Teotihuacan was forced to adopt the policy that highly developed industrial states employ today towards underdeveloped and dependent colonial territories: the selling of finished goods in return for raw materials.

In fact great quantities of Teotihuacan pottery and worked obsidian have been found in many different parts of Mesoamerica, often thousands of miles away from the city. Conversely, Millon discovered a dense concentration of foreign pottery in the eastern part of the city, some of it from the region of the Maya, some of it from Monte Alban; he takes the view that there may have been dwellings or storage places here, or the market place of foreign communities or of indigenous merchants who carried on trade with foreign parts.

At all events, Millon's excavations show the increasing importance of craft work and of the expansion of the principle of division of labour.

51

In Teotihuacan he discovered a number of areas in which an extraordinary accumulation of objects made from obsidian were unearthed. These districts, in which peasants may originally have manufactured obsidian tools as a sideline, moved from the periphery into the town centre. In the course of this displacement specialisation took place within the obsidian industry. A few craftsmen took up the production of knives, while others produced only arrow-heads or spear-heads and scrapers. The number of workshops in the centre of the city was constantly on the increase. Obsidian remains stemming from this period of Teotihuacan's development have been found in many parts of Mesoamerica.

Was this metropolis on the plateau of Mexico the capital city of an empire? This is a most complex question and never fails to give rise to sharp differences of opinion. Both the complexity and the controversy are partly explained by the fact that no traces of war have been discovered in Teotihuacan. The Mexican warlike gods of a later period do not appear in Teotihuacan. No fortifications have been found and the representation of a warrior occurs only once in the art of the city. The innumerable arrow-heads and spear-heads could certainly have been used as weapons of war, but they could equally well have been used for hunting. In the face of all the evidence of peace that exists, is it conceivable that Teotihuacan was a warfaring city?

Those who support the theory that Teotihuacan was a mighty state bent on conquest point to the tremendous influence that the metropolis exercised on the whole of Mesoamerica. Its influence is noticeable in all great centres of the classic period of Mesoamerica. The more excavations are undertaken the more evidence of this influence is brought to light. In the fifth century the indigenous culture of Kaminaljuyu, the modern Guatemala City, which was found to have existed up to then, was overlaid fairly suddenly by a Teotihuacan style that fully reflects the metropolis of the plateau. Most scholars therefore presume that there must have been a conquest by Teotihuacan.

Reliefs and representations in the style of Teotihuacan exist in Tikal, the greatest centre in the lowland region of the Maya. The influences exercised by the great plateau city may be seen very clearly in the Zapotec city of Monte Alban. Are these influences exclusively the results of propaganda by peaceful missionaries or merchants from Teotihuacan?

This hypothesis has evoked more and more criticism. The circumstance that warfare and warriors found no expression in art is no proof that they did not exist. 'There was nothing in the monuments of Java' [writes an expert on South East Asia] 'to lead us to have the faintest inkling about the wars between the islands, or about the tremendous campaigns of conquest waged by the kingdoms of Singasari and

Madjabahit in other parts of Indonesia. There is nothing in the monuments of Chan to disclose anything concerning the interminable wars which these people waged against their neighbours.'[31]

Doubts about this are not only increased by the unreliability of archaeological evidence. It is a pertinent question whether the ruling class of a city as great and rich as Teotihuacan could have defended its position both internally and externally over so many hundreds of years without some sort of apparatus of power, without war of any kind. Such cases are rare.

Nevertheless, how is it that there is so much less tangible evidence of war in Teotihuacan than in the later cultures of Mesoamerica? There is one possible answer. It is conceivable that by reason of its might and size, which excelled those of other cities in Mesoamerica for hundreds of years, the great city of the plateau maintained a sort of *Pax Teotihuacana*, which it was able to maintain over a long period of time with virtually no recourse to war.

If it is presumed that Teotihuacan's influence was not only religious, it is still doubtful whether it is possible to speak of a Teotihuacan empire. The Aztecs, who almost a thousand years later subjugated almost the whole of Mesoamerica, did not found a homogeneous empire such as that of Egypt or of the Inca. Their 'empire' contained the most diverse forms of rule: strict controls exercised in the immediate vicinity of the Aztec capital city, obligatory tribute exacted further afield without direct control, Aztec garrisons on the borders of enemy tribes or states and in important commercial centres. The 'empire' of Teotihuacan was probably a similar amalgam of very diverse forms of sovereignty.

The power of Teotihuacan in the central plateau of Mexico was so great that it was hardly possible for other cities to develop. The only exceptions to this rule were Cholollan in the Valley of Puebla, in which one of the greatest pyramids of Mesoamerica was built, and Atzcapotzalco on the shores of the network of lakes in Mexico.

Who were the rulers of Teotihuacan? For many years it was thought that a definitive answer could be given to this question. The idea that it was solely a ceremonial centre and the absence of any evidence of war resulted in its being regarded as a peaceful theocracy. But in view of copious evidence about the size of the city and the diffusion of its influence it is increasingly difficult to uphold the idea of its having been a peaceful theocracy. Surely, as history so often shows, a theocracy need not necessarily be peaceful.

On the eve of the Spanish Conquest five distinct ruling groups had developed in Mesoamerica: a warrior caste that slowly turned into a hereditary aristocracy, which usually supplied the ruler; a priesthood; a mercantile caste; a tribal aristocracy and – in the early stages – a state bureaucracy with ever-increasing powers. From a functional point of view all these groups were necessary in Teotihuacan. The presence of a priesthood need hardly be discussed. Commerce had increased to such an extent that it required specialists to conduct it. The administration of a city as large as Teotihuacan and its economic needs must have required a bureaucracy, all the more so if an intensive irrigation system existed. The expansion of Teotihuacan's influence over most of Mesoamerica in the fourth and fifth centuries AD and the defence of the city against the barbarian tribes in the north are inconceivable without soldiers. The problem is how to determine whether these ruling groups had already become institutionally differentiated. What was their relationship to each other? This is a complex matter that can scarcely be elucidated through archaeology. Comparison with another culture might possibly help, at least to sketch out a conceivable process of development for the social organisation of Teotihuacan. Robert Adams has undertaken the task of making a comparison between the social development of Mesoamerica with that of Mesopotamia. The early development of the state in Mesopotamia appears to have been of a theocratic character, exactly like that in Mesoamerica. In the early Mesopotamian cities the temples were the most important centres of power, and they were at the same time the granaries in which reserves were built up. The temples organised the life of the community, determining political, social and religious events. In Mesopotamia this domination by a theocracy is corroborated both by archaeology and by written evidence. As the cities grew in size a process of differentiation became increasingly noticeable in Mesopotamia. The development of a warrior caste and the increasing power of the merchants had the effect of concentrating more and more power in the hands of the secular rulers and thus of diminishing the authority of the temples and the priesthood.[32] Was there a similar process of differentiation in Teotihuacan? It is quite certain that as Teotihuacan grew and its influence in Mesoamerica strengthened more secular than religious buildings were erected. As we have seen, the greatest construction of the first two centuries in Teotihuacan was the Sun Pyramid, which was designed for religious purposes. The greatest building of the later period was the Citadel, which Armillas regards as a centre of temporal power. Trade-marks and symbols of jaguars and eagles that in Aztec times represented military castes stem from Teotihuacan's late period. This all denotes a far-reaching process of differentiation. Secular forces came more and more into the ascendant. Whether they ever succeeded in seizing power in Teotihuacan must remain an open question, but it is possible that conflict between religious and secular forces was one of the causes of Teotihuacan's downfall.

There were probably ever-increasing conflicts between rulers and ruled. Little is known about the position of the lower classes in Teotihuacan. As far as the majority of the population of Teotihuacan is concerned, there are unlikely to have been any slaves. On the eve of the Spanish Conquest the peasant population in the whole of Mesoamerica and the craftsmen were organised into clan-like communities. Land was the common property of the clans. The nobility lived on the services and tribute payments of these community members. A similar organisation probably existed in the great city of the plateau. To what extent was religious conviction or compulsion the basis of the services rendered by peasants or craftsmen? It is conceivable that in the last years of Teotihuacan's existence, with ever-growing demands from the nobility, compulsion played an increasing role. The resulting conflicts probably had a more powerful effect than anything else in causing the ultimate collapse of Teotihuacan.

THE CULTURE OF THE MAYA

. . . Soon we came to the bank of a river, and saw directly opposite a stone wall, perhaps a hundred feet high, with furze growing out of the top . . .

The wall was of cut stone, well laid; and in a good state of preservation. We ascended by large stone steps, in some places perfect, and in others thrown down by trees which had grown up between the crevices, and reached a terrace, the form of which it was impossible to make out, from the density of the forest in which it was enveloped. Our guide cleared a way with his machete, and we passed, as it lay half buried in the earth, a large fragment of stone elaborately sculptured, and came to the angle of a structure with steps on the sides, in form and appearance, so far as the trees would enable us to make it out, like the sides of a pyramid. Diverging from the base, and working our way through the thick woods, we came upon a square stone column, about fourteen feet high and three feet on each side, sculptured in very bold relief, and on all four of the sides, from the base to the top . . . The sight of this unexpected monument put at rest once and forever, in our minds, all uncertainty in regard to the character of American antiquities, and gave us the assurance that the objects we were in search of were interesting, not only as the remains of an unknown people, but as works of art, proving, like newly-discovered historical records, that the people who once occupied the Continent of America were not savages. With an interest perhaps stronger than we had felt in wandering among the ruins of Egypt, we followed our guide, who, sometimes missing his way, with a constant and vigorous use of his machete, conducted us through the thick forest, among half-buried fragments, to fourteen monuments of the same character and appearance, some, with more elegant designs, and some in workmanship equal to the finest monuments of the Egyptians; one displaced from its pedestal by enormous roots; another locked in the close embrace of branches of trees, and almost lifted out of the earth . . .

. . . We returned to the base of the pyramidal structure and ascended by regular stone steps, in some places forced apart by bushes and saplings, and in others thrown down by the growth of large trees, while some remained entire. In parts they were ornamented with sculptured figures and rows of death's heads. Climbing over the ruined top, we reached a terrace overgrown with trees, and, crossing it, descended by stone steps into an area so covered with trees that at first we could not make out its form, but which, on clearing the way with the machete, we ascertained to be a square, and with steps on all the sides almost as perfect as those of the Roman amphitheatre. The steps were ornamented with sculpture, and on the south side, about half-way up, forced out of its place by roots, was a colossal head, evidently a portrait. We ascended these steps and reached a broad terrace a hundred feet high, overlooking the river, and supported by the wall which we had seen from the opposite bank . . . We sat down on the very edge of the wall, and strove in vain to penetrate the mystery by which we were surrounded. Who were the people that built this city? In the ruined cities of Egypt, even in the long-lost Petra, the stranger knows the story of the people whose vestiges are around him. America, say historians, was peopled by savages; but savages never reared these structures, savages never carved these stones. We asked the Indians who made them, and their dull answer was 'Quien sabe?', 'who knows?'

There were no associations connected with the place; none of those stirring recollections which hallow Rome, Athens, and

'The world's great mistress on the Egyptian plain';

but architecture, sculpture, and painting, all the arts which embellished life, had flourished in this overgrown forest; orators, warriors, and statesmen, beauty, ambition, and glory, had lived and passed away, and none knew that such things had been, or could tell of their past existence. Books, the records of knowledge, are silent on this theme.[33]

John L. Stephens, American diplomat and passionate archaeologist, gave this account in 1835 of his first impression of the Maya city of Copán. Since Stephens's book appeared in 1835 and made the culture of the Maya widely known, more archaeologists have become interested in the Maya than in the civilisation of any other people of ancient America. What exactly inspired this interest? The superlative art of the Maya cannot be the only reason. The art of a number of other civilisations of ancient America equals that of the Maya. There are other factors that must account for the particular attraction of this culture.

The Maya demonstrate the highest intellectual achievements to be found in pre-Columbian America: the calendar, mathematics and graphology reached a stage of development among them that no other American people, except perhaps the Olmecs, equalled. Scholars from all over the world have been attracted by their scripts, two-thirds of which have not yet been deciphered.

The intellectual achievements of the Maya are in striking contrast to their methods of food production and their tools, the standard of which is typical of the lowest American cultures. Also surprising is the fact that they were surrounded by primeval forest. In most other areas of primeval forest in America not even the beginnings of civilisation exist.

The problem that so greatly stirred Stephens's imagination has also impressed many archaeologists since: the centre of Maya culture in southern Mesoamerica is the only one of all the cultural centres of the New World that shows no continuous settlement. Even today the most important cultural areas of Mexico are located in the regions of Teotihuacan and Tenochtitlan, and in Peru the Valley of Cuzco is a densely populated area. But the Maya lowland region remains almost totally deserted and has presumably been so for a thousand years.

It is not surprising, therefore, that research into the Maya took the form of an almost unprecedented international exercise, ranging from Siberia to Central America.[34] Archaeologists had to overcome great difficulties. Co-ordinated research is not made any easier by the virtual inaccessibility of the most important Maya centres, nor by the fact that Maya ruins lie in no less than five different modern states.

Nevertheless, important progress has been achieved in recent years by systematic excavations, for instance those carried out in the greatest Maya city, Tikal, which make it possible to reveal a new picture of the social organisation and life of the Maya. We are however still far from having any certain evidence concerning the rise and fall of Maya civilisation.

The civilisation of the Maya developed over a very extensive area of southern Mesoamerica. Even today it is inhabited, albeit in very varying degrees, by descendants of the Maya whose languages are inter-related. It covers parts of Southern Mexico and parts of Guatemala, Honduras, British Honduras and El Salvador. Certain archaeological similarities do exist in this region, but it is not possible to speak of a homogeneous Maya area. Most archaeologists distinguish between three different geographical regions, southern, central and northern, all of which display great cultural differences.[35]

Essentially the southern part covers the highlands and coast land of modern Guatemala. It constitutes the richest and most fertile area of the Maya region and is now inhabited by millions of people. On the Pacific coast of Guatemala it was possible to cultivate cocoa, one of the most sought-after crops, and the only one that served as an international currency. The highlands of Guatemala are in many respects reminiscent of the plateau of Central Mexico. They have rich and fertile regions and contain a similar medley of moderately high- and low-lying zones, with a great variety of agricultural possibilities in a relatively confined and narrow area. The southern region of the Maya possessed important mineral raw materials, jade and obsidian, which played a decisive part

in Maya civilisation. In addition there were great quantities of limestone, which was highly suitable for large buildings. In the highlands of
Guatemala there were no obstacles to a considerable flow of traffic,
and there were good communications between the various valleys.
This area is estimated to have been the most fertile and the most suitable
for human settlement.

The northern Maya region, which covered the peninsula of Yucatan,
is similarly densely populated today (and was in pre-Spanish times),
even though it is much less fertile than the southern region. This peninsula consists of a tropical plain with very little rainfall, but it is
adequately supplied with subterranean water caverns and rivers. These
made it possible to cultivate extensive areas of Yucatan. Maize could
be grown, as well as certain kinds of agave, in particular sisal hemp,
which was already used for clothing in pre-Spanish times.

Between these two areas is the central Maya region. For the most
part it is covered by dense tropical primeval forest and is almost uninhabited today. The soil is however suitable for maize, though conditions are difficult. In a slash and burn agriculture such as the Maya
probably practised, the soil could be cultivated only for two years and
then had to lie fallow for five or ten years. With the same agricultural
system prevailing in the central highlands of Guatemala, the southern
region of the Maya, the soil could again be used for cultivation in as
little as two years.[36] The luxuriant tropical vegetation constituted an
additional obstacle to human settlement, since it overran the crops
under cultivation and was a perpetual danger, as well as enhancing
the difficulties of communication. Between the areas of primeval forest
there were stretches of savannah that could not be cultivated with the
digging sticks used by the Maya, and swamps that were entirely
unsuitable for human settlement.

The tropical fauna of this region was and still is among the least
agreeable in Mesoamerica. A great variety of insects, especially flies,
and snakes cause danger to the traveller. Even today there is the ever
present risk of contracting tropical diseases. The region is also considered to be among the poorest in the Maya zone in its supply of raw
materials. Limestone alone is available in sufficient quantity. Yet it was
in precisely this region, which has remained uninhabited for hundreds
of years and is the least fertile, poorest and most difficult of access of the
Maya zone, that Maya civilisation attained its finest flowering. That it
should have risen as it did despite this poses one of the most difficult
problems facing scholarship today.

There is no doubt that the development that took place in the Maya
region displayed the most marked individual features, both materially
and culturally, not only in Mesoamerica but probably in the whole of
America. These were not immediately apparent, however.

As in the rest of Mesoamerica a proliferation of small agricultural villages preceded the appearance of the Maya civilisation. The inhabitants of the villages that sprang up during the first century BC lived, as on the Mexican plateau, mainly on maize, beans, pumpkin and game. In addition they presumably also cultivated cotton and cocoa. In about 300 BC the first religious buildings of any size began to be built. In the highlands of Guatemala pyramidal mounds of earth cover magnificently furnished graves. The rich offerings and even human sacrifices that were made to the dead, and were probably meant to accompany them into the unknown, indicate that a far-reaching social stratification had already taken place. A considerable number of such centres has been excavated in the central highlands of Guatemala. One centre in particular, however, seems to have excelled all others, both in size and probably in power. This was Kaminaljuyu, the modern Guatemala City. The number of religious buildings there is by far the largest, and it is estimated that a labour force of between twelve and fifteen thousand would have been required to erect them. This could suggest a degree of political centralisation. Indeed it is assumed by some that Kaminaljuyu constituted the cultural and perhaps also the political centre of power in the highlands of Guatemala.[37]

The rise of this city, as was the case in all the larger centres of Mesoamerica, was very closely associated with an expansion of trade. Objects have been found in Kaminaljuyu from extremely distant regions, and conversely pottery and other objects from this city have found their way into regions as far afield as the Mexican plateau.

At the same time the culture of Izapa, which lies in the state of Chiapas in modern Mexico, about twenty kilometres from the Pacific coast, was emerging. Most archaeologists consider it to be a late development of Olmec culture. Reliefs, sculptures and pyramidal mounds of earth have been found here that are strongly reminiscent of those of the Olmecs. The open, curling back lips of a god are closely related to the grinning jaguar teeth of the Olmec gods and the U sign that is so characteristic of Olmec sculpture can also be seen here. Hieroglyphs have not been found in Izapa itself, but some have come to light at another Olmec site, at El Baul on the Pacific coast. Very close links between Izapa and many parts of the Maya region have been substantiated by the presence of Izapa ware in the highlands and by the strong cultural influence exerted by Izapa.[38]

In the early centuries of our era a growing differentiation became apparent in the development of the various Maya regions. Izapa's importance diminished and after a period of decline, Kaminaljuyu came under the domination of Teotihuacan in the fourth century AD. The civilisation of the Maya proper shifted more and more into the central lowland region. From the first century AD a tremendous advance took place almost without transition, both in culture and in population. Archaeologists in general regard the construction of what is known as the Pyramid E-VII-sub – an archaeological term – in Uaxactun as the beginning of this development. It is the most ancient building in the Maya lowland region and has been preserved largely by virtue of being covered by a more recent pyramid, the façade of which was badly weather-worn. Beside a stairway leading to the summit of the fifteen-metre-high pyramid are representations of jaguars.

The construction of this pyramid introduced a development that reached its peak about AD 300. This is the date regarded by most scholars as the beginning of the classic period of the Maya. In a relatively short time over eighty large and many smaller Maya centres were constructed in the central lowland region alone. Dozens more were built in the northern region. Only a small proportion of these have been systematically excavated and evaluated so far, and there is little doubt that new excavations will greatly modify our present knowledge.

The classic period in the region of the Maya is distinguished by a spectacular flowering of architecture, sculpture, painting and learning. The architecture of the Maya centres was monumental. They contained great plazas bordered by tremendous pyramids, temples and palaces. Most archaeologists use the term 'acropolis' for these groups of buildings. Wide roads suitable for religious processions lead into these central plazas. The centres are in some respects reminiscent of Teotihuacan, though the differences between them and the great city in the centre of Mexico outweigh their similarities. To start with the external impression of these pyramids is quite different. The Mexican pyramids are broken by platforms and give the effect of a gentle incline. The pyramids of the Maya, which are in fact much smaller, give an impression of greater height. A steep stairway, uninterrupted by platforms, leads up to the summit of the pyramid, on which stands a temple, its roof decorated with a roof-combe. Wolf regards this as an architectural development of the roof-combe of a Maya peasant hut.[39]

Anyone ascending the great pyramid of Teotihuacan and a lower Maya pyramid very soon senses the difference. Although the Sun Pyramid in Teotihuacan is distinctly higher, the platforms that separate the stairways from each other have the effect of making the ascent relatively easy, so that it does not require much exertion and does not make the climber giddy. The Maya pyramids are quite different. An almost endless number of steps lead upwards without a break, causing a sensation of giddiness and of overwhelming height even during the ascent, and far more during the descent.

The corbelled vault gives Maya cities their particular stamp. It did not exist in other parts of Mesoamerica and is regarded as the most distinctive feature of classic Maya culture. It arose from the fact that rooms in a Maya building were vaulted by overlapping stones. Thick walls and roofs containing narrow, dark, windowless rooms were characteristic of Maya palaces and temples. It is therefore doubtful whether these rooms were suitable for habitation.

One of the most striking achievements of the Maya is their system of writing, the most advanced in pre-Columbian America. Maya hieroglyphs were executed as pictographs, either painted and illustrated manuscripts or engraved on stone. Almost all the pictographs were burned as works of the devil after the arrival of the Spaniards. Only three of these hieroglyphic manuscripts have survived and they are now in European libraries; they are known as the Dresden, Madrid and Paris codices, from the cities where they are preserved.

In contrast to the pictographs, the inscriptions on stone have largely been preserved. The hieroglyphs were found for the most part on stelae that had been erected in the centre of Maya cities of the period. Over a thousand such stelae have so far been accounted for. In addition hieroglyphs were also engraved on other stone objects, and there are over two thousand of them on the sixty-two steps of a stairway in the Maya city of Copan. Murals and smaller objects such as vases and jade plaques were also inscribed with hieroglyphs.

When Stephens first saw these hieroglyphs in the first half of the nineteenth century he was completely at a loss. There seemed to be no trace of anything by which to decipher them, but the example set by Champollion inspired the search for a 'Rosetta stone' for the Maya script. In 1865 the search was thought to be at an end. That year saw the first printing of a book, forgotten for centuries, by the first Bishop of Yucatan, Diego de Landa, *History of Events in Yucatan*.[40] Landa was responsible for burning hundreds of Maya pictographs, but he was nevertheless exceedingly interested in the Maya and asked a number of Maya scholars about the meaning of the hieroglyphic writings. In his book he recorded the Maya calendar, and introduced a phonetic alphabet of twenty-nine sounds. Was this the much sought-after Rosetta stone? The Maya script was not completely deciphered and Landa's alphabet did not become an 'open sesame' for the understanding of Maya hieroglyphic writing. Nevertheless with the help of Landa's book it was possible to set out their calendar and to understand their astronomy, so that about a third of the hieroglyphs that referred to these subjects could be deciphered by the end of the nineteenth century.

The remaining two-thirds of the hieroglyphs have not been deciphered with any certainty, and their decipherment has led to great controversy. In the main there were two schools of thought. One took the view that Maya hieroglyphs were not phonetic but ideographic, expressing ideas and not sounds, more or less like Chinese script. A second group took their stand on Landa's assertion that Maya script was phonetic. In the last few decades the latter trend has received fresh encouragement from Russian research. J.Knorozov tried to discover a phonetic solution, and a team from the Siberian Academy of Science attempted to decipher the script by means of computers. The results are nevertheless disputed[41] by scholars who do not believe in a purely phonetic interpretation of Maya script, though they also hold the view that a purely ideographic interpretation is no longer tenable. In many quarters it is thought that Maya hieroglyphic writing is a mixture of the most varied developments of graphology, containing pictographic, ideographic and phonetic elements.

For years there was also fierce controversy over the hypothetical content of the Maya hieroglyphs that still remained to be deciphered. Many scholars, basing their belief on the hieroglyphs that had been deciphered, assumed that they contained religious, calendrical and astronomical data. Recent research however has increased the probability that at least a considerable number of Maya hieroglyphs are historical. Tatiana Proskuriakov inaugurated a new age in the decipherment of the Maya script by finding historical data in it. In the Maya cities of Piedras Negras and Yaxchilan she described the entry into office, the life and battles of a hypothetical ruler called 'Bird Jaguar', then uncovered the lives of other historical figures.[42]

Will the Maya script ever be completely deciphered? No one dares to answer this question. At all events the increasing number of scholars who are turning their attention to the problem and the growing international interest in it is encouraging. The work of these scholars is all the more valuable in that Maya hieroglyphs present in many respects a thankless task. While archaeological excavations almost always produce some result – even if this does not correspond with the archaeologist's expectations – decades may be spent on deciphering Maya hieroglyphs without any visible result. The growing use of cybernetic methods of calculation may perhaps lead to greater progress. One of these days a Rosetta stone for Maya hieroglyphic writing may be discovered in a Spanish archive, in Yucatan or in one of the settlements of a religious order.

Fortunately information concerning the great achievements of the Maya in the realm of the calendar, astronomy and mathematics is much more complete. As with all agricultural peoples, preoccupation with the seasons was of decisive significance for the Maya and perhaps represented the most important function that the priesthood had to carry out. The Maya shared with other peoples of Mesoamerica a specific calendar system. There were two distinct measurements for the year: a ritual calendar year of 260 days, which was divided into 13 months of 20 days each; and a solar year of 365 days, which contained 18 months of 20 days each, with an additional period of 5 days. Each day had its place both in the solar and in the ritual calendar. The first day of the solar year coincided with the first day of the ritual year only every 52 years. A new cycle of 52 years then began. Such cycles are characteristic of all Mesoamerican calendars. Within such a cycle it was easy to fix every day with precision, since every date in the solar year corresponded only once in 52 years with a date in the ritual year. Among the non-Maya peoples of Mesoamerica these 52-year cycles were not related to a fixed order. A scholar considering a date in the ancient history of a central Mexican people is therefore able to establish the exact day within a cycle of 52 years, but cannot be certain which cycle is in question, that is to say, whether the relevant day is 52 or 520 years ago.

The Maya had solved the problem of the correct sequence and dating of these cycles by what is known as the 'long count'. They created the following divisions:

20 days equalled one Uinal
18 Uinals constituted one Tun (or 360 days)
20 Tun constituted one Katun (or 7,200 days)
20 Katun constituted one Bactun (or 144,000 days)
20 Bactun constituted one Pictun (or 2,880,000 days)
20 Pictun constituted one Calabtun (or 57,600,000 days)

Within such a calendar every day could of course be precisely dated by referring to an exactly fixed point of departure. The Maya had fixed such a point of departure, but its exact year is unknown. How is it possible to establish this fixed point? The Maya calendar was still in force at the time of the Spanish Conquest. Scholars have therefore made efforts to co-ordinate events that took place during the Conquest and were registered in the Maya calendar with the date of the same events in the Christian calendar. A second method consisted of checking astronomically determinable data, such as eclipses of the sun, against each other in the Christian and Maya calendars. Research has not yet been able to clarify this method in all its details. There are two different theories for the hypothetical point of departure of the Maya calendar. Most scholars adopt the Martinez-Goodman-Thompson correlation, according to which the point of departure is the year 3113 BC. Another calculation, by Spinden, puts the point of departure back two hundred years. Recently attempts have been made to confirm one of these hypotheses by results obtained by dating various objects by the radio-carbon method.

The astronomical attainments of the Maya, whose technical equipment was almost nil, went still further. The Maya priesthood had succeeded in calculating the exact dates of the Venus year and of solar eclipses, and at the time of the arrival of the Europeans in the New

World their calendar was more precise and accurate than the Julian calendar in use at that period in Europe.

Maya computations primarily served religious purposes. Some scholars have described the Maya as being obsessed by time and this description might possibly be justified, for the preoccupation with time seems to have been interwoven with every religious rite. Each day was regarded as the burden which a god had to carry. Life on that day would be governed according to the character of this god and of the constellation of the heavenly powers. Determining the favourable or unfavourable days constituted one of the main functions of the priesthood.

Obviously, an advanced knowledge of mathematics was necessary to accomplish these important achievements in astronomy. Maya mathematicians had reached a high degree of development in their field. They had mastered the positional notation system unknown to the Greeks and Romans. Their system was not decimal but vigesimal. Maya numbers could be expressed either by symbols or by dots and bars.

In the following examples the dot-bar system is set out. One dot represents one unit and one bar represents five units. The bottom line contains all numbers up to 20, the next 20 to 399, the following line 400 to 7,999. The next starting point is again twenty times greater, and so forth, thus:

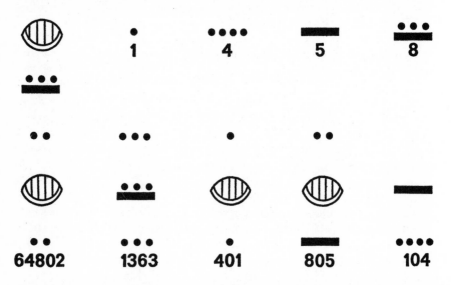

One of the greatest mathematical achievements was the invention of the figure 0. This was unknown to the Greeks and Romans and was

first introduced into Europe from India by the Arabs in the year
AD 1202. It is possible that the Maya knew the figure o before the
Indians.

The most glaring discrepancy that comes to light in these achievements of the Maya lies in their use of a highly developed system of
mathematics almost exclusively for astrological-religious purposes. So
far among the hieroglyphs no figures have been found for recording
everyday transactions. There must have existed a virtually unbridge-
able gulf between the outlook of the priests who mastered so complicated
a calendrical-mathematical system and that of the simple peasants.
This is also apparent in their religion, which in any case we know
relatively little about. The gods of nature on which it was based,
especially the rain god Chacs and the legendary hero Itzamna who
existed at least amongst the sixteenth-century Maya, were certainly
worshipped by the people, but it is extremely doubtful whether the
mass of the peasantry were able to understand their complicated
attributes. Every god possessed four personalities each expressing a
different point of the compass and a different colour. The connections,
based on complicated computations, between the gods and the stars in
their courses must also have been very difficult to grasp.

In any case there can hardly be a greater contrast than that which
existed between the intellectual achievements of the Maya and the
essentially primitive character of their material life. This contrast and
the environment in which the culture of the Maya developed, which
differed so fundamentally from that of all the other high cultures of
America and of the Old World, has led to an exceptional number of
theories regarding both the origin and evolution of the Maya civilisation, and also its end. The problem facing scholarship in this matter is
that many of these hypotheses must be taken seriously. They cannot
finally be adopted as proven, nor can they be rejected out of hand.

Scholars have been able to answer with a considerable degree of
certainty Stephens's urgent questioning of over a century ago as to the
identity of those who built the great Maya cities. Parallels and similarities between the Maya hieroglyphics of the sixteenth century and
those of the ancient Maya cities, physical resemblances between present-
day Maya and those of the classical period allow us to presume that the
inhabitants of the ancient cities were the ancestors of the modern Maya.
But the question of the spoken language of the classical Maya is still to
be answered. Which of the present dialects did it resemble? Was it a
sort of proto-Maya language which formed the common basis of all
these dialects?

The place of origin of the Maya civilisation is much debated. The
great intellectual achievements of the Maya, graphology, calendar and
mathematics, were fully matured from the moment that they appeared.

F

Prototypes of the form of their writing, calendar and mathematics have never been discovered. Nevertheless such achievements require a long period of evolution and development. Where did this process take place? One school of thought is convinced that Maya civilisation originated within the Maya region, and believes that the reason why no prototypes have been discovered of writing or of other intellectual achievements is only because the first attempts at writing and mathematics were executed on perishable material such as wood or paper. Engraving on stone only came into practice at a considerably later date.[43]

Recently the idea that the important intellectual achievements of the Maya originated among the Olmecs, where the first hieroglyphs and the earliest calendrical data were discovered, has been gaining ground among scholars. Many scholars see the connecting link between the cultures of the Maya and the Olmecs in the culture of Izapa.[44] Even if this theory is accepted however a final answer concerning the origin of these civilisations has still not been given since no prototypes of script, of the calendar or of mathematics have been found among the Olmecs either.

Other scholars are convinced that the Maya culture did not originate in the tropical lowland of Mesoamerica. Many of them believe that Mesoamerican high culture originated in the highlands,[45] either in the plateau of central Mexico or the highlands of Guatemala. They point out that nature in the highlands is much kinder, living conditions are easier and above all in the highlands there is a far greater possibility of increased production and of releasing a larger group of the population from agricultural work. Those who think that all Mesoamerican high cultures originated in the central Mexican plateau take their stand on the supposition that Olmec culture originated there and that it then became diffused over the whole of the lowlands.

Some scholars seek the origin of Maya culture outside the American continent, and point to similarities between the religion and art of the Maya and those of some South-East Asian peoples.[46] The pros and cons of this hypothesis have already been examined in the first section of this work.

But whichever theory or hypothesis is favoured, a fundamental problem still remains: how could a culture like that of the Maya develop in the highly unfavourable circumstances that prevailed in the southern Maya region, an area which is now almost completely deserted? There are vast stretches of America covered by tropical primeval forests, yet the Maya were the only Indian people living there to develop any sort of advanced culture.

William T. Sanders has investigated the ecological bases for the high cultures of both the Old and New World.[47] Among these he regards as most important the presence of fertile soil, which can be intensively cultivated, and enough water for irrigation, making possible intensive cultivation of the soil by a peasant population with an essentially neolithic technology. There should also be a large river capable of serving as a natural highway, and a scarcity of raw materials as an incentive to trade.

All this directly contradicts the ecological character of the tropical primeval forest area and that of the Maya particularly. The rivers which flow across the Maya region are unsuitable for transport and the primeval forest makes communication very difficult. The soil is of low fertility. As is still the case, on the eve of the Conquest the popular agricultural system was the slash and burn method already described. Although the *per capita* yield is no less than in many regions where intensive agriculture is practised, the individual requires much more land than is the case with intensive agriculture. It has been calculated that the maximum population density the central region of the Maya could sustain on the basis of such a system and given the nature of the soil was between fifty and eighty inhabitants per square kilometre.[48] These peasants were forced to live scattered lives and tended to change their habitations frequently since after a few years they had to leave the fields they had cultivated.

Was it then possible for a system with such a proportionately small population density, with people living scattered lives and with few economic incentives towards centralisation, to produce great cities and important cultural achievements? In theory, yes. As already mentioned, it has been estimated that a Maya family only needed to work 120 days in the year to produce twice the amount of food it needed. Its members could then spend the rest of the year on public works. It has also been established that about half the population in the region of Peten were in a position to feed the other half as well as themselves.

In fact, though, the lack of population density, its scattered way of life and the difficulty of communications were a definite obstacle to the development of a high culture in almost every primeval forest region in America. Although a great many Indian tribes of the Amazon forests were closely associated with the highly developed empire of the Inca, the influence exercised on them by the latter in cultural and social matters was small. Why were the Maya an exception? Why did such an important high culture develop in this region, in contrast to all other regions of primeval forest in America?

It is hardly surprising that this very problem has given rise to so many varied and contradictory hypotheses. Some historians believe that the Maya culture originated in the highlands and then for reasons which cannot be ascertained today – wars, for example, or emigration – shifted to the lowlands where owing to unfavourable conditions it slowly declined. Critics of this theory have pointed out with some justification that a thousand years is a long period for decline and that this period in any case cannot be regarded as a period of decline since it was precisely in this millennium that the Maya attained their most important achievements. Even if the Maya had originated elsewhere it is incontestable, given our present state of knowledge, that they reached the zenith of their development in the unpropitious lowlands rather than in the fertile highlands.

Other scholars consider that the Maya succeeded in overcoming the difficulties of their environment through religious faith. The faith of the population was such that the priesthood were able to use for their own purposes the plentiful spare time which the peasant population enjoyed. This utilisation of the peasant labour force may have taken place either peaceably or by force. Many scholars are puzzled nevertheless as to why, among the Maya alone, such an advanced culture could have originated against the background of such a primitive form of agriculture. The few examples of high culture known in the tropics, say among the Khmer of South-East Asia, are always associated with irrigation and intensive agriculture.

It was precisely these considerations that led Eric Wolf and Angel Palerm to suggest that some kind of intensive agriculture must have existed among the Maya as it did in Teotihuacan.[49] That hypothesis has been borne out by recent excavations in the Maya region. In addition, Wolf and Palerm believe that there may well have been some kind of commercial link between the Maya and Teotihuacan. Perhaps the large Maya centres served as market places where the highland and lowland peoples exchanged their produce. This theory had been given credence by the strong influences of Teotihuacan discovered recently in the great Maya centre of Tikal. If this were true, the development of Maya culture would no longer be so exceptional and we should be dealing with a development very similar to that in other regions of high culture, only in a rather less suitable agricultural environment. However, the fact that no proof of such intensive agriculture has been found so far, nor that it existed on the eve of the Conquest, throws some doubt on this theory.

Bennett Bronson[50] considers that it was not intensive agriculture, but crops other than maize on which a large population could still subsist which constituted the agricultural basis of the classic Maya culture. Possibly, the basic food of the Maya was tubers, which yield a far higher crop in primeval forest land, but so far no evidence for this has been found. Maize is not only the most important basic food – it occupies an important place in Maya religion.

Questions about the social organization of the Maya are no less contested. Reconstruction of their social conditions and organisation in some respects suggests a steep pyramid. At the bottom a man's position was relatively secure and no great harm could come from a fall. The higher an individual ascended, the less secure the hold and the easier it was to crash.

Life at the bottom of the social pyramid, best represented by village communities, is the easiest to reconstruct, largely from archaeological sources. The permanence of village communities in Mesoamerica as in many parts of the world makes it possible to draw conclusions from later periods which almost certainly apply to the classic period. The peasants lived, as they do today, in small huts generally covered with leaves. The huts seem to have been sturdier in the classic period and if anything more luxurious. In those days a platform was even erected as a foundation, which is hardly ever the case nowadays.

Maya dress usually consisted of richly decorated knee-breeches for men and a cotton skirt and blouse, also finely embroidered, for the women. The upper classes frequently used jade and feathers for decoration. The ideals of beauty among the Maya in some respects sharply contradicted those of Europeans. The skull of a new-born child was pressed between two boards, to bring about an elongated deformation, and squinting was considered particularly beautiful. To bring this about wooden balls were hung between the eyes of the newly-born. Ears, lips and the bridge of the nose were pierced in order to carry ornaments. Young people painted themselves black and adults painted themselves red.

The morals of the Maya peasants must in some respects have eased the work later carried out by the missionaries. Monogamy was the general rule, polygamy being reserved for the nobility only. Adultery was regarded as a crime, although separation was an exceedingly simple and informal affair.

The prevailing tribal organisation among the Maya, still in practice today, was more difficult for Europeans to understand. Land was common property of clan-like groups, whose members were forbidden to intermarry within their own group. Portions of land for cultivation were handed over by the tribe to every family. Most villages were not very large and consisted of twenty to forty families.

The work these peasants did was by no means light since to clear the tropical forest with simple stone tools must have been extremely difficult. Nevertheless a Maya peasant required less time for his husbandry than a European peasant, who at the same time bred cattle, or than a central Mexican peasant on the plateau, who had to bring in several harvests a year from intensively irrigated land. Bee-keeping and the rearing of dogs and turkeys were widely practised and hunting was another major source of food.

The Maya peasant used up a large proportion of the ample free time for building temples, and for work and services for the benefit of the upper classes. These burdens however cannot have been too oppressive during the most important era of the classic period. Gordon Willey's excavations in many of the smaller Maya villages led him to conclude that the Maya peasants had a comparatively high standard of living: he sees as evidence of this the richly decorated graves in the smaller villages and the presence of platform foundations in all the houses.[51]

For whom did these peasants work? Who made up the nobility, and who lived in the Maya cities? The first problem facing archaeologists was the question as to whether the dozens of Maya centres were actual cities, like Teotihuacan. The imposing acropolis which formed the centre of so many Maya centres could mislead one into believing that they were.

More accurate archaeological examinations have however given rise to a different conclusion. The Maya habit of erecting houses on platforms of which, in contrast to the houses themselves, vestiges still remain has made it possible to count the number of houses. This assessment, together with the examination of rubbish heaps, led to the conclusion that with one exception, only three to five thousand people lived in each of the Maya centres, a population density which can hardly be defined as urban. For this reason, most scholars regard Maya centres not as cities in the real sense of the word, like Teotihuacan for instance, but as ceremonial centres. The population of the outlying villages flocked into these centres only on religious occasions, on feast days and market days. Otherwise they were inhabited only by the upper classes, their servants and a few peasants. Even now there are several 'cities' of this kind in Guatemala where, apart from religious occasions and market days, only a very small number of religious and administrative officials gather.

Who then constituted the nobility? This is one of the most hotly disputed problems of Maya history. Did the Maya form a democratic tribal organisation, without any hereditary nobility? Egon C. Vogt discovered in the Maya township of Zinacantan a constantly changing religious organisation which in his view could also have existed in the classic period.[52] Zinacantan was a locality surrounded by many small villages. During most of the year the place was empty apart from a few Maya who carried out religious and administrative functions. The men responsible for these functions fulfilled them only during a limited period of time. The rest of the year they spent in the various villages from which they had come. The functions were distributed in accordance with a complicated system of services, of riches and of social prestige, which meant that they were not carried out professionally by one social group. Vogt suggested that such an organisation possibly existed, at least for a time, amongst the classic Maya, in which case the social organisation of the Maya must naturally have had a strongly democratic character. This theory nevertheless has been vigorously opposed. Vogt's opponents point to the many representations in frescoes and reliefs during the last century of the Maya, which portray a richly clad nobility sharply distinguished from the general population. Above all, they point out that the religion, script, mathematics and astronomy of the Maya demanded such a high standard of knowledge, that a democratic system involving constant change is hardly credible in this connection. At the time of the Conquest these intellectual achievements were the monopoly of a small circle of initiates. Consequently, most scholars believe in the existence of a nobility widely separated from the mass of the population. The point on which they do not agree is whether the nobility were of a religious or a temporal order.

There is scarcely an advanced civilisation in ancient America in which the proportion of religious and secular buildings is more strongly orientated towards religious buildings than among the Maya. In addition no ruling class of any other high culture expended so much energy on purely intellectual-religious ends as did that of the Maya. From the very earliest times hardly any signs of war have been discovered, and in contrast to later epochs, scarcely any fortifications were erected. Such representations of war as we have nearly all belong to a later period. All these factors caused many Maya scholars to term the Maya cities theocracies or hierarchies. They recognised the Maya cities as independent city states that led a comparatively peaceful existence governed by a priesthood.

Does history contain many examples of peaceful co-existence by theocratic states lasting centuries? How was it that on the eve of the Conquest not a single state of this kind was discovered in Mesoamerica? These questions are put by some historians who hold the view that among the Maya a secular, entirely military caste was in power as was the case among their descendants at the time of the Conquest – at all events after a central Mexican conquest in the eleventh century AD. In all the cities they conquered the Spaniards eventually met the supreme rulers, *Halach Uinic*. These men were temporal rulers, whose office was hereditary. They possessed their own estates, which were cultivated by slaves, and they exacted tribute and services from the peasants. Under them was a sort of village prince, the *Batab*, who represented a minor nobility, and a very complex hierarchy of priests who ranked beneath the temporal power. Cannot this social structure be transferred to the classic period? Are not the reliefs of warriors in Yaxchilan, the frescoes in Bonampak which represent bloody battles, evidence that in the late classic period at least the Maya did not enjoy absolute peace? For years scholarship was faced with these two ideas, each supported by plausible arguments.

Excavations recently carried out may help to reconcile these two theories which for so long have seemed irreconcilable. Archaeological work in Tikal, the greatest of the Maya centres, has confirmed that this city was more important than any other settlement.[53] It contains not only the largest buildings, but is the only centre that can be called urban. Some proof of this lies in the number of the population, estimated at about eleven to twelve thousand, a far greater number than that in any other Maya centre. At the same time much stronger influences from Teotihuacan have been discovered here. Together, these facts make it highly probable that Tikal, as a vassal or ally of Teotihuacan, ruled over a considerable portion of Maya territory, and that a sort of *Pax Teotihuacana* or a *Pax Tikaliana* guaranteed a peaceful development in the first centuries of Maya history. This theory is supported by the fact that representations of battles and wars do not appear until the last period of Maya history, when Teotihuacan's influence was receding and when Tikal was perhaps already overrun by enemy tribes. The ending of Teotihuacan's domination and the subsequent struggles for independence by the many Maya centres could have initiated a period of war.

THE CULTURE OF MONTE ALBAN

The cultures of Teotihuacan and of the Maya represent the two most clearly defined and at the same time most extreme forms of development of the classic period in Mesoamerica: in Teotihuacan there was a great city, in the Maya region there were ceremonial centres of which only one developed the characteristics of a city. In Teotihuacan there existed a culture and a civilisation based on an intensive agriculture that allowed for sophisticated methods of food production; in the Maya region there was a culture where agriculture was comparatively undeveloped, but where intellectual achievements far outstripped those of Teotihuacan. Alongside these two clearly defined high cultures of Mesoamerica, there were others that exercised less influence and had strong ties both with the Maya and with Teotihuacan. In the Valley of Oaxaca a culture developed in which a technically advanced agriculture was associated with high intellectual achievements. This culture shows strong ties with Teotihuacan as well as with the Maya, although it is impossible to say whether Oaxaca depended exclusively on foreign cultures.[54] Ecologically speaking, the Valley of Oaxaca resembles the central Mexican plateau. There is the contrast of tropical lowland, snow-covered mountain peaks and fertile valleys with a temperate climate, the largest being that of Oaxaca itself, and although it is warmer here than at the higher altitude of the Valley of Mexico, the temperature is certainly not tropical. Just as in the central Mexican plateau there is a combination of temperate and tropical regions where the various climatic zones verge closely upon one another. The geographical character of the Valley of Oaxaca facilitated communications both with the neighbouring lowlands and the Valley of Mexico. Consequently there was a far greater exchange here of the most diverse cultural influences than in any other region of Mesoamerica.

Archaeological research, in spite of the great progress that has been made recently, has not advanced so far in the Valley of Oaxaca as in Teotihuacan. One of the consequences of this is that the date of the beginning of human settlement in Oaxaca is still in doubt. Because of Oaxaca's proximity to the Valley of Tehuacan where, as has already been related, MacNeish discovered traces of human settlement going back to 7000 BC, the conclusion was drawn that the Valley of Oaxaca must have supported human settlement for approximately the same time. Nevertheless, incontestable evidence of very early human settlement has so far not been discovered. As in other parts of Mesoamerica, the first signs of a high culture in the Valley of Oaxaca likewise have no recognisable origins. These signs come for the most part from one place, which was for almost a thousand years the focal point and centre of the valley's life: Monte Alban, which stands on a hill. The first signs of religious architecture there are platforms supported by stone walls, on which there were representations of people generally known as *Danzantes*, that is dancers. They were so called because the stone figures were represented in a wide variety of distorted attitudes and seem to be performing strange dances. In reality, as Coe[55] presumes, they were more likely people who were either being sacrificed or killed for reasons which are still unknown. Because these dancers clearly have Olmec features, the culture of Monte Alban I is generally considered to have been closely connected with the Olmecs. Some scholars may go so far as to see Monte Alban as the place of origin of Olmec culture. At all events the population of this region may well have played a significant role in the development of writing and of the calendar. The script and calendar glyphs of Monte Alban are among the most ancient in Mesoamerica. The inhabitants of Monte Alban knew the dot and bar system of numbers and seem to have used both the ritual calendar of 260 days and the astronomical calendar of 365 days. Monte Alban must certainly have been an important ceremonial centre at that time and perhaps even had city status.

Who were the inhabitants of Monte Alban? The Maya, the Olmecs as well as the Zapotecs, who today dwell in the Valley of Oaxaca, have all been suggested.

About the year 300 BC a completely new architectural and artistic style appeared in Monte Alban and in a number of other places in the Valley of Oaxaca which archaeologists term Monte Alban II. The style of the earlier period persisted, but only at the level of folk art and in simple objects. The ceremonial buildings were erected in the new style. Typical of this period is a stone building known by the prosaic name of Construction J which resembles an arrow-head and contains dark rooms. Whether it was built as a palace or as an observatory is impossible to say. Script and calendrical glyphs found in this period have a particularly curious form. Heads on the glyphs are reversed and represented upside down. Alfonso Caso interpreted these symbols as representing the glyphs of places which had been overthrown.[56] In fact there are several indications that a foreign conquest took place. Only the upper class was influenced by the new culture, which bore a marked resemblance to the civilisations of the lowland region, especially that of the Maya. Conquest by a Maya people is even suggested as a strong probability.

About the third century AD there was another upheaval in Oaxaca. Parallel to the appearance of a new art style, known by archaeologists as Monte Alban III, there was a tremendous upsurge in Monte Alban which now developed into a great city. In the centre was a colossal plaza, bordered by four pyramidal buildings separated from each other by houses built on terraces. This plaza is considered one of the most beautiful in all Mesoamerica.

At this period the art and construction methods of Monte Alban show strong Teotihuacan influences. These influences however do not occur in a pure form as in other regions of Mesoamerica, but were intermingled with Monte Alban's own style. Consequently, many historians doubt whether there was a direct conquest of the city on the hill by the great central Mexican city. It is just as probable that religion and trade may have spread the style of Teotihuacan.

Monte Alban shows strong resemblances to Teotihuacan from a material point of view as well. It appears to have been one of the few genuine cities beside the great city of the plateau. A close network of dwelling houses surrounded the religious centre proper. The agricultural basis was also very similar to that of Teotihuacan. The discovery of a large dam, which indicates a vast irrigation system similar to one in the neighbouring valley of Tehuacan in the year AD 300, led experts for a long time to assume that something similar must have existed in neighbouring Oaxaca and the recent discovery of a complicated system of dams and terraces in the Valley of Oaxaca seems to have confirmed these conjectures. The existence of such an intensive agriculture becomes credible when the density of the valley population – which was very great on the eve of the Spanish Conquest – is taken into account.[57] Trade also played a considerable part in the development of the Valley of Oaxaca; it was the production centre in Mesoamerica for one of the favourite dyes, cochineal.

If the culture of Monte Alban closely resembled those of central

Mexico materially and also to a certain extent artistically, intellectually there was a much greater affinity with the cultures of the lowland: writing, much more predominant than in Teotihuacan, calendars and a highly developed mathematics. At the same time a number of characteristics appeared in the Valley of Oaxaca, which are typical of the cultures of this valley and which give them a particular stamp both as regards town planning and architecture.

While neither Teotihuacan nor the Maya centres could be described as fortresses, there are several signs that military considerations played an important role in the lay-out of Monte Alban. Situated on a hill high above the valley, Monte Alban was a natural fortress. This is confirmed by the many representations of war and conquest, which far outnumber those in Teotihuacan or among the Maya. Whether it is possible to speak of a military hegemony however is still doubtful, for these militaristic features are far scarcer than among later militarily orientated cultures of Mesoamerica. This theory is reinforced by the fact that on the eve of the Spanish Conquest the High Priest occupied a far more important position amongst the Zapotecs than among any other Mesoamerican peoples.

The Zapotec religion was very like the religion of other Mesoamerican peoples. The chief god Cocijo, like Tlaloc in Teotihuacan, appears to have been the Rain God. The Jaguar deity closely related to the Olmecs and the Maize God, Pitao Cozobi, played an important role. But the religion of the peoples of Oaxaca is distinguished from those of other Mesoamerican peoples by a special peculiarity. In no other part of Mesoamerica was the cult of the dead so much encouraged, nor was so much energy devoted towards this end as in the Valley of Oaxaca. Their extensive burial grounds were lavishly decorated with pictures and are among the richest grave enclosures in the whole of Mesoamerica. The burial urns discovered in Monte Alban are among the most characteristic and typical elements of Zapotec art, and are almost baroque in appearance.

Monte Alban dominated the whole Valley of Oaxaca and appears also to have exercised a strong influence on the neighbouring region of Mixteca. Mixteca stands out as the most turbulent and most warlike region of Mesoamerica. At the same time it is one of the regions in which the earliest historical evidence is to be found. The Mixtecan pictographs indicate that by AD 720 there already existed warlike states that embarked on campaigns of conquest in all directions. It is possible that the Mixtecans were used initially as mercenaries by the rulers of Monte Alban. They were soon to bring about the downfall of their former rulers.

75

CHAPTER 6

THE END OF THE CLASSIC CULTURES

In the period from the seventh to about the tenth century AD convulsions occurred in Mesoamerica which in extent and impact can only be compared with the fall of the Roman Empire and the Barbarian invasions of Europe. The great cities and ceremonial centres which had been dominant until then lost their power and influence, and were finally abandoned and in part destroyed.[1]

The end came for Teotihuacan in about the year 650, or 750 according to other estimates. The city was abandoned by its population and the signs of burning and the destruction of individual sculptures are evidence of the violence of these events. A similar fate seems to have overtaken Monte Alban about the year AD 900.

In the tropical lowland of the Maya one great cultural centre after another was abandoned during the century or century and a half between AD 750 and about 900. The Maya cult of erecting stelae which gave an exact record of events makes it possible to follow the process here more accurately than on the plateau. The last hieroglyphic monument was erected in the city of Copan in the year AD 800, and in Piedras Negras in 810. The last stele in the great centre of Tikal was erected in 869 and in Uaxactun the last stele is dated from 889. The last existing stele anywhere was erected in a small place in San Lorenzo. The end of the cult of the stelae was also the end of the cities, which were then abandoned and overrun by tropical primeval forest. Why and for what reason were there these radical convulsions? How did they happen?

The difficulty in answering this question is best understood by putting ourselves in the place of a historian compelled to explain the history of the fall of the Roman Empire and of the Barbarian invasions without the aid of a single documentary source. How could we possibly reconstruct the invasion of the Germans, the campaigns of Attila, only from potsherds and crumbling ruins? Such is the position of historians when describing the decline of Mesoamerican culture for so far no deciphered written evidence has appeared and it is doubtful whether any of the traditions of the sixteenth-century Mesoamerican peoples reach back to this period. Later peoples regarded Teotihuacan as a mythical centre where the gods were born. The decline of the Maya cities may well have been recorded but as already pointed out, Maya hieroglyphs have not yet been deciphered.

Not surprisingly, many different theories were formulated about these events and so far no definitive answer has been forthcoming. A number of ideas can at all events most probably be rejected. For a long time a few scholars assumed the cities were abandoned because of natural disasters, possibly extreme changes in climate or great earthquakes. No traces of earthquake damage can be detected in the architecture however, and although modern archaeological methods of examination make a far-reaching investigation into climatic conditions of the past possible there is no indication of radical climatic changes.

The theory that great plagues possibly exterminated a considerable proportion of the population has been met with similar scepticism. Those who support this theory point to the violent epidemics that came in the wake of the Spanish Conquest, bringing death to the majority of the Indian population of Mesoamerica and which according to some estimates, reduced the population of this region from twenty million to two million in the course of a few decades. All these epidemics however – malaria, smallpox, certain vermicular diseases, syphilis – are, in the view of most scholars, of European origin.

Many historians have drawn a definite line between the abandonment of the great central Mexican plateau centres and the fall and abandonment of the cultural centres of the Maya lowland. In fact the differences are considerable. In the plateau of Mexico the great cities were after all destroyed and left, but the end of these cities did not in any way mean the end of city cultures. After Teotihuacan had been abandoned other cities remained, such as Cholollan in the Valley of Puebla, Xochicalco or Atzcapotzalco, and were affected by these events in only a limited degree. In the Maya lowland, on the other hand, all cultural centres and cities ceased to exist, and there are indications that many villages underwent a similar fate.

In spite of these basic differences, Mesoamerican cultures are so closely interlinked that these various phenomena can hardly be considered in isolation from each other. When trying to define the reasons for the decline of a society, there must in the first analysis be an examination of its successors. After the end of the classic period societies appear in many places which were ruled by a military aristocracy and were obviously much more warlike than previous societies. This change from government by a priesthood to government by a military caste is not restricted to Mesoamerica. It took place in many other parts of the world, in Mesopotamia for instance,[2] and the causes are not hard to find: increasing populations were forced to expand outwards and in order to consolidate the ruling class and to protect it from without and within, a military force had to be created. At the same time the increasing wealth of the great centres attracted a variety of peoples who were at a lower level of development. In these circumstances warriors were necessary and they easily rose from having been the servants of a theocracy to become equal partners and finally the rulers. This kind of development would result from external attacks by warlike nomadic tribes. In Mesopotamia for example, this process took place extremely rapidly. The theocracies were inevitably forced to give way to the power of the warriors, sooner or later, and in Mesoamerica it is only surprising that the priestly rulers were able to keep their power for so long.

The theory already referred to of theocracies peacefully co-existing beside one another for hundreds of years is fairly unlikely. It is much more probable that the classic period's long-lasting stability rested on the firm foundation of a *Pax Teotihuacana*, on the enormous power of the plateau metropolis which overshadowed all other centres in Mesoamerica. It secured the boundaries against the nomadic tribes of the north and presumably also prevented the outbreak of internal dissensions. The end of Teotihuacan signified the end of the classic period of Mesoamerican culture.

What was the reason for the downfall of Teotihuacan? The fall and destruction of the Roman Empire were the result of a combination of external and internal problems. From outside the empire the barbarians attacked in gathering strength, their increased power possibly a result of contact with the culture of the state which they had served as legionaries or as frontiersmen. Internally social and national dissensions brought the Roman Empire to the very brink of collapse. The same combination of internal and external factors, albeit in a very different context, seems to have brought about the fall of Teotihuacan.

The feeding of the growing population must have presented the ruling class of Teotihuacan with a major problem, particularly since food production failed to keep pace with the population. No new plants were introduced during Teotihuacan's long history, and apart from the rudimentary irrigation system that took shape at the beginning of Teotihuacan's development, it appears that no other method for raising food production was developed. Moreover only limited amounts of foodstuffs could be imported from more distant regions to supplement local production. Since draught animals, carts and river communications did not exist, everything had to be carried by man. Since bearers had to travel great distances however, they tended to consume more foodstuffs than they were able to supply.

The scarcity of food and rising starvation must have caused the population to doubt the priesthood's ability to fulfil their main functions, namely to propitiate the gods so that they might endow the land with abundant crops. Increasing misery among the population, the apparent incapacity of the priesthood on the one hand and constantly growing demands by the upper class on the other, probably provoked the radical social convulsions within Teotihuacan. It is equally likely that the subject regions, as their populations increased and their strength rose accordingly, should have striven for independence; a struggle which was perhaps aggravated by Teotihuacan's rising demands.

Teotihuacan, weakened by such conflicts, was an easy prey to invading barbarians from the north. Who were these barbarians? It was thought for a long time that they were exclusively hunting and gathering tribes. Nevertheless scholars could not help wondering whether such small and scattered groups would after all be in a position to conquer an empire, even if it were crumbling. A theory that partially resolved this question was put forward by Armillas[3] who presumed that there had been an expanding peasant colonisation on the northern boundary of Teotihuacan from the sixth century.

It is possible that barbarian tribes became cultivated here and learned to practise agriculture. Teotihuacan may have set up military colonies here to protect its boundaries. These peasant colonists, like the barbarian mercenaries of Rome, had the material and military capacity to weaken Teotihuacan and together with northern tribes to overrun it, and to advance still further south. This seems to be exactly what happened. Teotihuacan was abandoned, and among the ruins of the city was found pottery that could be traced back to peoples of northern stock. Nevertheless the nobility of the great plateau city were not annihilated; they withdrew to a small city on the shores of the network of lakes in Mexico, Atzcapotzalco. The culture of this city, known to archaeologists as Teotihuacan iv, was nevertheless a mere shadow of the classic period of the great plateau city and it reflects with unmistakable clarity the fall of the upper class.

Elements of Teotihuacan culture also lived on in the city of Cholollan, which instead of declining went from strength to strength. Whether an ex-Teotihuacan nobility ruled here or whether – as some historical legends would have it – the city was occupied by conquerors from the south is not known. These centres played an important role in the civilising process of the northern barbarians who largely succeeded to the cultural heritage of the great city of the plateau.

The disintegration of Teotihuacan's domain had lasting effects on the whole of Mesoamerica. The coming of the barbarians and the ending of the *Pax Teotihuacana* led to a widespread increase in warlike activity. The Bonampak murals and the Yaxchilan reliefs in the region of the Maya, which represent warlike scenes, both belong to this period. The increase in military activity and the end of Teotihuacan's influence did not however lead directly to a cultural decline in the Maya region. On the contrary it appears that the Maya cities used their newly-won independence from the great city of the plateau for a tremendous cultural boom. New cities were built, new pyramids and temples constructed and the number of stone inscriptions increased dramatically. But this cultural burst lasted only a short time, and by the ninth and tenth centuries almost all the existing centres of high culture in Mesoamerica had seriously declined. Monte Alban was abandoned and more and more Maya cities in the northern and southern regions were occupied by foreign tribes from the central Mexican plateau. Here growing ecological difficulties and over-population – it has been estimated that the population in the Valley of Oaxaca had reached its maximum density shortly before Monte Alban was abandoned – could have undermined the position of the priesthood.

The decline of the classic centres by no means signified the end of settlement or the end of civilisation in all the regions referred to. It later flowered in a different form. A completely exceptional development however took place in one region only. In the rest of Mesoamerica cities persisted even when partly dominated by foreign invaders, but in the central Maya lowlands they disappeared completely. The population also seems to have diminished increasingly. It is possible to say without exaggeration that this problem is the greatest and the most mysterious facing the whole of Americanist study. A variety of explanations have been forthcoming, but in the main three kinds of causes are suggested: peasant revolts; invasion of foreign peoples; a return to a more primitive agriculture.

Thompson[4] took the view that great peasant uprisings in the Maya region finally led to the expulsion of the priesthood and to the abandoning of the ceremonial centres. Such an uprising could easily have been caused by the growing rift between the priesthood and the peasantry who were expected to meet their demands. Thompson believes that this combination of factors was further encouraged by the fact that the priests had increasingly become involved in abstract cults such as that of the planet Venus, which the peasants found impossible to comprehend. When the nobility fled the peasants who remained in the Maya lowland were no longer able to maintain the cities, although they still buried their dead there. This theory has however been sharply contradicted. Willey[5] and Bullard[6] both believe that the peasant population of the Maya lowland dwindled to the point where it all but disappeared. Does a peasant revolt account for so drastic a reduction of the population? Does it provide a satisfactory explanation as to why all the ceremonial centres were destroyed?

There also appear to have been uprisings in other parts of

Mesoamerica, but nowhere else did they lead to such a drastic reduction of the peasant population or to the disappearance of the existing civilisation. Nor are there any examples of such a development in other parts of the world. In China, where there were a number of successful peasant revolts, a new ruling class developed from the ranks of the peasantry, which in one form or another attempted to continue the customs and culture of the upper classes. Why did this not happen in the lowland region of the Maya? The towns were abandoned, they became deserted and isolated buildings were perhaps used only for a few religious occasions.

George L. Cowgill[7] takes the view that it was external reasons that brought about the downfall of the Maya civilisation. He maintains that conquering tribes from central Mexico deported the Maya, especially the nobility, and that the defeated population was settled in the peninsula of Yucatan where it could be easily controlled. However, if this was so, why was the population of the central Maya region the only one in Mesoamerica to suffer this fate? In a recently held symposium on the subject of the collapse of Classic Maya Civilisation a number of scholars noted that at the western confines of the Maya region where the decline of Maya culture began, signs which could indicate foreign intrusions can be made out. A pottery type, fine paste which was non-Maya in origin, was found there. This could indicate raids and border intrusions but not conquest since this type of pottery did not penetrate into the rest of the Maya region. Gordon R. Willey believes that such incursions could have provoked, in conjunction with internal conflicts, a crisis in Maya society.

The Maya scholars Cook[8] and Morley[9] believe that the particular development in this region must have been the result of special ecological factors which did not exist anywhere else. They believe that the population growth led to a progressive shortening of the fallow period that was such a vital part of the slash and burn method of agriculture. As a result trees no longer grew on the soil, which was then abandoned; grass replaced trees and savannah developed. The Maya whose only instrument was the digging stick and who were completely ignorant of the plough were unable to cultivate this sort of savannah-like terrain. As the amount of suitable soil for cultivation diminished, great famines must have occurred. The lowlands could no longer sustain the population which was obliged to leave its homeland and colonise the Yucatan peninsula. This theory also has met with considerable opposition. It has been pointed out that no savannah has been found close to the great centres, and in any case a number of experts are doubtful whether savannah can result from prolonged slash and burn agriculture. Above all it was established that some of the first cities to be abandoned were precisely those which stood on land periodically watered by rivers where such problems would never have arisen. There is also consider-able doubt whether the population of the Maya lowland did colonise the Yucatan peninsula, since recent archaeological research has demonstrated that this area had a limited population even in the classic period.

All these theories go to show how controversial the problem of the decline of Maya civilisation is even today. Possibly the problem is a complex one, and a combination of all three factors contributed to its decline: deterioration of agriculture, revolts and attacks from outside. In the present state of our knowledge it is only possible to say that not one of these theories can be finally accepted or finally rejected. Perhaps, and this is indeed the hope of all scholars who concern themselves with the Maya, the decipherment of the Maya script will one day help to solve this problem.

CHAPTER 7

THE CIVILISATIONS OF THE MIDDLE ANDES

Development in the second great cultural region of America, that of the Andes, revealed far-reaching resemblances to, but also marked differences from, that in Mesoamerica. The civilisations of the Andean region extended from the north of present-day Argentina over parts of present-day Peru, Bolivia and Ecuador as far as Colombia. This study will however be confined to a description of the development which took place in the key area in the central Andean region of Peru and Bolivia, and which finally constituted the basis on which the empire of the Inca originated.

It is necessary in order to understand this development to recall geographical and ecological similarities and differences between the Andean region and Mesoamerica. In both cases regions are involved whose heterogeneity is almost their most important characteristic: a lowland plain and a plateau, which however is not a level plateau but a jumble of mountain and valley in which although they are so closely adjacent there are striking ecological differences. So much for the similarities. The lowland of Mesoamerica consists of tropical primeval forest in which, for reasons so far not quite clear, an important civilisation originated.

In Peru and Bolivia also a wide plain of tropical primeval forest stretches along the foot of the eastern slopes of the Andes, and extends as far as the Atlantic. But a civilisation never developed here; small tribes of primitive peasants lived alongside hunting and collecting tribes.

On the western slopes of the Andes on the other hand there developed one of the most remarkable civilisations of ancient America. These coastal valleys of Peru display an almost unique character in America. Parallels exist only in the Old World, for instance in the Valley of the Nile in Egypt. In the same way, rivers flow quietly through desert to the coast of Peru. The sea and the rivers were indispensable to the life of the coastal inhabitants. To exceed a minimal level of production, agriculture required different prerequisites here from those necessary in the other regions of America. It could only be practised on a large scale with the aid of extensive systems of artificial irrigation: its extraordinary productivity in this region was entirely due to the use of these devices.

There are a number of not inconsiderable differences between the coastal valleys of north and south Peru. While it never rains in the south, in the north when the warm current moving towards the equator meets the Humboldt current over which the rain clouds empty themselves, typhoons or torrential rainstorms occur and surge over the coast about once every ten years. This can produce catastrophic results and lead to gigantic floods. Even though the north coast of Peru is thus more prone to natural catastrophes than the south, it does possess a compensating advantage. The valleys of the north coast are much more extensive than those of the south and it is not surprising that the most significant rudiments of civilisation were found to have originated there.

The central highland region of the Andes is of a completely different character from the lowland. Only a fraction of it – much less in comparison than in Mesoamerica – is suitable for agriculture. These areas are concentrated in the main in six regions which also represent the focal point of all cultural development in the Andean region: Cajamarca, Callejón de Huaylas, Huanuco, Mantaro, Cuzco and Titicaca.

Here important public works did not precede the formation of large population groups as on the coast. In these areas the already domesticated potato and other tubers of the Andean region were cultivable without artificial irrigation. Maize however, which only reached Peru rather late and did not play so decisive a role as in Mesoamerica, required artificial irrigation. Frost lasts longer in the Andean region than on the Mesoamerican plateau, and it was only possible to harvest the maize crop before the frost if the period of growth was shortened by artificial irrigation. The cultivation of maize therefore required comprehensive works of terracing and irrigation before it could be undertaken. But even with the aid of such irrigation it was not possible to cultivate it in the whole of the highlands.

The partly unfavourable climatic conditions of the Peruvian highlands, in comparison with Mesoamerica, were to a considerable extent compensated by the existence of cattle. The highest plateau, the Puna, in the southern part of the Andean highlands, proved to be most suitable as a grazing ground for the typical Andean animals which had been domesticated: llama and alpaca, both of which are classed in the category of *auchenida*. The most common animals, llama, however were not suitable for riding nor were they able to carry heavy loads; but it was always possible to load them up with about seventy-five kilograms, and this was already a factor of considerable importance. All three animals played a very significant role on the Peruvian highlands as producers of wool. This was especially the case in the southern part of these highlands. In the northern part the vegetation was scarcely suitable for the grazing of these animals, with the result that cattle-rearing played a much less significant role here.

The frontier, a factor of decisive importance for Mesoamerica, was much less significant in the Andean region. As in Mesoamerica, there was in the Andean region an extensive frontier with regions populated by nomadic hunting and collecting peoples and primitive peasants, who were scarcely touched by the civilisation although they were strongly attracted to it. As in the case of Mesoamerica, the Andean highlands lay along the frontier and its inhabitants had constantly to do battle with peoples from beyond the frontier, while the lowland was protected from attacks by nomadic tribes. However the resemblances end here. The frontier played a decisive role in the history of Mesoamerica. Whenever weaknesses in the social structure of the population of the high cultures became evident, the barbarians streamed over the frontier into Mesoamerica, carried out conquests and finally took over the civilisation themselves. In the Andean region the frontier played a far more subsidiary role. Admittedly the frontier people constantly carried out attacks against the areas where a civilisation had developed but those attacks were confined to plundering raids and constituted no serious threat. The frontier people of South America never succeeded in overrunning the civilisation in the Andean region.

The relationship between the highlands and the lowlands closed both in Mesoamerica and in the central Andean region with a victory for the highlands and a conquest of the lowlands. Thence began the development of the empire. Nevertheless this did not happen in at all the same way in the two regions. Differences were of decisive importance for the later evolution of the two great empires which came into being in ancient America: those of the Aztecs and the Inca.

In Mesoamerica there existed a clear central region, the Valley of Mexico, which offered unique conditions for the control of many regions lying both near and far: a most favourable strategic situation with possibilities for a particularly intensive type of agriculture which was able to sustain the most densely populated area of Mesoamerica, and a network of lakes which facilitated the integration of the population of the Valley. There existed no such centre in Peru. The regions in which intensive agriculture encouraged particular density of population and political integration existed on the north coast of Peru, and lay strategically, as far as the conquest of the Andean region was concerned, in a very unfavourable position. Campaigns from the lowlands for the conquest of the highlands were exceedingly difficult to undertake. The development of Andean states began in various regions, and the Valley of Cuzco, the central point of the Inca Empire, played a decisive role only in the last centuries before the Spanish Conquest.

A further and most important difference characterised the relationship between the plateau and the lowlands in Mesoamerica and that in the Andean region.

Products of the Mexican lowland, such as feathers, cotton and above all cocoa, were much sought after in the Mesoamerican plateau. The plateau had very little to offer in exchange, however, for the lowlands also produced the maize and other foodstuffs that it could offer. In order to acquire the sought-after products of the tropics, the inhabitants of the plateau had either to conquer the lowlands, which they repeatedly tried to do, or to use their labour to convert raw materials into consumer goods. It is not surprising that early in the development of Mesoamerica great quantities of finely finished pottery and obsidian tools were dispatched to many different regions of Mesoamerica.

In Peru the balance of supply and demand between the highlands and the lowlands was conditioned in a rather different way. In exchange for cotton and maize from the lowlands which was only cultivable in parts of the highlands, the highland areas were able to deliver potatoes, or *chuñu*, a certain kind of preserved potato, and the southern highland areas meat and wool. Metals were added somewhat later.

The significance of these differences should not be underestimated. They brought about a much stronger urge towards conquest of the lowlands in Mesoamerica than in Peru and an earlier beginning of these conquests. They also occasioned a completely different type of government as we shall be able to see from the examples of the Inca and Aztec empires.

One more important difference between Mesoamerica and the Andean region remains to be noted. The lowlands of Peru were essentially easier to conquer from the highlands than were the Mexican lowlands. This was not only due to the short distance between the highlands and the lowlands or to the fact that the lush primeval forests did not exist in the coastal lowlands of Peru, but also to the irrigation installations of the coastal area. Whoever controlled the irrigation systems of a valley was very easily able to control the whole valley. This was one of the decisive factors which facilitated the conquest of the Peruvian lowlands by the highlands.

ARCHAEOLOGICAL SOURCES AND RESEARCH IN THE CENTRAL ANDEAN REGION

Research in the central Andean region in comparison with Mesoamerica offers the archaeologist and historian some advantages but also some considerable disadvantages.

The advantages concern a very circumscribed area of the Andean region, the Peruvian coastal valleys. Thanks to their desert-like character and arid nature, objects have survived here which would have perished in the much damper region of Mesoamerica. This is specially true of the exquisite textiles of the south coast of Peru, which even today are regarded as the most important artefacts of this kind, not only in America but far beyond. This is also true of other perishable objects, which make it possible even now to reconstruct the daily life of the coastal inhabitants.

These natural advantages are reinforced by the fact that one of the coastal peoples, the Mochica, on the north coast of Peru, developed a perhaps unique art in ancient America. This exceptional position is due to quantity – tens of thousands of pottery objects have been discovered in this region – and above all to quality. The pottery of the Mochica exhibits a unique degree of realism. On it was represented the life of the people from the depictions of the gods to the most intimate events of personal life.

A further advantage of the Peruvian lowlands for scholars is that the relationship between environment and cultural achievements does not present such difficult problems as in the Mesoamerican lowlands. The nature of the Peruvian lowlands strongly resembles many regions of the Old World in which civilisations developed, such as Egypt for instance.

Against these advantages must be set the disadvantages. The people of the Andean region, in contrast to those of Mesoamerica, never developed a genuine script, so that this very important source is lacking for the Andean region. Of course, here as in Mesoamerica, there is comprehensive written evidence from the period following the conquest: accounts by chroniclers, reports by Spanish officials, depositions regarding historical traditions made by the Indians themselves. All these sources only just cover a span of two hundred years before the Conquest and are confined almost exclusively to the highlands. The most important archaeological evidence however is located in the lowlands and goes back thousands of years. There is therefore a deep gulf between the written and the archaeological evidence.

In view of this situation, it is not surprising that for a long time the Inca were measured by their own standards and all Peruvian cultures were attributed to them. Systematic research in the realm of Peruvian archaeology only began at the end of the nineteenth century. In this connection the German scholar Max Uhle won particular distinction for himself when he was able to show convincingly that important cultures had existed in the Andean region for hundreds, even for thousands of years before the Inca.

The interest of archaeologists was concentrated here as in other parts of America at first on monumental buildings and artistic splendours and they only attempted later – in particular just after the Second World War – to reconstruct the life of the population. In this connection the research carried out by American archaeologists, ethnologists and botanists in the Valley of Virú on the north coast of Peru, in which it was established that life in this region could in a large measure be traced back six thousand years, must particularly be mentioned. During the last decades the intensity with which research has been carried on has constantly increased and it has also taken on a more international character. Archaeologists of the Andean region were joined in their excavations by North Americans, Europeans and in the last ten years very largely by Japanese. There exists however a significant discrepancy between the achievements of intensive research in the lowlands and the far less developed research in the highlands of the Andean region.

In the opinion of most archaeologists the state of research in the Andean region has not yet equalled that in Mesoamerica. The reasons for this are various. One is almost certainly the greater economic power of Mexico and another the influence of the Mexican revolution of 1910 which stimulated interest in the Indian past of the country as never before. Perhaps also considerations of tourism played a certain role in the financing of aid for excavation – Mexico is more easily accessible to foreign tourists, particularly from North America, than Peru.

THE BEGINNING OF AGRICULTURE AND CIVILISATION IN THE CENTRAL ANDEAN REGION

In describing the evolution of agriculture in Mesoamerica, perhaps the most striking feature was its protracted evolution. The discovery of agriculture did not result in rapid changes in the social organisation nor in the economic life of the peoples who practised it. Its latent potentialities only began to be more or less fully exploited in Mesoamerica six thousand years after its discovery.

In Peru, development followed similar lines, even though differences are again discernible. In the Valley of Chillon on the central coast of Peru, the earliest traces so far of human settlement in the Andean region were found. There are stone scrapers and borers which date back to about 8500 BC.

The earliest finds in the highlands in the Cave of Lauricocha, four thousand metres above sea level, date back to 7500 BC. These were mainly stone tools found in the lowest strata of the cave, of very primitive workmanship. They were obviously made by hunters and gatherers who had also used this cave as a dwelling place. How are these hunters and gatherers of the highlands connected with the villages which sprang up several thousand years later on the Peruvian coast? Is there any connection, any transition of any kind? This problem remained unresolved for many years until recently fresh research carried out by Frederick Engel[1] and Edward Lanning[2] shed light on it. It very seldom rains on the desert-like coast of north Peru, hardly more often than about once in a decade. Vegetation there only exists on the banks of rivers which flow from the highlands through the arid coastal plain into the sea. There are also small oases called 'lomas' here and there but only for part of the year and they owe their dampness to the banks of fog coming off the sea. Lanning succeeded in showing that these oases were much more extensive eight to ten thousand years ago than they are today. In about 7000 BC hunters and collectors appear to have led a seasonal existence on these *lomas*. Stone tools have been discovered which primarily served to grind seed into powder and therefore prove that collecting was the main occupation of these peoples.

About 3500 BC climatic changes took place on the coast of Peru which brought about far-reaching consequences to the lives of these peoples. An icy current became increasingly noticeable off the sea coast. This resulted in the diminution of the damp fog cover and in the progressive desiccation of the *lomas*, so that the hunters and food-gatherers found it increasingly difficult to collect the plants and animals that were necessary for their survival. On the other hand this cold current resulted in a rapid increase in fish off the Peruvian coast which even today constitute one of the most important resources of the country. It is therefore not surprising that in this very period, fairly large groups of human beings found their way to the coast and lived largely off fishing. These fishing tribes did not live only on fish, but also on various other marine animals such as crabs, sea-eels, starfish, mussels and other moluscs.

Agriculture developed very early on the coast of Peru. Even in about 4000 BC linseed, peppers, lucuma fruit and bottle gourds were grown. Just as in Mesoamerica agriculture played only a secondary role to start with, maize, the basic food in Mesoamerica, was wholly absent at this time in the Andean region.

It is still not known for certain where the knowledge of agriculture came from, and whether or not the peoples of the Andean region adopted this knowledge from other parts of America or evolved it themselves is a very controversial question. While most scholars believe that the domestication of the wild form of maize took place in

Mesoamerica, it is generally presumed that the same thing happened in Peru with its most typical product, the potato. At all events it is not yet possible to establish exactly when this took place since research in the highlands is still not sufficiently advanced.

About 3000 BC a new and so far completely unknown product appeared on the coast whose cultivation brought about radical consequences both in the social life and probably also in the whole outlook of the coastal peoples. This product was cotton, although where it came from is still one of the most controversial problems of Peruvian archaeology. The cotton found in Peru, which thanks to the aridity of the coast was preserved for thousands of years, resulted from the crossing of Asiatic cotton with a type of American cotton. This has led to the wide belief that Peruvian cotton cultivation had its origin in Asia. This assertion was strengthened by striking resemblances established in recent years between the pottery ware of a later period of the coastal regions of Ecuador and Japan. Cotton appears soon to have played an important role in the life of the coastal peoples. It was used for ordinary clothing, and above all for ceremonial attire. Finely woven artistically impressive cotton textiles were already being produced in about 2500 BC. At the same time cotton played an important role in the production of fishing-nets and might thus have contributed substantially to the raising of food production.

It is possible with the aid of archaeology largely to reconstruct the life of these early fishing peoples. For nourishment they depended mainly on fish and mussels. Agriculture primarily served the purpose of cultivating cotton for textiles and bottle gourds. These served as vessels, since pottery was not introduced into Peru until between 1800 and 1500 BC, presumably from regions in present-day Colombia or Ecuador, where the art of pottery is more ancient than in Peru. Pottery ware in north Colombia dates from as far back as 3100 BC and in Ecuador from 2700 BC. The coastal inhabitants lived in small scattered groups and their social organisation was presumably somewhat similar to the later kinship organisations, the ayllu which existed throughout the whole of Peru at the time of the Spanish Conquest. Although we lack any detailed knowledge of their religion, their burial grounds, partly adorned with offerings, indicate that they believed in a life after death.

As in later times the finest specimens of textiles were found as mortuary offerings in graves and probably already possessed a particular cult significance. Generally, agriculture appears to have played a larger role among these Peruvian coastal peoples than in Mesoamerica at the same period.

It was presumed for a long time that many thousands of years elapsed after agriculture became known both in the Andean region and in Mesoamerica before its practice became sufficiently efficient to allow large groups of people to leave the task of direct food production, thus creating the premises for a centralised social structure. Recently however a number of finds have forced a revision of these conceptions.

An impressive outline of a temple was found in Chuquitanta on the central coast of Peru which goes back to about 1800 BC. It contains nine buildings constructed of stone and plastered with fine clay. Chuquitanta is a thousand years older than any similar construction in Mesoamerica but it is by no means unique: two pyramids of the same period were excavated on the banks of the River Seco, also in the central coastal region.

In modern Las Aldas, on the central coast of Peru, extensive buildings were found clustered round the ground plan of a temple which dates back to 1500 or 2000 BC. This lay-out is so extensive that John Rowe assumed it was a city and estimated that its population numbered ten thousand.[3] If he is correct Las Aldas would have been the first city on the American continent. Although this theory is contested by other scholars Las Aldas remains in any case the largest centre of the period when such particular features of ancient American civilisations as maize and pottery were quite unknown. The explanation for the rise of such a centre in so early a period of development in the Andean region probably lies in the success of the fisheries on the coast of Peru which made it possible to set free sufficient labour among the population for the building of temples.

Such an explanation is less valid in the highlands where a Japanese expedition excavated in Kotosh the remains of the foundations of a temple going back to 1500 to 1800 BC. Edward Lanning considers that maize was already known at that date in Kotosh and that its high rate of productivity released sufficient labour for the construction and maintenance of temples.

In the main these beginnings of a high culture were extremely limited in their range and extended only over a limited region. Almost a thousand years were to elapse before any similar degree of civilisation extended to the rest of the Andean region. Its rise exhibits almost staggering similarities with the beginnings of high culture in Mesoamerica.

After a gradual and difficult progression in agriculture in Mesoamerica that lasted thousands of years and increased very little from one millennium to the next, changes suddenly took place at the beginning of 1000 BC: great religious buildings, a new style in art and new kinds of intellectual developments appeared. The Olmec culture spread over a large part of Mesoamerica.

About the same period, shortly after 1000 BC, similar changes became apparent in Peru. Great temples appeared and a new art style spread over wide areas of the Andean region. As with the Olmec style in Mesoamerica, the first style to develop in the Andean region became the most widely established. This art style, with its wave of religious buildings, is known as Chavin. It derives its name from the place where one of the greatest temples in this style was excavated, Chavin de Huantar in the Peruvian highlands. There is nevertheless no evidence that Chavin was the centre of this style and the place may originally have been called by another name. It is not known who the inhabitants were, what their language was or where they came from.

Chavin de Huantar is one of the most impressive temples erected at that time. It consists of a number of rectangular structures which formed the foundations of temples which no longer survive. In contrast to the pyramidal structures in Mesoamerica, the rectangular foundations are not massive but honeycombed with rooms, passages and airshafts. Outside the temple is decorated with anthropomorphic and zoomorphic heads carved in stone.

Two different kinds of representations of gods have been found in Chavin. One, which was found in the middle of the temple, was probably the chief cult object and is known by archaeologists as El Lanzón. Although this deity is essentially anthropomorphic, the hair consists of snakes and the mouth resembles a jaguar's jaws. It is no longer possible to determine what it signified.

Another deity far less anthropomorphic in appearance is the so-called Raimondi Stone, a stele incised in relief almost two metres high. Here too snakes constitute the hair and the facial features are strongly cat-like. The Raimondi stele consists of a number of bodies and faces that have been piled up to create an almost monstrous form.

The cult structures of the Chavin period also existed in many other areas of the Andean region, on the coast as well as in the highlands. While art in Chavin itself found its highest expression in stone carvings, on the coast pottery and textiles predominated. Traces of the Chavin style have also been found in beaten gold. On the coast the temples often took the form of pyramids built of adobe bricks.

The Chavin style extended throughout the northern highland region and the northern coast of Peru. While its influence is hardly perceptible in the southern highlands, it is apparent later in a modified form, in the culture of the southern coast, the Paracas culture. As with the Olmec culture in Mesoamerica, so in the Andean region the Chavin culture appeared suddenly in its mature form without any visible origins. It is therefore not surprising that the Chavin culture gave rise to such a wide variety of theories and ideas.

Could the constantly recurring zoomorphic motif of a beast of prey point to an origin in the primeval forest region of the Amazon? The

Peruvian archaeologist Julio Tello[4] asked this question and pointed out striking similarities between Chavin culture and the religion of the primeval peoples on the eastern slopes of the Andes. In particular the cult of such beasts of prey as the jaguar, serpent and condor seemed to have certain affinities with the religion of these peoples.

However the beast of prey motif, and specially the cult of the jaguar, has led a number of scholars to draw opposite conclusions. The motif of the jaguar which plays so important a role in the Chavin style is also of decisive importance in the Olmec style which appeared in Mesoamerica at the same period. Would it not be more likely that the Chavin style was an offshoot of this Olmec style? The similarities between the Chavin and Olmec styles are not by any means confined to the jaguar motif. In pottery there are equally striking congruities. Michael D. Coe holds the view that Olmec merchants probably made the long sea voyage from the west coast of modern Mexico to Peru and that commerce and religious influences contributed towards a fusion of their culture with already existing elements of an indigenous high culture.[5]

The origin of Chavin culture may possibly lie a few thousand kilometres further away. Robert Heine-Geldern has suggested a Chinese origin. He detects in the art of Chavin motifs of decidedly Chinese character, belonging to the period of transition from the middle to the late Chou-style, a period which may be dated at about 700 BC.[6] Most Peruvianists dispute these theories and believe that the Chavin style originated in the Andean highlands where it achieved its finest flowering.

Perhaps even more important than the problem of the origin of Chavin culture is the question of the reasons for its spread. Why do Chavin characteristics occur in most parts of the Andean highlands? In the case of the two later occasions when cultures spread in the central Andean region it was the work of conquering peoples. But whether this was also the case for Chavin culture is extremely doubtful. Hardly any evidence of warfare or weapons has been discovered, and while in earlier times Chavin was considered to be a fortress or a castle, it is generally regarded now as a temple enclosure. A people capable of conquering so large an area as the central Andean region must at least have had a considerable population. Most of the settlements of that period are however so small that it is hardly possible to speak of a concentration of population. The possibility of such conquests cannot however be excluded and further archaeological excavation in this region may still reveal surprising results.

If the spread of Chavin culture was not the result of conquest, what could have led to the powerful extension of this culture? Most scholars believe in the rise of a dynamic new religion which spread over large parts of the Andean region. It is widely thought that Chavin and perhaps the other centres of this culture were great cult centres which became the focal points of pilgrimages. The pilgrims would then have carried the gospel of the new religion into the most distant villages. It is possible even today in fact to observe holy places and pilgrims travelling hundreds, even thousands of kilometres to visit them. Nevertheless, the question arises just why this cult should have become diffused in the eighth century BC. Were there special impulses which made the spread of this new religion possible in this way? It was impossible to answer this question until after the Second World War when the most far-reaching archaeological research ever undertaken in Peru was carried out in a valley on the north coast of Peru, especially in the Valley of Virú. The archaeologists made an illuminating discovery. In the Guañape period closely associated with the Chavin maize appeared in the Valley of Virú. Maize was certainly known in the Andean region before the beginning of the Chavin period. There is considerable evidence though that its use spread during the Chavin period. Some scholars believe that at this time a new and more productive type of maize became known in the Andean region.

The association of the new religion with something so abundant and productive as maize would largely explain the widespread diffusion of the new cult. It could also be one of the reasons why the new cult did not spread in the southern highland region, in particular the region of the Lake of Titicaca which the high altitude made less suitable for the cultivation of maize.

In about 300 BC the culture of Chavin vanished just as abruptly as it had appeared. The exact reasons for this decline are still not clear. In its place there appeared no uniform culture but a number of diverse local developments. Nevertheless it had a certain amount of influence on the further development of this region.

The culture of Chavin in the Andean region like that of the Olmecs in Mesoamerica introduced a millennium in which art, technology and culture reached their zenith. This millennium is described by many archaeologists in both regions as the 'classic period'. Nevertheless the classic period in the Andean region is characterised by totally different features from the classic period in Mesoamerica. There cities rose suddenly at a time of limited progress in methods of food production. In the Maya region even such advances are questionable and in Teotihuacan the system of agriculture developed was relatively modest. In the Andean region things were quite different. Here revolutionary developments in the matter of food production occurred first. Large-scale irrigation systems were created that are without equal in Mesoamerica. Urban development came much later and it appears that the largest centres only came into being a thousand years later than in Mesoamerica. In Mesoamerica the city developed first and was then followed by the territorial state that grew up round it. In Peru on the contrary the city appeared long after the state.

The Mesoamerican classical period was not for many years a spectacular era of peace. Yet war did not, seemingly, play an important role until a later epoch. In the Andean region on the other hand wars and battles appear to have been inseparable from the rise of classic cultures from the very beginning.

The great classical cultures both in Mesoamerica and in the Andean region were not the work of one single people: rather they were rather the result of a great rise in the number of tribal groups. This upsurge did not take place within the framework of one homogeneous state, but in a large number of independent communities. Nevertheless in Mesoamerica the classical period evolved under the dominating political influence of one region: Teotihuacan. In the Andean region, a dominant power such as this did not exist. The region containing the densest population and with the highest degree of state integration was the northern coast of Peru, but it was so poorly placed strategically that a conquest of the Andean region from there was hardly conceivable. Those regions on the other hand which were particularly strategically well placed developed only slowly and haltingly into large states.

The differences between the highlands and lowlands of Peru were on the whole much more considerable than in Mesoamerica, probably because of the cattle-breeding in the southern highlands.

Both the Andean region and Mesoamerica produced tremendous achievements in the realms of art and architecture. However, beyond this the directions of their activities diverged sharply. In Mesoamerica, primarily in the Maya region, intellectual achievements took first place: graphology, mathematics and astronomy. These were dedicated first and foremost to religious purposes, and were hardly applied to any other object. In the Andean region developments were on a different level and dealt mainly with the control of nature and the continuous improvement of food production. Changes in this field were so tremendous that they could almost be termed revolutionary.

Their principal manifestation was the spread of maize cultivation and large-scale irrigation schemes. The significance and form of these works varied a great deal according to the region in which they were built. They reached their zenith on the northern coast of Peru and were generally least developed in the southern highlands of the Andean region. It is very difficult for archaeologists to date irrigation works exactly. The type of building changes in style very little, as in the case of pottery, for instance. Even the presence of clay shards of a certain epoch may merely mean that the builders of a later period had used old shards.

These difficulties only applied in a very limited degree on the Peruvian coast. In that area there existed a very clear and straight-forward criterion for judging the age and extent of irrigation installations. Since it very seldom rains in the coastal valleys, agriculture is entirely dependent on irrigation except for small areas of soil immediately beside rivers. Wherever the population density exceeded a certain minimum an intensive form of agriculture must have existed. The greater the density the greater the extent of these installations.

Starting from these premises it was possible on the basis of intensive research in the Valley of Virú, a small valley on the north coast, to reconstruct the history of irrigation step by step. In the period following the decline of Chavin culture in this valley, termed Puerto Moorin by archaeologists, a dense concentration of population settled in the top end of the valley. It is therefore presumed that irrigation works first appeared here, and that a substantial increase in population followed almost immediately. In the following Gallinazo period new villages cropped up all over the valley: this would support the assumption that a network of irrigation channels was constructed, embracing the whole of the Virú valley. The population density as a result rose to about twenty-five times that which it had been barely four hundred years before.

A similar development took place in other valleys of the north coast of Peru, and in the longer valleys particularly, the irrigation works were of tremendous size. An example is a canal of 130 kilometres in length that was built to irrigate the Chicama valley. After comprehensive installations had been constructed in every valley, the irrigation works in various valleys were then often connected with each other. The archaeologist Paul Kosok discovered such a system of truly gigantic proportions in north Peru[7] where a uniform irrigation network connected the valleys of Jequetepeque, Zana, Lambayeque, Leche and Motupe with each other. Together they embraced a third of the whole cultivated area on the coast of the Andean region. It is however impossible to ascertain whether this extensive system belonged to the classic period or whether it was of later date.

The valleys on the southern coast of Peru are much smaller than those in the north and the rivers that cross them only contain enough water for a few months in the year. The irrigation works were commensurately smaller, although from a technical point of view they represented a more significant achievement than many in the north. In the Nazca Valley large subterranean canals were constructed which conducted the water from the mountains into the valley.

In the highlands there were different problems which were also more complicated. Here it was a question not only of creating irrigation works but of reclaiming the mountain slopes for cultivation.

To this end, and to avoid the danger of erosion, great terraces were constructed. They were shored up by walls and were thus able to retain moisture.

The importance of the irrigation systems in the Andean region can only be appreciated if it is realised that even now irrigation in Peru has not reached the proportions it had in the pre-Inca period. On the north coast irrigation works almost two thousand years ago were twenty per cent more extensive than is the case today.

The peoples of the Andean region used other means of increasing agricultural production besides irrigation: the fertiliser known as *Guano*. This fertiliser consisting of the excrement of birds which breed on the small islands off the coast of Peru is still one of the most important fertilisers in the modern world.

The classic period of the Andean region was characterised by war from its very inception. Evidence of this is encountered in all spheres of life and death. The large number of arms laid in graves, the many pictographic representations of wars and battles, especially on the north coast, and the fortified buildings that appear almost all over the Andean region speak in unmistakable terms.

The development of fortified buildings has been most extensively studied in the Valley of Virú, already mentioned, on the northern coast of Peru. In the period following the decline of the Chavin culture small fortifications immediately began to spring up on the crested fringes of the valleys. These small fortifications surrounded by walls are then replaced by larger piles, among which pyramids occur. As these hill fortifications increased in number palaces began to appear on some of them which were surrounded by great walls. At the same time walls are thrown round various localities, which could equally have served defensive purposes. Similar lay-outs of smaller or larger dimensions are to be found in most of the valleys of the lowlands and highlands of the Andean region. In the southern part of Acari Rowe even discovered a fortified city, Tampo Viejo.[8]

The classic period in the Andean region was not characterised by the appearance of an all-embracing empire any more than in Mesoamerica. After the decline of the Chavin culture almost every valley of the Andean region first developed its own culture, which cannot nevertheless be considered in isolation from that of neighbouring valleys or regions. In the centuries following the beginning of our period some parts of the Andes appear to have developed large political networks which were also important from a cultural point of view. The Andean region may be divided ecologically mainly into four areas: the north coast, the south coast, the northern highlands and the southern highlands. Political and cultural evolution would seem to have run alongside these regional divisions.

THE CIVILISATIONS OF THE NORTH COAST OF PERU

The most pronounced unity of political, ecological and cultural factors lies on the north-west coast of Peru, a region which contains the best source material in the whole of the Andean region. The Mochica culture, called by some the Proto-Chimu-Culture, was the expression of this unity and flourished from AD 300 first in the Chicama valley and the Moche valley and later in most of the valleys of the north-west coast. Two peculiarities, one ecological and economic, the other artistic, distinguished the Mochica culture from all other classic cultures of the American continent.

The state built by the Mochica on the north-west coast of Peru was the only great state structure of the classic period in America that depended almost entirely on artificial irrigation. No great state had developed on the south coast of Peru, while the highland regions, especially in the north, depended on irrigation only in a limited degree.

The influence exercised on social structure and organisation by artificial irrigation is one of the most debated anthropological and historical problems existing today. Did the necessity of constructing great public works such as irrigation systems lead to the development of the state or did a state have to exist before such undertakings were begun? This is only one of the many hotly debated problems in this field. Despite wide differences of opinion many scholars, having examined in detail the great cultures of the Near East, of India and China, which were based on intensive irrigation, have agreed on a number of distinctive characteristics which appear in almost all cultures of this type.

A marked degree of state centralisation is a decisive characteristic of all these cultures and the appearance of a bureaucracy that soon dominated the structure of all sectors of life, religion and art. This bureaucracy owed much of its power to its control of water supplies and to the social needs imposed by the works for which it was responsible.

The economic, social and political gulf between rulers and ruled grows even deeper. This symptom alone would not have been exceptional since it also existed in ancient Rome and in the medieval feudal states in Europe. What did make these irrigation states unusual was the fact that most of the land was not owned privately by the nobility as was the case in ancient Rome or among the feudal landlords of the Middle Ages in Europe, but was vested in the state. Most of the state income was distributed among the members of the bureaucracy who themselves however owned limited land and property.

The state was so powerful that it frequently concentrated trade and handiwork under its control. Its greatest wealth lay not in the land but in its right to dispose of the labour of its subjects who were compelled to place a large measure of their time – and sometimes their earnings – at the state's disposal.

One of the most striking features that made this sort of state so different from a slave or feudal state was the survival of the original kinship organisation. The great mass of the population, especially the peasants, continued to live in kinship associations, which practised far-reaching economic, social and religious functions, the division of land among their members, the regulation of marriages, mutual help and common religious observances. They showed an increasing tendency however to evolve from democratic largely independent structures into state administrative units that controlled public works and military service.[9]

There is considerable evidence that development on the north-west coast of Peru followed a similar pattern. First of all small local fortresses sprang up in the coastal valleys. They obviously provided protection for the small groups within the valleys against other rival groups. As time went on the fortresses became larger until a uniform series of fortifications surrounded a whole valley. Power in individual valleys became vested in the hands of a ruling group, the construction of the great irrigation works began to take place, and there was a sudden increase in the population. In the third century AD there was a fresh development when the indigenous pottery of all the valleys of the north-west coast was replaced by another ceramic type from the valleys of Moche and Chicama. The conclusion has accordingly been drawn that a campaign of conquest from these valleys overran the north-west coast of Peru. The first important state emerged in the Andean region.

What was life like within this state? Thanks to the unique type of pottery the Mochica produced we have more information about the life of its inhabitants than about any other culture of the Andean region of that period. All aspects both of the supernatural world and of the daily life of the Mochica were represented either in the form of plastic representations or painting of what must certainly be unique diversity.

These representations prove the existence of a privileged ruling class. Recognisable dignitaries are very clearly portrayed. They wear a particular turban-like head ornament and are accompanied by lesser orders. Entertainments, such as hunting scenes, are represented in which only the ruling class were able to take part. They are also represented at religious occasions and above all in war. It is not clear from these representations whether there was any difference between priests and warriors or whether there was still only one uniform ruling class. It is impossible to reconstruct from the pottery only the life led by their subjects, portrayed in war, in farming, in religious ceremonies. When it is remembered however that on the eve of the Conquest the entire population of the Andean region was organised into clanlike communities it is not difficult to guess that a similar organisation must have existed in the state of the Mochica. Do the individual and comparatively rare representations of men in chains point to the existence of slaves? It is impossible to say for certain.

Mochica pottery however represents much more than just the relationship between rulers and ruled. Details can be seen of social and personal life in a manner scarcely displayed at this period by any other American people. Did there exist between the ruling class and the peasantry a group of professional merchants, as there undoubtedly did in Mesoamerica? There can scarcely be any doubt that there was trade or at least a form of barter between the state of the Mochica and the highlands in view of the many objects from the highlands that have been discovered in the coastal region. How did this trade operate? Was there a commercial monopoly as there was under the state of Chimu, the successor state of the Mochica, just as there was in pre-dynastic Egypt, or was there a regular professional group of merchants? The latter possibility seems unlikely. No figures which could possibly represent merchants have been discovered on the enormous numbers of Mochica pots which depict all groups of the population. And apart from this there were no cities that could have been called trading centres. Exactly as in classic Mesoamerica the energies and labour forces not required for agriculture seem to have been devoted largely to religious projects. The most important buildings of the Mochica period are gigantic pyramids that served exclusively religious purposes. The two greatest but by no means only ones are in the Moche valley on the north-west coast of Peru. The most important, known as the Pyramid of the Sun although this title has not been authenticated, is of impressive proportions: the platform on which it stands is 228 metres long and 136 metres wide and the pyramid stands 18 metres high. It is estimated that 130 million clay bricks went into the building of it. The smaller pyramid – also unauthenticated – is called the Pyramid of the Moon; it stands on a smaller platform 82 metres long, 60 metres wide and 21 metres high, which makes it somewhat higher. Temples were erected on the summits of the pyramids as in Mesoamerica.

Despite the greater size of the Pyramid of the Sun, the moon and not the sun was the most important deity of the Mochica. In a wide variety of representations the god of the moon is always shown overcoming rival deities and emerging victorious from every encounter. In the torrid, dry coastal valleys exposed to the scorching rays of the sun it is not surprising that his rival, the moon, was regarded as the most important deity. The god of the moon was never solitary or isolated. In a universe filled with innumerable and diverse deities he had always to fight for his supremacy. Gerdt Kutscher[10] divided up the repetitious multiplicity of demons which occur in the representations into four groups: the first includes zoomorphic demons usually armed for battle, such as fox demons and stag demons. The second group consists of plant spirits, especially bean and maize demons. A third group displays highly animistic features. Godlike properties were attributed to weapons and to the clothing and arms of the warriors. Demons in the fourth group have predominantly human features.

Among the many cult rites which were practised three kinds stand out in particular: many representations show human sacrifices, particularly of children and of prisoners of war. Some of these sacrifices appear to have been offered up to animals. Thus, a ceramic representation shows a jaguar falling upon a hypothetical prisoner of war. However the sacrifices never reached the dimensions they had in Mexico under the Aztecs. Nocturnal ceremonies accompanied a completely different cult rite, in which the drug coc, cultivated in the lowlands and still chewed by millions of Indians today in the Andean region, was taken.

In some respects, sporting competitions of a religious character are reminiscent of Mesoamerica. While in Mesoamerica however these competitions were ball games, ceremonial races were held on the north-west coast of Peru.

The secular buildings of this period with the exception of the irrigation works are much less impressive than those of a religious character. Great cities are completely absent at this period. Dwelling houses were generally built of clay bricks. While the peasants dwelt in small huts, larger buildings were erected for the nobility. The many rooms that were grouped round a central patio had floors of raised clay slabs covered with mats and cushions made out of the wool of the *ceiba* tree. Hooks were used to hang clothes on, and jewellery was kept in baskets or wooden caskets. The bareness of the rooms was partly broken by finely decorated blankets.

The high proportion of surplus energy that was devoted to religious construction by the Mochica has led historians to conclude that there must have been a theocracy. As has already been stated this could have been the case. It must be added, however, that it could not have been a peace-loving theocracy. The evidence of the numerous fortresses discovered is supported by the many representations of war and of warriors in Mochica pottery. The lively battle scenes between warriors point to battles between the inhabitants of a valley or between individual valleys. In some of the fights the warriors are attired completely differently bearing heads as trophies and may have come from the region of the Amazon. The Mochica warriors wore richly ornamented helmets and cotton wool armour, and carried shields. Their most important weapon was a club with a copper point. Spear throwers were also employed.

Art concerning religion, wars and the acts of the ruling class is frequently met with in pre-Spanish America. What makes Mochica art unique is the detailed description of every detail of life both by night and day of the ruling class and of the people as a whole.

Mochica food was of unexampled richness in ancient America. The extraordinary variety of agricultural products included maize, sweet potatoes, chile peppers and a wonderful variety of fruit and vegetables. These products were supplemented by fish and meat dishes. Meat included llama, guinea pig, dog and many kinds of game. Due to the ever increasing progress in artificial irrigation and the abundance of meat and fish, the Mochica do not seem to have had the acute problems of famine that always faced the inhabitants of Mesoamerica. It plays no part in the historical traditions of the Andean peoples on the eve of the Spanish Conquest nor in the representations in the pottery of the Mochica. This fact probably resulted in the absence of outbreaks either of rebellions or of radical social conflicts as in Mesoamerica. Confrontations of a more or less serious nature must however have occurred. The draconic penalties illustrated so often in the pottery are evidence of this. The penalties extended from the chopping off of noses or upper lips to flaying and stoning.

The material achievements of the Mochica went hand in hand with the high level of their art. Indeed their pottery is unique among the ceramics of ancient America. Three characteristics are particularly significant: the first is the unique degree of realism in representations that cover all aspects of life; the second is its dynamic character: no other people in America have succeeded in depicting movement and massed scenes so expressively as the Mochica. The third feature is its eroticism. The candid representations of all forms of sexual intercourse has made Mochica pottery extremely popular with archaeological smugglers.

Weaving was also highly developed. The Mochica did not only spin cotton, but also vicuña and llama wool which was often mixed with cotton. Weaving – probably done by women if we go by the representations in pottery – seems to have attained a refinement which the people of Mesoamerica never achieved. The most beautiful pieces were kept not for women but for men. Male attire consisted generally of loincloths, richly embroidered shirts with and without sleeves, and jackets which were also highly decorated. Members of the nobility wore in addition circular mantles with round collars and a head decoration in the shape of a turban. Feminine attire was much simpler and always consisted of a plain shift reaching to the knees. To compensate for the effect of this simplicity the face and the feet were painted and a variety of jewellery was worn. Textiles also played an important role in the cult of the dead, and graves were decorated with all kinds of fabrics.

The peoples of the classic period in the Andean region, in contrast to those in Mesoamerica, were already familiar with metallurgy. Among the Mochica, where it had already reached an advanced stage of development, gold, silver and copper were worked. Alloys of gold and silver, and inlays of gold and turquoise or gold and lapis lazuli were also produced, although bronze was still unknown. Metal objects served primarily as ornaments but had already begun to be used as weapons and for agricultural purposes.

While the material culture and the artistic achievements of the Mochica took a great step forward, there was considerably less progress in intellectual development. It seems to have been characteristic of certain branches of knowledge in pre-Colombian America that they stood in inverse ratio to the development of a number of the material aspects of culture. In other words the more advanced food production became and the more intensive agriculture, the more rooted in practical problems knowledge remained and the less its comprehension of abstract theories.

In Mesoamerica it was the Maya who practised the most primitive form of agriculture but who revealed the greatest achievements in the realm of the calendar, mathematics and graphology. On the other hand in central Mexico where food production reached a much higher level, intellectual achievements were on a far lower level. The same seems to apply to the Mochica. Knowledge was concentrated primarily on practical problems such as the construction of large irrigation systems which, in view of the primitive tools available and the difficulties of the terrain, must have been far from simple.

The Mochica also produced results in the equally practical science of medicine. In the pottery of the Mochica not only are various diseases represented in detail, but also the operations that were undertaken. Among the most important is trepanning.

At present scholars are hotly debating another problem concerning the intellectual development of the Mochica. Did the Mochica possess a script? On the basis of the drawings of beans which constantly recur in Mochica pictograms and ceramics, Rafael Larco Hoyle has erected the hypothesis that these beans represented glyphs which closely resembled Maya glyphs. In fact there are various recurring representations of messengers hurrying on their way with beans in their hands. In view of the fact that on the eve of the Spanish Conquest no evidence of such a script was discovered, many scholars doubt this theory and believe that the beans were only toys. Other scholars however admit that there might have been the beginnings of a script here, although they are extremely doubtful whether a script as such had already come into existence. They believe rather that the beans might strongly resemble the later quipus of the Inca which were always mnemonic.

Whatever significance the script may have had, no beans of the Mochica period have been discovered. Therefore, in contrast to the Maya, no written evidence of this period will ever be found. Fortunately archaeological evidence and artistic representations are so rich and expressive that they largely make up for this lack.

In considering the development of the state of the Mochica, two problems always present themselves. Why did this people, the first to create a state structure in the Andean region, fail to exert greater influence on the region? Hardly any signs of Mochica influence have been discovered in the highlands or on the southern coast of Peru. The answer is almost certainly connected with the fact that the Mochica were hardly in a position to undertake conquests of any size in the highlands. This was primarily a result of the unfavourable strategic situation of the Peruvian coastal valleys. The conquest of the highlands from the low-lands is always a difficult undertaking and becomes more so when climatic variations are so great that those used to the hot climate of the coast can barely tolerate the cold of the highlands. In addition the coastal inhabitants of Peru, on ecological grounds, were bound to fear invasions from the highlands rather than the reverse. Lastly in the event of invasion water could be cut off and their lifeline severed. This is probably the reason, as will be shown, why the state of the Mochica and its successor the state of Chimù had in the last resort to surrender to the people from the highlands.

The second question is much more difficult to answer. Why did no cities develop in the state of the Mochica? The basis of every urban development is a highly productive agriculture that allows a consider-able proportion of the population to be freed from direct food produc-tion. A highly productive agriculture undoubtedly existed in the Mochica region. It was presumably even more highly developed than that of Teotihuacan or, for that matter, the region of the Maya, yet there was no development which could be compared with Teotihuacan or with Tikal. Comparison with Teotihuacan might help to clarify this problem. In Teotihuacan urban development is clearly discernible. From a ceremonial centre which attracted thousands of people there inevitably developed a trading centre. Merchants from many parts of Mesoamerica came to Teotihuacan to exchange their goods. At the same time or shortly afterwards Teotihuacan became the administrative centre of a great governmental region. Here there lived priest princes, the nobility, bureaucrats, their numerous servants and craftsmen and peasants.

The absence of a similar evolution in Mochica may be attributed to two factors: in the first place the development of commercial centres was hindered by the fact that trade in the state of the Mochica, just as it was later among the Chimù and the Inca, was presumably a state monopoly in the hands of a bureaucracy. None of the cities of the Andean region known to history on the eve of the Spanish Conquest bore the character of a commercial metropolis. They were all administrative state centres dwelt in by the ruling classes. The second reason why no such centre developed in the Chimu state that succeeded the Mochica on the north-west coast of Peru might be due to a rather lax organisation in the state of the Mochica. Possibly the various valleys were given their independence and their nobility continued to live there in the larger villages. It is also not unlikely that if a theocratic hierarchy ruled the state of the Mochica, it was afraid that other large secular centres might endanger its power. This problem remains one of the most important unresolved questions concerning the development of the north-west coast of Peru.

THE CULTURES OF THE SOUTH COAST OF PERU

On the way down the Peruvian coast from north to south striking differences become apparent. The valleys grow smaller and the rivers shallower, so that the possibility of artificial irrigation with its aim of raising productivity is increasingly diminished. The population density is less than in the north and it is not surprising that the buildings should be smaller and the extent of state integration far behind that of the north coast. On the southern coast of Peru there is no evidence of a great centralised state. It is possible though that some limited urban development did exist. This is to be seen in the fortified city of Tampo Viejo in the Acari Valley and Cahuachi in the Nazca Valley. While the state organisation in the north offered its inhabitants protection from external attacks, the inhabitants of the south coast must have led a precarious existence. Possibly these cities were primarily places of refuge in the case of attack from outside.

This drop in food production and population density was not however accompanied by a drop in artistry; although the ceramics of the south coast do not equal those of the Mochica culture either in craftsmanship or in expressiveness, and although subject matter was far more restricted and contained religious motifs and abstract decoration, weaving on the other hand reached a level of development unparelleled elsewhere in the Andean region.

In contrast to the north coast of Peru, it never rains on the south coast. Accordingly textiles have endured here over thousands of years completely intact. In the years from 1925 to 1930 two large burial-grounds in the middle of the desert were excavated, Paracas Cavernas and Paracas Necropolis, in which a number of mummies were found. These had remained intact, thanks to the dryness of the climate, just like the woven fabrics in which they were wrapped. Additional fabrics and ceramic and precious metal objects were added to these woven textiles as burial offerings. While the textiles of Paracas Cavernas must be attributed to the pre-classic period and are in part coarsely woven, those of Paracas Necropolis are among the most beautiful and the richest found in America and perhaps in the whole world. Over a hundred shades of colour were used and a great diversity of materials – cotton, wool and even human hair. The creators of these textiles are still unknown. Since the places where the burial enclosures are situated seem to have been uninhabited it is generally thought that corpses were transported there from far away. The similarity of some of the Paracas motifs to those of the Nazca valley a hundred kilometres further south indicates that the dead came from there.

Labour which was not employed in agriculture, instead of being expended in great temple enclosures or the maintenance of a comprehensive bureaucracy, was devoted to the cult of the dead. The textiles discovered in the graves show a high degree of skill that must have required a tremendous amount of labour. There is also less evidence of differences in status and wealth among the dead than on the northern coast. This fact, and the lack of evidence of any strongly integrated state which might have embraced several valleys, leads us to conclude that the social organisation of the southern valleys was more democratic than that of the north. It was probably also more strongly theocratic in character. Not only does the religious orientation of art suggest this, but also the fact that it was precisely here that astronomical achievements were the most strongly developed.

When a few decades ago Paul Kosok[11] flew over a desert not far from the valley of Nazca, he noticed from the aeroplane some strange markings. They were animal figures engraved in the soil and round about them were a great variety of lines and markings, shapes of triangles, trapezes and so on. The unique feature of these markings is that they are only visible from the air and not at ground level. Archaeologists regard these markings therefore as drawings of animals which were intended as pictures to be looked upon by heavenly beings. The significance of the trapeze and the markings is a perplexing question. They have been interpreted as representing pathways running between graves, but such graves have so far not been discovered. When these lines were examined however for possible astronomical significance, it was discovered that a number of markings pointed to solstices and others to equinoxes. This suggests that the astronomical attainments of the peoples of this valley must have been comprehensive and they must have made preparatory studies. Kosok believes that he discovered similar astronomical markings in various textiles in the region of the Nazca. Should such astronomical markings prove to be correct the fact would be confirmed once more that progress in the realm of astronomy and in a number of other areas of knowledge stood in an inverse ratio to the degree of state integration. Such progress was probably associated with the more strongly theocratic orientation of the peoples, who were not yet significantly integrated into the state and who still lacked a comprehensive bureaucracy. It is certainly no accident that in places where the power of the ruling class increased interest invariably shifted from problems concerning heavenly bodies to much more mundane affairs and that interest in astronomy diminished correspondingly.

THE HIGHLAND CULTURES OF THE ANDEAN REGION IN THE CLASSIC PERIOD

The falling off already noticeable in the evidence of archaeological remains as one travels south is even more apparent in the highlands. Here nothing as highly expressive as the ceramic art of the Mochica is to be found, although this could be due in fact to the absence of an arid climate like that of the south coast where many perishable things survived. Also far fewer systematic excavations have been undertaken than on the coast.

In this region therefore we still have to depend very largely on surmise. This is particularly true of the northern Peruvian highlands. Were there already large integrated states in this region in the classic period? The finds made so far, stone statues of warriors and women, and above all pottery decorated with hunting motifs like the one of Recuay, and also stone buildings of two to three storeys in various parts of the northern highlands, have failed to shed any light on these questions. How advanced was the technique of irrigation and terracing at that time? Was there a religious or secular ruling class?

No less problematic, even though the finds are richer, is an understanding of the social structure in the southern highlands, especially in the region of Lake Titicaca. There was a completely different kind of ecological structure here than in the rest of the Andean region. In contrast to the other regions of the middle Andean region, in which a high culture developed, artificial irrigation played no part. The waters of Lake Titicaca – the largest lake at this altitude in the world, which today separates Bolivia from Peru – could have provided water but the climate is far too harsh for an irrigation economy. Maize, which was cultivated almost everywhere in the Andean region under conditions of artificial irrigation, was only able to flourish here in exceptional cases. Artificial irrigation on the other hand was scarcely necessary for the potato.

The absence of an intensive irrigation system was compensated for by a number of other factors which made it possible for just as dense a population to exist as in the most fertile coastal valleys. The first of these factors was the productivity of the potato and the fact that the peoples of the highlands knew how to extract a substance called *chuñu* from the potato which could be preserved over a long period. The fact that the miserable looking steppes of the highlands, the Puna, were highly suitable for cattle breeding was equally important. This is probably the area in which llama and alpaca were first domesticated, for hundreds of thousands of these animals lived here in the classic period.

The cultivation of the potato and the breeding of the llama did not require a strong centralised organisation, as did the irrigation system of the coast. Centralising tendencies appear to have begun later and were primarily concerned with external conquest rather than internal economic consolidation and great public constructions.

In view of this state of affairs, it seems at first remarkable and highly problematical why some of the most important centres of the classic period should have originated precisely in this region. One of the earliest of these centres is Púcara on the north-west coast of Lake Titicaca. In the middle of this centre there is a large stone terrace surrounded by walls and a sunken patio with subterranean grave vaults. The whole complex of buildings was presumably a temple. All around further remains of unidentifiable buildings were found. In view of the size of these precincts, John Rowe affirmed that Púcara was a city, although other scholars contest this. Because Púcara's influence is only slight, it is not thought to have been the capital of a large state.

The most important and by far the best-known centre of the southern highland region of the Andes is not Púcara but Tiahuanaco, fifty kilometres away on the opposite bank of Lake Titicaca.

As with the Maya in Mesoamerica the question of Tiahuanaco in the Andean region provoked a vast number of scientific hypotheses and controversies, and provided an almost magical attraction for widely different fantasies.

Lying at a height of about four thousand metres, in modern Bolivia, twenty kilometres away from Lake Titicaca, are the ruins of Tiahuanaco. One of the most impressive groups of buildings in the Andean region, they include four large and a number of smaller buildings and numerous sculptures. Stone was the chief building material.

Two of the four buildings are pyramids that are considerably lower than those of Teotihuacan. The first pyramid, called Akapana today, is 180 metres long, 135 metres wide but only 15 metres high. The second pyramidal building, known as Pumapumku, stands on a platform only 6 metres high. The flat blocks of stone weighing a hundred tons each which were used for their construction are their most impressive feature. In contrast to the buildings of classic Mesoamerica, pieces of metal in the form of T-shaped copper clamps were used to bind the stones together.

A third great building in Tiahuanaco known today as Kalasasaya is quite different. It contains a great platform 135 metres long and 130 metres wide, in the middle of which there is a patio. At the entrance to this stands a monolithic gateway which is the most famous construction in Tiahuanaco, the so-called Gateway of the Sun. This monument, hewn from a single rock, 3 metres high and 3·75 metres broad, is decorated by a relief with a principal theme that is found over the whole of the Andean region. At the centre of this frieze is a figure known to most scholars as the Sun God. It has anthropomorphic features in contrast to the deities in Mesoamerica. The head is surrounded by rays which indicate that this figure is a personification of the sun. Representations of puma and condor also play an important role in this relief. Traces of tears in the form of puma fall from the eyes of the central figure, and some of the rays round the head begin as puma heads. The deities hold staffs (rays) in their hands which end as condor heads. In addition there are forty-eight subsidiary figures all hurrying towards the main figure. They are partly human and partly animal, with masks of predatory animals and birds.

In contrast to the reliefs of the Sun Gate which are both monumental and life-like in effect, the stone statues in Tiahuanaco are still and life-less. A number of the motifs of this Gateway of the Sun, especially the geometric representations of puma and condor heads, recur with few variations over the entire Andean region.

What exactly caused the culture of Tiahuanaco in the Andean region, like that of the Maya in Mesoamerica, to become the object of so many theories both scientific and fantastic?

Just as the peoples of Mesoamerica at the time of the Conquest were able to explain little of the historical background of the classic cultures of, say, the Maya or of Teotihuacan, so the inhabitants of the Andean region when the Spaniards arrived knew very little about Tiahuanaco. For the Inca it was a legendary centre where once upon a time the god Viracocha had dwelt. They knew less than archaeologists today about its builders and inhabitants.

As the Maya cities suddenly unfolded and developed without ascertainable antecedents, so the culture of Tiahuanaco seems in the light of existing research to have developed in a similar way. Although traces of an earlier settlement have been found in Tiahuanaco most archaeologists consider that there were hardly any connections with later Tiahuanaco culture.

As in the Maya region there seems to have been a striking contrast between harsh natural environment and tremendous cultural achievements. Among the Maya the antithesis was between tropical primeval forest and a high culture; among the builders of Tiahuanaco it was between great buildings and an inhospitable region at an altitude of four thousand metres.

The present-day inhabitants of the Bolivian high plateau are among the poorest people in the whole of America and the region is unsuited to intensive agriculture. Why did a centre rise here, even if it was only made possible by tremendous labour? Some of the blocks of stone used in the building of Tiahuanaco weigh up to a hundred tons and the nearest site this stone could have come from was five kilometres away. Obviously their transport must have required enormous combined effort. This seems to presuppose a population density and a degree of social integration that is difficult to imagine in such an inhospitable region. Moreover, the artistic finish of the buildings of Tiahuanaco points to the existence of a large class of skilled artisans. Could such a group have developed in the region of Lake Titicaca? If the highland Indians were not by themselves in a position to construct such a centre as Tiahuanaco its builders must have come from outside. Was Tiahuanaco the religious or political centre of the Andean region, whose inhabitants were recruited for the building of the highland centre? This hypothesis seemed very likely in view of the fact that the Tiahuanaco style is spread over the whole Andean region.

In the case of the Maya a sophisticated calendar prevented excessive speculation and vague hypotheses. In the case of Tiahuanaco however, the various theories about the age of the city differ very widely. Did the great stone buildings not bring to mind the megaliths of the ancient world which are thousands of years old?

It is not surprising that the most fantastic theories were advanced. The archaeologist Posnansky took the view that the Temple of Kalasasaya was intended for cosmic purposes. Since the orientation of the temple did not correspond with the points of the modern compass, Posnansky assumed that the earth's axis at the time when Kalasasaya was built had shown a different slope to the ecliptic plane that it shows now. He concluded accordingly that this temple was built seventeen thousand years ago and he saw in Tiahuanaco the origin of every civilisation in the world.[12] These theories appear almost conservative, however, when compared with the theory held by another archaeologist, Bellamy, who estimates Tiahuanaco to be 250,000 years old. As in the case of the Maya, those who supported the theory of Atlantis also had their say. They believed that the builders of Tiahuanaco may have been the surviving members of the population of the sunken continent of Atlantis.

Even though up to the period of the Second World War there seemed to be no possibility of ascertaining the exact age of the city, such speculations were rejected by most scholars. When archaeologists resumed work at Tiahuanaco after the Second World War they were equipped with new methods and renewed interest that enabled important breakthroughs to be made which clarified a number of problems.

With the radio-carbon method it was established that the rise of Tiahuanaco began at the outside early in the Christian era and that the greatest buildings of Tiahuanaco had already been erected by the third or fourth century AD. It was also established that the Tiahuanaco epoch manifested itself in the rest of the Andean region a few centuries later.

These facts not only put an end to all speculation about the age of Tiahuanaco but proved that its erection could not have been the result of a conquest of the remaining Andean region. The Tiahuanaco style first appeared in the Andean region hundreds of years after the highland centre was built. The theory that the building of Tiahuanaco was the result of a local development in the southern highland region of the Andes becomes increasingly probable.

Recent ecological and historical studies have shown that the antithesis between the grandeur of Tiahuanaco and the inhospitality of its environment was not as great as had widely been presumed considering the low living standards of the present inhabitants of the region. Llama breeding in the pre-Spanish Andean region was a highly productive branch of the economy. Wool and textiles were extremely valuable. Recently discovered Spanish reports of the period immediately following the Conquest have shown that the inhabitants of Chucuito in the highlands of the Lake Titicaca were among the richest Indians of the pre-Conquest period as well as of that immediately following the Conquest.[13] The idea that, with the aid of these rich cattle breeders such a centre as Tiahuanaco could have been created cannot be dismissed. However further excavations in the region of Lake Titicaca are necessary to confirm these presumptions.

Despite all the advances achieved in the last few years, there are still a number of very important questions left: what exactly was Tiahuanaco? Was it a city or only a religious centre? Was it the capital of a state? Was it a commercial centre? The excavations in Tiahuanaco have, alas, not gone so far as for instance excavations in Teotihuacan, and one is therefore a long way from having any definite answers to these questions. So far the excavations have revealed no traces of large dwelling settlements or of any great population density which could justify the term 'city', although fresh research could completely alter this impression. It is not surprising, given our present limited knowledge, that there should be a variety of theories concerning Tiahuanaco's significance. Edward Lanning believes it was a regular city, the capital of a large state stretching over important parts of the southern highlands of the Andes to the north of present-day Chile and Argentina. Other archaeologists consider that Tiahuanaco was in the classic period primarily a religious centre which the population of the highlands visited as pilgrims. Tiahuanaco may in addition have fulfilled other functions.

The highland region of Lake Titicaca was one of the areas in the Andean region where it was difficult to grow maize. The needs of the highland inhabitants for maize and other products of the lowlands were nevertheless very great. Maize played a decisive role not only as a food but also in the preparation of chicha beer, and in religious life. Cotton presumably could also have been needed. Conversely wool, meat and the potato flour *chuñu* were much sought after in the lowlands. Is it not possible therefore that important markets developed in the ceremonial centres of the southern highlands to which at certain times of the year the highland peoples flocked in order to exchange their products for those of the lowlands? It will probably never be discovered who transacted this exchange; whether they were merchants unknown to us from later periods of Andean history, or representatives of the coastal states who carried maize into the highlands in exchange for animals and other highland products. No exact answer is forthcoming. At all events it may be presumed that the cities in the southern Andean highlands were commercial centres. The fact that both Púcara and Tiahuanaco lay near Lake Titicaca made them accessible by land and by boat. No archaeological confirmation of all these theories has as yet been found. The excavations however are nowhere near finished.

THE END OF THE CLASSIC CULTURES IN THE ANDEAN REGION

The classic cultures in the Andean region came to an end at the same time as those in Mesoamerica. The process of disintegration is not supported by historical evidence either in the Andean region or in Mesoamerica. Most of the high cultures of the Andean region ceased to produce their ceramics and other artefacts between the sixth and tenth centuries AD. A kind of Tiahuanaco art style seems to have overlaid everything, probably as the result of a conquest. Where the conquerors came from, whether Tiahuanaco or another region under the influence of Tiahuanaco culture, is still a matter for dispute and will be considered later.

The close of the classic cultures in the Andean region lacks the dramatic and overwhelming character of the disintegration of the classic Mesoamerican cultures. There is no evidence of any radical overthrow of the cultures or of great migrations of population and there is nothing to point to a massive abandonment of the existing cultural centres. The final years of the Andean region consequently present fewer problems and questions than the decline of Mesoamerica. It was not the decline of classic cultures but the dominance of one civilisation in particular which brought about the end.

The absence of radical social upheavals in the Andean region as compared with Mesoamerica is largely comprehensible. The permanent antithesis within Mesoamerican cultures – constant increase of population against limited increase in food production – does not seem to have existed in the Andean region. The continuing construction of irrigation works on the coast, the growth of the herds of llama in the southern highlands probably ruled out such a possibility. It is significant that in the coastal region of the north just before the classic culture ended the land suitable for cultivation had not been entirely used up. On the eve of the Spanish Conquest even the key region of the Aztec Empire was perennially threatened by famine, the last time being in the year 1505, and all traditions and legends mentioned overwhelming famines; in Peru there was scarcely any reference to such disasters. The peoples of the Andean region would appear largely to have solved this problem.

The special powers of the ruling class were a second factor which also prevented social upheavals. The ruling classes in Mesoamerica, particularly in the Maya region, fulfilled primarily a religious role of mediation between mankind and the gods. Their secular functions were relatively insignificant. Great installations such as the irrigation works of the north-west coast of Peru did not exist. The largest installations of the kind in Mesoamerica, those of Teotihuacan, were of insignificant size by comparison with the installations on the coast of the Andean region. Whatever point of view is adopted regarding the importance of war in Mesoamerica, it undoubtedly played a much smaller role there in the early years of the classic period than in the Andean region. Accordingly the functions of the nobility in relation to war were less significant which meant that their position could be much more easily upset than in the Andean region. A new religion which called in question the role of the ruling class as mediator between mankind and the gods was enough to threaten its entire existence. The more comprehensive secular role of the nobility in the Andean region offered correspondingly greater stability.

Consequently it is not surprising that the classic cultures of the Andean region were only overcome by a well organised power of great strength, while the failing cultures of Mesoamerica were not equal to the pressure of barbarians from across the frontier. The almost inevitable result was a far-reaching disintegration of the high culture of Mesoamerica while in the Andean region, a high culture continued to exist under a new ruling class.

When considering the 'classic period' in the Andean region and in Mesoamerica, the question at once arises whether the conception of 'classic' is justified. A 'classic period' is a time when the development of a culture is at its zenith. The term was initially coined to refer to artistic achievement, and in this respect it is fully justified both in Mesoamerica and in the Andean region. The pottery of the Mochica, the textiles of Paracas.Necropolis, the giant pyramids of Moche on the north-west coast of Peru, the stonework of Tiahuanaco, the cities of the Maya, the stupendous buildings of Teotihuacan, the achievements of the Maya in the realm of graphology and astronomy undoubtedly justify the term 'classic' both from an artistic and an intellectual point of view. The cultural and intellectual achievements of these regions were never surpassed in later times.

The question takes on other aspects when considered from the standpoint of food production and technology. Irrigation had certainly made tremendous progress even in the classic period in the Andean region, but had in no way reached its zenith. There is strong evidence that a considerable part of the irrigation channels connecting several valleys to each other were only constructed in the post-classic period. The same goes for the tremendous terraces constructed in the highlands. The impressive network of roads which covered the whole Andean region dates only from the later Inca period.

In the realm of technology equally the zenith had not yet been reached. In the field of metallurgy the working of gold, silver, copper and even some alloys was already known, but knowledge of bronze was only added in the post-classic period.

A similar situation may be established, perhaps with greater clarity, in Mesoamerica. The technology of intensive agriculture by irrigation had already existed in the classic period and is confirmed by all research so far carried out. But the largest, most comprehensive and important irrigation installations, particularly in the lakeland area in the present-day Valley of Mexico, were only constructed in the post-classic period. Metallurgy too was unknown during the classic period. With regard to social integration also, the greatest empires both in Mesoamerica and in the Andean region stem from the post-classic period.

For all these reasons, it is questionable whether the term 'classic', although justified in connection with art, may be used as unambiguously in other fields such as food production, general technology and social integration.

In some respects the high cultures in Mesoamerica and in the Andean region developed in similar ways: they did not follow immediately upon the knowledge of agriculture but only thousands of years later. Their origin, as far as it is archaeologically possible to ascertain, was sudden. The leading and responsible class of the classic high cultures both in Mesoamerica and in the Andean region seems to have been a priesthood. The rise of classic cultures in Mesoamerica and in the Andean region was associated with an important economic advance. In the

Andean region new methods of food production were developed primarily through the construction of tremendous irrigation systems. Trade on the other hand developed much more slowly. In Mesoamerica the introduction of new methods of food production and the construction of large irrigation schemes were on a considerably smaller scale, against which trade played a far more important role than in the Andean region. There were probably three radical differences between the classic cultures of Mesoamerica and the Andean region that have a certain bearing on the forms of evolution.

Firstly the main preoccupation of the ruling class of Mesoamerica was with theoretical problems such as graphology and the calendar, while the nobility of the Andean region was concerned much more with practical and technical questions; secondly great cities were raised in classic Mesoamerica in contrast to the Andean region; and thirdly the significance of militarism in the Andean region was greater than in Mesoamerica.

Theories to explain the first two differences have already been suggested. But why did war play so much greater a part in the classic period of the Andean region than in Mesoamerica? One of the explanations given for this phenomenon is the fact that in the Andean region there was less land suitable for cultivation, and as soon as the available land in a valley had been settled the temptation arose to conquer fresh land in neighbouring areas. In Mesoamerica, where by comparison there was more land available for cultivation, there always existed the possibility of colonising fresh land peaceably. There is something to be said for this explanation although if the situation in the Virú Valley region of the Andes, where archaeologists have made the closest examinations, is taken into account it appears that there had existed fortresses and a military tendency long before the whole of the available land was settled.

The problem should perhaps consist less in establishing why in the Andean region militarism developed so early – such a development exists almost universally – than in determining why there was less evidence of militarism over such a long period in Mesoamerica. One of the most credible explanations is the transcendence of Teotihuacan, the existence of a *Pax Teotihuacana*, under whose protection the classic cultures of Mesoamerica attained their zenith.

CHAPTER 8

THE POST-CLASSIC CULTURES OF AMERICA

The classic period was followed by a new era which lasted from about the tenth to the sixteenth centuries and closed with the conquest of America by the Europeans. The differences between this period and earlier ones are less material than social in character. It is an epoch in which great empires developed; a time in which large-scale wars became a permanent feature of society. Innovations in the material sense not relating to food production occurred only in two fields: in the Andean region objects were made of bronze for the first time, in Mesoamerica metal working was introduced. These developments however did not lead either to important social or economic upheavals, and their effects remained relatively insignificant until the arrival of the Europeans.

The most important innovation consisted in the erection of large public buildings, especially irrigation works and water-control installations, on an unprecedented scale. Were these installations the cause or the effect of the evolution of the state? This hotly debated problem will be examined in greater detail.

In the post-classic period a number of the differences between Mesoamerica and the earlier Andean region vanish. Others diminish. The contrast during the classic period between the importance of militarism in Mesoamerica and in the Andean region becomes a thing of the past. In both regions militarism is now of decisive and pre-eminent importance; warriors in Mesoamerica may have played an even more important role than those in the Andean region.

The trend towards greater urban development in Mesoamerica and towards an even greater degree of state integration in the Andean region remains, but it is less pronounced. In the Andean region large new cities develop but judging by their scale and the degree of their urbanisation they appear to have lagged behind those of Mesoamerica. Unified states develop in Mesoamerica, but never reach the degree of integration achieved by the Inca states in the Andean region.

The thrust in Mesoamerica towards intellectual achievement –

graphology, the calendar and mathematics – and the urge so characteristic of the classic period in the Andean region towards irrigation
and other methods of increasing food production remain although in a
lesser degree. In Mesoamerica, in comparison with the classic period
there are no further developments in the calendar, in graphology or in
mathematics. On the contrary there appears to be a general retrogression in this respect. In the Andean region however there appear
presumably for the first time in this period the *quipu* knot symbols, a
kind of substitute for some of the functions of writing.

In the Andean region developments in irrigation and terracing
construction surpassed in scale anything which had previously existed.
Despite this the variance with Mesoamerica is not increased: for in the
Valley of Mexico the largest works ever constructed in Mesoamerica
for the control of water make their appearance. The feature that most
distinguishes this period, at least the latter part, from all preceding
periods is the existence of copious written records. In Mesoamerica
these included hieroglyphs of the pre-Spanish period as well as reports
and descriptions which were written down after the Conquest either in
the language of the victors or in that of the conquered. In the Andean
region there existed only the second type of source.

The sources in Mesoamerica reach further back in time than those
of the Andean region. In the central plateau, there are traditions going
back to the tenth century AD and in the Mixteca region in Oaxaca
they can be traced to the seventh century AD. Traditions handed down
in the Andean region go back to the thirteenth century but credibly substantiated evidence exists only from the middle of the fifteenth century.

For the remoter periods it is often extremely difficult to sort out the
historical core from the tangle of myth and legend. The significance of
the archaeological material as historical evidence is often increased
while the available archaeological materials decrease. And this is no
paradox. On the contrary it thus becomes possible to co-ordinate the
history with the archaeology, checking the findings of the one science
against those of the other, which greatly increases the historical value of
the archaeological evidence. At the same time however, and this is
especially true for Mesoamerica, fewer buildings and artefacts survive
from this later period than from the classical period. This is not because
less was built or made but because most of the centres of the classical
period had already been abandoned by the time the Spaniards arrived.
They were not resettled and consequently survive to the present day as
archaeological monuments. The position of many great cities which
still existed at the time of the Conquest was different. Like the Aztec
capital city of Tenochtitlan, the dwelling places of the Spanish
conquistadores and those ancient buildings which were not destroyed in
battle were torn down and replaced by new ones.

In the Andean region the position in this respect was more favourable, with the result that in the Inca capital city of Cuzco many more buildings of the pre-Spanish period survive than in Tenochtitlan in present-day Mexico.

CHAPTER 9

THE FIRST POST-CLASSIC CULTURES OF MESOAMERICA

THE TOLTECS

After the destruction of the great classic centres of Mesoamerica the last remnants of the classic cultures withdrew into small fortified centres. But they were not strong enough to keep the territory of their forefathers. All over Mesoamerica there is evidence, supported by historical tradition and confirmed by archaeological monuments, of new bands of conquering tribes which overran the old civilisation. In some instances these bands settled down in the cities of the classic period. Most of them however built new centres and used the classic cities, which they already regarded as holy places, as burial grounds for their dead. These waves of conquest originated from the south and south-east as well as the north of Mesoamerica.

In the south-east the Mixtecans threatened the successors of the classic culture of Monte Alban and erupted into the Valley of Oaxaca. Likewise another group of conquerors appears to have come from the south-east of Mesoamerica and settled themselves in the city of Cholollan. They are traditionally known as Olmecs. Scholars call them 'historical Olmecs', to distinguish them from the Olmecs who founded the first high culture of Mesoamerica at La Venta as already described.

Cholollan, now called Cholula, is one of the strangest, most interesting and, comparatively speaking, the least excavated centres of Mesoamerica. It is one of the few cities which have been continuously settled since the time of Teotihuacan until the present day. On the eve of the Spanish Conquest, Cholollan was a holy city, a place of pilgrimage which was traditionally reputed to have contained four hundred temples to which pilgrims from many parts of Mesoamerica journeyed. It was also the site of one of the largest pyramids ever built in ancient America.

In contrast to the great pyramids of Teotihuacan this temple was not constructed all at once. As so often happened in Mesoamerica, the existing pyramid was at various times covered with new layers. A tunnel which archaeologists bored into the pyramid revealed structures of many different periods and cultural influences.

Systematic archaeological research in Cholula was hindered by the fact that the city, even after the Spanish Conquest, remained a kind of holy place. The Catholic Church had clearly wished to create a certain continuity and to make use of the sacred character of the city in a Christian sense. On the foundations of the temples which had been pulled down and destroyed more than three hundred churches were built which give the city a unique appearance in Mexico, even today. There is even a tiny church on the top of the gigantic pyramid which now looks more like a weather-beaten mountain. Consequently the difficulties facing archaeologists here are much greater than in the abandoned cities of the Maya or in Teotihuacan. This is probably one of the main reasons why the excavations in Cholollan lag behind those in other regions of Mesoamerica.

Excavations so far carried out confirm the historical traditions regarding the arrival of foreign conquerors from the south in about the ninth century AD. In accordance with these traditions, the 'historical Olmecs' founded in Cholollan a strong, compact, militarily orientated state which exerted its influence far beyond the city itself.

Nevertheless it was not the conquerors from the south, who came chiefly from the civilised region, who left their mark on both central Mexico and on the whole of Mesoamerica in the following centuries, but conquerors from a completely different cultural region and a totally different area, the Toltecs from northern Mexico.

There are many traditions, legends and myths about the Toltecs contained in a number of chronicles and pictographs some of which complement each other while others are contradictory. They are usually represented as a people who came from the north under the leadership of a mighty and terrifying conqueror, Mixcoatl, or 'Cloud Serpent'. Cloud Serpent conquered a large region of central Mexico and built a first capital near to the later city Culhuacan, among caves on the mountain of La Estrella. He married a wife, Chimalman, 'Prostrate Shield', who bore him a son, Ce Acatl Topiltzin, 'Our Lord One Reed'.

Our Lord One Reed, who was to become the greatest hero of Toltec history, was obliged to begin with to live in exile, since his father was murdered by one of his junior leaders who then took over the leadership of the Toltecs. Our Lord One Reed succeeded in killing his father's murderer and returned to his tribe where he became the High Priest of the god Quetzalcoatl, the Feathered Serpent, whose name he also adopted. He is described in some chronicles as the spiritual and temporal leader of the Toltecs, others report that he had to share his power with a temporal ruler. Under his leadership a new capital city was built, Tollan, which in splendour and richness surpassed anything that had existed before. 'And he had dwellings which had been built of green precious stones called "Chalchihuites". He had other dwellings built of silver, some built of dyed and white sea shells ... dwellings of turquoise and of rich feathers ... The afore-mentioned Quetzalcoatl had all the riches of the world, gold, silver and green precious stones ...'[1] It was a golden age in which there was nothing lacking:

Under his rule maize was plentifully available, gourds were very plump, an armful in circumference, and the maize cobs were of a gigantic length ... Cotton of all colours was harvested, red, yellow, brown, white, green, blue and orange. These cotton colours were natural colours. So cotton flourished exceedingly ... cocoa trees of the most diverse colours grew plentifully ... Quetzalcoatl's subjects were exceedingly rich and they lacked for nothing. There was no hunger, maize was not lacking, indeed it was so abundant that the small maize cobs were not consumed, but used for heating baths.[2]

The Feathered Serpent was represented as the greatest bearer of civilisation in the history of the Mesoamerican peoples. He had discovered script and the calendar, and according to some chronicles, agriculture. Tollan's golden age soon came to an end.

And it is related and told that at the time in which Quetzalcoatl lived, malicious demons often tried to tempt him that he should atone for himself with human beings, that he should sacrifice human beings.

But he never wished to do this. He said, 'He would not go so far,' for he greatly loved his subjects who were the Toltecs. His sacrifices always consisted only of serpents, birds, and butterflies.

That means, so it is said, that he thereby angered the demons, so that they began to deride him and to mock him, while they said that they wished to plunge Quetzalcoatl into misery and to chase him away, which is just what happened.[3]

The war of his enemies against the Feathered Serpent is variously described. There is a description of how a hostile magician disguised himself as a doctor and went to the ailing Quetzalcoatl. 'My Lord, drink of this medicine', he said, and Quetzalcoatl replied: 'Noble sir, I have no wish to drink', and the old man replied and said, 'My Lord, drink of the medicine, for if you do not do so, you will rue it later, try at least to put a little on your forehead or drink a little of it.'

And aforesaid Quetzalcoatl tasted and then drank the medicine and said 'What is this? It seems to be something very good and tasty. It has already taken away my illness. I am cured.' 'Drink once more, for the medicine is very health-giving and you will become still better.'

And when the said Quetzalcoatl had drunk once more, he became drunk and began to weep bitterly and his heart grew tender and he was unable to forget the deception which the old magician had practised against him. The medicine which Quetzalcoatl had drunk was white wine made out of Maguey, called 'Teometl'.[4] While he was making himself drunk he broke the vow of his priestly office.

Another legend goes still further and relates that when Quetzalcoatl had lost control of his senses a maiden was brought to him whom he violated. Now he had lost his chastity which as a priest he was bound to maintain and was forced to leave Tollan with his followers. He travelled far away to the land of Tlillan Tlapallan, as the peninsula of Yucatan was called by the central Mexicans, but declared that he would one day return. The day of this return was exactly established in the fifty-two-year cycle of the Mesoamerican calendar. How deeply this belief was rooted is shown by the fact that when the Spanish *conquistador* Hernán Cortés landed in Mexico in the year 1519, the presumed year of the return of the Feathered Serpent, the Aztecs were firmly convinced that the god had now returned. After the departure of Quetzalcoatl, Tollan fell. In some chronicles the end of the city followed hard on the banishment of its spiritual ruler, while in others Tollan went on for another two hundred years. The last ruler Huemac also became the victim of hostile magicians. One of these magicians, the chronicle relates, disguised himself as a

strange Indian, called Toueyo, who like all his tribe went about stark naked. He sold green peppers and sat himself down in the market place in front of the palace.

Huemac, the temporal ruler of the Toltecs – in contrast to Quetzalcoatl who was a High Priest and had no children – had a very beautiful daughter who was desired, on account of her beauty, by all Toltecs, who wanted to marry her; but Huemac had no wish to give her to these Toltecs.

When the Lord Huemac's daughter looked into the market place and saw the said naked Toueyo and his phallus, she ran into the palace and her desire for Toueyo's phallus was so great that she became lovesick. Her whole body swelled. When Huemac the Ruler discovered how ill his daughter was, he asked the women who served her: 'What is the matter with my daughter? What illness is she suffering from, that her whole body is swollen?' And the women answered and said, 'Lord, the cause and reason of her illness was Toueyo the Indian, who went about naked, and when your daughter saw his nakedness, she became lovesick.' Huemac thereupon called the pepper seller to him and gave him his daughter to wife.[5]

Thus began, as the chronicle relates, the undermining of his authority amongst the Toltecs. He had given his daughter not only to a foreigner but also to a member of the lower class.

Under Huemac's rule a number of catastrophes supervened which forced him to flee the city. '. . . Then came drought and aridity, and a great number of people died. Worms . . . ate the corn which they had garnered into their granaries and many other catastrophes happened as well. It seemed as though fire rained down, and there was such drought for twenty-four years that rivers and wells completely dried up.'[6] Tollan, thus weakened, was laid open to foreign conquerors who occupied the city.

Thus far go a few historical and mythical accounts about Tollan which exist in a number of other versions. Where lies the core of historical truth? Did such a core exist? This is a difficult problem to solve when it is considered that nearly all the historical personalities mentioned in the legends were at the same time gods in the pantheon of the central Mexican peoples. Cloud Serpent was among other things the god of the northern stars and Prostrate Shield the earth goddess. The 'Smoking Mirror' was, in addition to possessing various other attributes, the god of the night-sky. Innumerable significances can be assigned to the Feathered Serpent. It was the tribal god and the cultural hero of the Toltecs, the god of the morning star, the god of maize and of the wind – to name only a few. Tollan itself represented the centre of the universe. Are all Toltec legends simply a mythical interpretation of the war of the powers of nature, an allegorical portrayal of the pantheon of the gods? The many contradictions appearing in these myths gave rise to many different interpretations. A long list of kings was drawn up, all of whom ruled for exactly fifty-two years – the length of a Mesoamerican calendrical cycle. A statement like this is more than doubtful. How can we explain why almost every chronicler cites different calendrical data? There is no doubt that maize, the calendar and script were known in Mesoamerica long before the advent of the Toltecs. What credibility can be assigned to the myth of a hero of civilisation who is alleged to have made all these discoveries himself?

It is only possible to separate the kernel of historical truth, at least in part, from the mythical shell which surrounds it with the aid of the scientific use of archaeology. The first and most important problem solved by these means was the location of Tollan. Only then was it possible to correlate history and archaeology. The wonderfully preserved art of Tollan – reports constantly reiterated that all the greatest achievements of Mesoamerican culture originated there – resulted in the grandest and most beautiful city in pre-Aztec Mesoamerica, Teotihuacan, being attributed for years to the Toltecs. The size, grandeur and richness of this city, its position in the centre of the Mexican Plateau, the fact that the Feathered Serpent had played so great a role in Tollan, all this seemed naturally to identify Teotihuacan as the historical Tollan. Such an idea would place Teotihuacan in the realm of recorded history and would seem to resolve one of the greatest puzzles of Mesoamerican culture. Nevertheless the more written sources were compared with archaeological evidence the greater became the contradiction between historical versions of the annals of the Toltecs and the reality. Teotihuacan was constructed at a much earlier period than that given in almost all historical sources for the origin of Tollan. It was impossible to find any connection between the many regions which according to historical accounts were overthrown by the Toltecs and Teotihuacan. Legendary and historical references to the geography of Tollan did not coincide with that of Teotihuacan. These contradictions caused two scholars, Wigberto Jimenez Moreno[7] and Paul Kirchhoff,[8] to reconsider the problem. Jimenez Moreno came to the conclusion that Tollan could only be identified on the basis of historical sources with the ruins of present-day Tula in the Mexican province of Hidalgo. Kirchhoff succeeded in identifying eight of the twenty localities which were supposed to have constituted the empire of the Toltecs, in the centre of which historical Tula was also situated.[9] Excavations carried out in the ruins of this tract of land, which had attracted little notice until then, confirmed the results of this research. Remains were found showing the closest connections with all the centres known to have been of Toltec culture, such as Chichen Itza in the Yucatan peninsula.

Archaeological research in Tollan was seriously complicated by the fact that it had suffered much greater destruction than, for example, Teotihuacan. Early conquerors seem to have almost destroyed the city. These excavations revealed the ruins of a city, neither as important nor as large as Teotihuacan, and smaller than the later Aztec capital city of Tenochtitlan, but none the less of monumental character and considerable dimensions. As in Teotihuacan, its centre consisted of plazas surrounded by pyramids and palaces. The geographical orientation of the pyramids also resembled that of Teotihuacan. Nevertheless Tula revealed a number of completely new characteristics. Evidence of war was much more predominant than in any of the classic cultures. The many sculptures and portrayals of warriors on the Temple of the Morning Star on the largest pyramid of Tula depict warriors marching with completely expressionless faces as well as symbols of jaguars and eagles. These prove that among the Toltecs the military orders of jaguars and eagles – which were to play such an important role in the later history of Mesoamerica – already existed. Long wide stone colonnades on the great plazas of the city were a new architectural feature in comparison with the cities of the classic period.

Equally typical of the art of the Toltecs were the so-called Chac-Mols. They are sculptures in stone of deities leaning backwards and supporting huge altars on which presumably sacrifices were laid. Unfortunately there have been so far no systematic researches made into the range of the city, the density of its population or the extent of urbanisation in Tula. Such an examination is the only possible way of evaluating the real importance of this city. Nevertheless the excavations so far undertaken have established the existence of a great city centre. Even if Tula's grandeur did not equal the mythical grandeur of Tollan, it would have been perfectly capable of carrying out the general functions of the capital city of an empire.

The location of Tollan was to a certain extent the key which made it possible to correlate history and archaeology and to extract, even if incompletely, the historical facts from the myths surrounding them in the Toltecs' annals.

The Toltecs presumably belonged to the Nahua-speaking peoples, a group that later included the Aztecs and most of the inhabitants of central Mexico on the eve of the Conquest. They came from north of the border of Mesoamerica from the same regions which the Aztecs in the sixteenth century designated contemptuously as the stronghold of the uncivilised Chichimecs, the barbarians. Nevertheless in contrast to the peoples who populated this region in the sixteenth century, the Toltecs, before their arrival in Mesoamerica, had not been collectors and hunters. Far north of the boundary of Mesoamerica, close to the present city of Zacatecas, a huge complex of fortress-like buildings was found called La Quemada. Situated in a highly favourable strategic position on a hill, it consists of pyramids and thick fortress-like walls. The builders of this fortress cannot possibly have been small hunting and collecting tribes. They must already have been familiar with agriculture and have achieved a certain degree of integration. In view of this it cannot be ruled out that they were also capable of carrying out conquests. Many scholars therefore consider that the Toltecs, before their appearance in Mesoamerica, were the builders of La Quemada.

In the ninth or tenth centuries AD the Toltecs, under the leadership of the conqueror Cloud Serpent, invaded the central Mexican plateau. Scarcely a century later they had pushed forward deep into the south of Mesoamerica. Clear evidence of Toltec culture has been discovered in almost all regions of Mesoamerica. The city of Chichen Itza contains buildings which are exactly identical with those of the Toltec capital of Tula. In the Valley of Oaxaca as well as in the highlands of Guatemala there are similarly clear signs of Toltec culture. This archaeological evidence is confirmed by historical tradition, containing references to conquests by the northern followers of the Feathered Serpent.

The incursion of the Toltecs into the Mexican regions of high culture is reminiscent in some respects of the invasions of the Roman Empire by the barbarians. Just as was the case in the Roman

Empire, a large part of the area of high culture in Mesoamerica was in such a state of dissolution owing to internal strife so that it fell with little trouble into the hands of the invaders. Exactly as the first barbarian tribes had widely adopted Roman culture even before their invasion of the Empire, the Toltecs appear before their invasion of Mesoamerica to have been exposed to the strong influences flowing from the central Mexican region of high culture.

The invading Toltecs were just as unsuccessful as the barbarians who invaded Rome in their attempts to create an empire out of the whole conquered territory. The regions taken by the Toltecs fell apart into a number of states most of which were independent. In addition to the state situated in the central Mexican plateau with its capital city Tula, other Toltec states were found in the peninsula of Yucatan whose centre was the city of Chichen Itza, and presumably also in the south-east Mexican state of Tabasco and in the highlands of Guatemala. Apart from the fact that they were states where warriors played a predominant role, we know very little about their social organisation. Were the warriors a hereditary aristocracy owning private property and lands or simply a privileged meritorious aristocracy within the framework of a tribal organisation? However rich the sources are in other respects, they give no information on this question.

As the first tribes of barbarians which invaded the Roman Empire were pressed southward by other invading tribes behind them, fresh waves of invading tribes from the north seem to have pressed towards the south those Toltecs who had already settled in Mesoamerica. The arrival of other tribes from the north could help explain the contradictions and conflicts that occur in the traditional legends and chronicles.

Just as in Europe where the Church was the guardian ot an ancient culture which she transmitted to the newly-arrived barbarians, so the priesthood in Mesoamerica was the guardian of the finest achievements of the high culture: of writing, mathematics, the calendar and probably also of a number of technical and manual skills which were transmitted to the new arrivals in the shortest possible time. The comparison must not however be exaggerated. The Christian Church succeeded in converting the invading barbarians to their faith, but in Mesoamerica a similar attempt appears to have almost completely failed. Most historians regard the followers of the Feathered Serpent as the disciples of the ancient priestly religions, and their suppression is regarded as a victory for the new Toltec concepts. Yet even where this religion was able to survive and even to flourish, as among the conquerors of the Yucatan peninsula, it had to accommodate itself substantially to the new circumstances. On the reliefs in Chichen Itza beside the many representations of the Feathered Serpent may be seen men bearing the hearts of human sacrifices. The practise of human sacrifice had also become customary amongst the followers of the Feathered Serpent.

Just as the states which followed the dissolution of the Roman Empire in Europe failed to reproduce the social organisation of Rome, so the Toltec states failed to reproduce the social conditions of the classic period of Mesoamerica. Instead of being in the hands of priests, the state was ruled by the military caste. The great fortresses built at this time are decorated with representations of warriors; the historical traditions which repeatedly point to war and warriors as the most important group among the Toltecs are eloquent witnesses of military rule.

There is however a significant difference between the Toltecs and those barbarians who overthrew the Roman Empire. The urban culture that existed in the western empire of Rome collapsed. Many cities disappeared; others became less and less important. The Toltecs in Mesoamerica on the other hand founded new cities such as Tollan, or developed centres such as Chichen Itza into metropolises. This difference in development is closely linked with another phenomenon. The barbarians who overthrew the Roman Empire disrupted or greatly complicated the trade routes within the former imperial territory and between Rome and the Orient. Trade declined, cultural communications became stagnant. Exactly the opposite happened among the Toltecs. They opened up to commerce the trade routes which had been disrupted after the fall of Teotihuacan and a tremendous trade boom followed between the north and the south, between the plateau and the lowlands. In this respect the Toltecs only followed the rule common to all the peoples which had inhabited the central Mexican plateau since the rise of the high culture. The development of trade with the tropical lowlands was of decisive importance for them. The south appears to have held an attraction for the peoples of the north not unlike that of overseas territories for the Spaniards of the sixteenth century. There were three products which specially attracted the inhabitants of the north: cocoa, feathers and cotton. Cocoa was not only the favourite drink of the inhabitants of central Mexico at the time of the Conquest and presumably even before; it was – at least in the sixteenth century – a sort of universal currency that could buy almost anything and against which everything was balanced. Debts could be written off with cocoa, slaves bought, jewellery acquired, food products paid for on the market. Cocoa was the means by which great feasts could be organised and prestige acquired in the eyes of others. Feathers constituted the most valuable ornaments in Mesoamerica, and the feather handiwork of the Mesoamerican peoples is regarded even today as one of their greatest artistic achievements.

The feathers came for the most part from birds only to be found in the tropical lowlands or in the highlands of Guatemala. Cotton was important not only for the production of clothing, but for use in warriors' armour. Among the most important cocoa-producing areas of Mesoamerica were regions in the northern state of Oaxaca, on the Gulf coast in the present state of Tabasco and on the west and east coasts of present-day Guatemala. Clear traces of the Toltecs may be found in nearly all these regions. Cotton was produced on the peninsula of Yucatan, and a few of the birds with the most valuable plumage came from the Guatemalan highlands.

Trade was so widespread in this Toltec period that the Mesoamerican peoples may well have come into contact through central America with the Andean cultures. This could explain their knowledge of metallurgy, which first appeared in Mesoamerica at about this time. Likewise the similarities with Peruvian art-forms and techniques are so great that these skills must have come from there. Metallurgy nevertheless was of secondary importance for economic or military techniques in Mesoamerica. With few exceptions tools and weapons continued to be made of wood or stone. Metal objects served for personal ornament and might also have had meaningful religious significance, but they possessed limited practical value.

The opening up of the trade routes between the central Mexican plateau and the tropical lowland regions already mentioned could explain the trend towards urbanism in the Toltec period, and the tremendous prosperity of Tollan in the first century of its history. Tollan's prosperity did not however last long. Two or three centuries after the foundation of the city the prospect loomed that had been at the back of all social upheavals in Mesoamerica: famine. However much traditions may vary on other matters, they are in almost universal agreement as regards famine, catastrophes and drought. Some scholars believe that the famines and droughts which destroyed the Toltec Empire were caused by climatic changes in the twelfth and thirteenth centuries AD. This factor cannot be excluded. Quite apart from this however, it must be stated that the Toltecs had not discovered any means for increasing their food production, or any new ways of utilising intensive agriculture. Potentially the most productive region of Mesoamerica, the plateau of Mexico was situated cheek by jowl with the developments in the Toltec region. In the valley of Teotihuacan the size of population receded so much that it was not only much smaller than it had been at the time of Teotihuacan's ascendancy, but also than it was later in the Aztec period. This might be due to a failure of the existing irrigation systems.

History seemed to be repeating itself. Once more the regions of central Mexico fell as a result of major internal conflicts: traces of violent destruction were found in Tollan. Once again the bearers of the high culture withdrew to small city states – some of the inhabitants of Tollan were to build a state like Culhuacan in the Valley of Mexico – and once again barbarians from the north overran the region of high culture.

THE CHICHIMECS

The invaders who now entered Mesoamerica from the north were far more like 'barbarians' than the Toltecs had been. Yet it was precisely these people who were to erect the largest and most powerful state structure ever to exist in Mesoamerica. This had less to do with the invaders themselves than with the region in which they settled, the Valley of Mexico, which was to become the centre of the economic, social and political development of Mesoamerica. Anyone crossing the vast city of Mexico today, now that its population has risen to six million inhabitants, would find it hard to imagine that a few hundred years ago a large part of this area was covered with water. Only a few rather miserable looking traces of lakes, such as the half dried out Lake Tetzcoco or the 'floating gardens' of Xochimilco, bear witness to the former geographical features of the high valley and give some idea of the network of lakes and canals which once existed. Only when between the skyscrapers in the city centre one sees the national theatre, the Palacio de Bellas Artes, whose ground floor is slowly sinking, is one reminded that once upon a time there was water here.

On the eve of the Conquest an extensive network of mostly inter-connected lakes stretched over a large area of the Valley of Mexico. On their shores the soil was exceptionally fertile. Using irrigation it was possible to produce two harvests a year. Perhaps even more favourable for agriculture than the soil on the lake shores, however paradoxical it may sound, was the lake itself. The inhabitants of the Valley of Mexico practised a system of cultivation called the Chinampa system. The Chinampas were erected on lakes like artificial islands. In the shallow waters of the lakes rafts were made of branches, roots and brushwood which were then covered with soil from the lake bottom. This soil was unusually rich and resulted in a uniquely pro-ductive agriculture. In this way a far greater population could be maintained than in other regions of Mesoamerica. Recent research has demonstrated how productive this agriculture was and the kind of results which it was possible to obtain. With the use of the slash and burn system of agriculture, which was practised primarily in the low-lands of Mesoamerica, 1,200 hectares of land were necessary to feed a hundred families. In the central plateau, where the soil was more fertile, and in places where irrigation was not necessary, only 650 ha were necessary for the same number of families. Against this 86 ha of irrigated land was sufficient to keep a hundred families. With regard to food supply the lakes offered further advantages. Fish and lake eels, whose eggs were regarded as special delicacies, enriched their diet and replaced the meat which formed only a very small part of it.

Besides the possibilities of an intensive agriculture and a dense concentration of population, the network of lakes in the Valley of Mexico had special advantages that the greater part of the rest of Mesoamerica were not able to enjoy. In a region where there were no draught animals and transport facilities were unusually bad, the lakes constituted a unique means of facilitating transport. This acted as a wonderful stimulus to trade, to specialisation and to economic, political and social integration. The Valley of Mexico also occupied an extremely favourable strategic position. It was easier to reach other lower lying parts of Mesoamerica from there than to ascend to the plateau from the lower lying regions.

The full realisation of all the potential in the economic, social and political fields that the Valley of Mexico contained with its network of lakes necessitated in the first place overcoming a number of perils which nature had concealed. These perils differed in kind but were mainly due to the constantly varying rainfall. If less rain fell than usual the level of the water sank and some of the Chinampas dried out. This was not alarming in itself. It was much more disastrous when rainfall was too heavy and the lakes burst their banks and flooded the surrounding countryside. The greatest danger of all arose when the eastern lake, the Lake of Tetzcoco, burst its banks. This lake differed from the others in the high valley in that it was not a sweet but a salt water lake. The burns and rivers which fed it flowed over a salty region, so that its waters were useless for agricultural purposes. The other lakes were sweet water lakes. In normal times the level of the salt water lake was lower than that of the sweet water lakes. In times of flood however it could happen that the waters of the salt water Lake of Tetzcoco over-flowed into the sweet water lakes and caused untold damage to plants.

The full use of the potential of the Valley of Mexico necessitated extensive measures to counteract these dangers. Dams had to be erected between the sweet water lakes and the salt water lake. Dykes had to be built to prevent flooding. A system of water channels was necessary to convey water from highland sources in times of water shortage into the lake district. These were all immense constructions in which thousands of people had to be employed. The full potential of the Valley of Mexico had not been fully exploited even by the fifteenth century. This is not to say however – reference has already been made to this – that the Valley of Mexico was not one of the most ancient of

Mesoamerica's cultural regions. Large settlements had already existed in the archaic period. The culture of Teotihuacan embraced a part of the lake shores, and the last inhabitants of Teotihuacan moved their homes to a city which stood right on one of the lakes of the high valley, Atzcapotzalco. Settlements likewise existed in this region during the Toltec period. Yet settlement was much less dense than in later times and the great network of dams and dykes that was necessary to regulate the waters of the lakes was not constructed until the fifteenth century. The reason why this process was so long drawn out also constitutes one of the most discussed problems of Mesoamerican history. Was it because the states of the classic and Toltec period did not possess the necessary manpower in order to carry out such projects? This is hardly likely since the constructions in Teotihuacan, for example, required no less a concentration of manpower than the water control works in the Valley of Mexico. Was it because the extraordinarily fertile Chinampa system was only discovered in the fourteenth or fifteenth centuries, as is widely surmised? This is contested by some scholars who believe that Chinampa systems existed in the classic period. Was it because of climatic changes which took place in Mesoamerica? This hypothesis is widely accepted today. On the one hand it is thought that a diminution in rainfall in the north resulted in a reduction of cultivable agricultural land. Where fresh land could have been freely occupied before, new methods had to be found to get more out of the available soil. On the other hand it is widely thought that a change in the water level of the lakes took place in the thirteenth and fourteenth centuries AD so that the level rose. As a result, although more soil and more water thus existed for the fertile Chinampa cultivation the danger of flooding increased and with it the necessity for water control works. Whatever the reason one phenomenon stands out clearly: there was an ever increasing shift of the cultural, political and economic centre of Mesoamerica into the Valley of Mexico.

This valley in the post-Toltec period consisted of many small compact city states which were constantly doing battle with each other. Their structure was presumably not very different from those which the Spaniards found on their arrival in the small states of Mesoamerica: a 'capital city' or a 'capital village' in which the nobility lived and which the Spaniards called a *cabecera* (capital city) and small dependent localities which they called *estancias* (settlements). At the same time groups of invaders from north of the cultural border of Mesoamerica constantly streamed into the high valley.

The invaders from the north were known collectively as 'Chichimecs'. This expression means 'Race of Dogs' and probably goes back to a totemistic origin. Jimenez Moreno discovered a legend among the people of Huichol which points in this direction. This legend tells how the mother of the gods foretold to a woodcutter that the earth would be laid waste by a flood. In order to save himself he must hide in a hollow tree stump and take with him a she-dog. In this way the woodcutter succeeded in saving himself and the she-dog. He then led a solitary life in a cave with the bitch. While the man felled trees the bitch prepared his meals. Unable to understand how such a bitch could cook, the man hid one day in front of his cave and watched how the bitch, who thought he was away, shook off her pelt and turned herself into a woman. The man took away the furry pelt and burned it, whereupon the woman felt terrible pains. When the man poured water over her the pains vanished and the spell seemed to have been broken. They were then wedded and their children became known as 'Race of Dogs'.

The name Chichimec is reminiscent of the expression 'barbarians' which the Romans used for the people on the far side of the border. In the sixteenth century people who lived in the north or who came from the north were all called by this name. But the name was never applied to one single people or to one single tribe. The Chichimecs who after the fall of Tula invaded the plateau and who also invaded the Valley of Mexico cannot be reduced to a common denominator. Among them were people who had lived in close association with the Toltecs and had presumably served as mercenaries of the Toltec Empire and who knew about agriculture. There were other smaller groups made up of hunters and gatherers who likewise invaded the area of high culture. In the Valley of Mexico they found the most fertile land already occupied by other tribes. If they were strong enough they were able to erect independent states in the less fertile parts of the valley and in certain circumstances to make conquests. If they were weak they were obliged to enter the service of the already existing city states of the high valley. The Chichimecs never succeeded in overrunning and conquering the already existing city states. Whether they came into the valley as autonomous tribal groups or as groups which had been conquered, they all shared one experience: they were speedily drawn into the existing battles among the city states, either as allies or as mercenaries of the old and settled inhabitants and very rapidly assimilated their cultures. The destiny of two of these groups was of decisive importance for the whole of the later history of Mesoamerica. They were the ancestors of the inhabitants of the two greatest city states which governed almost the whole of Mesoamerica on the eve of the Spanish Conquest, namely Tenochtitlan and Tetzcoco.

There are many, one might almost say too many pictographs about the evolution of these peoples. The later rulers of Mesoamerica shared with many a ruling class of the Old World the tendency not only to know their early history, but to reconstruct it according to their own wishes. Consequently there was a pronounced tendency to represent their past as having been much more difficult than it was and to exaggerate certain achievements. These historical traditions must therefore be handled with a certain amount of care, especially since they often contradict each other. Nevertheless they are a valuable aid in reconstructing the history of these nomadic peoples.

The strongest group of Chichimecs which invaded the Valley of Mexico was led by a chieftain called Xolotl. They succeeded in conquering a large part of the north-east of the Valley of Mexico. This was the region least suited to the practice of agriculture. Instead there existed here most of the game and wild plants. It was thus possible for these Chichimecs to continue their hunting and gathering existence. In the chronicles it is told how the inhabitants of Culhuacan – the successors of the Toltecs – turned to the Chichimecs and asked for their military assistance against a rival state. In exchange they offered 'to fetch them out of the hills and caves',[10] that is to say to bring them the benefits of civilisation. In the pictographs civilisation represented practically everything from agriculture to house building. A sort of Toltec 'development officer' is depicted who showed the Chichimecs how to plant corn or maize and how to weave textiles.

Reinforced by fresh groups of Chichimecs who invaded the Valley of Mexico and intermingled, militarily secure thanks to the mercenary services which they performed for the stronger states of the high valley, the successors of Xolotl very soon constructed one of the most powerful and strongest states in the Valley of Mexico. Its centre was the city of Tetzcoco on the north-east shore of the network of lakes of Mexico, a city which was soon to become one of the most important in Mesoamerica. Despite the infertile soil, every possible opportunity for cultivation was used and a virtue made out of necessity by drying and utilising the salt from the lake. This trade in salt – in other parts of the plateau of Mesoamerica it was a very rare commodity – contributed in no small measure to the economic power of Tetzcoco, to the development of a trading class and to closer relations with many Mexican states of the plateau.

It is probable that it helped Tetzcoco to become a great power.

CHAPTER 10

THE AZTECS

THE BEGINNINGS

Information and reports about the development of a second group of northern immigrants are just as detailed as in the case of Tetzcoco: namely the Azteca or Mexica who were to have the hegemony over the greater part of Mesoamerica on the eve of the Spanish Conquest. The early history of this group is not easy to unravel. It is hidden in a veil of myth which even the later Aztecs found difficult to penetrate. Furthermore the Aztecs were inclined to make their history fit the existing circumstances of the time and to garble it. It is not surprising therefore that there are a number of theories with regard to this early period of Aztec history. The Aztecs themselves believed that their ancestors came from a place called Aztlan. Was there such a place and if so, where was it located? This is one of the most hotly debated problems of Aztec history.

Jimenez Moreno holds the view that the Aztecs came from the west of Mexico, far beyond the boundary of Mesoamerica.[1] This group, he explains, originated in a region of the present state of Nayarit. After wandering for a long time southwards, it came into contact with the Empire of Tollan, and the Aztecs became mercenaries of the Toltecs. After the collapse of Tula they advanced into the region of the central plateau. For some time they even held Tula, at any rate the ruined city of Tula, in order to reach the plateau from it.

Paul Kirchhoff on the other hand considers that the Aztecs who reached the Valley of Mexico were already a mixed group of Toltecs and Chichimecs.[2] The Chichimecs were a nomadic group of hunters and gatherers living in the western part of the Toltec Empire who were subject to the supremacy of a Toltec group, the Azteca, whom Kirchoff calls the real Aztecs. Other Toltecs who advanced from the west and were known as Mexica succeeded in subjugating the Chichimecs. Both groups then migrated together to Tula and from there to the Valley of Mexico where they arrived as a completely integrated group. Whichever version is accepted, one thing seems to be certain: the fortunes of the Mexica after their arrival in the Valley of Mexico were much more sombre and much less easy than those of the Chichimecs under Xolotl, who lived as mighty conquerors and sought-after allies in the valley. The Aztecs for years led the existence of outcasts and at best as conquered subjects in the Valley of Mexico.

After their arrival they first tried to settle on the hill of Chapultepec. Anyone today visiting the hill on which rises the palace of the Emperor Maximilian has a unique view over the whole of the Valley of Mexico. Whoever occupied it seven hundred years ago must in addition have possessed a unique strategic position. It must have been easier to attack the localities below than vice versa. In addition there were in Chapultepec any number of fresh water springs which were much coveted by the inhabitants of the lower lying areas, especially in times of drought. It is not surprising therefore that a number of city states joined together in the valley in order to drive the Aztecs out of their settlement area. This undertaking succeeded. The Aztecs were driven out of Chapultepec and their leader Huitzilihuitl was taken prisoner by the aggressors and put to death.

The history of the Aztecs over the next hundred years was characterised by two outstanding features: they were forced to settle in regions which were acknowledged to be unprofitable and infertile and at the same time they had to pay the city states to whom these territories belonged a high price for the right of settlement. The price, at least in the early years, was less economic – the soil hardly produced anything – than military in character; the Aztecs were forced to do military service for their overlords.

It is not known whether the first place settled by the Aztecs after they were driven from Chapultepec, Atetelco, belonged to any of the valley city states or whether it was so poor and unprofitable that nobody took the trouble to claim it. Here the Aztecs scraped a miserable living as hunters and gatherers, according to tradition for fifty-two years. As the chroniclers relate it was the gloomiest and most wretched period of Aztec history, a period in which they lived constantly on the brink of famine. The next site in which they are found appears to have been slightly richer and more fertile. It was a place called Tizapan in the south-western part of the Valley of Mexico.

This place belonged to the city state of Culhuacan. How the Aztecs came there is not clear. Did they go of their own free will because Atetelco no longer supplied a subsistence level for them? Were they forced by Culhuacan to settle within its territory because Culhuacan required mercenaries? Were the Aztecs (in view of their consistent poverty it seems possible) forced to raid the surrounding localities so that it was desirable to hold them under tighter control? No definite answer exists. One thing only seems certain: Tizapan was no paradise either. In fact it had become famous in the Valley of Mexico because of its unrivalled number of snakes. According to one tradition the ruler of Culhuacan, Coxcoxtli, is said to have declared in regard to the Aztecs: 'We are not dealing with human beings but with military maniacs. Perhaps they will perish and be devoured by snakes, of which there are such a great number there.'[3] The Aztecs at all events made a virtue out of necessity. Tradition has it that snake hunting became their favourite pursuit and snake dishes became the greatest delicacies.

It was not long before the Aztecs had to pay a price in order to acquire Tizapan. In a war against Xochimilco the Aztecs had to join battle on the side of Culhuacan. They did this with great success and Culhuacan won the war. The result however was that shortly after this victory the Aztecs were driven out of Tizpan by their overlords. A number of legends seek to explain why this happened.

A pictograph shows that the Aztecs were required by their overlords to bring evidence of how many of the enemy they killed. Thereupon they cut off the ears of all the dead and brought them to the ruler of Culhuacan. When he saw the terrifying result he was so horrified that he ordered the Aztecs to be driven out. Another legend contains equally gruesome details. It tells how the Aztecs took the daughter of the ruler of Culhuacan prisoner and sacrificed her to the gods. She was flayed and a priest dressed up in her skin. Then the Aztecs invited the ruler of Culhuacan to a feast and in the middle of the festivities the priest entered, dressed in the princess's skin. The father's reaction is not difficult to imagine. The ruler of Culhuacan ordered the intruders to be driven out.

Whichever of these legends may be correct, there is one fact that stands out clearly: in their bloodthirsty rites the Aztecs differed from the other peoples of the valley. It is not unlikely that the increasing power of this people, who already had a reputation for exceptional brutality, constituted an ever growing danger to the ruler of Culhuacan whose own power was declining.

Again the Aztecs were forced to emigrate and again their history seemed to repeat itself. Once again they were allotted a region regarded as impracticable and infertile, and forced in return to render military services to a powerful city state. Nevertheless the territory handed over to them placed at their disposal powers of a quite different order from the regions they had settled in previously and the city state to which they surrendered – Atzcapotzalco – was to become the predominant power in the Valley of Mexico, and to draw the Aztecs in its wake.

The region now settled by the Aztecs was an island in the middle of the lake district of the Valley of Mexico, which they called Tenochtitlan. This island – the site of today's Mexico City – was to become their

capital city. Tradition relates that the tribal god, Huitzilopochtli, said
to the elders of the tribe, 'Go thither where the cactus Tenochtli grows,
on which an eagle sits happily . . . there we shall stop, there we shall
wait, there we shall meet a number of tribes and with our arrow or with
our shield we shall conquer them. There will our city Mexico
Tenochtitlan be, there, where the eagle its wings outspread calls and
eats.' In actual fact they discovered the place and cried out: 'At last
we have been worthy of our god, and we have deserved the reward.
We have joyfully discovered that this is where our city shall be.'[4]

At first this place probably did not strike the Aztecs as particularly
satisfactory, at least not from an economic point of view. The soil was
marshy, there was hardly any timber and the chronicles relate how at
first the Aztecs were clad only in materials made of agave fibres and
were forced to gather plants and to hunt in order to eke out their
miserable existence.

This island however possessed amazing potential. Situated in the
middle of the lake, it was difficult to attack. It lay on the borders of the
most important city states of the Valley of Mexico. If on the one hand
this presented a threat to the Aztecs as long as they remained weak, as
their strength increased it was an excellent jumping off ground for
making conquests. Nor were the economic possibilities of the island
small. Their exploitation to the full nevertheless demanded great
expense of labour. The marshes had to be reclaimed, and above all
artificial islands had to be created – the Chinampas already described.

It would appear that the Aztecs made full use of all the possibilities
which Tenochtitlan contained: a century after the foundation of their
city in the year 1427, they had become one of the most important city
states in the Valley of Mexico. For this they were indebted to two very
different circumstances: first, to the reclamation works on the island of
Tenochtitlan and above all to the setting up of the Chinampas, which
increased their wealth and economic power; and second, but no less
important, to the alliance with Atzcapotzalco, which soon became the
most important city state of the Valley of Mexico. Under the rule of
Tezozomoc, who traditionally ruled for the almost incredible span of
sixty-three years, the inhabitants of Atzcapotzalco – the Tepanecs –
succeeded in bringing the whole of the Valley of Mexico under their
control. At the beginning of the fifteenth century, during the last years
of the reign of Tezozomoc, they appear even to have succeeded in
undertaking expeditions outside the valley and to have conquered
among others the region of Cuauhnahuac, which was rich in cotton.

The Aztecs played a significant role in all these conquests, although
their status is difficult to define. Presumably they represented a mixture
of mercenaries, vassals and allies. They were mercenaries and vassals
in so far as they were subject to Atzcapotzalco and paid tribute to this

state, primarily in the form of military services. In proportion to the rate at which the conquests grew, the importance of the Aztecs also increased. They were treated less and less as ordinary vassals and mercenaries and more and more as allies. A number of regions which they had conquered for Atzcapotzalco were made over to them and from there they obtained the timber which they lacked and a constantly increasing supply of food. As their strength increased their influence in the making of political decisions seems also to have risen. Nevertheless until the year 1427 they remained an integrated if highly uncomfortable and wilful component of the Tepanec empire.

However correct the terms 'mercenaries', 'vassals' and 'allies' may be, they sometimes suggest too European a picture of the Aztecs. It is not possible to understand the incentives for their rise by relying only on such concepts. Their social organisation and their religion must also be closely examined. This is more easily obtainable from source material than is the case for all previously discovered peoples and cultures of ancient America: since the Aztecs were the last ruling people of Mesoamerica their legends, traditions and history survived into the time of the Spanish domination.

THE SOCIAL ORGANISATION OF THE AZTECS UNTIL THE CONQUEST OF ATZCAPOTZALCO

The basic social units of the Aztecs at the time of their arrival in the Valley of Mexico and at the time of the Spanish Conquest – even though their significance had changed by then – were the *calpulli*, just as they were among most of the peoples of central Mexico. *Calpulli* means large house and is the name given to a community endowed with far-reaching functions. It was a settlement community in the sense that its members lived together in one place. It could refer to the population of a whole village, part of a village or a small section of a city. The land on which the members lived was their joint property. It was handed over to the members for their use. They were in duty bound to work the soil regularly. Anyone who left it untended for two years lost all claim to it. The members of the *calpulli* were not permitted to sell or lease their land. If they regularly worked it and did not leave it, the use of it was also handed on to their heirs. Should members of a *calpulli* possess no land, land was handed over to them from a reserve of free land.

The *calpulli* were also religious and military units, and in later times administrative ones. From the religious standpoint the *calpulli* had its own god, there was a *calpulli* temple and the members practised common ceremonies. Militarily the members of the *calpulli* appear, at least in the early period of the Aztec advance, to have been a closed unit. This was emphasised by the fact that they received their military training and instruction in the history of their people in schools – *telpochcalli* – which were under the *calpulli's* authority.

At the head of the *calpulli* was the *calpullec*. He acted partly as a judge in minor controversies, partly as an administrator – with the responsibility for allocating land – and as representative of the *calpulli* in the tribal council. It would appear that he himself was not required to work any land, but that a piece was put at his disposal which the other members of the *calpulli* worked jointly. This *calpullec*, who was elected by the members of the *calpulli*, always had to be a member of the same family, which means that the choice was limited. He was supported by a council of elders, whose composition is unclear.

There are still sharp differences of opinion among scholars concerning the nature and significance of the *calpulli*. For some the *calpulli* remains the prototype of a clan, a community of kinship which until recently many anthropologists considered a universal phenomenon. It was regarded as a patrilinear exogamous clan, in other words a group whose members believe they are descended from a common ancestor. This type of tribal organisation is very widespread. One of its most important features is the prohibition of marriage amongst each other. It is also characterised by strong democratic qualities. All members consider themselves to have equal rights and feel bound to help each other in times of need. If a member of the clan is attacked by an outsider his clan must come to his aid or avenge him.

Did the *calpulli* constitute such a community? This is extremely unlikely. There is no evidence that marriage was forbidden among its members and furthermore, there was no belief in one common ancestor. Accordingly opponents of this theory deny that the *calpulli* had any tribal character. Only domiciliary conditions – a group dwelt together in one place – determined the character of the *calpulli*. Even this theory however has met with serious opposition. Chroniclers repeatedly emphasise that the members of the *calpulli* in some way or another felt themselves to be related to each other. Although there were no direct relations of kinship, *calpulli* members were evidently aware of them. So the question again arises, what is the *calpulli*? The ethnologist Paul Kirchhoff[5] has given the most interesting answer. He described a new type of clan whose characteristics were quite different from those already mentioned above. Its members considered themselves to be interrelated, even to have descended from a common ancestor, but the degree of kinship with this ancestor differed widely. The more closely related to him a man was, the more important was his position in the structure of the clan and vice versa. In order to represent this inequality graphically, Kirchhoff used the term 'conical clan'. The apex of the cone represents the privileged minority especially closely related to the ancestor, while the base represents the mass of other members.

With the exception of the belief in a common ancestor there are decisive features of this conical clan which apply to the *calpulli*. The most important feature was the inequality of its members. This was primarily expressed by the existence within the community of a privileged hereditary group – the chief and his family – from whom the *calpullecs* had to stem. Pedro Carrasco took this idea further and suggested that the *calpulli* were composed of families of varying rank whose members tended to marry members of other families of the same *calpulli*. In addition there were other symptoms of inequality. The hereditary character of land tenure and the fact that land was not, as so often among other clans, freshly divided up at regular intervals caused differences in wealth within the *calpulli*. Such differences could very easily lead to other more pronounced differences. As a result important presuppositions existed in the *calpulli* which governed the social status of its members.

A further characteristic typical of most clanlike organisations in the world, a strong sense of communal solidarity, seems to have been absent among the *calpulli*. Its members were in no way obliged to protect a member from outside attack or even to avenge him, and vendetta seems to have been completely unknown. Internal solidarity appears also to have been of a limited character. There is no mention of any responsibility of the *calpulli* for disabled, ill or old members. These problems, which face every human community, were the concern either of the closest members of the family or of the larger organisation, the tribe or the state, governing the *calpulli*.

While important features of the *calpulli* remained constant, the forms of organisation controlling them were constantly increasing. Until their settlement in Tenochtitlan the Aztec *calpulli* were kept together largely by a loose tribal organisation. They seem to have been led on the one hand by the chiefs of the *calpulli* – the chronicles are not in agreement as to their number, some refer to seven *calpulli* and to their corresponding seven chiefs, others speak of fifteen and others even of twenty – and on the other hand by a priesthood, the representatives on earth of the ancestral god Huitzilopochtli. Within two centuries this god was to become the transcendental deity of central Mexico, the most feared symbol of Aztec power and the ideological justification for Aztec imperialism. He was to function as absolute ruler in an ever growing pantheon of deities. Yet in the period of the Aztec migrations he was only the modest ancestral god of a small people.

Government through a loose body of priests and *calpulli* chiefs did not in any way correspond to the conventions and usages of the rest of the people of the Valley of Mexico. There largely centralised forms of government with supreme rulers, who enjoyed far-reaching authority and power, had developed. The Aztecs rapidly adapted themselves to the organisational forms of the other peoples of the plateau. This process of adaptation was on the one hand doubtless inspired by the determination of the newcomers not to be inferior to the old established and more powerful groups. On the other hand the permanent waging of war and the great reclamation and drainage schemes that were necessary to make the sterile soil of Tenochtitlan productive equally required a highly organised and centralised power.

Part of this process of adaptation appears to have been the division of Tenochtitlan into four urban quarters, *nauhcampa*, that is the four directions of the wind. This was a principle which had enjoyed a very long tradition in the Valley of Mexico. As already mentioned, recent excavations in Teotihuacan have revealed a similar division. The same held good for the Toltecs and for almost all the peoples of central Mexico. This division had a ritualistic significance since the figure 4 was sacred. The four directions of the wind were represented by the four most important deities in the pantheon of most of the peoples of the plateau. But this division does not appear to have depended solely on religious considerations. Paul Kirchhoff believes that he has discovered among one people of the plateau, the Acolhua, a functional division of these four groups: that the first specialised in religious services, the second in political government, the third in administration and the fourth in agriculture. Such a division does not indicate complete equality among *calpulli*.

Whichever group wielded the political and religious power belonged to the ruling class; that concerned with agriculture usually belonged to the ruled. This would mean that inequalities existed between the *calpulli* very early. This theory may generally be accepted in the case of Tenochtitlan. If, in fact, the Aztecs consisted of a grouping together of various *calpulli*, some of which originated from a ruling Toltec group, others of whom had previously been Chichimec nomads, such a presumption is not improbable. As a result of excavations which have been carried out in Tenochtitlan it has been established that most members of the ruling class came from certain parts of the city. Another significant fact is that the population was not equally divided over the four city quarters. A considerable portion of the *calpulli* appear to have lived in only one of the four quarters; these presumably were the husbandmen.

The social stratifications which had already existed before the settlement of Tenochtitlan were greatly strengthened after the city's foundation. This differentiation in class structure took place in both an upward and a downward direction. In the year 1376 the Aztecs proclaimed a supreme leader for the first time, called Huey Tlatoani, the 'Chief Speaker'. This first leader, Acamapichtli, was the son of an Aztec and a princess of Cuhuacan. The rulers of this city state were descendants of the Toltecs, and the Aztecs, as newcomers to the High Valley, doubtless attempted by this means to establish a connection with the old Toltec tradition and with the ruling class. The rights and functions of this Chief Speaker fluctuated between those of a petty tribal chief and those of a state ruler. Economically he enjoyed a privileged position. Particular lands, *tecpantlalli* were assigned to the palace and the peasants living there were obliged to provide for the Chief Speaker and his family. In addition every *calpulli* had to till a piece of land for the benefit of the ruler, or of the central authority and the Chief Speaker owned his own lands which were not tilled by members of the Aztec people, but probably by foreign bondsmen, *mayeques*, of whom we shall speak later.

The Chief Speaker was the leader in battle, chief justice, and administrator of the ever increasing state revenues. Yet all these privileges, at least at the beginning, were limited in such a way, both by tradition and by advisory bodies, that his powers were those of a tribal chieftain rather than of a despot.

This was made clear even during the Chief Speaker's election. His successor was chosen from among his family. He himself did not determine on which member the choice should fall, nor was his successor determined by rules of heredity but by election. In the early stages of Aztec society the full meeting of the members of the tribe constituted the electors or else the representatives of the *calpulli*. The choice generally fell on the brother or son of the Chief Speaker.

The limitation of the power of this Aztec leader is shown most clearly in three of his most important functions: the declaration of war, the distribution of tribute and state revenue and the appointment of dignitaries and officials. Regarding the declaration of war, the Chief Speaker had in a large measure to bow to the decisions of a war council consisting of the representatives of the *calpulli* and the most eminent warriors. Only if this council agreed could a declaration of war follow.

Still tighter limits were placed on the distribution of the great revenues that came to the rulers. It was the ruler's duty to care for 'the poor, the widows and orphans'. Thus on the feast day of the goddess Xilonen all the poor and fatherless were given clothes and food. Every new ruler on his appointment was emphatically reminded by the priests of these duties: 'Do not forget the poor, dying of hunger . . . distribute food to the aged', he was firmly admonished. Still more important was the instigation of great ceremonies at which the bravest warriors were rewarded.

The ruler then summoned all the brave men of the Order of the Knights of the Sun together . . . and after they had assembled, he placed upon them rich apparel . . . then he had the Knights which were called Tequihuaque summoned and did the same with them . . . Then other warriors came who were called Otomi . . . to these he gave yet other apparel and jewels . . . Then he clothed all old and young priests . . . He also provided the watchmen and servants of the temples with clothing . . . For the same purpose he had summoned to him the old people of the four quarters of the city and the poor and the orphans.[6]

The ruler was also responsible for laying in reserves against years of famine.

Recipients of gifts from tribute moneys and also candidates for the most important offices of state were chosen according to a particular code – distinction in war, since this was to a large extent ascertainable and had little to do with the personal wishes of the Chief Speaker. Beside this meritorious aristocracy consisting mainly of warriors, there was a second kind of nobility which already contained the germ of the aristocracy. These were the descendants and members of the family of the Chief Speakers, known as *pipiltin*. They were very numerous since the Chief Speaker and his family, unlike the ordinary people, had the right to polygamy. The *pipiltin* lived in the palace and the ruler was obliged to feed them. It appears even at this early date that certain if limited functions were their exclusive responsibility. At all events anyone who had distinguished himself in war always had the chance of acquiring state appointments and other honours. Part of the riches that he won in battle or by reason of his new office had to be spent on great banquets at which he had to entertain and bestow presents on a number of guests. In the early years of Aztec history there were probably members of most social classes among the guests but later on participation was increasingly reserved for the nobility only.

A stratification in the social structure now began to take place in a different direction. In this period the settlement of craftsmen who were attracted from widely differing areas of Mesoamerica began; they were given the right to organise themselves into their own separate corporations. In addition a new dependent class developed among the Aztecs, the *mayeques* or bondsmen. This group may have been of very long standing in the Valley of Mexico. These *mayeques* were not members of the *calpulli*; they possessed no land or soil of their own, but tilled the land of the nobility. They were bound to this land and were transferred with it to the owner's heirs. Their labour belonged exclusively to the landowner, and they paid no tribute to the central authority. Who were these *mayeques*? Did they belong to conquered regions? There is no proof of this. They were probably of varying origins in different parts of Mexico. It is very possible, and this is also confirmed in some legends, that they were late immigrants into the Valley of Mexico who no longer had the strength to acquire their own land and were ready, under conditions of serfdom, to till the soil of peoples who were already established.

The most important social change which took place during the first century of Aztec history was the increasing power of the military caste. War became the most important occupation – it was the only one which held out the promise of advancement, social esteem and riches. Already in those days the adage which a later Mexican ruler expressed may have been in current usage: 'Are not war and victory the true profession of a Mexican, and is it not more worthwhile to win victory even against a thousand perils than sit at home like a woman, and work?' This is still more clearly stated in the answer given by a woman to a youth, who dared to address her before having accomplished deeds of war:

And you coward, you dare to speak, you greenhorn? You of all people dares to speak? Ponder rather how you may accomplish some heroic deed so that the locks which you now wear in the nape of your neck to show you are a coward with little courage may be cut. You coward, you greenhorn; there is nothing for you to say here, since you are a woman just like me and have never left the fireside.[7]

In the beginning of Aztec history, when the tribe was small and battles were waged nearby, all able-bodied men were probably drawn into the fighting. Arms and ammunition were distributed to all men from the state stockpiles. The weapons consisted in the main of spear slings (*atl atl*), arrows and bows and *maccahuitl* (these were sticks tipped with obsidian points; they were exceedingly sharp and dangerous at the first stroke but very quickly became blunt). The Aztec warriors in addition carried wooden shields and wore breast plates made of cotton wool which offered such effective protection that some of the Spaniards during the Conquest of Mexico laid aside their heavy metal cuirasses in order to wear these cotton-wool shirts instead.

The *calpulli* was and remained for a long time the basic unit of the army. In time however élite units of the bravest warriors also appeared. These units, constituted on the basis of deeds which at this early period are not precisely known (in later periods they were exactly ascertainable as will be demonstrated), consisted of members of military orders, in particular those of the eagle and the jaguar. These kinds of orders appear to be older than the Aztecs, and may have already existed at the time of Teotihuacan.

The most important state officials were nominated from the members of these orders. They were fully aware of the fact that they belonged to an élite. This was also emphasised by a number of outward distinctions. In battle members of the military orders wore the uniform of their order, and in peacetime they were compelled to wear cotton clothing only and specified jewellery. With the exception of members nominated for state duties, members of the military orders were not allowed to leave the *calpulli* community and dispose of their own land and soil. But differences not only in prestige but also in wealth and prosperity may well have increased between them and the other members of the *calpulli*. In the campaigns in which all took part they were awarded richer honours than the ordinary members of the *calpulli* in the army. Above all, there were many wars in which not all members of the tribe were involved. Either the battles were waged far away from Tenochtitlan, so that it was not possible for reasons of transport and supply to engage all able-bodied men, or these battles took place at a time when a considerable proportion of the men were required for agriculture. For such campaigns members of the military orders and the young men of the *telpochcalli*, the house of youth (yet to be described), were chosen as recruits. Consequently the difference between the military caste and the rest of the population not only in standing but also in wealth became more sharply distinguished. Nevertheless it was not until a century after the foundation of Tenochtitlan that this meritorious aristocracy of warriors developed into a new class. This moment in Aztec history was very exactly registered, a thing which does not often happen, and was closely associated with the rise of the Aztecs to the hegemony of the Valley of Mexico.

In the year 1426 after a rule of sixty-three years, according to tradition, the legendary Tezozomoc of Atzcapotzalco died. He had succeeded in overthrowing all the high valley regions but his kingdom survived him by only two years. His successors did not possess his powerful personality and the integrating factors of the domain of Atzcapotzalco had in any case never been very strong. Tezozomoc had never introduced any important economic measures which would have brought about an effective integration of the Valley of Mexico. His rule seems to have been based on a narrow and brittle foundation: Atzcapotzalco was itself too weak to dominate the High Valley and Tezozomoc had therefore had to recruit subject peoples – the most important among them were the Aztecs – to do battle for him. They had little share in the spoils of the victories.

On these grounds it is not surprising that after the death of Tezozomoc the Aztecs should have wished to shake off the domination of Atzcapotzalco and themselves enter into the heritage. But because they were too weak on their own they first had to look round for allies. The last city state which Tezozomoc had conquered with the vigorous aid of the Aztecs – Tetzcoco – seemed to be the most appropriate choice. The last ruler of Tetzcoco, Ixtlilzochitl, had been killed, but his son Netzahualcoyotl, was still living in exile. Netzahualcoyotl, the 'Hungry

Coyote', is one of the most outstanding and clever personalities known in ancient Mexican history. From his exile he succeeded in keeping alive in Tetzcoco the spirit of resistance – it was after all one of the most powerful city states in the Valley of Mexico and this had been its first defeat; previously it had always overthrown others. He immediately understood the possibilities an alliance with Tenochtitlan would open to him and did all he could to bring it about.

He allied himself with the Aztecs to proceed against Atzcapotzalco and in a number of decisive battles in the years between 1429 and 1433 Atzcapotzalco was conquered and its power destroyed. Tenochtitlan and Tetzcoco, joined by a smaller city state of Tlacopan (present-day Tacuba, a suburb of Mexico City), now entered into the heritage of Atzcapotzalco. In a mere twenty years they succeeded in transforming the domain of Atzcapotzalco for their own use. The conquest and destruction of Atzcapotzalco was the signal for the Aztecs to grasp at world power. Radical changes took place both within Tenochtitlan and outside.

Internally the conquest of Atzcapotzalco finally cemented the supremacy of the military aristocracy and paved the way from an élite to a regular aristocracy. These far-reaching changes are repeatedly confirmed by tradition. For instance it is recorded that shortly before the battle against Atzcapotzalco serious differences of opinion occurred between the leaders and most trustworthy warriors of the Aztecs and the common people. The leaders and warriors supported the battle but the common people were afraid and spoke out in favour of surrendering to Atzcapotzalco. A stormy discussion followed and a sort of pact was agreed. The leaders and warriors declared to the people: 'If we are not successful, we shall surrender ourselves into your hands . . . that you may eat our flesh and take vengeance upon us.' And the people answered:

We undertake, if you are successful, to serve you, to pay tribute money to you, to be your bondsmen, to build your houses and to serve you as veritable lords and to place at your disposal our sons, brothers and nieces and while you are waging war, to bear your loads and your arms and to serve you everywhere, wherever you may go and finally to sell you our possessions and persons for your service for ever.[8]

This pact was solemnly sworn by both sides.

The chronicles then relate that after the overthrow of Atzcapotzalco the pact came into force. The immediate results appeared in the division of the territory of Atzcapotzalco among the victors:

After lands had been given to the crown, the first to receive land was Tlacaellel, the general of this battle, who received ten *suertes* of land, all in Atzcapotzalco.

146

To other important leaders two *suertes* of land each were given. To the common people who had shown themselves in this battle to be cowardly and fearful and had sworn to serve the lords and victors . . . no land at all was given. Land was also given to the quarters of the city (this was what the Spaniards called the Aztec *calpulli*) for the cult of the god, to each quarter one *suerte*.[9]

In this way the great mass of the military aristocracy received the economic basis of their power for the first time.

Did events in fact play themselves out like this? Can such social changes be brought about by means of such a pact. It is questionable to say the least. But all traditional accounts agree that with the conquest of Atzcapotzalco, far-reaching social changes did take place which effectively put economic and political power into the hands of the military aristocracy. Whether such a pact was ever made is another question. There is some evidence that we are dealing here with a very exactly planned and prescribed official account which was meant to confirm and justify later events. This is supported by the fact that the first Aztec censorship in the period after the conquest of Atzcapotzalco began to function under the Aztec ruler Itzcoatl. On his order all pictograms recording the previous history of the Aztecs were destroyed. A tradition which the Aztec informants transmitted to the Spanish priest Sahagun says:

They held fast to their history. But at the time that Itzcoatl ruled in Mexico the records were burned. The decision to do this was taken at that time. The lords of Mexico said it is not good that the whole people should know the pictures. Those who have been overthrown will be corrupted by them and then the world would be turned upside down; for much untruth is contained therein.[10]

It is easy to imagine how the foundations of social changes were laid by this official ideology, just at the time when the military aristocracy were receiving power and wealth, while all traditions recalling earlier and more democratic forms of government had to be rigorously suppressed.

The results of these internal upheavals in Tenochtitlan were most clearly seen in the shift of authority to the military caste. The supreme council consisted of military representatives and in the last resort they deliberated with the rulers over matters of war and peace. A change also took place in the composition of the electoral committee which had to decide on the succession to the Chief Speaker. It no longer consisted of representatives of individual *calpulli*, but of representatives of the military aristocracy. At the summit the power of the central authority was strengthened but divided between two men.

Before and after the conquest of Atzcapotzalco a second personality appears at the summit with whom the Chief Speaker had more and more to share his power. This was Cihuacoatl, the 'Snake Woman'. The chronicles relate that the Chief Speaker took no decision without consulting the Snake Woman, and no decision was valid if Cihuacoatl had not given his consent. Was this division of power a lasting institution? It would seem so since this dichotomy in fact reflected the religious conception of the Aztec universe. The Aztecs believed, as we shall demonstrate later, that the world had been created from a male and female principle. The fact that Snake Woman was a feminine name indicates that it was meant to represent the female principle. The problem is made more difficult by the fact that only one personality is known to have exercised real power as the Snake Woman. This was Tlacaellel, who lived until he was about eighty years old and was the power behind three Chief Speakers. Before his appearance hardly anything is heard of the Snake Woman; after his death there was such a leader, but he seems to have been only one among many.

Apart from this dichotomy the power of the central authority increased in strength both internally and externally. The victors over Atzcapotzalco did not repeat the mistake made by their predecessors, of trying to rule the High Valley with insufficient forces and so involving themselves in quarrels which would have allowed their opponents to snatch away their hardwon victory. The coalition which had defeated Atzcapotzalco was strengthened by the formation of a triple alliance between the rulers of Tetzcoco, Tenochtitlan and Tlacopan. This provided for a common military leadership and a common sharing of booty and of the conquered territories. Tenochtitlan and Tetzcoco were each to receive two-fifths of the spoils, and Tlacopan one-fifth. The treaty also ensured close collaboration between the three rulers of these city states and equality of status. They were in collaboration with each other for a century – until the arrival of the Spaniards – but equality of status, as will be demonstrated, did not last. Until 1450 the Triple Alliance was extraordinarily successful in reconquering the old domain of Atzcapotzalco, in extending its dominion over the whole of the Valley of Mexico and neighbouring regions and in placing it on a firmer footing than Atzcapotzalco had ever known.

The leading power of the Triple Alliance in the early years after the conquest of Atzcapotzalco if not the one responsible for all major decisions, appears to have been Tetzcoco. Many factors go to explain the particular role played by this city: the dynamic personality of its Chief Speaker, Netzahualcoyotl, the 'Hungry Coyote' of whom more will be said later; the tradition and history of this city state, which was already independent and powerful at a time when the Aztecs were still a small and dependent people; and the fact that Tetzcoco constructed large irrigation works earlier than any other city state in the High Valley, which led to a stronger economy and to a rapid increase of population. In addition the position of Tenochtitlan *vis-à-vis* her allies was steadily weakened by the social composition of the Aztec state.

As the cities of the Triple Alliance grew, there was naturally a substantial increase of population which led to greater social stratification. The development of the military aristocracy, the increase of its power and its liberation from the daily routine of food production have already been described. The growing wealth of the cities of the Triple Alliance resulted in the vigorous development of a second group: the craftsmen. They flocked into the cities of the Triple Alliance from all parts of Mesoamerica and also from the lowlands. Netzahualcoyotl in particular invited craftsmen to come to his city and offered them the most favourable conditions of work and settlement. Thus textile handiworkers who manufactured cotton clothing, leather workers, gold and silversmiths, sculptors and many other craftsmen arrived in the cities of the Triple Alliance.

They did not come to Tenochtitlan in such large numbers as Tetzcoco. This was partly because Tetzcoco was the centre of the artistic and intellectual life of the Mexican plateau at this time, and partly because of the peculiar and one-sided social development of Tenochtitlan. Closely connected with the craftsmen was the rapid development in Tetzcoco and in Tlacopan of a second social group, whose significance was to be decisive for the status, the existence, the further development and the wealth of these cities; this second group was the body of merchants. They delivered raw materials to the craftsmen for their manufacture, raw materials that came for the most part from distant regions, especially the tropical lowlands which were not subject to the Triple Alliance. In exchange they delivered to the lowlands the manufactured products of the plateau, and also the few raw materials that it was able to export, salt, fish and other lake produce.

This important social group, which spread as it grew rich both in Tetzcoco and in Tlacopan and in most of the city states of the plateau was almost wholly absent in Tenochtitlan due to the development of an island neighbour of Tenochtitlan, Tlatelolco. This island, today a suburb of Mexico City, was in pre-Spanish times situated immediately beside Tenochtitlan. It appears to have been settled at the same time as its larger neighbour but it is not clear where the first settlers came from. Some scholars believe that they were closely related to the Aztecs, possibly a part of the Aztecs themselves; others state that they were a population group which had migrated from the coast. The destiny of this island city, which was for a time united with Tenochtitlan only to separate again, displays some similarities with Tenochtitlan but also some fundamental differences. Like their neighbours in Tenochtitlan the inhabitants of Tlatelolco also had to eke out their scanty existence at first on an equally inhospitable and barren island. Just like its stronger neighbour, it was for many years subject to Atzcapotzalco and had to do military service for the great city state. It developed however in a completely different direction from Tenochtitlan. Even though it made war, the warfare played a much smaller role in Tenochtitlan. While the chronicles of the other city states dwell constantly on conquests, rulers, battles and conflicts, the tale of Tlatelolco, quoted in an old chronicle, is quite different, for the ruling class in this city state were merchants.

Here follows the report, of what the custom of the merchants was in the old days, when Quaqualhpitzaua began to reign, when they, the chiefs of the merchants, Itzconatzin and Tzuatecatzin called the guild of merchants into existence.

When they began to trade, it was only in quetzal feathers and blue tail feathers and chamol feathers. They only traded in these three things.

Second to succeed to the throne of the ruler was Tlahcateotl; in his time Cozmatzin and Tzontantzin were installed as chiefs of the guild of merchants. They opened up trade, not only in long quetzal feathers and feathers of the Caqua bird, but also in turquoise and green precious stones, in fine cloaks and fine loin cloths. Earlier people had only worn small cloaks and dresses made of agave fibres, agave loin cloths, agave shirts and small agave cloths.

The third ruler to mount the throne was Quauhlahtonatzin the honourable warrior, in his time Tollamimichtzin and Mixcohchtzin were installed as chiefs of the guild of merchants.

They opened up trade in little golden lip plugs and golden earrings and rings for the fingers, which were called Matzatzaztli rings, and in shining golden jewellery and heavenly blue turquoise and quite large pieces of green precious stones, and in long quetzal feathers and in the skins of wild animals, the long feathers of the Caqua bird and of the *turquoise* bird and of the great heron.[11]

All these products came from the tropical lowland which had not yet been conquered by the Triple Alliance. If Aztec warriors wanted to wear the rich feather ornaments to which their offices entitled them, they had to go in person to the market place of Tlatelolco to buy them or to exchange their own costly products for them.

In contrast to Tetzcoco and Tlacopan, where the wealth of the merchants benefited the state in every direction, either by taxation or by means of the growing wealth of the whole city, Tlatelolco came to be a permanent site for creaming off the trade destined for Tenochtitlan. The greatest beneficiaries of every conquest, of every thrust forward made by Tenochtitlan, were its merchants, whose power increased with spectacular quickness. Their presence prevented the emergence of a merchant class in Tenochtitlan. Despite a close alliance with

Tlatelolco, this city state was for years a thorn in the flesh of the Aztecs.

THE CONQUESTS OF THE TRIPLE ALLIANCE

The history of the Triple Alliance after the overthrow of Atzcapotzalco may be divided into three periods, the first from 1428 to 1450, the second from 1450 to 1502 and the third from 1502 to the Spanish Conquest in 1519.

In the first period the Triple Alliance succeeded in conquering most of the Valley of Mexico and the neighbouring regions, thereby reinstating the old domain of Atzcapotzalco and on a more secure foundation. Nevertheless even this foundation was not strong enough to exorcise the danger which recurred time and again in all the legends, myths and religious representations: that of famine. In the years 1450–54 according to the chronicles the Valley of Mexico suffered the greatest famine in its history. Seventy years later, when almost all the survivors had died, the chroniclers wrote with horror of the consequence of this famine, which had led to the death of thousands of the inhabitants of the cities of the Triple Alliance and had caused thousands of others to sell themselves into slavery in the tropical lowlands in order to survive. Even the control exercised over great tracts of Central Mexico was unable to save the inhabitants of the Triple Alliance from this famine. It became, as famines so often did in Mesoamerica, the catalyst for rapid new developments. In order to raise food production three very different methods were chosen, the combination of which was not only to change the face of Tenochtitlan fundamentally, but also that of the whole of Mesoamerica.

The first method was military in character. After 1454 the Triple Alliance began great campaigns which were carried out far and wide from the Valley of Mexico. First of all the provinces adjoining the valley in the south and east were conquered, then the armies of the Triple Alliance advanced into the region of Mixteca and after that they overthrew the rich food producing regions of Totonacapan in the modern state of Veracruz. From there the victorious armies drove as far as the Isthmus of Tehuantepec and this way conquered large tracts of the Atlantic and Pacific coasts of modern Mexico. At the end of the fifteenth century the Aztecs ruled over an area which embraced the majority of the population of Mesoamerica.

The campaigns of conquest, even when they differed individually, were always carried out according to a certain plan. First of all scouts were sent to discover the strategic situation of the region to be conquered and its wealth. For this work merchants were selected who acted both as scouts and spies. They disguised themselves and insinuated themselves into specified areas. Their reports probably decided what strategy was adopted, and how many warriors were mobilised and also what demands could be addressed to the newly conquered territory. Once the reports were received the rulers of the Triple Alliance conferred with each other and were advised by their respective councils of war. If war was decided an ambassador was usually, but not always, despatched to the ruler of the territory to be conquered. The latter was summoned to pay tribute and to submit to the Triple Alliance. If he accepted, and many rulers of smaller states saw no other alternative but to surrender peacefully, the Triple Alliance often agreed to discuss the question of the amount of the tribute to be paid. The tribute having been fixed, a receiver of tribute for the overthrown territory was then appointed. The ruler remained in office with full honours and continued to exercise political and economic power.

If he refused to agree to this submission a weapon was handed to him as a sign of war and the Triple Alliance prepared for the campaign. If the locality in question was small, only the members of the military orders and the young men in the houses of youth, the *telpochcalli*, were sent into battle. If the region was larger, all the inhabitants of the Triple Alliance were mobilised and the smaller city states of the Valley of Mexico which had already been overthrown were also recruited for the war. The news of a declaration of war was usually greeted with joy. 'And everyone was so glad', a chronicle relates, 'to go to war, that no more warriors remained in the cities, for all wanted to go to war since they fared so well in it.'[12]

Weapons were issued to the warriors from the state stockpiles and certain foodstuffs were prepared as reserves for the campaign. These rations however were only meant for the moment when the armies of the Triple Alliance were already mustered before the enemy village. The villages through which they marched had to feed them. 'Every village into which the Mexicans and their entire army came went out to meet them, they were given shelter and richly fed. . . .'[13] The chiefs and head men of the village appeared with flowers and food and all kinds of other presents. 'In places where this did not happen, and where the soldiers were not provided with all necessities, they robbed and laid waste the villages.'[14] Since the decision as to whether a village had in fact provided 'all that was necessary' to the advancing army was a very subjective one, the combination of eagerness and fear with which the inhabitants gave everything conceivable to the advancing warriors in order to escape plunder can be easily imagined.

Having reached the enemy village, the opposing armies frequently met on a battlefield chosen in advance on ritualistic grounds. Both armies confronted each other and the members of the military orders stepped out to lead the armies of the Triple Alliance. Insults were exchanged by the different sides with loud cries, accompanied by musical instruments and drums, in order to intimidate the enemy and to give themselves courage. Thereupon they attacked each other with arrows, spears and stones and finally met in close combat. If the attackers failed to break through, attempts were made to lure the enemy into a trap. The battle formation would become dispersed and warriors pretend to flee. Then they would resume the attack on all sides. Once the enemy line, which was generally near the defending capital, was broken, the attackers flocked into the city confines. While some fell upon the enemy who had retreated on to the steps of the temple pyramid, others began to plunder the houses and kill their inhabitants. This plundering and killing lasted until the leaders of the defeated army sued for peace and offered tribute. If the tribute was sufficient and met the wishes of the Triple Alliance, the order was given to stop the fighting. Otherwise the battle was continued and also the plundering and massacre of the civilian population. If the conquered army finally made an offer acceptable to the leaders of the Triple Alliance, it was by no means an easy matter to convince the troops to stop massacring and plundering. Often the officers and the members of the military orders had to round on the troops whose rejoinder was 'that it was their reward and their pay, that they had not come risking so much in order to die'.[15]

After the victorious troops had withdrawn from the locality receivers of tribute, sometimes governors, were left behind. The plunder and booty, especially the captives, were taken away by the victors. Their fate will be described later.

The victories of the Triple Alliance were the result of the full exploitation of the strategic and ecological advantages which the Valley of Mexico had to offer. Besides this, one factor that proved decisive was that the Triple Alliance had triumphantly understood the aim of unifying all the peoples of the plateau. This unification was not only the result of the power and dominance of the Triple Alliance within the Valley of Mexico. It was based also on the fact that the Triple Alliance had perceived in a remarkably astute manner the advantage of allowing the conquered city states of the plateau to participate to a considerable degree in the conquests. Finally a completely new factor after 1450 had led not only to a greater incentive towards integration but also to an important increase in population: the great revolutionary constructions built to alter the water level in the valley.

Tetzcoco completed pioneering works in the field of irrigation, as in all others which were not directly connected with war. This state was not particularly interested in works designed to control the level of lake water, since the salt lake of Tetzcoco did not come into question for

agricultural purposes. It was much more concerned with building a
network of aqueducts and canals which made the water from the
surrounding mountain springs available for agriculture. The most
impressive and also the most widely known is the system installed at
Tetzcotzingo, where the great network of aqueducts and channels
irrigated the agricultural terraces as well as the gardens which had been
laid out for the ruler of Tetzcoco. It was a system which was still
admired by the *conquistadores* many years after the Spanish Conquest.

Thanks to the greatness and industry of the ruler of Tetzcoco [to quote a
Spanish priest] water was led into canals from a distance of 2 leagues in order
to irrigate the hill. Mountains were removed and valleys filled up in order
that water might flow by its own impetus until it reached the top of the hill,
where it could then pour downwards in order to water all trees and plants,
which it still does today.[16]

The inhabitants of Tenochtitlan then invoked the aid of the ruler of
Tetzcoco, Netzahualcoyotl, for the installation of irrigation systems on
the lakes themselves, the enormity of which put all the constructions of
Tetzcoco in the shade. A number of great dykes were built by the Aztecs
with the object of dividing the sweet water lakes from the salt water
lake of Tetzcoco, and so in the case of flood to prevent the salt water
polluting the sweet water. In addition these dykes were intended to
regulate water level and prevent floods. A number of causeways were
built connecting the island of Tenochtitlan with the mainland. The
dykes were interrupted by breeches through which water could flow
from one lake into the other when necessary and the openings were
spanned by removable bridges. Thus Tenochtitlan was converted into
an almost impregnable citadel in time of war or siege, as the Spaniards
were later to discover to their cost.

The construction of these dykes required tens of thousands of
labourers, that the surrounding cities were compelled to supply. Woe
to them if they dared cast doubts on the correct execution or the
purpose of these constructions. The irrigation works carried out by the
Aztecs were not confined to the building of dykes. Great aqueducts
were laid from the mountain tops in the vicinity of Tenochtitlan in
order to supply the city with fresh water and at the same time to
regulate the level of the water in time of drought.

All these constructions served a double purpose. On the one hand
they made it possible to extend the productive Chinampa system to the
network of lakes and allowed additional foodstuffs for many thousands
of people to be cultivated. At the same time they brought about an
unprecedented degree of integration among the various cities and city
states of the Valley of Mexico. The unification of the plateau after 1427
by conquest and later by combined expeditions into the lowlands was

now reinforced by economic means and by a common dependence on the great irrigation works. The important conquests made by the Triple Alliance beyond the Valley of Mexico and the irrigation works within the valley itself helped raise food production and made it possible to feed many more people.

The great famine of 1450 had one remarkable consequence: the Aztecs now aimed not at increasing the amount of foodstuffs but at radically reducing the number of consumers. We are referring to the practice of human sacrifice, which increased enormously. This phenomenon, so characteristic of the Aztecs and so repellent to posterity, can be understood only in the context of the religion of the Aztecs as a whole.

THE RELIGION OF THE AZTECS

It is far from simple to describe the religion of the Aztecs. In it are reflected even more clearly than in their social organisation the radical changes which took place within a very short period in their history. The most important elements of the beliefs of the peoples of the plateau were added to their religion after they had settled in the Valley of Mexico. The conquests resulted in a continuous expansion of the religious ideology, into which the gods and practices of the conquered peoples were assimilated. In Tenochtitlan there was a special temple that housed all the idols of the conquered peoples. They were taken there partly as prisoners to guarantee the loyalty and devotion of their peoples, and they also provided a subject of study for the Aztec priest-they were at pains to increase the veneration accorded to their deities into their religion. This religious syncretism most probably encouraged a massive increase in the number of priests. By adapting new practices they were at pains, to increase the veneration accorded to their deities and to enhance the power exercised by them. The capacity of the Aztec religion for absorption is demonstrated by the fact that it was even found possible to absorb Christianity. During the colonial period – and to a large extent up to the present day – Christianity represented for many Indians only a disguised form of their old religion.

The difficulties in studying Aztec religion, due to the multiplicity of deities and the changes in religious conceptions, are increased by the fact that the official religion became separated from the much simpler religion of the people in proportion to its increasing complexity. On the other hand it is a positive advantage that there are few elements of Aztec culture so well known as their religion. In their efforts to root out 'the devil and heresy' the Spanish priests who came to Mexico made a close study of the religion which they wanted to destroy.

Aztec ideology was extremely complex concerning the powers which created and ruled the universe, but very straightforward in regard to man's right behaviour towards these powers. The gods of the creation of the world were a male and a female principle, Ometecuhtli, the 'Ruler of Duality' and Omecihuatl, the 'Wife of Duality'. They were only indirectly the creators of the world however, in that they helped to bring to life the four deities which then created the real world. These four deities represented the four directions and appear originally to have embodied exclusively the forces of nature. With time they mingled with tribal gods or cultural heroes. One of the most important of these gods was the creation god Quetzalcoatl, the Feathered Serpent, who was also the wind god. Quetzalcoatl, as already described, was partly identified with the Toltec ruler Ce Acatl Topiltzin who had at the same time been the high priest of the Feathered Serpent. The black Tezcatlipoca, the Smoking Mirror, was god of the night and darkness and the war god of the eastern Nahua tribes. Likewise the tribal god of the Aztecs, 'Humming-bird on the Left' Huitzilopochtli, was promoted into this foremost group of creation gods.

The process of creation accomplished by these gods did not all take place at the same time. The world was created five times and destroyed four times. Each of these periods was known as a 'Sun'. During the first Sun giants, who did not yet possess the knowledge of agriculture and only lived by gathering various plants, inhabited the earth. After 676 years, according to the legends, the god of night, Tezcatlipoca, changed himself into a tiger and ate up all the giants so that no more human beings were left in the world.

During the second Sun Quetzalcoatl reigned. He recreated man, who inhabited the earth for a period of 364 years. Then there was a terrible storm, and the wind swept almost all the human beings away. Only a small number were able to save themselves, and were changed into monkeys.

The third period began under the lordship of the god of rain. This period, which the legends say lasted for 312 years, ended in a rain of fire. Only a few human beings, transformed into birds, managed to survive.

The fourth period, the fourth Sun, also ended in a natural catastrophe, this time as a result of tremendous floods, and only a few people who changed themselves into fish were saved from extinction. The world was now wrapped in darkness. There were no human beings and there was no sun. The gods, whose number had meanwhile increased, met in Teotihuacan in order to help create a new sun. They lit a fire and called upon the rich god Tecuciztecatl to cast himself into the flames so that he could thus become the sun. The legend relates how this god approached the fire, but when he saw that the fire was burning 'he felt its great heat, grew fearful and dared not to cast himself in and stepped back'. Thereupon the gods turned to the small and despised god Nanauatzin and said to him:

'Now, Nanauatzin, you try.' Since the gods had addressed him, he took great pains, shut his eyes, ran forward and cast himself into the fire, which then began to burn brightly and to glow. When Tecuciztecatl saw that his predecessor had cast himself into the fire and was burning, he also seized courage and likewise cast himself into the flames . . . After both had cast themselves into the fire and had burned up, the gods sat down and waited, to see where Nanauatzin would appear. After waiting a long time, the sky began to colour and the light of dawn shone over everything. It is said that the gods thereupon threw themselves on their knees, to wait and see whence Nanauatzin, who had turned into the sun, would appear.

No god knew in which quarter of the heavens the sun would finally appear until 'a few looked to the east, and said the sun will rise here. And they were right.'[17] But the sun remained still and did not move. When the gods asked the reason the sun replied that he was waiting for his sacrifice. And one god after another cast himself into the flames, and only then did the sun begin to move in the sky. This myth was to become one of the most fundamental in Aztec culture. The sun could only be kept in motion by sacrificial death, first of the gods and later of human beings.

This last period, the fifth sun, was that in which the Aztecs believed they were living. It differed from earlier periods in that the god Quetzalcoatl had given mankind a completely new basis of life: maize. This had until then been stored up by ants and only when the Feathered Serpent changed itself into an ant did this god succeed in stealing a grain of maize and bringing it to mankind.

This fifth sun was also finally doomed to set. Famine and floods would precede its setting, after which monsters would descend from the heavens and eat up mankind. It was impossible to prophesy the date of this catastrophe but it would in any case take place at the close of a fifty-two-year cycle. The Aztecs were always afraid when such a cycle was coming to a close that the end of the world would follow. All lights were extinguished, the population kept to their houses and trembled and only when daybreak came would the priests, after they had made a human sacrifice to the gods, light a new fire and the people know that the sun had triumphed and that the world was saved again for at least the next fifty-two years.

At the height of Aztec power it was not the creation gods who occupied the highest ranks in the Aztec pantheon, but the tribal god of the Aztecs, Huitzilopochtli, Humming-bird on the Left. From a tribal god of a small people he was promoted to be god of war and god of creation. There is another creation myth concerning him which tells how the

earth goddess Coatlicue, who already had one daughter and four hundred sons, one day swallowed a small berry: she forthwith became preg-
nant, and her sons and daughter who did not believe in an immaculate
conception decided to kill her. Just as they were about to fall upon her
Humming-bird on the Left leapt from her womb and killed in one
deadly flashing stroke his sister and his four hundred brethren. This
legend symbolises the victory of the sun over the moon – the sister of
Humming-bird on the Left and the stars – the four hundred brethren –
who were annihilated by the rays of the sun.

The Aztecs called themselves the People of the Sun, or the People of
Humming-bird on the Left. In the capital city of Tenochtitlan he was
assigned a place on the largest pyramid of the city. Only one other god
was worshipped there, the god of rain, Tlaloc. His role illustrates the
importance of rain and agriculture as well as the growing significance
of the network of lakes in Mexico in the lives of the Aztecs – for purposes
of irrigation and transport.

Besides these gods there were a great many deities which fall into
various groups: there were the gods of certain social groups, tribal gods,
gods of individual professional groups and the gods of individual
calpulli; often deities represented the forces of nature or heavenly bodies.
These various gods were often confounded with one another. The most
rapid changes took place among the tribal gods whose destiny was of
course closely bound up with that of the tribes they represented.

The phenomenal rise of Humming-bird on the Left from a small
tribal god to become the god of the sun is the clearest and best-known
example but by no means the only one. The extent to which the Aztecs
identified themselves with the Toltecs and their heritage was paralleled
by the growing significance of the Feathered Serpent. Fresh attributes
were constantly being assigned to him. Not only was he the god of
creation and the bearer of culture; he was also often regarded as the
god of maize, and the merchants appear to have chosen him to be one
of their patrons and protectors.

The adoption of this god by the Aztecs was not without its problems.
In the early Toltec period the cult of Quetzalcoatl to a certain extent
opposed the ever increasing practice of human sacrifice. The legends
relate that at this time only butterflies were sacrificed to the god
Quetzalcoatl. In later Toltec history and in Aztec times, the cult of
Quetzalcoatl ceased to oppose human sacrifice. Nevertheless among
some opponents of the practice of human sacrifice there seems to have
remained the memory of Quetzalcoatl's earlier role. They saw in him a
redeemer who would one day return and abolish human sacrifice.

The concept behind the god Mixcoatl, Cloud Serpent, is also very
complex. Varied elements became confused. He was the god of the
northern stars. The inhabitants of Tlaxcala worshipped him as the

original and only god of their city. In the Aztec pantheon he also plays an important role, and he was regarded as the god of the northern hunting peoples. At the same time his history was closely identified with that of a historical personality, who was believed to be a manifestation of him on earth: Mixcoatl, Cloud Serpent, the first leader of the Toltecs.

The prospect becomes simpler and clearer when we turn from the tribal gods to the gods of individual professional groups. There were clearly defined gods of the various handicrafts and of the merchants. The patron deities of individual *calpulli* were probably simpler still although not a great deal is known about them. In many respects they must have been very close to the peasants.

There were far fewer metamorphoses among the gods symbolising the powers and forces of nature than among the gods of social groups. Some of them may be traced back to the times of Teotihuacan and some even earlier. The chief among these is Huehueteotl, the god of fire, and another was Tlaloc, the rain god.

Among the most important deities of this group were the gods of maize and vegetation, namely the god of maize and the goddess of the maize-ears, Cinteotl and Xilonen. Closely associated with these gods are two of the most agreeable figures in the Aztec pantheon: the goddess Xochiquetzatl, the personification of love and beauty, goddess of flowers and housekeeping and at the same time patroness of women of easy virtue. The masculine counterpart was the god Xochipilli, the god of love, sport and summer. In terrifying contrast to these gods was the god of spring, Xipe Totec, who originated in the tropical and eastern lowlands. This god symbolised the anticipation of spring, the revival of vegetation: the rites practised in his honour were among the most ferocious in the Aztec religion.

The diversity of these gods is clearly expressed in the representations made of them. These are to be found particularly in pictograms or carved in stone and range from gods represented in human terms to those almost wholly devoid of such features. The flower god Xochipilli is represented as a radiant youth adorned with flowers and jewellery.

The god of rain, Tlaloc, although human in form, instead of a human face has a mask made out of two snakes which form a circle round his eyes and join their mouths in front of his mouth. The god of spring, Xipe Totec, was represented by a mask made of flayed human skin. Often it was more than just a mask represented in stone or on paper. On religious occasions priests dressed themselves in flayed human skins.

The earth goddess and the mother of the gods, Coatlicue, had no human features. She is represented in one of the greatest surviving Aztec works of art, a stone sculpture $2\frac{1}{2}$ metres high which is preserved in the National Museum of Mexico. In this statue the idea of death and birth, of destruction and creation were combined equally. The goddess wears a girdle in the form of a snake from which hangs a skirt made of intertwining snakes. She carries a terrifying looking chain made out of hearts, hands and a death's-head. Her hands and feet are claws since, as Alfonso Caso has written, she 'feeds off the corpses of human beings'.[18] The head has no human features at all, it consists of two snakes' heads joined together. The only human attribute in the whole conception are the two pendulous breasts which clearly symbolise the life-giving function of the earth mother, for at her breasts both gods and mankind have fed. This deity makes a particularly strange, abstract and monstrous impression on the modern viewer. How very close she was to the Aztecs, even more so than the other gods and goddesses, is impressively demonstrated by the fact that many of the practices and rites dedicated to her still survive. At the site in present-day Mexico City where the temple of the mother of the gods, Tonantzin, stood (she was probably a manifestation of Coatlicue), the Spaniards built the church of the Madonna of Guadalupe. Thousands of Indians from all over the country flock to this temple and on certain days execute dances and ceremonies which their ancestors instituted hundreds of years ago, even if in a somewhat different form, in honour of the mother of the gods, Coatlicue.

What did the world in which these gods lived and ruled look like? At the centre was the earth, shaped like a wheel and surrounded by sea on all sides. The Aztecs called it Cemanahuac: 'That which is completely surrounded by water.' The water reaches as far as the sky where it becomes the Holy Water. The universe stretched horizontally over the earth in Four Directions which the Aztecs believed represented various aspects. The west where the sun had his dwelling-place was the red land. Opposite was the east, the symbol of light, fertility and of life, which was always represented in white. The north was represented in black and symbolised the end of life and death, while the south appeared generally to be blue in all Aztec representations.

Besides this horizontal arrangement of the universe there was also a vertical one. Thirteen heavens stretched upwards over the earth and below them were nine hells. The heavens were in the first place the dwellings of the gods and of a few privileged human beings who were allowed to join them after death. More will be said about them later. These heavens were conceived as storeys in a house, the two highest inhabited by the creation gods. Below the earth the nine hells stretched downwards, the habitation of the god of death, Mictlantecuhtli and of the souls of the dead.

What was man's role in this cosmos? What destiny had he been chosen for? Man was given a greater significance *vis-à-vis* the gods by

the Aztecs than in the Christian religion. On the other hand, the fate
that awaited him on earth and after his death was in their belief much
sadder and gloomier. Hardly any religion is so pessimistic, indeed at
times so despairing as the Aztec religion. This is already expressed in
the myth of creation. Mankind was created four times by the gods, only
to be destroyed in natural catastrophes, either to be consumed by the
gods or at best to be transformed into animals. Mankind of the fifth Sun
was created by the god of creation and of life, the Feathered Serpent.
To this end the god had descended into the realm of the dead, Mictlan,
in order to fetch precious bones. He encountered great obstacles which
he had to overcome. The god of death, Mictlantecuhtli, had a deep pit
dug into which the Feathered Serpent fell and died. But he awoke to
new life and brought the bones to the paradise of the gods, Tamoamchan.
There they were ground by the Snake Woman goddess and laid in a
richly jewelled casket. Thereupon the Feathered Serpent appeared again,
mortified his flesh and sprayed the powder with the blood that was
drawn. He then fasted together with five other gods, and from the
powder of the bones man arose.

A hard fate, filled with gloom and privation, awaited man upon
earth. The babe at his mother's breast was told of this immediately
after birth. 'Thou wilt know and taste sorrow, thou wilt experience
misfortune and misery. Thou hast come to the abode of perpetual
mourning and of affliction where there is pitiful suffering.'[19] Aztec
poets saw life as a dream which is swiftly over. 'We only come to sleep,
to dream. It is not true, that we come to earth to live. We are as the
grass in Spring. Our heart comes, it blooms and opens, our body causes
some flowers to blossom, and then all withers.'[20] Life was a brief dream
that could be cut short at any time by the end of the world, the end of
the fifth Sun, which must inevitably come. Famine and earthquakes
would sweep mankind away and what remained would be devoured
by the gods of the stars who had changed themselves into tigers.

Only a fraction of mankind expected a better after-life to follow the
gloomy present. The hope of hereafter did not depend on the way they
lived their lives on earth but on the way they met their death. These
were the warriors who fell in battle or were sacrificed as prisoners to
the gods, the women who died in childbirth and all people killed by
natural catastrophes, such as floods or lightning. Children who died
young also belonged to this group.

Warriors would rise with the sun in the east and climb every valley
with warlike songs. Likewise the women who died in childbirth would
find their rest where the sun sets in the western quarter of the world
since they too had died in battle. Perhaps the fate of those who died as a
result of natural catastrophes was even more interesting. They discovered a god of rest in the kingdom of the water gods where perpetual

spring reigned, where there was an overabundance of things to eat and drink and everything blossomed and flourished.

Everyone else on the other hand awaited a sombre fate after death. They had to wander through eight hells for four long years before reaching the ninth. The way through the eight hells was strewn with obstacles. In the first the souls of the dead were met with a turbulent and rushing river which they had to cross. Then they had to pass between two mountains which constantly butted against each other. In one of the other hells a cutting icy wind blew which the Aztecs said was as sharp as the sharpest obsidian blade. In the seventh hell wild beasts lay in wait to eat up the dead. The soul finally came to rest in the ninth hell. Whether the soul continued to exist in a realm of shades as in the Greek Hades or whether it was completely annihilated is not clear. The ashes of the dead were put into urns together with a number of objects that were intended to ease their way through the eight hells. Thus a small dog was always buried with the dead to help them cross the rushing waters of the river. Before burying or cremating the dead a piece of jade was placed between the lips to offer the wild beasts in the eighth hell as something to eat. Paper and the clothes of the dead were burned so as to warm them while they crossed the hell in which the icy wind blew.

It would be a mistake however to deduce from this fundamental pessimism of the Aztec religion that the Aztecs were ascetics who despised the pleasures of life. As the following description of the city of Tenochtitlan and of the life of the ruling class of the Aztecs proves, the very opposite was the case. There were many contradictions between the official religion and actual life. During the last years of Aztec rule various religious principles appear to have been revised and doubt cast on others. It is thus widely believed that the conception of a warriors' paradise was a new idea in Aztec religion that only appeared shortly before the Spanish Conquest. New and differing points of view came into being concerning the hereafter. Epicurean conceptions developed. To quote one poem: 'Therefore sweet scented flowers only continue to live on this earth, just as the songs which spell joy. Enjoy them now.'[21]

Others believed in an eternal life, more substantial than the life of shades offered by Mictlan. 'In fact', to quote another poem, 'the place where blessedness is to be found is not on this earth: one must seek it elsewhere. There one will find joy. Or are we treading this earth in vain? Surely there is another place where life will be found.'[22] How could man influence the gods in order that they might determine his destiny on earth? There were some rites at least outwardly similar to Christian rites that were later seized on by the Spanish priests in order to convert the Indians to Catholicism. Prayers were addressed to the gods for a variety of reasons. Some of these prayers have survived, and some of them testify to the existence of a wealth of poetry.

Like the Catholics the Aztecs were also familiar with confession, although in a somewhat different form. Through confession not only heavenly but earthly absolution and freedom from punishment could be received for certain crimes. But confession was a rare and precious gift which a man was allowed to receive only once in a lifetime.

My son [said the priest to a penitent, to quote from a chronicle], thou art come before the presence of God, who is the protector and helper of us all. Thou art come to show him thine evil smell and thy rotten inward parts. Thou art come to lay before him the secrets of thy heart; beware, go not to perdition by lying in the presence of our Lord; strip thyself naked and make thy confession. Now confess everything of which thou art ashamed in the presence of our Lord Yoalli Ehecatl, that is Tetzcatlipoca.

After the confession was over, the priest turned again to the penitent and said:

My son, thou hast spoken before our Lord God. Thou hast confessed thine evil deeds. I now desire to tell thee in his name what thou must do. When the goddesses Ciuapipiltin descend upon the earth, or when the festival of the goddesses of carnality, called Ixcuiname, is celebrated, thou wilt fast for the whole of four days and thereby punish both thy stomach and thy mouth.

As soon as dawn breaks . . . thou wilt draw through thy tongue the small fibres Teocalcacatl or Tlacotl. If this does not seem to thee enough, thou wilt do the same to thine ears in atonement in order that thou mayest receive absolution for thy sin, and not to acquire any merit. Thou wilt carry out this operation on thy tongue with a thorn of the Maguey; through this hole thou wilt then draw the fibres . . . thou mayst, an thou willst, bind all the fibres into a bunch, so that about three to four hundred pass through thy tongue. Once thou hast done this, the evil which thou hast committed will be atoned for.[23]

The principal aspect of the relationship between mankind and the gods was represented neither by prayer nor by confession. If man wanted to determine his own fate and to influence the gods and heavenly powers to this end, he had to tread other paths. It was very important to choose the right moment for everything. Because the world existed under the sign of everlasting conflicts between the various gods it was necessary to fix exactly which day, even which hour, was under the control of which god. To make these calculations the Aztecs depended on their calendar which was known to all Mesoamerican peoples and which has already been described in connection with the Maya civilisation. There was a calendrical year consisting of eighteen months of twenty days and five extra days, and a liturgical year consisting of thirteen months of twenty days. Every fifty-two years the same days of the liturgical and the calendrical year coincided. So time was divided into cycles of fifty-two years. In contrast to the Maya of the classic period the Aztecs had no knowledge of the so-called 'long count', that is they had no fixed point from which time could be calculated with any exactitude. By the use of their calendar it was possible to establish the day of an event exactly within the fifty-two-year cycle but not to state in which cycle this event had taken place. One can imagine a historian being told of a revolution in 89 without knowing whether the revolution took place in 1789, 1889, or 1989. Every day in the calendar was fixed under the sign of a god, whose properties could work for good or ill on any project which had been planned. In the case of events which could not be fixed for a certain day, such as a birth, efforts were made to counteract the influence of the gods bringing ill fortune by practising a sort of circumvention. Thus a child born on an unlucky day was given its name on a later day under more fortunate auspices.

The most important method by which man could influence the gods was not through prayer nor by calendrical manipulation, but by nourishing the gods, especially the sun. Just as the gods after the coming of the fifth Sun had to sacrifice themselves so as to allow it to continue its journey across the heavens, so human beings had to be sacrificed and their blood offered to nourish the Sun. Without this nourishment the Sun could no longer exist, light would go out in the world and the world would be destroyed. The holy mission of the Aztecs was always to provide the Sun with nourishment. This mission was most clearly formulated by the Snake Woman Tlacaellel, the Chief Speaker's deputy:

Sacrifice these sons to the Sun . . . A convenient market must be sought and just as men go to the market to find their warm tortillas [flat maize cakes which are still the national dish of Mexicans] so shall our god come to market with his army, to buy sacrifices and human beings, which he can eat; our people and our armies must reach this market in order to buy with their blood, their hearts, their heads and lives the jewellery, the precious stones, and the beautiful feathers required for the service of Humming-bird on the Left the wonderful.[24]

All prisoners without exception were sacrificed to the gods. In one of the many Aztec ceremonies they were drawn up in front of the pyramids. They sometimes even had to dance in honour of the gods. They then mounted the steps to the top of the pyramid where the priests were waiting for them. On their way up they were sprayed with a kind of narcotic which dulled their senses. Four priests laid the prisoners on their backs on the sacrificial stone and a fifth tore out their hearts from their breasts after gashing them open with an obsidian knife. The effect of such a ceremony on the horrified Europeans is described by one of the *conquistadores* of Mexico, Bernal Diaz del Castillo, who during the siege of the city of Tenochtitlan had to watch, powerless to intervene, how some of his comrades were sacrificed.

There was sounded the dismal drum of Huichilobos [distortion by the

Spaniards of his real name Huitzilopochtli] and many other shells and horns and things like trumpets and the sound of them all was terrifying. We all looked towards the lofty Pyramid where they were being sounded and saw that our comrades whom they had captured when they defeated Cortés were being carried by force up the steps and they were taking them to be sacrificed. When they got them up to a small square in front of the oratory where their accursed idols are kept, we saw them place plumes on the heads of many of them and with things like fans in their hands they forced them to dance before Huichilobos, and after they had danced they immediately placed them on their backs on some rather narrow stones which had been prepared for sacrifice and with stone knives they cut open their chests and drew out their palpitating hearts and offered them to the idols that were there. Then they kicked the bodies down the steps and Indian butchers who were waiting below cut off the arms and feet and flayed the skin off their faces and prepared it afterwards like glove leather with the beards on and kept those for the festivals . . . In the same way they sacrificed all the others and ate the legs and arms and offered the hearts and blood to their idols.[25]*

It is true that parts of the bodies of the sacrifices were eaten, but this was not a case of simple cannibalism; it was a ritual meal, a bloody communion with the gods. The mass sacrifices were the most usual but not the only form of human sacrifice.

Specially courageous warriors who had been taken prisoner were given the opportunity to fight for their lives. But it was only an illusory fight. The prisoner was bound to a post and given a wooden club. With this he had to fight simultaneously four fully armed warriors wielding swords with obsidian points. The odds were so uneven that the prisoner had scarcely any hope of winning. Tradition cites only one case where a prisoner from Tlaxcala, Tlahuicole, succeeded in killing his attackers. He was set free by the Aztecs, but had to pledge himself to fight for them, although not against his own people.

Rather different concepts underlay the sacrifices offered to the vegetation gods. It was not a matter of offering nourishment to the gods, but of the victim becoming the very god incarnate. His sacrifice symbolised the death and the resurrection of the gods. The chosen victim enjoyed a better fate than the other prisoners for at least a year. He was worshipped as a god during this time, lived in a palace with numerous servants, and the most beautiful women were placed at his disposal. His last day on earth was the occasion for great rejoicing in the whole city, for a reincarnation of the gods was at hand.

The unfortunate beings who had been selected for this purpose [a chronicler says] were solemnly attired and with great ceremony and to the sound of rejoicing were led through all the streets and plazas. On the way

---

* I have used Alfred Percival Maudesley's translation of *The Conquest of New Spain*, ed. Genaro Garcia (Mexico) IV. An edition is published by the Hakluyt Society (London, 1910), p. 149 (translator's note).

everyone that met them entrusted to them their wishes and needs so that they might carry them to the god before whose throne they must surely come to fulfil their destiny. They were accordingly offered food or given some other present, so that they took with them to the temple many things from this procession through the city, which then fell to the share of the priests performing the sacrifice. After their return, feasts and dances were organized during which again every possible honour was done to the poor sacrificial victims. Once this rejoicing was over, the high priest undressed them in turn and led each one separately onto the platform of the temple, where a stone statue of an idol stood in front of the towers. Here the unfortunate man was laid upon his back and bound hand and foot. Once again dancing took place around him and all sorts of commissions were entrusted to him for the god. Finally the priest who was to carry out the sacrifice and who enjoyed no small esteem among the rest of the priests, stepped up, slit open the breast of the wretched man with a sharp stone knife, accompanying this act both before and after with cruciform signs, tore out the heart still warm and palpitating and offered it to the high priest. He pressed the bleeding heart to the idol's mouth, sprayed a few drops towards the sun, or if it were at night, towards the stars, sprinkled blood into the mouths of the rest of the idols, and finally smeared the lintel of the temple door of the chief idol. Once this holy deed was accomplished, the heart was burned and the ashes kept as a relic. In the same way certain other parts of the body of the sacrificial victim were burned, and these ashes too were preserved, though separated from the first.[26]

At another ceremony in honour of the god of spring, Xipe Totec, the victim was flayed after death and the priests of the god of spring dressed themselves in his skin which symbolised the new skin that the earth acquires in spring.

Women and children were also sacrificed, usually slaves delivered up for this purpose by the peoples who had been conquered. The women executed a solemn dance and while the dance was still going on priests dressed in black glided up to them and cut off their heads. Child sacrifices offered to the rain god Tlaloc were often particularly cruel; for it was considered that children who cried particularly loudly and shed many tears helped to make the earth fertile.

The attitude towards death of those being sacrificed, in so far as they belonged to the culture of the Nahua and largely shared the religion of the Aztecs, was paradoxical. The natural fear of death and every man's will to live was mingled with the firm belief that by means of their sacrifice there would be an escape from the shadowy existence of Mictlan and as warriors they would ride through the heavens side by side with the sun. The warrior from Tlaxcala mentioned already, Tlahuicole, whose life was spared by the Aztecs and who commanded an army for them in distant Michoacán, asked on his return from his victorious campaign that he should now be sacrificed so that he might take his place beside the sun. Those Aztecs who were captured by others and who succeeded in escaping into their own ranks were, as far as the members of the nobility were concerned, sacrificed by their own people since they were now dedicated to the sun.

The human sacrifices were the aspect of Aztec culture that most repelled the Spaniards and other Europeans. They finally constituted for the Spaniards the moral justification for the conquest of the Aztec Empire. It must however be stated that from a moral standpoint there is hardly any perceptible difference between the Spanish priests who burned a heretic in order to save his soul and to protect the faithful from his heresy and the Aztec priests, who sacrificed a prisoner in order to send his soul to paradise and to offer food to the gods. It should be added that after the Spanish Conquest the number of Indians who perished as a result of Spanish ferocity far exceeded the number of Aztec sacrifices.

Human sacrifices were not invented by the Aztecs, and similar practices were carried out by many peoples in other parts of the world. In Mesoamerica the Toltecs practised human sacrifice and so did the Maya in the post-classic period, and there is reason to suppose that such sacrifices had already existed in Teotihuacan. Nevertheless it was only among the Aztecs that they developed such massive proportions. It is said that on the occasion of the dedication of the great temple in Tenochtitlan in the year 1487 between twenty and eighty thousand human sacrifices were made. Chroniclers relate that prisoners waited in four long columns which stretched over a distance of four kilometres in order to be sacrificed. The Chief Speaker Ahuitzotl and his deputy, who performed the sacrifices, tore bleeding hearts out of bodies for hours until they collapsed from exhaustion. Conservative estimates of the number of human sacrifices are reckoned to have been about fifteen thousand a year during the last decades of Aztec rule. The question naturally arises how there came to be this many prisoners. Were the Aztec campaigns of conquest sufficient to account for so great a number? It must be said that Aztec military strategy was largely directed towards the taking of prisoners. The rewards a warrior received, the esteem he enjoyed, the pay he received and the possibilities of advancement open to him were all subject to one single yardstick: the number of prisoners he had taken. This was soon to become the only criterion for achievements in battle. This strategy of not killing the enemy but taking him prisoner could result in military successes so long as the enemy followed a similar policy. But as soon as the Aztecs encountered enemies whose first aim was to annihilate their adversaries and to take no prisoners, they were bound to be at a serious disadvantage. This proved to be the case when the Aztecs came up against the Spaniards.

Despite a strategy that was exclusively directed towards obtaining prisoners of war, it must have become increasingly difficult to find the desired number of sacrifices. The problem became proportionately worse as the distance of the battlegrounds from the cities of the Triple Alliance increased: the stronger the Aztecs became the more states voluntarily joined their ranks. And since the population density was less in the lowlands than on the plateau the number of warriors who could be used in sacrifice was proportionately reduced. Moreover the great distances made it inconvenient to bring great numbers of prisoners to Tenochtitlan. There was of course the possibility of substituting other sacrifices and this did in fact happen. Slaves were often sacrificed, and some peoples had to deliver tribute in the form of men and women intended for sacrifice. The Aztecs however were not willing either on religious or political grounds to allow this kind of sacrifice to become too general. From a religious point of view the sacrificial value of a slave was incomparably less than that of a warrior taken prisoner in battle. In the ritual eating of the sacrifices there was a conviction that their strength was being absorbed. Therefore, a very special value was attached to the sacrifice of a valiant warrior who had defended himself to the last. From a political point of view the possibilities of sacrificing slaves – at least until the end of the fifteenth century – were limited by the structure of slavery itself, as will be described.

The insistence on increased sacrifice beyond a certain minimum from the conquered peoples would have resulted in a serious shock to the whole Aztec governmental structure. So long as the number of sacrifices demanded was low the conquered states could usually offer foreign or asocial elements from their own ranks to the Aztecs. If however the demand for victims exceeded a certain minimum, it would become necessary for subject states to seize innocent members of their own people, and this would undoubtedly have led to riots and revolts. The Aztecs might even so have resorted to this means had they not seen a much more convenient solution. A number of city states close to the Valley of Mexico had not yet been overthrown by the Aztecs. This applied in particular to Tlaxcala and Huejotzingo.

Human sacrifice was a feature of the religion of both of these city states and with them the Aztecs made special treaties, probably unique in history, with regard to a 'War of Flowers'. It was agreed that battles should take place at stated times between the members of these states and the Aztecs, the sole aim being to enable both sides to take prisoners of war. The battle was not intended to lead to operations of conquest, and in times which were not suitable for war, either on economic grounds or because of natural disasters, it should not take place. The idea behind this unique kind of warfare was very clearly expressed by the Chief Speaker's Deputy of the Aztecs, Tlacaellel. He compared the place where the ritual battle was fought with a market, at which the food for the gods was acquired:

This Tianguez [Aztec for market] . . . shall take place in Tlaxcala and Huetzingo, so say I, Tlacaellel; for, if we were to place it further away, for instance in Yopitzingo, Michoacan or in Huasteca, or near those coasts . . . it would be transferring it to very distant provinces, not easily accessible to our armies. They are very remote regions, and we must admit that our God does not care for the flesh of those barbarians. He considers it to be bad and tasteless food instead of white and wholesome since, as I say, they speak a foreign tongue and are barbarians. Therefore our markets and our festivals shall only take place in these six cities which I have named . . . the inhabitants of which will constitute warm food which has only just left the oven tender for our God. And this war shall be so organised that our aim will not be to destroy these cities, but that they shall always remain standing so that whenever we might wish to do so and whenever our God might desire to eat and to enjoy himself, we can come there just like anyone who goes to the market in order to buy food.[27]

These battles, which might perhaps be compared to medieval jousts in Europe had the price not been so bloody, lasted until the arrival of the Spaniards.

Did the Triple Alliance spare Tlaxcala which alone of these cities kept its complete independence until the sixteenth century, as they later maintained, in order to have a permanent supply of sacrifices for their war? Or was the War of Flowers a recognition of their inability to conquer this city, as its inhabitants later told the Spaniards? It is difficult to give a definite answer to this question. Whatever the case, these wars brought about a very peculiar relationship between the Triple Alliance and their opposite numbers in the War of Flowers. For instance after the battles with Tlaxcala and Huejotzingo their rulers were secretly invited to Tenochtitlan. There they attended the great ceremonies at which most of the members of their own army were sacrificed, and returned with rich gifts from the Aztecs to their homeland. This kind of attitude, which seems unthinkable to a European, was not at all illogical to the peoples of the Mexican plateau. The sacrifice of their own followers was after all in a certain sense also a celebration; they thereby contributed towards the food for the gods and the sacrifices turned out to their benefit in the last resort through their journey into a better life.

With regard to human sacrifice among the Aztecs, a fundamental question must be postulated. Many peoples throughout the world have practised human sacrifice, especially agricultural peoples, where sacrifices were closely connected with fertility rites. Nevertheless there are few instances where human sacrifice attained the massive proportions it did among the Aztecs. Above all they usually ceased the moment that larger states became consolidated and the execution of prisoners of war was seen to be an economically unsound policy since they could rather be used for the benefit of the entire population or of the ruling class. In such cases the importance of human sacrifices diminished and they were largely replaced by animal sacrifices, or the sacrificial ceremony was carried out symbolically. Did religious faith in fact transcend powerful and important economic interests among the Aztecs? Or did no fundamental contradiction exist between the economic and political interests of the Aztec Empire and the mass execution of prisoners of war?

It must be emphasised at once that human sacrifices, through the terror that they spread, helped to consolidate the power of the Aztecs and prevented subject peoples from rebelling. This reign of terror was all the more important to the Aztecs in that they maintained no garrisons in most of the conquered territories to enforce their power. The fear of possible human sacrifices played a far from insignificant role among the subject peoples. The Spanish *conquistadores* described this very meaningfully after they had begun to negotiate with one of the Aztec subject peoples, the Totonaca, in Cempoala, in the present state of Veracruz.

While we were holding speech with the captain [writes Bernal Diaz], a few Indians came out of the city in great haste, in order to tell the captains who were speaking with Cortés that five Mexicans, tax collectors for Montezuma, had just arrived. When the captains heard this, they grew pale, trembled with fear, left Cortés forthwith and hurried to receive the Mexican. In a trice they had decorated a room with flowers, prepared a meal for the Mexicans, especially a great deal of cocoa which is their best drink . . .

As soon as they had eaten, the Mexicans called the fat captain [the Spaniards had so named the captain of Cempoala with whom they were treating] and the other captains and expressed their annoyance that they should have received us in their houses; for now they would be forced to ally themselves with us, which would not please their Lord Montezuma; they should not have received us or given us any jewellery without his consent and without his orders and they therefore hurled many threats at the fat captain and at the other leaders and at once demanded that they should place at their disposal 20 Indians, men and women, in order to silence the gods because of the wrong which had been done to them.[28]

Cook in an interesting hypothesis describes human sacrifices as 'population planning'. He presumes that after the great famines there were attempts to reduce population and he has estimated that human sacrifices increased the death rate among the plateau peoples by fifteen per cent, a not inconsiderable figure.[29]

But however this idea is viewed the question still remains: was not the sacrifice of so many people in stark contradiction to the economic interests of the Aztec state and of the upper classes of the Triple Alliance cities? Surely they lost a great deal by not selling these prisoners of war, who represented a powerful labour potential, in the slave markets as in ancient Rome? Was it not in their interest to divide them among the rulers of the cities of the Triple Alliance in the same way as the land and jewellery? Would it not have been to the state's advantage if prisoners had been used as state slaves for the great public building programmes, as was the case in Greece or Rome? One can only say that slaves of this kind found no place in Mexican society. Both the ruling class of the cities of the Triple Alliance and the state itself disposed in the matter of tribute dues and bondsmen of far cheaper, more diligent and less dangerous labour forces. The reason for this will be further described below when considering the problem of tribute and of slavery.

Would it not have been more rational, as in the case of the Inca, to send the slaves home so that they might work for the Aztecs there? The chance to do this was very small. A considerable number of slaves came from areas such as Tlaxcala or Huejotzingo or from the still more distant region of Tarascan Michoacan which had never been subject to the Aztecs. There they would merely have increased the number of warriors. A considerable number of the prisoners came from regions which, although subject to the Aztecs, nevertheless belonged to the more distant provinces of the 'Aztec Empire'. The tribute paid by these provinces was however so little that the presence or absence of these men made very little difference to the capacity for payment.

Without exaggeration it can be stated that there was no fundamental contradiction between the economic and political interests of the nobility in the cities of the Triple Alliance and the mass executions of prisoners of war. Such a contradiction might have occurred if the cities of the Triple Alliance had conquered the whole of Mesoamerica, if their empire had reached a completely different level of integration than it showed at the time of the Spanish Conquest. As it was the gods were able freely to grow fat on their bloody nourishment. Their servants on earth had no use for it.

Was the religion of the Aztecs suited to be an imperial cult maintained by the state? The religions of great empires, however much they may differ, nearly all have certain tendencies in common: a close administrative association between the religious and the temporal hierarchy coupled with divine justification of the existing social order, particularly the power of the ruling classes. At the same time they offer the comfort of religion to the conquered, which could extend from the promise of a better life in the hereafter to the performance of activities ordinarily forbidden in the shape of religious ceremonies.

Administratively the religious hierarchy of the cities of the Triple Alliance was closely associated with the temporal power, but in content the religion of the peoples of the Valley of Mexico bore the features of an imperial religion only in a very limited degree. The Aztecs were convinced that they were a chosen people, whose mission consisted in feeding the sun with human sacrifices. This faith justified their campaigns of conquest but did not legalise their overlordship. It could even be turned against them. A conquered people which rose up and sacrificed Aztec warriors to the gods had equally done its duty by the gods. Essentially it was a religion with a dual aspect by which conquests and revolts against the conquerors were equally justified. It offered religious comfort to those who were sacrificed, but not to those who were overthrown, who worked and did forced labour for the Aztecs all their lives. Furthermore the continuously developing state bureaucracy – except for those members who were killed in wars – was rewarded for its services in this life but not in the next world.

It is therefore not surprising that in the fifteenth and sixteenth centuries great efforts were made to change the religion of the cities of the Triple Alliance. These efforts assumed two different aspects, depending on the city state concerned. The first and most radical attempt to revise existing religious ideas sprang from the city state of Tetzcoco, which was allied to the Aztecs. The originator was the Chief Speaker of the city, Netzahualcoyotl. He advocated a belief in one almighty god, In Tloque Nahuaque. The conviction was expressed that life after death did not depend on the way of dying but on the way of living. Netzahualcoyotl spoke at the same time in favour of reducing human sacrifice. These efforts came about partly as a result of the fact that Tetzcoco had become the intellectual centre of the Valley of Mexico and partly because Netzahualcoyotl was undoubtedly the greatest thinker of ancient Mexico. It was an attempt to rationalise and systematise the existing religion. At the same time there was the desire to link it more closely to concrete imperial requirements. The growing bureaucracy and the conquered peoples were now assured of being rewarded for their loyalty in this life by a better life in the hereafter. The concept of one almighty god would halt the endless rise of the Aztec god Huitzilopochtli, Humming-bird on the Left, and lead instead to the erection of an almighty god in whose creation no state could claim a monopoly. In view of the ever decreasing power of Tetzcoco in comparison with its mighty allies these efforts remained largely illusory. The cult of the Almighty Being, In Tloque Nahuaque, remained confined to a small clique round Netzahualcoyotl, and never received imperial recognition.

The religious aspirations which finally gave the Aztec religion a new stamp and the chance of adapting itself to the requirements of the empire came not from Tetzcoco but from Tenochtitlan. No abstract godhead, but the deification of the Chief Speaker of the Aztecs was to legitimise Tenochtitlan's dominion not only over the conquered peoples but over the allied cities as well. The deification of Aztec rulers took place towards the end of the fifteenth and the beginning of the sixteenth centuries. The Chief Speaker was now regarded as the divine successor of the sun and the government ordained by him was believed to be willed by the gods. This super-human character gave colour to the origins of the whole of the upper class, which was now regarded as a creation of the gods. It also appears that certain beliefs developed that allowed these ruling classes of divine origin to expect a better life after death.

At the time the Spaniards arrived in Mexico, the ideology of this divine ruler bore the stamp of the official religion although neither among the Aztecs themselves nor among the peoples conquered by them had it succeeded in superseding the old ideas entirely.

THE RULERS OF THE CITIES OF THE TRIPLE ALLIANCE

The comprehensive historical traditions of the peoples of the central Mexican plateau enable us to describe the personalities who contributed decisively to the rise of the cities of the Triple Alliance.

The following held the office of Chief Speaker of the Aztecs after the overthrow of Atzcapotzalco until the end of the fifteenth century:

Itzcoatl (1427–40)
Moctezuma Ilhuicamina (1440–69)
   Often known to historians as Moctezuma I, a son of the earlier Chief Speaker Huitzilihuitl. He was succeeded by three brothers, all of whom were descendants of the first Chief Speaker of the Aztecs, Acamapichtli.
Axayactl (1469–81)
Tizoc (1481–6)
Ahuitzotl (1486–1503)

The two most important personalities who paved the way for the Triple Alliance to become a world power are nevertheless not among them. These were the Chief Speaker of Tetzcoco, Netzahualcoyotl, 'Hungry Coyote', and the deputy of the Chief Speaker of the Aztecs, Tlacaellel.

There is no personality in the history of Mesoamerica about whom there are more legends, incidents and stories told than about Netzahualcoyotl. Fortunately for the historian they are not obscured by the mythological and religious undercurrents so characteristic of the descriptions of Toltec rulers. The ruler of Tetzcoco lent wings to the romantic representations of his contemporaries and successors to an extent that was unique in Mesoamerica. This may have had something to do with the fact that none of the leading personalities of the cities of the Triple Alliance had fallen so low before his ascent. As an eighteen-year-old boy Netzahualcoyotl had to flee his native city of Tetzcoco and live to see the murder of his father by order of the ruler of Atzcapotzalco.

He lived in exile for many years and from there built up Tetzcoco's resistance against the foreign conquerors. After he had allied himself with the Aztecs, and the Triple Alliance had beaten the armies of Atzcapotzalco, he returned victorious as Chief Speaker to Tetzcoco.

The romantic destiny of Netzahualcoyotl does not, however, fully explain his popularity or the special role that he played in Mesoamerica. This is accounted for by the particular situation of his native city and by his extraordinary intellectual abilities. Although the same rights in the Triple Alliance were granted to Tetzcoco as to Tenochtitlan, its power fell further and further behind that of the Aztec capital. Its situation on the salt lake of Tetzcoco made a productive chinampa system of agriculture impossible, thereby reducing the density of population of that town below that of Tenochtitlan. In addition the military organisation and experience of the Aztecs, thanks to their activities as mercenaries over many years, were more significant than that of other peoples in the Valley of Mexico.

Could these disadvantages be evened out? Was it possible to avoid being swallowed up by one's ally? Netzahualcoyotl wanted to avoid a confrontation with Tenochtitlan that from the outset would have had no chance of success. On the contrary he encouraged the warmest and best possible relations with the Aztecs, and as long as he lived differences of opinion were reduced to the minimum. The method he chose to stand up to Tenochtitlan was different. Industry and the exercise of inelligence were to make up for natural disadvantages. Tetzcoco became the largest and most important scientific and artistic centre in Mesoamerica and the first city of the Triple Alliance to build comprehensive irrigation works, those of Tetzcutzingo already described.

Netzahualcoyotl sent for representatives of more than thirty different crafts from all parts of Mesoamerica to come to Tetzcoco. There the craftsmen received houses and land and were settled in their own quarters of the city. Together with the merchants they were allowed representation and a voice in the authoritative city councils.

At this time Tetzcoco was unique in the Valley of Mexico in its achievements in science, technology and art. The great technical innovations such as the mighty irrigation works in the network of lakes in Mexico were created with substantial co-operation from skilled artisans from Tetzcoco. In addition Tetzcoco became the centre of poetry and literature, and the most important works were written there. No wonder, for the greatest poet ancient Mexico produced was the Hungry Coyote. Not without reason have his poems been described by modern critics as philosophical. They are especially unexpected in view of the bloody sacrificial rites practised in the cities of the Triple Alliance. They show great depth of feeling and represent a combination of mourning over the brief transitoriness of life, epicurean cries after the joys of earthly life and a striving to discover the meaning of life, and aspirations towards a creed – sensations which differed widely from the customary and official conceptions of the inhabitants of the Valley of Mexico.

I can descry that which is secret, that which is hidden from us. My Lords! We are but mortal men. All of us must go hence. All of us here on earth must perish.
We shall be rubbed out like a drawing.
We shall wither away on the earth like a flower.
Think thereon, ye Lords, ye Eagles and Tigers,
Even though ye are made of jade, even though ye had been made of gold, ye too must go thither, where ye will find those who have been flayed.
We shall one day all of us perish, and none of us will be left.

The search for an almighty god was in some measure an answer to the above plea.

O Creator of Life, happiness comes down from Thee. It is Thou that givest us beauty, sweet scented flowers, beautiful flowers.[30]

Other poems that are in startling contrast are hymns to life, fortune, happiness and flowers which add beauty to the whole of life. Poems which sing of human sacrifices and the divine mission of feeding the gods are not among his works. Netzahualcoyotl succeeded in gaining for Tetzcoco a leading position which lasted for several decades within the Triple Alliance, and later an outstanding position therein. No decision was taken by the Aztecs without Netzahualcoyotl's agreement. Throughout his reign, he succeeded in gaining for Tetzcoco two-fifths of all rich booty captured thus contributing to a significant boom in the fortunes of his city.

The most outstanding personality among the Aztecs was quite different. The differences between him and Netzahualcoyotl in some respects symbolise the differences between Tetzcoco and Tenochtitlan. This personality was never Chief Speaker of the Aztecs, but a man who outwardly always acted as the Chief Speaker's deputy, as the Snake Woman, the brother of the Chief Speaker Moctezuma I, Tlacaellel. This man, who lived from 1400 until about 1480, influenced three Chief Speakers during his term of office. He appears to have been the *eminence grise* behind them though some historians doubt this. Several chronicles emphasise that no decision was taken without his agreement and it is constantly related that he was able to contradict the Chief Speakers, who invariably followed his advice. When an attempt was made after the death of one of the Chief Speakers to elect him to this office, he replied 'I am the ruler and you have regarded me as such. How can I be still more of a ruler?'[31]

His power was primarily the result of his personality. Neither before nor after him had an incumbent of the Office of Cihuacoatl even approached such a role. If we attempt to apply current expressions to the pre-Spanish past of Mesoamerica, we would call him the 'ideologist of Aztec imperialism'. The three great tendencies which characterise the development of Tenochtitlan in the second half of the fifteenth century, internal government by the military caste, external expansion and the religious conception of human sacrifice, may not be attributable to his influence. But he indubitably made a significant contribution in providing them with an ideological justification. The treaty already mentioned between the military caste and the Aztec people, made before the overthrow of Atzcapotzalco and which gave power into the hands of the military caste, was attributed to him. He was the first leader clearly and unequivocally to formulate the demand for human sacrifices, which then served equally as a justification for Aztec conquests and for the making of sacrifices. Finally it was he who ordered all pictograms to be destroyed so that no other account of the past or of the history of the Aztecs but that formulated by himself could exist. Beside this 'ideological' activity he seems to have busied himself with being a planner of all wars, a strategist and tactician of the first order. Every campaign undertaken by the Aztecs was discussed in detail between him, the war council and the Chief Speaker.

However bloody his theories were, it would be wrong to insist that he was a fanatic obsessed with killing. Where killing was contrary to the economic interests of Aztec expansion he commanded that it should stop. There is a story that after the outbreak of a rising against the Aztecs in the recently conquered city state of Cuetaxtla the Chief Speaker expressed himself in favour of exterminating the whole population as punishment. Tlacaellel very sharply opposed this plan. He declared that after the rebels of Cuetaxtla had been overcome their tribute should be doubled and this punishment would have to suffice: 'For it would be inconvenient, indeed impossible, to annihilate localities which were so rich: for there would be nobody who would be prepared to settle there.[32]

This Machiavelli of Aztec politics died when he was over eighty years old. He indicated, more than any other Aztec leader, the way that was to lead Tenochtitlan from being a down-trodden, tribute-paying village to becoming a world power.

All other men who played a leading role in the Triple Alliance in the fifteenth century pale in comparison with these two powerful personalities. The three first Chief Speakers of the Aztecs, Itzcoatl, Moctezuma I and Axayacatl, who ruled in Tenochtitlan during and following the overthrow of Atzcapotzalco, were greatly overshadowed by Tlacaellel. The first two are recognised as having been conquerors, while the third does not quite fit in with them. Under his leadership the Aztecs suffered their greatest defeat since the conquest of Atzcapotzalco.

A great army led by Axayacatl attempted to conquer the realm of the Tarascans west of the Valley of Mexico in the modern state of Michoacan, and was literally put to flight. This defeat not only spelt the collapse of the Aztec aspiration to conquer the Tarascan realm but at the same time severely damaged their prestige in the eyes of the conquered peoples. This is clearly expressed in a poem left by Axayacatl:

I, your grandfather Axayacatl am ashamed, I have come to the end, I despise myself . . .
The true Mexica, my grandsons, hold fast and stay in rank and file.
Their drums sound and their shields remain firmly in their hands.

But he quite clearly replies to critics at once with the lines:

We, your grandfathers, still live on. Our spear-slings, our spears are still mighty. How many victories have they not helped us to win?
I, your grandfather, scoff at your effeminate weapons, at your effeminate shields.
Conquerors of olden days, arise.[33]

Axayacatl's grief was well founded. He suffered not only because of the lost might of the Aztecs, not only because of his lost prestige among his own people, but because, in addition, he had forfeited his own life. The power of a Chief Speaker depended to a great extent on his success in war. Other conquests which Axayacatl had made and the power of Tlacaellel, who was still alive at the time, probably protected him from a violent death. His brother and successor, Tizoc, however, who had no conquests to show, was poisoned five years after succeeding to office.

Tizoc's successor, his brother Ahuitzotl, was determined to put an end to the stagnation that had taken place under the rule of his brothers. While he was in power conquests and human sacrifices reached an all-time peak. It was Ahuitzotl who dedicated the great pyramid of Tenochtitlan with the sacrifice of between twenty and eighty thousand human beings. His armies advanced furthest into the lowlands: great tracts of the present state of Oaxaca and of the Huaxteca in modern Veracruz were conquered. Aztec armies reached the frontier of modern Guatemala. He was so feared among the peoples of Mesoamerica that even today in some parts of Mexico a feared opponent is called a *huizote*.

Inwardly however this ferocious conqueror was a man of peace and reconciliation. Under his rule peace was made with the merchants of the neighbouring city of Tlatelolco which had meantime been conquered. They received extensive privileges, and even battles were waged to protect them. At the same time, Ahuitzotl tried to re-establish certain aspects of the original democratic administration of the Aztecs, which had slowly begun to disappear. Service rather than birth largely determined his choice of people nominated for the highest offices of state. This was carried to such lengths that his successor Moctezuma II complained bitterly that Ahuitzotl had appointed 'men of low birth' to be his advisers. It is typical of this man's character that the sentimental lyrical poems composed by so many rulers of the cities of the Triple Alliance are not associated with him. When he died, the Aztec Empire had reached the zenith of its development.

A completely different spirit informs the descriptions of the Chief Speakers of Tetzcoco and their court. In the case of Tetzcoco one is strongly reminded of the courtly intrigues of a medieval palace. Not that the son of Netzahualcoyotl, Netzahualpilli, Chief Speaker of Tetzcoco from 1472 to 1516, may not have been a considerable conqueror. He took part in all the great Aztec campaigns and constantly extended the domain of Tetzcoco. All the same he is known rather in other connections: for his achievements in the spheres of jurisprudence, art and poetry and for his singular and unhappy emotional life, sung in innumerable legends and poems of the peoples of the Valley of Mexico. He had the misfortune to marry a Mexican 'Messalina', Chalchiuhnenetzin, the 'Heart of Green Stone'. This woman had a sinister habit. She made love with any man who happened to take her fancy and then had him murdered. In order however not to forget him, she had a statue erected of the murdered lover. When Netzahualpilli discovered more and more of such statues in his wife's apartments, he asked her what they meant. She replied that they were statues of her gods. When the betrayed husband finally discovered the truth he had her executed, just as Claudius executed Messalina.

Netzahualpilli continued his father's policy of making Tetzcoco the centre of art and science. Great new palaces were erected under his rule and the town made more beautiful and finely decorated. Like his father, he was one of the most important poets of his age and like his father he mourned the transitoriness of life.

My heart is filled with grief,
I am the young Netzahualpilli.
I seek for my captains.
The Lord of the glorious Quetzal, the young and mighty warrior has gone from us.
The blue sky is now his dwelling place.
Will Tlatohuetzin and Acapipiyol perchance come hither where I stand weeping to enjoy with me a heady draught?[34]

Again like his father he largely opposed the existing religion and sought comfort in a higher divinity, In Tloque Nahuaque. In contrast to him however he lived to witness the decline of his city and the ever increasing power of the Aztecs. When he died, Tetzcoco had declined into being almost a province of Tenochtitlan.

THE ZENITH OF AZTEC POWER

When in 1502, seventy-five years after the conquest of Atzcapotzalco, Moctezuma Xocoyotzin, who was to be defeated by the Spaniards, was elected Chief Speaker, the cities of the Triple Alliance and the regions under their rule had very little in common with those which had existed seventy-five years earlier.

Tenochtitlan had developed in three-quarters of a century from a small city state into a world city in the true sense of the word. This was clear from the size and structure of the population and from the external appearance of the city, which had grown both in height and in breadth. Its growth upwards was apparent in its gigantic and mighty buildings, which tens of thousands of people, assembled from all parts of the valley, helped to build. Its expansion was the result of the overthrow of the neighbouring island city of Tlatelolco in 1473, which was then annexed to Tenochtitlan. Perhaps even more important was a further conquest, that of the waters of the lakes. New Chinampas, the artificial islands already mentioned, were always being constructed. The city has been estimated to have covered about 750 hectares.

No one can give so clear an impression of the grandiose character of the city as the *conquistadores* under Cortés, who were the first, last and only eyewitnesses from the Old World. As a measure of comparison many of them were also familiar with Rome and other Italian cities and some had even reached Constantinople. Bernal Diáz describes his first impressions after he had reached, with Cortés's troops, the city of Itztapalapa on the shores of the Lake of Mexico.

. . . In the morning we arrived at a broad causeway and continued our march towards Itztapalapa, and when we saw so many cities, and villages built in the water and other great towns on dry land and that straight level causeway going towards Mexico, we were amazed and said that it was like the enchantments they tell of in the legend of Amadis, on account of the great towers and pyramids and buildings rising from the water and all built of masonry. And some of our soldiers even asked whether the things that we saw were not a dream?

Gazing on such wonderful sights we did not know what to say or whether what appeared before us was real; for on one side on the land, there were great cities and in the lake ever so many more, and the lake itself was crowded with canoes, and in the causeway were many bridges at intervals, and in front of us stood the great City of Mexico, and we – we did not even number four hundred soldiers.[35]*

* I have again used Maudesley's translation of Castillo, II, pp. 37–40 (translator's note).

Three very different clusters of buildings formed the centre of the city. The religious centre was the great *Teocalli*, a huge complex of buildings consisting of temples and pyramids, surrounded on all sides by a wall 1½ metres high, decorated with serpents' heads.

The chief mosque [thus Cortés described the temple of the Aztecs] stands on a great plaza, whose circumference is surrounded by an eight-foot high wall. Its extent is so great that houses to hold 500 people could be built within its confines. The wall is laid out as a large square, and is furnished with huge towers and pinnacles. Houses are built along them with long alleys for the priests and monks. The Temple itself is higher than the Cathedral of Seville. It has the appearance of a four cornered pyramid of four tremendous stairways. At the summit of the wide platform, which is reached by a wide exterior stairway, there stand two tower temples made of polished stone and carved woodwork, in which the huge idols are enthroned. The walls around them are richly decorated and painted with all manner of monsters and singular figures. Here too are the graves of the Kings. Each of these two temples was dedicated to a different idol . . .

From the main hall of the Temple narrow doorways lead to small chapels, where smaller idols stand. Those rooms were all full of human blood which had been spilled during the sacrifices.[36]

Beside this giant pyramid, which rose above the whole city of Tenochtitlan, there were a wide variety of other buildings in the great *Teocalli*. The Spaniards noticed particularly a circular building in a style used nowhere else in Tenochtitlan, which was dedicated to the Feathered Serpent.

A little way apart from the great Pyramid there was another small tower which was also an idol house, or a true hell, for it had at the opening of one gate a most terrible mouth such as they depict, saying that such there are in hell. The mouth was open with great fangs to devour souls, and here too were some groups of devils and bodies of serpents close to the door, and a little way off was a place of sacrifice all blood-stained and black with smoke, and encrusted with blood, and there were many great *ollas* and *cántaros* and *tinajas* [names of various large pottery vessels for holding water and cooking] of water inside the house, for it was here that they cooked the flesh of the unfortunate Indians who were sacrificed, which was eaten by the priests.[37]*

In addition there were a number of other temples in this *Teocalli* as well as the school for priests, *Calmecac*, and a great plaza for the ritual ball-game.

The city's secular and administrative centre nearby consisted of the palaces of the ruler, of his deputy and of his predecessors. With never-ending astonishment the Spaniards describe the luxury, the size and proportions of the palaces of the last Moctezuma. The palaces were gigantic two-storey buildings. Access to air and light was available

* Maudesley's translation, II, pp. 80–1 (translator's note).

mostly through doors that opened into the inner patios of the palaces. They contained the living-quarters of the rulers, mostly on the second floor, the quarters of some of the higher officials and a number of the most important official rooms such as those used for legal sessions.

In the patios large gardens were laid out, and the palace of the last Moctezuma contained a huge menagerie.

Now I must tell you a few things about the court of the Lord Moctezuma, which I must freely admit to your Imperial Majesty [wrote Cortés], that I do not know where I should begin or end. I am only able to recount very little about it. How great must the power of this barbarian prince be and how immense must his wealth be in that he, as I have already told you, possesses everything under the sky, idols of gold, silver, precious stones and feather work.[38]

The economic centre of the city consisted of the huge market of Tlatelolco, where the Spaniards estimated that between sixty and eighty thousand people traded daily.

The city has many plazas, where there are always markets being held dealing in foodstuffs and all manner of merchandise [Cortés writes]. The main plaza in the middle of the city, twice the size of the one in Salamanca, is surrounded by columns. Day after day 60,000 people congregate here to buy and sell. Every imaginable kind of merchandise is available from all parts of the Empire, foodstuffs and dress, and in addition objects made of gold, silver, copper . . . precious stones, leather, bone, mussels, coral, cotton, feathers: finely polished and unpolished stones are on sale, burned and un-burned clay bricks, chalk, planed and unplaned beams and boards of every description. In a particular plaza, all sorts of birds are sold: turkeys, wild fowl, quails, . . . all kinds of vegetables are also obtainable, salads, onions, garlic, hellebore, artichokes, water-cress and so on . . . Maize is offered for sale either as grain or also in loaves. Game and fish are available raw, cooked or salted . . . The various wares may only be sold in the appointed plazas, a rule strictly kept. Everything is sold by the piece or by measurement, never by weight.

In the main market there is a law court in which there are always 10 or 12 judges performing their office and taking decisions on all marketing con-troversies. They also have the power to administer punishment. Furthermore overseers always go round and examine the measures of the salesmen and I have frequently seen them taking away a false measure and breaking it.[39]

Bernal Diaz was no less impressed by the market than Cortés:

When we arrived at the great market place, called Tlatelolco, we were astounded at the number of people and the quantity of merchandise that it contained, and at the good order and control that was maintained, for we had never seen such a thing before . . . I could wish that I had finished telling of all things which are sold there, but they are so numerous and of such different quality and the great market place with its surrounding arcades was so crowded with people that one would not have been able to see and inquire about it all in two days.[40]*

Tenochtitlan was in some respects not unlike Venice; the city's streets consisted mostly of canals, and the principal means of transport was by boat. Even where there were solid footways, a canal ran alongside and there was hardly anywhere in the city that could not be reached by water. A considerable proportion of the upper-class houses were near to the palaces and the great *Teocalli* and were built in two storeys. The houses of the ordinary people had one storey. A feature common to them all was the complete absence of windows, and the fact that they were mostly whitewashed and built round inner patios. Apart from the market and the great *Teocalli*, where the people flocked together for religious ceremonies, and in front of the small temples and pyramids which existed in every quarter of the city and housed the local deities, life was carried on not in the streets but primarily in the inner patios. Even the simplest were richly decorated with flowers.

In the life of such an enormous city there is a great variety of problems, from the provision of food and fresh water for the population or the question of communication between the island city and the mainland, to the disposal of sewage and refuse. Despite the highly productive *Chinampa* system of agriculture practised by the peasants of Tenochtitlan, probably only a fraction of the city's food requirements could be provided domestically by the end of the fifteenth and the beginning of the sixteenth centuries. Most of the supplies had to be brought from the mainland. The chief means of transport by which they reached the city was canoe. It is estimated that between fifty and sixty thousand canoes operated daily between the mainland and Tenochtitlan. Refuse was thrown into the water, while human excrement was carefully collected and used for manure.

Unlike the European cities that flourished at the same time, there do not appear to have been any epidemics in the Aztec cities. The only epidemic reported was smallpox which broke out after the arrival of the Spaniards. The greatest natural danger for the inhabitants of Tenochtitlan was that of flooding. Until the end of the fifteenth century hardly a decade passed in which floods due to heavy rains did not wash away parts of the city. The great dams that were built in the last years of the fifteenth century appear to have lessened but not entirely to have removed this danger.

Tenochtitlan was the largest city in the Valley of Mexico. It extended from the middle of a great network of neighbouring cities, some of which stood on islands although most were situated on the mainland on the shores of the lake. What was Tenochtitlan's population? Probably by the end of the fifteenth century it had nearly reached the

---

* Maudesley's translation, II, pp. 70–1, 73 (translator's note).

proportions it had in the year 1519 at the time of the Conquest. There are in any case unusually wide differences of opinion regarding the size of the population not only of Tenochtitlan but of the whole of Mesoamerica at this time. A study published about thirty years ago estimated the population figure for Mesoamerica on the eve of the Conquest at about three million;[41] a more recent study published in 1966 increased this figure to thirty million.[42] How can these differing views be explained? Without going into the details of demographic calculation, which could fill many volumes, it is necessary at this point to take note of certain problems. In the course of this work some population estimates have already been given, as in the case of Teotihuacan or the Maya city of Tikal. These are estimates that have so far met with little or no opposition, largely because they are based on archaeological excavations. Houses have been dug out, counted and evaluated, or at least attempts made to assess how many people could have inhabited a house at one and the same time and how many dwellings were inhabited in the same period. These methods were however impossible to apply to most of the cities of the Aztec period, and to Tenochtitlan particularly. Tikal and a large part of Teotihuacan were ruined cities that had either been completely abandoned or were only covered by sparse peasant settlements. Since the overthrow of Tenochtitlan, however, the capital city of Mexico has risen in its place making a detailed archaeological excavation quite impossible. What then has been the basis for calculating the population of these cities and of the whole of Mesoamerica? The Aztecs did not carry out a census, but had exact tables of the tribute due for payment by each separate province. But these bore only a conditional relationship to the number of inhabitants in a province. For instance provinces which resisted conquest had to pay a far higher tribute, irrespective of their population, than those that submitted voluntarily. How was it possible in these circumstances, to arrive at a credible estimate? This is one of the most controversial problems. Another concerns the credibility of Spanish sources.

To arrive at the population figure it would be necessary to depend on the testimony of those who had seen the Aztec Empire either at its peak or shortly after the Conquest. These were the *conquistadores* themselves and the priests who followed them to convert the population to Christianity. How reliable are their statements? Were they in any case in a position to estimate the size of the population? If so, did they have an interest in overestimating the number of their enemies in order to place their own deeds in a better light? Did the Catholic priests not tend to exaggerate the number of their converts in order to show how many souls they had set on the right path?

The first reliable census carried out by the Spaniards after the

Conquest of Mexico was made in the year 1565, when the Indian population had greatly diminished. How heavy was the death rate after the Conquest? Did not the priests tend to exaggerate this rate too in order to place more blame on their compatriots whom they held largely responsible? Do the later statements made by various historians regarding the death rate of the Indians after the Conquest not stem from the wish to condemn Spain and to create a dark legend regarding Spanish colonial rule?

A further estimate is based on agricultural productivity in pre-Spanish Mexico. How many people anyway could this agriculture nourish? Are we in a position to estimate exactly where high productivity and less productive forms of agriculture existed?

These are some of the problems that have led to discussion on a very wide scale. As already mentioned there is a tendency now to raise the figure for the population of Mesoamerica on the eve of the Spanish Conquest higher than the three million mark estimated thirty years ago. This is partly because extensive studies of the agricultural system practised in pre-Spanish times have more and more emphatically pointed to its unusual productivity. A number of new documents containing hitherto unpublished accounts of the period following the Conquest bear out the statements of the *conquistadores* and of the first Spanish priests to come to Mexico. Exhaustive examination has increased doubts as to whether all the Spanish *conquistadores* and priests were at pains to exaggerate the number of Indians whom they had either conquered or converted. On the contrary: after the Conquest some of the *conquistadores* tried to give as low a figure as possible in order to avoid taxation charges. Again some of the priests probably recorded the number of Indians within their sphere as lower than it really was in order to prevent too many of them being pressed into the service of Spanish *conquistadores*. Finally recent discoveries made in Mexico and in Brazil, where previously unknown groups of Indians have come into contact with 'civilisation' for the first time, have more than confirmed statements made by earlier chroniclers about the mortality of Indians in such cases. Whole tribes, in the course of a few or often of one decade, were wiped out by illnesses against which they had no powers of resistance. Even the efforts of modern medicine – which of course did not exist in the sixteenth century – were little help in such cases. Most scholars concerned with the problem today believe that a figure of three million for Mesoamerica and sixty thousand for Tenochtitlan is untenable. Nevertheless there is no one opinion concerning the new assessments. The most exhaustive work undertaken recently in this field is a study by Borah and Cook[43] who give a figure of over twenty-five million for the population of central Mexico on the eve of the Conquest and about three hundred and sixty thousand for the united cities of Tenochtitlan and Tlatelolco. These assessments have led to one of the most violent controversies in the history of American studies, controversies which still persist. Borah and Cook proceed from the standpoint that no matter how much individual methods of assessment may differ, taken together they point to a similar figure that probably corresponds with the facts. Their opponents again have doubts as to both the reliability of Spanish sources and the capacity of agriculture practised in pre-Spanish Mexico to feed such a dense population.[44] Undoubtedly further researches into ecology and agriculture in pre-Spanish Mexico will strongly influence these discussions.

In contrast to the differences of opinion about the extent of the whole population of Central Mexico there is greater agreement concerning the population of the capital city. Most scholars incline towards an estimate of about three hundred thousand. This assessment is supported by the fact that the foodstuffs which annually flowed into Tenochtitlan as tribute probably sufficed to feed several hundred thousand people. In that case Tenochtitlan was not only the largest city in pre-Spanish America but one of the largest cities throughout the world in the sixteenth century. It was larger than Madrid or Seville, Rome or Florence. And this at a time when technologically speaking it had no wheel and no draught animals, no metal tools and no plough. Should Borah's and Cook's assessments of the total population of Mesoamerica be confirmed entirely, or as many of their opponents believe, if only fifty per cent of their estimate were confirmed, then many previously held conceptions would have to be revised in the writing of Latin American history. Mexico only reached the twenty-five million mark in the twentieth century; its population in the nineteenth century was eleven million. How was it that a 'neolithic culture' was able to feed a much denser population than a society provided with iron and steel, with the wheel, with horses, cattle and pigs, with wheat and rye, with ships that could sail round the world?

THE LINKS BETWEEN THE CITIES OF THE TRIPLE ALLIANCE

Since the union of Tenochtitlan, Tetzcoco and Tlacopan in a Triple Alliance was founded each city was independent, even though there was no question of full equality. Tlacopan was unquestionably weaker and smaller than its allies, a fact that probably explains why it received only one-fifth and not two-fifths of the tribute paid by conquered territories to the other cities. On the other hand equality of legal status was largely recognised between Tenochtitlan and Tetzcoco, while it was openly conjectured that Tetzcoco functioned as *primus inter pares*.

By the sixteenth century the situation had completely changed; Tenochtitlan and not Tetzcoco was the leading power in the Triple Alliance. This leadership was no longer that of a *primus inter pares* but an unequivocal primacy, continuously developing stronger and clearer features. It expressed itself, *inter alia*, in the fact that only in Tenochtitlan could the final decision be taken concerning war or peace, and above all in that more and more of the tribute intended for the Triple Alliance arrived first of all in Tenochtitlan. It is more than doubtful whether the portions due to the other city states were paid over to them in full measure. Why did this shift in power take place? After the death in 1472 of Netzahualcoyotl his successor Netzahualpilli possessed neither the drive nor the prestige of his father and this was certainly a contributory factor. Furthermore, as many authors have emphasised, the enforcement of militarism in Tenochtitlan played a considerable role in making its army the strongest and most important in the Valley of Mexico.

But the most important reason behind Tenochtitlan's predominance in the Triple Alliance lay elsewhere. During the time of Atzcapotzalco's overthrow Tenochtitlan was hardly larger, perhaps even smaller, than Tetzcoco, but by the end of the fifteenth century its population was double the size of that of Tetzcoco. The disproportionately rapid growth of this city is partly accounted for by the large drainage and irrigation works in the High Valley which made it possible to construct more and more *chinampas*. *Chinampas* of this sort did not of course exist in the salt water lake of Tetzcoco. Tenochtitlan was therefore able to grow much more rapidly than its ally. Perhaps even more important was the conquest of the neighbouring island of Tlatelolco in 1473. The reason for this conquest as told in the chronicles sounds rather peculiar. There is a story that the ruler of Tlatelolco, Moquihuix, had married a sister of the Chief Speaker of the Aztecs, the 'Little Precious Stone'. Since the Little Precious Stone did not alas live up to her very promising name – the chronicles relate that she smelt terrible and was quite thin and ugly – Moquihuix wanted to have nothing to do with her and exiled her to a palace nearby, while he enjoyed himself with his concubines. Deeply shocked by such neglect of his sister, big brother Axayacatl, the Chief Speaker of Tenochtitlan, decided to overthrow Tlatelolco and to punish its ruler. The decisive battle took place in 1473, and Moquihuix was hurled down from the highest pyramid of his city.

The campaign against Tlatelolco was in fact the result of long years of rivalry. In proportion as Tenochtitlan grew and spread, Tlatelolco also grew, probably at the expense of its big neighbour, for the biggest client of Tlatelolco's merchants was undoubtedly the great and rich neighbour to the south. It is not difficult to imagine how the warriors of Tenochtitlan, after a victorious campaign, spent an ever increasing proportion of their spoils in the market place of Tlatelolco on the many kinds of riches on sale there from all parts of Mesoamerica. Nor is it difficult to understand how, exactly as among the European aristocracy of the Middle Ages, hatred against the 'rapacious' merchants grew. The rulers of Tenochtitlan tried several times, but in vain, to stop this 'currency drain', to use a modern expression. The Snake Woman Tlacaellel, declared:

> I, Tlacaellel, would fain fire the brave hearted warriors and also encourage the cowards by rewards which are bestowed on them for special deeds. And to this end I would fain draw a comparison. When ye go to the market and see jewels or fine feathers . . . do ye not desire them and would ye not give all ye possess for them? Now ye should know that it is the will of your ruler in this place, as regards jewels and feathers . . . that brave warriors should no longer buy them, but that the ruler will bestow them in payment for brave . . . deeds. And every man must understand that when he goes to war and does doughty deeds, it is exactly as though he had gone to market, where he then caught sight of all these objects. For after his return, all will be given to him, according to his deserts, in reward for his exertions.[45]

However in face of the enticements of the market in Tlatelolco, these words must have remained a pious hope. It is not surprising therefore that Tenochtitlan set out to overthrow its neighbour, but rather only that it was such a long time before this campaign was put into effect, in fact in 1473. Probably Tenochtitlan waited until it ruled over considerable areas of the lowlands and was no longer exclusively dependent on the merchants of Tlatelolco for products from the tropics. It is also possible that Netzahualcoyotl rejected such a campaign against his ally. Although there is no evidence for such an attitude it is nevertheless significant that the Aztecs only began the conquest of their northern neighbour a year after Netzahualcoyotl's death.

After its defeat Tlatelolco lost its political independence. A military governor was installed, and the merchants in the market were compelled to deliver tribute. Nevertheless the city did not remain merely a conquered city, another addition to the long list of other regions already paying tribute. The enormous importance of trade for an aspiring world city such as Tenochtitlan and perhaps also the strategic position of Tlatelolco in the middle of the network of Mexican lakes, meant that it was very soon absorbed as an almost integral part of Tenochtitlan itself, presumably under the rule of Ahuitzotl. The ruling class of Tlatelolco, the merchants, soon enjoyed privileges and rights in Tenochtitlan, which far surpassed those of a large section of the city's native population.

Finally the shift in power of Tenochtitlan, derived from its rapid growth, resulted in even greater tributes so that it was able to expand far more rapidly than the other cities of the Triple Alliance.

THE AZTEC 'EMPIRE'

By the end of the fifteenth century the Triple Alliance had succeeded in bringing most of the inhabitants of Mesoamerica under its control in one form or another. The area under its control is estimated to have supported between five and fifteen million people. Consisting of thirty-eight provinces, it comprised the major part of the centre, the south-east and the south-west of present-day Mexico. The armies of the Triple Alliance had reached the coast of both the Atlantic and the Pacific Oceans. Yet in spite of these successes the cities of the Triple Alliance were still far from ruling the whole of Mesoamerica. Extensive regions of the Mixtecs and Zapotecs, who inhabited the area of the modern state of Oaxaca, and the Maya city states in the southern part of Mesoamerica were still independent. In the west of Mexico the Tarascans, who inhabited the region of the present state of Michoacan, won a devastating victory in 1480 over an invading army of Aztecs. In the plateau of Mexico finally city states such as Tlaxcala enjoyed an independence from the cities of the Triple Alliance even though they were in a dangerously exposed position.

Nevertheless the region under the dominance of the cities of the Triple Alliance represented the greatest conglomeration of territory, population and power in the history of Mesoamerica; a region demonstrating extraordinary richness and diversity of peoples, languages, religions and forms of social organisation, a diversity which for the most part, in spite of centuries of European occupation, has survived to the present day. Very frequently populations of different ethnic origins and speaking different languages coexisted in one city or village. Many of these states were composed of a centre which could be a large city as well as a small village where the ruling classes lived, and of dependent agrarian regions. They were ruled in very different ways. In some states one Tlatoani held supreme power, in others power was divided between several Tlatoanis. The regions overthrown by the cities of the Triple Alliance ranged from small independent villages through larger city states to regular states, containing hundreds of thousands of inhabitants. Did the victors create out of all this a cohesive, consolidated, viable empire? The degree of integration in these regions was so varied that it is very difficult to give any single answer.

For a long time the difficulties lay in the fact that there was not one but three capital cities in the conquered territories. The organisation of the conquered regions in so far as it existed was in the first place economic in character and directed towards exacting tribute and other benefits from these territories. Tribute was fixed very precisely and entered on pictograms. It was paid every eighty days, or in some cases annually. The Aztecs left behind tribute collectors called *calpixques* in all regions. They were treated with great deference by the inhabitants of the conquered region, and a piece of land was cultivated for them.

Pictograms recording the tribute due by individual provinces have survived, and throw light on the diversity and extent of the wealth that flowed annually into Tenochtitlan from all parts of the empire. Hundreds of different kinds of merchandise, raw materials and worked products, different foods, gold, silver, cotton, cotton textiles, armour made of feathers and cotton, precious stones, rubber and rubber balls, pipes for smoking and so on, reached the capital city in massive quantities. A few figures can give a rough impression of this wealth. A calculation of these foods, based on the average daily consumption of a well to do inhabitant of Tenochtitlan, demonstrated that they fed annually more than 360,000 people. No less comprehensive were the deliveries of clothing. Over 123,000 cotton blankets were delivered every year to the city. All this wealth was stored in special repositories and recorded in pictograms.

Although there was no uniform system of imposing tribute, it is possible to distinguish three different groups of provinces. The first were those areas in the plateau and round about the Valley of Mexico subject to Tenochtitlan or the other cities of the Triple Alliance. In this region there was the greatest diversity and also the most significant degree of integration. Some regions owed tribute only to Tenochtitlan, others only to Tetzcoco or Tlacopan. There were also great differences in the kind of tribute given. Besides the land which they were compelled to cultivate for the Chief Ruler the subject peoples also had to cultivate additional land for the nobility, the officials and other members of the ruling class. Those who worked for the latter were freed from the duty of working for the Chief Ruler. Besides these forms of tribute the inhabitants of the plateau had to perform work of other kinds. This extended from labour on the great public works such as dams and canals to maintaining the garden of the Chief Ruler, feeding the wild animals in the palace menagerie, providing servant girls and attendants for the households of leading citizens and so forth. Their duties also involved war service on behalf of the cities of the Triple Alliance.

The more distant a province was situated from the Valley of Mexico, the less its duties in the matter of labour towards tribute payments. It was simply too costly to bring labour from distant regions into the plateau and feed them – unless for special occasions or in the case of specially gifted craftsmen. For this reason these provinces had in the first place to deliver merchandise. This also varied with the distance from Tenochtitlan. The regions close to Tenochtitlan delivered primarily foodstuffs and other goods. Those further away were responsible primarily for textiles. The reason for this is not far to seek. Since there were no draught animals and everything had to be transported on men's backs, a point was reached where the transport of foodstuffs no longer paid since the bearers ate more than they delivered. Finally the provinces which lay along the boundaries of the Aztec domain were either not obliged to deliver any tribute at all – this was the case on the boundaries with the Maya region where the provinces were primarily regarded as transit routes for merchants – or were required exclusively to man frontier garrisons and provide supplies for frontier troops.

A further duty imposed on most of the overthrown territories was the organisation of markets at certain regular times of the year. The merchants of the cities of the Triple Alliance were to be able to trade with them there without hindrance, to purchase merchandise and to sell merchandise from the plateau.

The political integration and administration of these regions is much less clear. There appears to have been a marked dichotomy between the organisation within the plateau and that in the other areas of the Aztec Empire. In the Valley of Mexico the cities of the Triple Alliance began to exercise political dominion to an ever increasing degree over the remaining city states – which in part themselves ruled over smaller villages. Sometimes this found expression in direct annexation, but usually it took the form of indirect rule. The city states, while being granted nominal independence, were nevertheless restricted in certain definite fields. There was scarcely a ruler who could be elected without the consent of the Aztecs, and Tenochtitlan alone took decisions in matters affecting war or peace. The same held good for all matters relating to irrigation. The ruler of Coyoacan, who had dared to cast doubt on the works that had been undertaken by the Chief Speaker of Tenochtitlan to regulate the waters of the lake, was murdered out of hand by order of the Chief Speaker.

In most of these city states the members of the ruling class of Tenochtitlan had their own landed property and appear to have lived there part of the time and exercised their office. The dependence of all these regions on Tenochtitlan was noticeably on the increase. In those regions lying further away from Tenochtitlan and from the plateau, things were completely different. Whoever looks for institutions, laws and modes of behaviour as they existed in the great empires of the past will look in vain. The administration of the conquered territories remained in the hands of the ruler or of the ruling social groups who were sometimes constrained to intermarry with members of Aztec nobility. With few exceptions no garrisons were installed in these areas.

There was no staff of administrators, no state bureaucracy went from the capital to the conquered provinces to uphold the law, to control finance or to keep the government under supervision. Only a small staff of tribute collectors, who scarcely carried out these functions and did not dispose directly of armed military forces, resided in these territories.

The Aztecs sent no colonisers in strength to support their rule in a foreign environment. A spiritual expansion was only present in a very weak and rudimentary degree. The cult of 'Humming-bird on the Left' was introduced into a number of areas, but was not intended to supplant the indigenous cults. There was no desire to throw out the old religion, only to keep it in control, and the Aztecs attempted to achieve this by bringing representations of the most important idols to Tenochtitlan and imprisoning them there in a temple specially designed for this purpose, in the immense *Teocalli*. No attempts were made either to introduce the Nahuatl language into all regions. How limited the cultural influence of the Aztecs was in the last resort is revealed by the fact that no archaeological evidence of Aztec rule was found in most of the territories which had demonstrably been subject to their dominion.

There were only two exceptions to the general treatment of over-thrown regions. At the end of the fifteenth century Aztec garrisons began to be installed along the boundary with the Tarascan Empire and at the stations on the trade route leading to the region of the Maya. Colonists from the cities of the Triple Alliance were settled there. It appears to have been extraordinarily difficult to find such colonists and the chronicles repeatedly tell of the unwillingness of the plateau inhabitants to move away from home. Attractive privileges, from tax-free living to service by the overthrown peoples of the vicinity, were offered but they appear to have had limited success in persuading the dwellers in the plateau to leave the wealth and brilliance of life there in favour of the outlying provinces.

The regions that revolted against the Aztecs constituted a second exception but a completely different one. For a time the Aztecs took extremely rigorous steps in such cases. The inhabitants of the rebellious territories were simply slaughtered and the region settled by plateau people. As it became increasingly more difficult to find such settlers – since with the growing wealth of the cities of the Triple Alliance the inhabitants of the plateau were even less anxious to part from their homeland – the Aztecs had to resort to other means. One of these methods was the same as that used half a century later by the Spaniards against the Aztecs: a revolt was instigated, virtually a social revolt of the peasantry against the upper class. If the ruling group of a region encouraged revolutionary aspirations in another region however there was always a considerable danger of the revolution flowing back to the very spot where the original instigators least wanted it, into their own region. It is therefore not surprising that the Aztecs set out on this road with some misgivings. These are described with almost amazing naïvety in one of the chronicles, which tells how the Aztecs used such a tactic for the first time. The city state of Cuetaxtla, which had already been overthrown by the cities of the Triple Alliance, revolted against them. The ruler of Cuetaxtla and the military class of this locality had not only dared to withhold the tribute due to the Triple Alliance, but they had murdered the collector of tribute. In a conference held in Tenochtitlan between Moctezuma I and his deputy Tlacaellel the two men considered what should be done with the rebels. Moctezuma demanded the slaughter of the entire population. Tlacaellel who was much more astute in economic matters was strongly against such a move. Finally agreement was reached on a military campaign, and on doubling the tribute the conquered had to pay.

An Aztec army set out for Cuetaxtla and it quickly succeeded in annihilating the enemy. While the warriors took flight representatives of the Macehualtin, that is of the ordinary peasants, turned to the Aztecs. The words they used, as reported by the chroniclers, are in many respects reminiscent of similar utterances by peasant revolutionaries in medieval Europe.

Ye gentlemen of Mexico [they called] wherefore do ye kill us? What guilt do these poor ignorant simple people bear who have no interest whatever in this war? Why do ye avenge yourselves on us, who never have turned against you nor insulted you? Why do ye let our accursed overlords who are nothing but a pack of thieves and who have only brought death to us continue to live? Have we then not delivered unto you all the tribute which ye demanded? Was it our rulers perhaps who gave it to you? Is it not all the result of our sweat and toil? If we give blankets do our rulers do the same? Is it they who weave the blankets? Is it not we and our women-folk? And if they give cocoa, gold, precious stones, feathers and fish and tribute, do they not come from us and do we not offer them to our Lord Moctezuma and to our Lords, the Mexicans . . . ? We desire that you should help us to acquire justice to be done by our overlords. We desire that they be killed, annihilated and punished for they are responsible for our misery.[46]

They also indicated that their overlords had treated them with the greatest possible ferocity, that they had tyrannised them and burdened them with tributes that were much too high and 'that these lords had only one aim in life; to eat, drink and be merry, and they indulged in the most varied and dubious entertainments at the expense of the people'. Truly a manner of speech not often met with in the chronicles.

The Aztec military commanders who usually had no qualms when it came to killing suddenly exhibited in this case a striking restraint.

'We have no right to kill anyone except in battle' they replied. 'First of all Moctezuma must be asked for his counsel.' And as a matter of fact, Moctezuma, who had previously wanted to have all the inhabitants of Cuetaxtla slaughtered, showed equal restraint. In discussion with his deputy, Tlacaellel, he stated that the execution of the nobility of Cuetaxtla seemed to him problematical, 'since they were nobles and created in the likeness of the gods. Would the gods not consider the execution of these nobles as sacrilege?' The far more astute and machiavellian Tlacaellel replied 'that these had rebelled against almighty God and his presence on earth and that they therefore deserved punishment. The peasants demanded justice which could not be denied to them.'[47]

The nobles were then actually put to death by the Aztecs, and the peasants were allowed to choose new rulers. But in order to prevent any possible uprising an Aztec governor was installed in Cuetaxtla. Such a procedure seems only to have happened in the most extreme cases for the Aztecs knew only too well what dangers such a social upheaval could bring with it.

This insignificant degree of integration of the territories overthrown by the Aztecs makes it seem inappropriate, at least in so far as the greater part of the territories is concerned, to speak of an empire. The term 'domain' would be more apposite. What then is the reason for the lack of integration? Was it due to the inability of a neolithic people to create a real empire? The examination of the second great civilisation of ancient America, that of the Inca in Peru, will show that this was not at all the case. The Inca developed forms of integration that would have made every Roman administration green with envy. By making a comparison with this second great domain on the American continent, which can in fact be called an empire, an attempt will be made to illustrate the factors and forces which prevented the rise of a true empire in Mesoamerica.

What attitude did the overthrown peoples take towards their conquerors? Is it indeed possible to speak of a solid Aztec domain? The solidity, the security of an empire or of a domain depended on a variety of factors: on the strength of the state to be overthrown, on the allies which could be assured within the conquered territories, superior technical achievement, the degree of political, economic and cultural integration, the severity of the burdens laid on the conquered peoples and the question of whether these burdens were constant and predictable or arbitrary and constantly changing. Furthermore the relations between the conquerors as recipients and the conquered as the givers was decisive. How much compensation was offered to the underlings for all that was demanded of them? Was there, like the *Pax Romana* in Rome, a *Pax Azteca* in Mesoamerica, offering protection from external aggression and assuring peace between the members of the Aztec 'domain'? To what extent did the conquerors erect major constructions and large public works which the conquered had not until then been able to create because of the sums which would have to be raised? To what extent did the conquerors propagate new techniques that enabled the peoples they had conquered to increase radically their own productivity? To what extent were the conquered peoples enabled to join a large market, which gave them the opportunity of receiving products that they had hardly been able to attract before?

In dealing with all these questions, it is necessary to distinguish very clearly between the peoples and states of the plateau and those of regions lying further afield. In the High Valley the Aztecs appeared in fact as both takers and givers. Here a sort of *Pax Azteca* became established and the constant wars between the small city states of the High Valley gave way to wars waged abroad, in which the conquered states of the Valley of Mexico participated. But these wars appeared to them to be of a completely different character. The city states themselves were not threatened and the enthusiasm and pleasure of taking part in such Aztec campaigns was in general very great. The wars were almost always successful and resulted in rich booty.

The enormous irrigation works which the Aztecs had undertaken in the network of lakes in Mexico benefited all the surrounding states which were now protected from the dangers of constant floods. Although the Aztecs did not introduce any new techniques into the Valley of Mexico the irrigation works enabled the lake cities to cultivate far more land through the *chinampa* system of agriculture than had previously been possible. Finally the Aztec conquests opened up new markets to the merchants of the overthrown cities of the Valley of Mexico, enabling rare lowland products to flow into the High Valley at an unprecedented rate. By means of these factors the Aztecs won over the ruling groups of the city states of the High Valley. The heavy burdens of tribute were partly compensated for by the profits of the common victories and also by the economic and other advantages arising from the great irrigation works. The proximity of Tenochtitlan proved to some extent to be a protection against the arbitrariness of individual Aztec officials in these areas. Finally integration was probably facilitated by the fact that these people had strong cultural, linguistic and religious links with the Aztecs.

This integration of the Valley of Mexico was not only the result of certain ecological factors and the general proximity of Tenochtitlan. It was also undoubtedly the result of a conscious policy arising from the dependence of Aztec rule over Mesoamerica on the unity and compactness of the High Valley. As long as the Aztecs dominated the High Valley, which supported a substantial part of the population of the entire plateau region and which was in a unique economic and strategic position, their domination over great tracts of Mesoamerica was assured. Any division of the peoples of the High Valley would certainly have endangered their whole rule.

The relationship between the Aztecs and the conquered peoples outside the High Valley was totally different, notably in the balance between giving and taking. The Aztecs scarcely appeared any more as givers, but more and more exclusively as takers.

It is possible that the Aztecs introduced a sort of *Pax Azteca* here as well, stopping wars between individual city states and protecting the inhabitants from external attack. Nevertheless in this case the *Pax Azteca* was much more precarious than in the High Valley. There were with a few exceptions no Aztec garrisons that could guarantee such a peace. The chronicles hardly refer to any campaigns aimed at protecting subjugated territories from external attack. The instability of Aztec rule is probably best illustrated by the fact that many regions which had been overthrown by a Chief Speaker had to be overthrown again by his successor.

Unlike the inhabitants of the High Valley, the rest of the conquered peoples only seldom appeared as partners in Aztec campaigns of conquest. Consequently they were all the more exposed to the danger of plunder by the Aztec armies on the march. An Aztec commander only needed to be convinced that the inhabitants of a village through which he was passing had brought too few gifts and foodstuffs for his troops, to give the order forthwith to set about plundering. And even if this did not happen, Aztec armies seem frequently to have stripped villages through which they passed and plundered. Arbitrary elements generally showed a marked increase. The Totonacs living in the modern state of Veracruz complained bitterly to the Spaniards that the Aztec tribute collectors went much further than only collecting tribute. They constantly demanded fresh gifts and offerings for their gods, assaulted women, robbed dwellings and so on. Appeals to the central authority in Tenochtitlan seem to have been in vain.

In addition no large scale public works in connection with irrigation schemes are known to have been carried out by the Aztecs in the conquered territories. One of the principal functions which devolved on the central authority in many empires, the storage of reserves against periods of drought and famine, seems to have been left by the Aztecs to the city states themselves in these territories. In times of severe famine these city states were always absolved from tribute payments to Tenochtitlan. Food supplies were only sent to stricken areas in exceptional cases. Large roads and other means of communication which would have secured the Aztecs' dominion and strengthened the economic and cultural connections of the subject peoples were not built.

These peoples also found the Aztec conquests oppressive because of the completely different language and culture of the victors. If the peoples of the Valley of Mexico were able in some way to regard the human sacrifice of those they looked upon as their own kith and kin as a sinister necessity, the attitude of the more distant peoples to this matter was of course entirely different. For all these reasons it is not surprising that the reaction of these people to the Aztec conquests was very different from that of the conquered peoples in the High Valley. While the latter hardly rebelled at all against their Aztec overlords until the end of the fifteenth century, there were constant revolts against Aztec rule among the more distant peoples.

CHANGES IN THE SOCIAL STRUCTURE OF TENOCHTITLAN

The Chief Speaker

The radical social changes which took place in Tenochtitlan and in the regions immediately adjacent to the city apparently found their expression in the enormous growth of those sections of the population not directly engaged in agriculture. A few social groups had increased so much in power and size that they were scarcely recognisable. New groups had appeared and other traditional groups had conversely diminished significantly in status, wealth and power. The changes which took place in Tenochtitlan extended from the apex of the social pyramid down to its lowest level. The power of the Chief Speaker was growing constantly as the controls to which he was subject diminished progressively. The Snake Woman ceased after the death of the most distinguished holder of this office, Tlacaellel, to exercise any power that could represent any kind of a counterweight against that of the Chief Speaker. No chronicle after the death of Tlacaellel mentions any resolution taken by the Snake Woman or suggested to the Chief Speaker by him. The Chief Speaker's former opposite number or rival had turned into a second-class official; the only relics from the past remaining to him were a number of superficial privileges, such as the right to wear the same insignia and costumes as the Chief Speaker. The supreme council appears to have developed increasingly from ruling group to a collection of councillors whose advice was in no way binding on the Chief Speaker. By the end of the fifteenth century the first indications appeared that the Chief Speaker was no longer regarded as a human being but as a god incarnate.

The Bureaucracy

The most important element contributing to the Chief Speaker's power and which came increasingly between him and the population was the growing military aristocracy and the state bureaucracy which developed very suddenly. Both these factions were primarily responsible to the Chief Speaker. The development of such a bureaucracy was the result of the conquest by the Aztecs of a territory containing millions of people and of the rapid growth of the cities of the Triple Alliance. As these events took place so the Aztec bureaucracy grew in proportion. It assumed or at least controlled more and more of the functions which the *calpulli* had exercised until then. It increasingly showed tendencies towards a caste system of separation and isolation, which had not become fully effective by the end of the fifteenth century.

It was characteristic both of the military aristocracy and of the closely associated bureaucracy that they had both largely detached themselves from the *calpulli* communities. They developed in the fullest sense of the word into servants of the state, to which they were exclusively responsible and on which they were economically dependent. The development of this bureaucracy manifested itself in the change and elaboration of existing tribal institutions and in the creation of completely new state systems.

The most conspicuous and extensive changes and developments naturally took place among the military caste who enjoyed the greatest esteem and the greatest power in Tenochtitlan. Most of the fruits of conquest flowed towards them with the result that a wholesale reconstruction of the army took place.

The Army

In the period preceding the overthrow of Atzcapotzalco it is scarcely possible to speak of a professional army amongst the Aztecs. Until the overthrow of Atzcapotzalco the Aztec military forces consisted of three main groups: a small officer class, the broad mass of the population, which was mobilised in the event of important campaigns, and a class of élite warriors who were grouped together in special military formations. Until 1428 the numerically small officer class was freed from direct food production. Both the mass of soldiery as well as the warrior élite when not engaged in campaigning were members of the *calpulli* and had to perform agricultural or handicraft work. The most significant development in the Aztec army after 1428 consisted in members of élite formations being largely set free from every form of work when they were not fighting, constantly increasing in numbers and tending to develop into a regular social class of society. Among the most important military orders of Tenochtitlan were the military associations of the Eagle and the Tiger, those of the Cuachic and those whom the Spaniards designated as Brown Knights. While only the children of the aristocracy, who in any case had to distinguish themselves in battle, were accepted in the first two, the other two were open to all warriors who had performed outstanding deeds. The number of prisoners which had been taken was the main criterion by which these outstanding performances were measured.

From a military standpoint the members of these military orders constituted the backbone of the army. They were placed in the most dangerous posts and had sworn never to retreat. Viewed from a religious standpoint, these associations, whose origin was much older than Aztec rule in Mexico, performed their own ceremonies. They regarded themselves as warriors who had been endowed by the gods with the special mission first and foremost of being responsible for feeding the Sun with captives. The members of most of these military orders were provided with incomes by the state that enabled them to devote themselves exclusively to war. The form of this income varied widely.

Similarly the members of Aztec garrisons stationed on the frontiers of their domain and on the trade routes southwards can on the whole be termed professional warriors. They were not however warriors stationed temporarily outside their capital city, but in reality colonists who emigrated together with their families and settled down permanently in their garrison posts. They appear in part to have cultivated the land themselves, but for the most part they were cared and provided for by the members of the tribes who had been overthrown. The members of the garrison did not count as members of the military aristocracy or of the military orders. Usually they were impecunious peasants who hoped to improve their position by emigrating. Garrisons were kept relatively small and never exercised any significant influence on the destiny of the Aztec domain. In the last years of the Aztec Empire an ever increasing number of former peasants in Tenochtitlan seem to have become full-time warriors and to have given up their other activities.

Economic Administration

A second group that developed both in Tenochtitlan and throughout the overthrown territories in the second half of the fifteenth century might best be described as an 'economic bureaucracy'. They were the collectors, administrators and distributors of tribute. The great Aztec conquests and the formidable tributes that reached Tenochtitlan necessitated a very rapid, one might almost say a spectacular increase in this bureaucracy. It was the only part of the state bureaucracy that bore a truly pan-Mesoamerican stamp. Its representatives were to be found in almost all the territories that the Aztecs had overthrown. There was a *calpixque* in all the larger villages dependent on the Aztecs, whose function it was to collect tribute and to control its amount and the date for its delivery. These *calpixques* were subordinate to a tribute collector appointed for an entire province. At the head of the whole system was the *Huey Calpixque*, who was responsible for the collection of all tribute.

A second department of this economic administration was stationed in the capital city. It contained controllers responsible for each province who checked exactly whether the *calpixque* had in fact delivered the amount due to them.

Another extensive system consisted of the administrators of tribute headed by an official called *petlacatl*. These officials noted in pictograms the exact amounts of incoming tribute and made sure it was kept in good condition. But they did not make decisions on the distribution of tribute. This was done by order of the state authority.

Posts in the administration of tribute seem to have been highly sought after in Tenochtitlan. There is a story that the last Aztec Chief Speaker, Moctezuma II, when he heard of the advance of the Spaniards, sent out one of his warriors to observe the foreigners from nearby. In the event of the warrior being killed, Moctezuma promised one of the members of his family a post as tribute collector, clearly a significant reward which he had the power to bestow. The popularity of this post is entirely explicable and has little to do with any opportunities the tribute collectors might have had to fill their pockets from the state tribute payments. There were the strictest punishments for this and any thief discovered was punished with a gruesome death. The possibilities of becoming wealthy were simpler and involved less friction. The overthrown peoples were compelled to cultivate a piece of land for the *calpixque*, and to provide him with foodstuffs. The exact amounts to be delivered however were not laid down, and the *calpixques* in general demanded the highest contributions from the tribes under their control. It was not only a question of material deliveries. Many peoples who were overthrown by the Aztecs complained to Cortés bitterly that the tribute collectors always demanded women from them and simply carried off anything that took their fancy.

The conquered tribes were hardly able to offer any resistance in this matter. There is not a single known instance of a people conquered by the Aztecs being able to address complaints successfully in such cases to the Chief Speaker. But even if this had been possible it is hardly likely that the power of the *calpixque* would in any way have been effectively restricted. They were after all more than collectors of tribute; they were the overseers on behalf of the Chief Speaker in the conquered territories, reporting on the attitude of the overthrown tribes. A report to the Chief Speaker about a planned rebellion could have led to a destructive campaign from Tenochtitlan against the unruly province. If the *calpixque* were murdered, then the most fearful punishment was certain. Accordingly the fear of the tribute collectors amongst the overthrown tribes, as Cortés was able to experience at first hand, often amounted to panic.

While the collectors of tribute in the provinces were supported by the overthrown peoples, the Chief Speaker ensured that this was also the case for the body of officials in the capital city.

THE LEGAL SYSTEM AND ADMINISTRATION OF JUSTICE

It was typical of the whole character of the Aztec state that the army and the administrative machinery concerning tribute developed the most rapidly. Legal administration was also developing although its growth was much less rapid than in both the other spheres. This was because Aztec law only extended over a relatively restricted area of the conquered territories of the Valley of Mexico. It is also not clear how far this legal system embraced the city states of the High Valley in spite of their undoubted independence. Presumably in earlier times the *calpulli* had undertaken to resolve conflicts themselves between their members, whereas only cases that exceeded the competence of a *calpulli* or that concerned the whole tribe were dealt with by a tribal court. Traces of this were still to be found at the end of the fifteenth century. Cases of minor importance, of concern to individual *calpulli*, came before local judges. These however were no longer the heads of the *calpulli* but officials appointed by the state for this purpose.

In a society however in which an ever increasing proportion of the membership no longer belonged to the *calpulli*, more and more class distinctions were arising and with social differences and tensions on the increase, a legal system of this kind was no longer adequate. Accordingly a complicated network of law courts developed. The tribunals sitting in the *calpulli* constituted the lowest court. All other more serious cases were addressed to a higher court, the *Tlacxitlan*. This court consisting of three judges was also competent to judge all cases concerning members of the ruling class. Cases which concerned the highest offices of state, or those concerning capital punishment, came before an even higher court under the direction of the 'Snake Woman'. Every twelve days the Chief Speaker personally took over the conduct of this court.

Some chroniclers even describe a sort of professional advocate who represented the accused. These descriptions are however sporadic and confused, and it is difficult to say how far the chroniclers who wrote everything down after the Conquest may have been influenced by European realities. A comprehensive bureaucratic machine was at the disposal of the courts: scribes noted important points of the proceedings; the *Tequitlato* summoned the accused before the court, and if they refused to come, a sort of police officer, the *Topilli* was charged to arrest them by force.

Finally, the *Achcacauhtin* lived in a special house – 'the men of courage who were the *Tlatoani*'s executioners; they executed those whom the *Tlatoani* had condemned to death'.[48] The designation of the executioners in an old chronicle as 'men of courage', one of the most honourable distinctions which existed in Tenochtitlan, indicates that the executioners not only inspired terror but that they also enjoyed social esteem.

Only two categories of people were exempted from appearing before this legal hierarchy: warriors who had committed some crime during a war and were taken immediately before a field court; and the merchants who had their own courts.

Cases which earlier had presumably come within the competence of the *calpulli* now came increasingly within the competence of the state law courts. They covered civil cases such as divorce and disputes about property and crimes such as robbery, murder and treason. There were strictly drafted laws with clearly prescribed punishments. As in many other fields the pioneering work in this field also may be attributed to Netzahualcoyotl in Tetzcoco. The laws proclaimed by him remained the prototypes for Tenochtitlan as well.

The hardest and harshest punishments were directed against those who attacked power, property or the dignity of the state. Traitors were cut in pieces, their houses destroyed, their land covered with salt and their children sold into slavery up to the fourth generation. Anyone who wore jewellery that was not appropriate to his office was executed. The wish to ensure the dignity of the state led the Aztecs to execute high priests and officials who got drunk while others, not members of the aristocracy, only had their hair shaved off for the same crimes. Murder was also punished by death, but there was some differentiation in the handling of robbery. In cases of petty larceny the thief was sold into slavery; if he had stolen more valuable property he was executed. Punishment for adultery was exceedingly severe. The adulterer was stoned to death. If an adulterer killed his rival in a fight he was roasted and salt and water were poured over him.

It fits into the pattern of Aztec culture that warriors who did not obey the commands of their officers were also severely punished. It is significant that such punishment was much harsher for élite warriors than for ordinary soldiers. If the former were taken prisoner and succeeded in escaping, they were executed by their own army. On the other hand, ordinary soldiers who did the same were given prizes and recompensed. Anyone who did not carry out orders was flayed, and anyone who laid claim to a foreign prisoner of war for himself – a crime which, in view of the importance which prisoners of war had for the Aztecs, was very sternly avenged – was hanged.

It is significant that all these laws protected in the first place the authority of the state and the members of the Triple Alliance. However there was no protection for those who had been overthrown, no kind of regulation that restricted the arbitrariness of Aztec officials.

When considering the composition and the operation of this state bureaucracy, when examining – as we shall do below – its recruitment and its remuneration the impression gained is certainly not that of a machine operating without friction or with fixed standards. New institutions replaced old, old forms persisted but with new content.

THE PRIESTHOOD

Such problems must have occurred, perhaps to an even greater extent, in the second of the great Aztec institutions, the priesthood, which experienced a development similar to that of the state bureaucracy and was closely connected with it. The powerful increase of this class is already clear from the enormous numbers of temples and temple enclosures that were erected in the second half of the fifteenth century in the cities of the Triple Alliance. Added to the practical difficulties arising from such a sudden increase there must have been serious theoretical problems. In a polytheistic religion like that of the Aztecs it is impossible to speak of clearly defined transcendental qualities among the gods. Humming-bird on the Left was the most important and significant of the Aztec gods. Each deity had a particular field of operation. But how and above all by whom was the relative significance of individual deities assessed? Who decided how much wealth should be offered to one or other deity? What happened when there were overlappings as in the case of the several maize gods? All these problems and difficulties must have hindered the development of a homogeneous priesthood organised on strict principles. Nevertheless in the second half of the fifteenth century there appear to have been strong centralising tendencies among the priesthood.

At the summit the priesthood was closely bound up with the government. Both the Chief Speaker and the Snake Woman were at the same time important priests. Beyond this there was a particular priestly organisation separate from the state, that was also largely independent economically. The most venerated priests, who appear to have performed considerable executive functions, were the high priests of Humming-bird on the Left and of Tlaloc the rain god. These two priests nominated a number of officials, who carried out a sort of control over the entire priesthood. While one functionary, the *Tlaquimilotecuhtli*, represented a sort of treasurer, others supervised ritual or were responsible for education. How much autonomy was left to individual temples cannot exactly be ascertained. Each temple had a high priest and a complicated hierarchy of underlings whose functions were strictly specialised. This specialisation corresponded with the functions which the priesthood performed in the life of the Aztecs. The fulfilment of these functions necessitated an enormous increase in the number of priests. These assistants in the temples probably had little to do with cult practices; they were more concerned with collecting the enormous sums received by the temples, their registration, their control and finally the administration of their distribution.

The tremendous increase in human sacrifices also constantly required fresh priests, although the priesthood no longer had to feed and supervise the captives up to the time of their sacrifice. With the exception of those captives who were incarnations of the gods themselves and who lived for a year as such, all future sacrificial victims were looked after and supervised in the various *calpulli* and only led to the temples on the day of their execution.

A crucial function of the priesthood was soothsaying. This applied to all events whether important or utterly insignificant. The priests were consulted by all sections of the population for even the most trivial reasons, and as the city grew this type of priest had necessarily to grow too. By the end of the fifteenth century the soothsayers appear to have become completely independent of the rest of the priesthood and to have set up a sort of corporation of their own.

All these functions were traditional in character and their increase corresponded with the increase in the population, but did not signify the undertaking of new functions, with the possible exception of human sacrifices. These were already taking place by the beginning of the fifteenth century, and their tremendous increase had created a completely new situation.

The most important new functions of the priesthood towards society existed in two fields: the control over foreign deities and the training of the state bureaucracy. The first function was primarily carried out by bringing idols of all the deities of the conquered peoples to one temple in Tenochtitlan. There the religion of these peoples was closely studied, in order to absorb elements from it into the indigenous religion and to place the deities under the tutelage of the Aztec deities. It was a religious imperialism that was not, like that of the Spaniards later, designed to propagate their own religion at the expense of a foreign one, but was intended to bring the foreign deities into a conscious and dependent relationship with the indigenous gods.

Perhaps the most important new function that the priesthood practised, one which enormously raised their position, their power, their influence and the esteem in which they were held by society, was educating the children of the nobility and training them to take over the leadership of the Aztec state. While the male members of a *calpulli* were educated in special youth homes, *telpochcalli*, where they chiefly learned agriculture and soldiering, the children of the nobility had their own schools, the *calmecac*.

In the second half of the fifteenth century future priests were trained in these schools as well as future members of the ruling class. The life in this school would not evoke very enthusiastic responses from present-day schoolchildren.

They swept and tidied the house every day at 4 o'clock in the morning . . . The older boys went out to look for Maguey (a sort of agave) . . . They brought wood required for making a fire every evening, . . . down from the mountain on their backs.

A little earlier they stopped work and went straight into their cloister (as described by the Spanish chronicler), to attend divine service, to do penance and to bathe . . .

The meal which they consumed they made for themselves in the house of the *calmecac*.

At sundown they began to make everything ready . . . At midnight they all rose to say their prayers, and any one who did not waken and get up was punished, by being chastised on his ears, his breast, his muscles and his feet.[49]

Further harsh punishments were added as well as periodic fasting.

Besides training in warfare, the scholars learned first and foremost, as Sahagun describes

to speak well, to salute and to make obeisance . . .

All the verses of songs were taught to them so that they could sing them. These were hymns the verses of which were recorded in their books. In addition, they were taught Indian astrology, the interpretation of dreams and the counting of the years . . .

The grounding for these last subjects was reading, writing and arithmetic, which was learned in the *calmecac* in contrast to what was taught in the *telpochcalli*. Especially interesting and significant is the great importance placed on the teaching of history, that is on national tradition. Not only does the proportionate length of time spent on these subjects testify to their importance, but also the very strict control exercised by the state regarding the contents of this instruction. A description has already been given of the destruction after the overthrow of Atzcapotzalco of the old pictograms, the foundation of the teaching of the *calmecacs*. All new songs learned by the scholars of the *calmecac* had first to be submitted to a Tlapixcatzin, the 'overseeing censor'. Only when he gave his consent could the songs be sung either in the *calmecac* or in the city generally.

Departure from the *calmecac* took place either after marriage, or in the case of priests, as soon as they had entered their religious orders.

In proportion as the Chief Speaker, his deputy, the state bureaucracy, the warriors and the priesthood increased their power, so the influence and power of the old traditional aristocracy of the *calpullec*, the heads of the *calpulli* receded. They lost the right to nominate the Chief Speaker at a meeting of the leaders of the *calpulli* summoned to discuss the most important affairs of state. State officials were appointed to act instead in every *calpulli* by the Chief Speaker, and they themselves were down-graded to the lowest level of the ruling class.

THE INCOME OF THE NOBILITY AND THEIR RIGHTS

Apart from the fact that members of the ruling class no longer engaged in agriculture, it is not possible to say that their income came from any one source alone. Their incomes could derive either from their own landed property or from state subventions or from both.

The landed estates of the nobility had multiplied and become extraordinarily diverse compared with what they had been in the first half of the fifteenth century. The very varied forms of land tenure of the nobility fall into three categories:

(1) Land tied to a public office. In this case lands were attached to a particular office, for instance that of judges, who practised in a certain circuit. The land was either farmed out or was cultivated by peasants who had lived there for generations. Should the judge change, the tenure of the land went to the new owner.

(2) Land tied to a profession. This type of land tenure was usually tied to the profession of warrior. If a warrior distinguished himself in battle, the Chief Speaker would promise him a piece of land in a conquered territory. The peasants living in the vicinity or on the land had to pay state tribute to him instead of to the Chief Speaker. It was more a case of having a right to tribute than a right to land.

Both these kinds of land tenure were limited types of ownership. The land was granted by the Chief Speaker and could only be inherited in certain conditions. If the Chief Speaker appointed the sons to the office of their father, which was usually but not always the case, they received the land with the office. If a warrior's son distinguished himself in battle, he was given preference before all other candidates in taking possession of his father's land. But there was no automatic inheritance of this land that could be taken for granted. Furthermore the land could on no account be alienated, leased out or sold.

The peasants who cultivated such land depended on the owners to a very limited degree. They were members of *calpulli* who exercised all the rights and duties of such membership.

(3) The situation in regard to the third type of private tenure was completely different. In this type, land tenure was tied neither to an office nor to a profession. Here we are dealing with land that had been granted to the nobility of Tenochtitlan and other cities of the plateau at the time of their foundation. It was cultivated by certain bondsmen, the *mayeques*, and the owner always had to be a member of the nobility. The inheritance passed automatically to the eldest son and did not have to be endorsed by the Chief Speaker. Unlike the other types of land tenure, this land could be sold or alienated. The peasants cultivating it enjoyed a special status more like that of vassals than of members of a *calpulli*. Special services were often tied up with landed property and performed by the *mayeques*. These services covered work done in the nobleman's household and the carrying of heavy loads and transport service for him.

Subventions made by the Chief Speaker, which could vary a great deal, constituted the second type of income enjoyed by the nobility. Basically the lion's share of the massive tributes which flowed into the Valley of Mexico were earmarked for this class. Many members of the nobility received free food and a certain amount of free lodging in the ruler's palace. The enormous numbers of people who were fed daily at court left a lasting impression on the Spanish *conquistadores*: 'After Moctezuma, the sentries and servants ate' writes Bernal Diaz, 'and it appears to me that more than 1000 meals were served.'[50] Cortés, who had witnessed this procedure from even closer at hand and was equally astonished, wrote as follows: 'When day breaks, hundreds of persons of rank take their places in the palace, ... The retainers of all these noblemen alone fill two or three large courtyards. When Moctezuma comes to table, the underlings are fed just as well as he; the servants also receive their share; the kitchen and the cellar are open to all.'[51] A record of the annual consumption at the ruler's palace in Tetzcoco, which was smaller than that of the Chief Speaker of Tenochtitlan, has survived. The figures quoted, which are not at all unlikely, tell their own story:

Generally speaking [as appears from royal accounts], the annual consumption at the palace was 31,600 fanegas of maize, 243 loads of cocoa, 8,000 chickens, 5,000 fanegas of chili, 2,000 measures of salt; and for the clothing both of the ruler and of the rest of the nobility in his house and the other persons mentioned 547,010 blankets are registered all made of the finest materials and of great value.[52]

The chronicler appears to have added a nought too many against the blankets, otherwise the figures seem to be probable. The quantities of maize mentioned were enough to feed ten thousand people annually.

This type of support like all other types of 'payment' was designed among the Aztecs to constantly emphasise the close ties between the Chief Speaker and the nobility and to underline the dependence of the latter on the former. This became especially apparent during the frequent feasts, at which the Chief Speaker and his deputy spent hours in distributing presents to the members of the nobility. A chronicler describes the entry into office of the Chief Speaker Ahuitzotl: 'All the gentry of the neighbourhood were invited . . . the *calpixques* and administrators, working in various localities, brought together all the necessaries for this feast . . . The ruler himself arrayed the nobles in rich blankets, and he told them that this was the reward for their brave deeds . . .'[53]

Similar dispensations took place after every victorious campaign. This practice emphasised the dependence of the state bureaucracy and of the nobility on the Chief Speaker in his role as a sort of paternalistic provider, while at the same time upholding it as one of his most important duties.

From all this it emerges very clearly that there were considerable discrepancies in wealth not only between the nobility and the rest of the population in Tenochtitlan, but also within the ranks of the nobility. On the one hand there was the high official, the judge, the administrator or the military leader who possessed lands by virtue of his office or profession and presumably also by inheritance, for many of these officials were descendants of former Chief Speakers. In addition he received rich gifts at every feast and was given special honours in the palace. The villages under his administration provided him with household servants who kept up his palace, who possibly built him new houses and transported his possessions from one place to another. In direct contrast to him was the petty official, who sat a long way away from the Chief Speaker at his board in the palace, with whom he had presumably spoken only once or twice. He awaited every new festivity with impatience in the hope of acquiring a rather better blanket that he could barter for other things on the market. Only through bravery in battle could he rise from being a petty official to become an important official, a significant change in social status. If he distinguished himself particularly, he might be nominated by the ruler for a higher office or at least be richly rewarded. Even if he distinguished himself less, there was the chance of gaining rich plunder. Should he win a lot, he may even be able to purchase land with bondsmen attached and at least ascend economically into a higher social category.

The rights of a member of the nobility far exceeded the power his office gave him and the wealth that he enjoyed. He could always emphasise the prestige of his position by displaying special marks of distinction. Only members of the nobility were allowed to wear fine cotton materials and jewellery of jade and gold, to have two-storey houses. Juridically they possessed their own law courts, but – as far as it is ascertainable – they were more strictly punished for their crimes than were members of the lower classes for similar offences.

A privilege enjoyed by the nobility in domestic matters had specially pronounced and rapid social consequences: the right to polygamy. Only members of the nobility were allowed to have several wives, whose number was not clearly limited. The general practice was to have a few 'wedded' wives, while the rest counted as concubines. Their sons nevertheless had a wholly legitimate status. This became specially clear in the case of the Chief Speaker Itzcoatl, whose mother had been a slave. Although a considerable proportion of the nobility – the priesthood – were not allowed to marry and a comparatively high percentage of warriors fell in battle, the nobility increased, thanks to polygamy, more rapidly than any other social group in Tenochtitlan. This inevitably led in the long run to difficult social problems. These were closely connected with the character and form of ascent into Aztec nobility.

THE ASCENT INTO THE RULING CLASS

Aztec nobility was neither a closed caste nor an open meritorious aristocracy. It represented a mixture of both where the relationship of the various groups to each other were in a constant state of change.

By the end of the fifteenth century there were three main ways of becoming a member of the nobility.

The first may be called direct inheritance. This covered the sons, descendants and relatives of all the Chief Speakers who had ruled up to date. They carried the name Pipiltin, 'Sons of Lords'. They attended the *calmecac*, inherited the lands of their parents, lived in the palace and were maintained there. Although they did not automatically inherit the office of their parents, they had a privileged right to offices of state dependent on services rendered, especially in battle.

A second type of inheritance was rather more veiled. It applied to the sons of members of the nobility who did not come from the families of the Chief Speaker. They did not inherit the land of their fathers, nor were they automatically members of the nobility. They received however a privileged claim to membership of the ruling class. This was evident in the fact that they were allowed to attend the *calmecac* and that, provided that they had distinguished themselves in battle, their fathers' honours were awarded to them.

Finally there was a third type of ascent, from below. This was indissolubly linked with battle. Anyone who had taken a certain number of prisoners could be received into the nobility, but not into its top ranks. He was received into membership of the military order of Brown Knights. The highest orders of this kind, the Orders of the Eagle and the Jaguar, remained closed to him. Only a few men, who demonstrated quite outstanding capabilities, seem to have risen higher.

These three possible ways of ascent ran parallel with each other from the middle of the fifteenth century up to its close. The corresponding significance of each group within the nobility nevertheless changed very rapidly and very clearly.

Shortly after the overthrow of Atzcapotzalco, while Aztec armies were overrunning increasing areas of Mesoamerica, and ever growing riches were pouring into Tenochtitlan daily, the nobility tried to increase its membership. It needed new members urgently in order to handle the tasks which resulted from the conquest of such large areas. Accordingly, Tlacaellel made the following proposal to the Chief Speaker Moctezuma i:

> You must invite second-grade warriors into your royal palace, who have merited reward on a lower scale. They must be granted the right, after they have been selected by the generals, to wear the insignia, the ornaments and jewellery which are the privileges of the highest nobility. But in order to merit such distinction, a man must have distinguished himself in battle and to have taken prisoner some warriors of Tlaxcala, Huejotzingo and Tiliuhquetepec. The nobility will be restored by this order of knights . . . Moctezuma promised that they and their children should always be considered to be nobles.[54]

In the second half of the fifteenth century a gradual shift in favour of the hereditary principle may have taken place. The number of those having a right of inheritance increased and pressure to consolidate this right grew. The increasing amount of administrative business required more and more officials trained in the *calmecac*. This growth of the hereditary nobility did not necessarily directly prejudice the possibilities of ascent in the meritorious aristocracy. As long as conquests went on at breakneck speed, and as long as new members of the nobility were required for the consolidation of the vanquished there was room equally for a hereditary and meritorious aristocracy. Only when the rate of conquest slackened was there bound to be a confrontation between the two groups. At the beginning of the sixteenth century there in fact appeared symptoms of this kind, which will be described below.

Anyone studying the development of the Aztec nobility in the second half of the fifteenth century is immediately impressed by two apparently contradictory features: on the one hand the highly complicated relationships between the nobilities of the cities of the Triple Alliance, their extremely rapid development, the constant change in their social, economic and political basis and the introduction of completely new institutions, which were all apparently fuel for constant conflicts and confrontations within the ruling class; on the other hand however there is a peaceful, orderly evolution that could hardly have been expected in

P

face of these sudden changes. Despite the shift in power within the Triple Alliance the three cities on the whole lived peaceably with one another.

With one exception, not a single Chief Speaker was murdered. Little is known of bloodthirsty cliques or diadochian fights for the succession of a dead Chief Speaker. Edward Calnek has found some references to strong rivalries between different candidates for the post of Tlatoani. Moctezuma is said to have fled to Huejotzingo because he was threatened by Itzcoatl. Some rulers are reported to have sent potential rivals on extremely dangerous expeditions where everything was arranged to have them killed or captured. On the whole the chronicles contain relatively scant information on such struggles until the end of the fifteenth century. Of course the reports of the chroniclers are not wholly reliable. Perhaps the love for censorship in the Aztec writing of history may have simply caused such events to be silenced. On the other hand at the time of the Spanish Conquest many people were still living who had grown up in the fifteenth century and knew this period of Aztec history from their own observation. There are few reports of such events.

This absence of conflict and fighting has been attributed to the very strong feeling of solidarity among the Aztecs, a feeling that was partly the result of centuries of subjection. To this must be added the tremendous power of their religion, the sense of mission that the Aztecs felt as the representatives on earth of Humming-bird on the Left. In fact these factors played a tremendously important role. Nevertheless there have been other peoples in history whose solidarity during the time of their oppression was no weaker than that of the Aztecs, and whose sense of mission was just as strongly developed, who despite it went through a period of bitter internal conflict soon after their rise to power. That this did not occur among the Aztecs until the end of the fifteenth century is due to several factors. Sharp fights among cliques in many cases indicate a society that has reached saturation point or is in a state of decline. This was not the case among the Aztecs. They were still in full ascent. The power of the nobility was constantly on the increase, probably because they were being successful. In the course of half a century they had helped the Aztecs to become literally a world power. This success meant that the social changes which took place in Tenochtitlan were almost painless for all the groups involved. The rising nobility did not have to deprive the other social groups of anything. They simply gave them a slightly lower share of the wealth which had been acquired. Even the most disadvantageously placed inhabitants of Tenochtitlan received something from the crumbs of riches and power. Only when these crumbs became scantier in the beginning of the sixteenth century did the situation change.

Finally there was one more factor that must be taken into account. Palace revolts and fights among cliques probably reveal the complete isolation of the ruling class from the people. The Aztec nobility was no longer to be the tribal aristocracy it had so long been taken for. For a long time the most important officials had not been chosen by the clans nor could they be deposed by them; they were not responsible to them in any way. On the other hand the Aztec nobility did not constitute a closed caste system. The driving harnesses ran increasingly from above downwards but there were always still some that worked in the opposite direction. As long as these driving harnesses remained, palace intrigues and fights among cliques were less likely to take place.

THE MERCHANTS

The hereditary aristocracy and the priesthood, the military order and military aristocracy had, as far as their functions, influence and power were concerned, changed very rapidly during the fifteenth century, but nevertheless they had still developed organically out of Aztec society. There was another group however which for the most part forced their way into Tenochtitlan as outsiders, and despite the greatest esteem being shown to them by the nobility and the close ties that were forged, they were basically to remain outsiders until the fall of the city. This group was that of the merchants, the *Pochteca*.

The importance which the peoples of Mesoamerica attached to commerce is clear from the size and central position of the market-place. The huge market of Tlatelolco already described, although the largest in Mesoamerica, was not exceptional. Every city had a similar market. By the end of the fifteenth century extensive specialisation had taken place in the Valley of Mexico. In the market of Atzcapotzalco slaves were the main commodity sold, in Cholollan jewels, stones and feathers. Certain kinds of pottery were sold in Tetzcoco, and if anyone wanted a dog, he had to go to the market of Acolman.

The importance of the market is emphasised by the fact that it had its own gods and its own laws. Disputes in the market were referred to permanent market judges, who had the power to punish and usually gave judgement on the spot. The organisation of the market was extremely strict; each form of merchandise could only be sold in the appointed place. The quality of merchandise was constantly examined by market inspectors. As far as the common people were concerned, it was forbidden under threat of the strictest punishment to buy or sell outside the market. Spanish chroniclers described with astonishment how heavily laden peasants on the way to market refused to sell their merchandise even when offered more than the usual price.

Trade could only be carried on in the market. Although there were no coins, currency already existed which largely took the place of coins. Cocoa beans represented the most important of these currencies. Many years after the Conquest they were still regarded as money, just as much as the Spanish coins were. Small, handy, valuable and above all a special delicacy, they were admirably suited to this purpose. In addition cotton blankets, small copper hoes and occasionally gold, silver and jade were used. Were the market prices fixed or were they left to the discretion of the vendors? There are so many contradictory reports about this that it is impossible to be conclusive.

Only a fraction of those who sold merchandise in the market were merchants in the true sense of the word. The great majority of marketeers consisted of peasants and craftsmen who laid out the products of their work. There were no middlemen acting between the peasants of the High Valley and the purchaser in the city. The function of the merchants was different and more limited. They were the long distance traders, who brought into the High Valley the sought after products of the distant lowlands: feathers, cocoa, cotton textiles, gold, silver, jade, dyes and so on.

Trade between the plateau and the lowlands was many thousands of years old in Mesoamerica. Long before the rise of Teotihuacan the peoples of the plateau had tried to obtain the cotton, cocoa and feathers they coveted by barter, if not through conquest. But the organisation and importance of this trade changed according to whether or not the peoples of the plateau had political control over the lowlands or at least over the trade routes leading into it. It is therefore not surprising that until the advance of the Triple Alliance into the lowlands the importance of the merchants of the High Valley was very different from what it was afterwards. Guilds of merchants existed in almost all the cities of the plateau. Only Tenochtitlan appears to have been an exception owing to the particular development of Tlatelolco already described.

As long as the lowland regions were not under the control of the plateau, trade must have been a difficult and hazardous undertaking. Difficulties for the merchants began straightaway owing to the primitive state of technology: there were no draught animals, and no great waterways. Everything had to be managed by human porters, *tamemes*. This seriously restricted the variety and bulk of the merchandise to be handled, and resulted in the transportation of only high value products.

How was the crossing of hostile territory accomplished? Two main methods were used; one of them was disguise. The merchants were masters of this art. They crossed the enemy province dressed mostly as peasants or as members of the relevant tribe. Such disguise of course required a knowledge of the language of the people. The merchants must therefore have been the interpreters and language experts of Aztec society.

The second method consisted of setting up strong military convoys. The merchants of all the plateau cities united for this purpose and set out for the lowland provinces. They did not hesitate at times to fight battles and make conquests on their own account.

Once the lowland province had been reached the difficulties were not over by a long way. The highlanders had nothing comparable to offer in exchange for the valuable products of the lowlands since the plateau produced no raw materials. Consequently the merchants were forced to offer the inhabitants of the lowlands costly and valuable manufactured products of the plateau or to talk them into buying largely worthless plateau 'delicacies'. They mostly chose the second method which led to great bitterness among the lowland nobility. Repeated bloody confrontations resulted, as is clearly related in one of the chronicles:

Since the provinces of Tehuantepec, Xolotla, Izuatian, Minantlan and Amaxtlantan lay at a great distance from Tenochtitlan, and since they felt confident of their size and strength, they resolved to bar the way to the Mexicans, so that these should not come every year as usual to mulct the wealth of these cities by introducing delicacies and other worthless objects for which they received gold, jewels, feathers and other valuable products which they carried away with them. This happened every year, and there were so many of them that the roads were almost filled by these merchants. Indeed they were not only Mexicans who came, but merchants from Texcoco, Atzcapotzalco, Xochimilco, Chalco, Tlahuac and other places, and from all the provinces which lay round about the volcano, and it was not only one from each city, but there were hundreds of them. They arrived heavily laden with worthless merchandise, such as cheese which they made out of lake mud, foodstuffs which were made of worms, sacks full of lake flies which they call Aautli, potted ducks and many other tit-bits which the inhabitants of this province did not have. In addition they also brought toys, which they made themselves. In exchange they received cocoa, gold, feathers, and precious stones. When the inhabitants of these provinces became aware of what was happening, they determined to prevent this plundering of their cities for the benefit of the Mexican cities and provinces, which only brought in tit-bits and worthless objects.

After this resolve had been taken an army was raised, and surprise attacks were undertaken against the Mexicans and the peoples of the other provinces travelling by these trade routes in order to kill them.[55]

Let us suppose that the merchants had accomplished their laborious expedition and returned with their merchandise despite all obstacles. What then happened to their profits? This is just the kind of question that shows how dangerous and superficial it is to compare one merchant with another and to identify Aztec dealers with European merchants of the same period. In an economy which was not monetary, merchants must have played an essentially different role.

The possibilities of accumulating wealth were already very limited.

It is possible to keep sacks of gold coins, but it is not possible to store indefinitely great masses of cocoa-beans and blankets. As one chronicler tellingly remarks in regard to cocoa: 'Oh happy gold, which offers mankind a sweet and nourishing drink and protects its innocent owners from the hellish plague of avarice, because it cannot be buried, or kept for long.'[56] Nor were the merchants of Mesoamerica in a position to invest their profits in such a way as to revolutionise the economy and ensure decisive political and economic positions for themselves in all spheres of society.

State loans did not exist. In theory it was possible to buy land, but this possibility seems to have been very limited. Only a small portion of existing land in Mesoamerica was alienable and this in any case belonged to the nobility who were hardly ever prepared to part with it. Certain possibilities of usury existed. It was possible to loan money at interest. The payment of debts was among the duties that the state itself controlled. But the individual (with certain exceptions) could not pledge either his land or his house. The only things that he was allowed to pledge in the event of his being unable to pay his debts were objects of jewellery, his children or himself. Accordingly the influence and efficacy of usurers in Mesoamerica were very limited.

The setting up of manufacturing industries was hardly feasible because of low technical development, and both the state and the powerful guilds of craftsmen obstructed the control of craftwork by the merchants.

Were the merchants, allowing that they were unable to invest their profits gainfully other than by buying new merchandise, at least able to expend them for their own personal use? Here too there were narrow limits. Much of the merchandise that merchants brought back, such as different types of jewellery and feathers, they were not allowed to use. This merchandise was earmarked for the warriors. On no account could the merchants build finer houses or be better dressed than the warriors. Such a thing would have led to serious social tensions which in all likelihood would have brought about, after expropriation, the expulsion or even the end of the merchants. It was precisely these obstacles to luxury consumption that caused the urge for prestige among the merchants to express itself in a completely different way, in the form of rich banquets. In the first place other merchants were invited to them. However in order to exclude any hint of presumptuousness representatives of the nobility were also invited. It was a custom so deeply rooted that its effects were still felt years after the Spanish Conquest. Shortly after the conquest of Mexico, a Spanish chronicler gave a surprised and indignant description of the custom:

There is a devilish custom among these Indians, especially in Cholulan (the idol of which they worshipped) by which merchants wander around for ten or twenty years and save 200 or 300 pesos, and after all their exertions, having suffered hunger and sleepless nights, and without rhyme or reason, they hold a solemn banquet for which they expend all they have earned. What saddens me most, is, that they do this just as of yore, to bring honour to their name and to be highly esteemed. It would, after all, not be so bad if they did not, at the same time, wait for the day on which in the old days their idol was worshipped; this our Lord in his infinite mercy should indeed not allow, and should banish the memory of Amalech from their heads and lead them into his own service. Amen.[57]

All these restrictions on the permissible expenditure of profits must have limited the influence of the merchants. On the other hand so long as the cities of the Triple Alliance had not overthrown the entire lowlands, their influence must have been considerably strengthened by the fact that they were the most important purveyors of tropical products to the plateau. It is not at all surprising therefore that in Tlatelolco they became predominant and in Tetzcoco merchants sat with equality of rights on the Economic Council of the city, which dealt with all economic questions.

During the great campaigns of conquest conducted by the cities of the Triple Alliance, important changes occurred with regard to the rights, spheres of influence and economic possibilities open to the merchants. Thanks to the penetration by the Triple Alliance into the lowlands and the economic development of the cities of the plateau two of the most important problems facing the merchants were brought nearer solution. The security of the trade routes was largely guaranteed, so that increasing numbers of merchants could go on expeditions, and the problem of payment was facilitated. Owing to the flourishing craftwork in the cities of the plateau it was now possible to bring raw materials into the Valley of Mexico, have them manufactured there in order to re-export them and purchase new products with the profits. Even more lucrative must have been the trade in the war booty that the inhabitants of the cities of the Triple Alliance brought home with them after every successful campaign. The most notable example of this development was the great boom in Tenochtitlan's neighbouring city Tlatelolco.

It is precisely this development that explains why the nobility of the cities of the Triple Alliance were at pains to bring this profitable business under their control. This aspiration led to the overthrow, already described, of the greatest trading centre of the High Valley, Tlatelolco, by the Aztecs in the year 1473. The victors at first appear to have had the intention of refusing to grant special status to their newly won territory. Instead they treated it like any other subject regions that offered them resistance. A military governor was nominated and

Tlatelolco lost every vestige of independent administration. Heavy tributes were laid on the merchants and on all who sold in the market. The Aztecs were contemptuous about the activities of their subordinates in Tlatelolco and declared 'For the only trade we know is to throw into the battle our heads, our limbs and bodies in order to acquire wealth, rich plumage, gold and jewels.'[58]

A few years later there was hardly a sign of this despicable and harsh treatment of the neighbouring city and its merchants. Tlatelolco, despite the continued presence of military governors, was practically affiliated to the city of Tenochtitlan. Its subjects had access to the highest offices of state in Tenochtitlan, the merchants were introduced on all official occasions as pillars of the state and repeatedly honoured. The Chief Speaker declared to his officials: 'And in all districts devote your special attention to protecting the merchants, who trade with Xoconochco and Guatemala and the whole country; for they enrich the land and provide food for the poor and for the people, and anyone who molests or ill-treats them will pay for it with his life.'[59] And in fact, if merchants were killed anywhere, the Aztec armies were called up and major campaigns initiated in order to punish the murderers.

What was the effect on the merchants of so rapid and radical a change in the state's attitude towards them? The central administration had discovered that taxing the merchants was not the only, nor even the chief advantage that they could extract from them. One of the most useful functions which the merchants performed, as already described, was that of espionage. Disguised as another people, they went before every campaign that was planned into the relevant region. Who better than they could evaluate the economic potential of the region? And what more suitable place in which to collect information than the market-place? In this way the merchants made themselves useful to the military and the deep gulf which at first existed between warriors and merchants was diminished.

The state had yet another use for them: that of state trading. The massive tributes that reached the cities of the Triple Alliance constituted a large capital sum for instituting state trading. The balance could be applied to the exchange of products from the lowlands, especially from areas not subject to the Triple Alliance such as the Maya regions. Accordingly the merchants were increasingly required to trade in state merchandise along with their own. It even appears that merchants appeared who only traded for the state. Large expeditions, chiefly equipped by the state, went into the small neutral townships that lay between the Maya region and the conquered territories subject to the Triple Alliance. These small townships, whose independence from the large cities was respected in order to secure a neutral trading centre, are called by most historians ports of trade.[60]

The merchants demanded high payment for the expanding services they performed for the state. The merchants' guild in some respects constituted a state within a state, so extensive were its powers. The merchants in Tenochtitlan were the only social group to possess their own judges, and were not subject to the state judiciary. This legal autonomy went so far that the merchants even appointed the judges in the market of Tlatelolco. Thereby they regained many aspects of the independence that they had enjoyed before the overthrow of Tlatelolco. They possessed similar privileges in regard to tribute. Although they had to pay a great deal to the Aztec state, the method of payment and the extent of the tribute were not arbitrarily fixed by the state, but determined only after discussion with the chief of the body of merchants.

The merchants of Tenochtitlan and Tlatelolco were also granted special privileges in the newly conquered territories. The Chief Speakers of these regions had to hold markets on certain days to which they were bound to invite the merchants from the plateau. A considerable monopoly was granted to the merchants of Tenochtitlan and Tlatelolco in trading with certain districts of the Aztec domain and with the Maya across the Aztec border. Whoever molested the merchants was punished severely; if a city state did so the Aztecs went to war against it. A network of garrisons lined the most important trade routes to protect the merchants.

It is no wonder that the merchants' wealth constantly increased. They were showered with honours and received into the Aztec nobility. Their children attended the *calmecac* and merchants could apply to be received into the military order of the Brown Knights. Above all membership of the nobility gave them the right to invest their profits in purchasing their own land, which secured for them great power and prestige.

Despite all these rights, wealth and honours, the merchants remained *parvenus* in the eyes of the Aztec nobility. One chronicler writes:

Many tried in every possible way, to procure a title to their name . . . to found noble families . . . There were three possibilities of achieving this in the state:
The first and surest means . . . was that of distinguishing oneself in battle and performing spectacular and doughty deeds of courage . . .
The second means of becoming 'noble' was to enter the priesthood . . .
The third and of the three the least esteemed was through trade. The families of merchants became noble on account of their wealth.[61]

Until the Spanish Conquest merchants were regarded as doubtful and in the long run not full members of the nobility.

THE CRAFTSMEN

A second group in Tenochtitlan who engaged just as little in the traditional Aztec activities of agriculture and warfare as the merchants were the craftsmen.

They had not developed from Aztec society any more than the merchants had. While the merchants in the first place belonged to Tenochtitlan by reason of conquest however, most of the craftsmen were immigrants who had been imported by the rulers of the cities of the Triple Alliance from regions all over Mesoamerica. The activities of the craftsmen, like those of the merchants, were exclusively concerned in satisfying the needs of the state and of the nobility.

The Aztec peasant did not in fact require any craftsmen to satisfy his needs in housing, clothing, and agricultural implements. The houses constructed of dried adobe bricks were built by communal labour by members of the *calpulli*, articles of clothing woven out of maguey fibre were mostly made by the women and the agricultural tool – the digging stick, called coa – was so simple to make that nobody was required for this purpose. As yet no real division of labour between town and country existed in Mesoamerica. The craftsmen manufactured essentially luxury goods for the nobility and helped to build great state buildings.

The most highly regarded craftsmen were not, as one may imagine, the gold and silver smiths or the stone masons, but the *amantecas* or featherworkers. This was due to the extraordinary signicance of feather ornamentation in Mesoamerica. After them came the gold and silver smiths, the cutters of gems and workers in precious stones, stone masons and wood carvers, tailors who primarily made up cotton textiles, painters and pictographers, potters, builders and carpenters. They worked almost exclusively for the nobility and for the state and the priesthood – only members of the nobility were permitted to wear feather ornamentation, gold and silver, cotton clothing and precious stones and only they were allowed to dwell in two-storey houses and palaces, to construct which the aid of craftsmen was necessary. Sculptures and major buildings were again almost exclusively carried out by order of the state and the priesthood.

As with the merchants, the state aimed at making craftsmen dependent on it and in this it was largely successful. The majority of craftsmen by the end of the fifteenth century were either employed in the palaces and worked for the state or were maintained on the tributes exacted from various parts of the city. This dependence however was not absolute. All *conquistadores* report that craftsmen of all kinds could be found in the markets, where they offered their services to customers. Craftsmen were highly regarded. 'Mexico is famous above all by reason of the skill of her craftsmen, goldsmiths, builders, cutters of gems . . .'[62] the Snake Woman remarked on various occasions. They also enjoyed a number of privileges. The profession was handed down from father to son. The craftsmen were organised under their own guilds and their chief dealt with the central Aztec administration in all questions concerning them. These guilds, similar to those of the merchants, had their own gods with their own temples and ceremonies. Nevertheless their position was very inferior to that of the merchants: they did not have their own judiciary or belong to the nobility. This is undoubtedly connected with their economic dependence. They lacked the dynamic character of the body of merchants, which constituted a state within a state.

The craftsmen of the Valley of Mexico were the creators of an art form of which Albrecht Dürer said after having been shown some of the objects which Moctezuma II had given to the Spaniards: 'I too have seen the objects brought to the King from the new golden land . . . All these things were magnificent, and in all my life long I have never seen anything which moved my heart so much with joy as did these objects.'

THE MACEHUALTIN

The increasingly powerful summit of Tenochtitlan's social pyramid, the Chief Speaker, the military aristocracy, the priesthood and the merchants rested on two pillars: one consisted of the conquered peoples, the other of the common people of Tenochtitlan who consisted of three main groups: the *macehualtin,* or freemen, the *mayeques* who may be called bondsmen and the *tlacotin* who were regarded as slaves by most chroniclers and historians. The most extensive social group in Tenochtitlan consisted of the *macehualtin* – the term *macehualli* means he who acquires merit or makes atonement. They were members of the clan-like *calpulli,* which were still conducted strictly according to their traditions and foundations.

Thanks to a certain trait in the Aztec character we are very well informed about the course and manner of life of the various classes of their society. This trait is the Aztecs' fondness for long, rhetorical formal speeches that were delivered on every occasion. These speeches have largely survived and make a detailed reconstruction of the Aztec way of life possible.

Even infants were made aware of the oratorical artistry of the Aztecs. The umbilical cord which had been cut off at birth was given, if the child was a boy, to the warriors so that they might take it with them to the battlefield. 'It is said that the youth would thereby be much devoted to warfare.' This was not allowed to happen before the motives behind this procedure were explained to the new-born infant. It was the midwife who turned to him:

And that which I am cutting off thy body, off thy belly belongs to thee. It is something which thou dost owe to the *tlatecutli,* who is earth and sun.

And when war starts and the warriors assemble, we will place it in the hands of those who are brave warriors, in order that they may give it to thy father and thy mother, to the earth and to the sun. They must bury it in the middle of the battlefield where the fighting is carried on, and that is a sign that thou art dedicated and promised to the sun and the earth, a sign that thy name is scored into the battlefield, so that thou personally may not fall into oblivion.[63]

The education of youth was the business of the parents until puberty. Although the child could be sternly punished, the most important medium of education was again the speech-making, and on every appropriate and – judging by Old World standards – inappropriate occasion the child was reminded of his duties in life in long flowery admonitions by the parents.

When the youth reached the age of puberty he left his parental home and the *calpulli* took over his education. This must have been a very old custom among the Aztecs since we find the same sort of education among many North American peoples who never reached the state of development attained by the Aztecs. The youth moved to an institute for young men, a *telpochcalli*, where he lived with his contemporaries. An official, the *telpochlato* specially appointed for this purpose by the *calpulli*, took over the education of the young men.

If the youth was not familiar with agricultural labour, he was taught it there. The *telpochcalli* owned their own land and had to feed themselves by the practical efforts of their own members. These tasks however were of only secondary importance. The chief aim of education in the *telpochcalli* was to train youth for war. Only highly respected warriors were selected as instructors. Fighting was practised for many hours each day.

If the training in warfare was considered to be sufficiently advanced, the youth was taken along for the first time to the battlefield. On this first occasion he stayed apart as an observer. Only the most competent students were allowed to participate in the battle. They mingled with warriors belonging to the military orders whose duty it was to watch over them.

Besides the profession of arms and the knowledge of agriculture the youth was taught something about the traditions and history of the Aztec people, and in particular the religion of his people was explained to him. Prayers were said regularly to ensure the youths did not forget their union with the gods. Other skills, such as reading and writing, the study of the calendar or craftsmanship do not appear to have been taught in the *telpochcalli*.

When a student first went to the house of youth he was kept under the strictest moral control. Friendships with women were forbidden. This changed from the moment that he took part in his first battle, particularly if he had succeeded in taking a prisoner. Then he enjoyed the rights of a warrior and if he invited girls of easy morals into his quarters, the *telpochtlato* turned a blind eye.

Young men left the *telpochcalli* at the age of twenty to twenty-two. Their departure was always for the purpose of marriage. Great ceremonies were instituted, for which the permission of the *telpochtlato* had to be asked. They were attended by the young man's relatives, his school fellows and of course his instructors. Everybody was richly entertained at his family's expense and afterwards a hatchet was laid before the guests which the young man had used in the *telpochcalli* and which was a symbol of his membership of it. A relative of the young man now began to speak and said: 'Instructors and directors of the young who are here present, do not grieve that your brother and son wishes to leave your association and take a wife. Here is the hatchet. It is a sign that he wishes to leave your association. Take it, in accordance with the custom of Mexicans, and release our son to us.' Thereupon the *telpochtlato*, the instructor of the young, replied: 'All of us, I and the young men with whom your son has grown up over a period, have heard that you have resolved to marry him and from now onwards he will be separated from us for ever. So be it, as you have commanded.'[64] Then the instructors and the young men took the hatchet, went away and left the young man in his father's house.

The marriage which was resolved upon by the family, who also chose the marriage partner, had to take place at this precise time, but not until the son or daughter had been questioned. Again certain prescribed rites and long flowery speeches were laid down. The bridegroom's parents visited the bride's parents three times and the latter repeatedly evaded coming to a decision by prevaricating. But this evasion made it very clear to the bride-seekers that they would receive a different answer on the fourth day. And so it was: when they arrived on the fourth day, the parents replied:

This little one seems to have impressed you, since you want her so obstinately to be the wife of the man of whom you speak; we do not understand why he should indulge in such illusions; for she is a good-for-nothing and stupid into the bargain. But since you are so obstinate it is necessary – since the young girl has uncles, aunts and other relatives – that they may consider what must be done; you must hear what they say. It is also necessary that our daughter should be acquainted with the decision. Come tomorrow and we will give you our decision.

After further visits and flowery speeches, the marriage was finally agreed and this was an occasion for a great festival and a rich banquet. Long rhetorical admonitions by the older relatives prepared the girl for the event:

My daughter, thou wilt add to the number of old women: thou hast ceased to be a young girl, and hast already begun to grow old; it is time that thou didst abandon childish things. Thou wilt not in future behave as a child, but wilt greet everyone as a grown up in accordance with precepts which have been written down. Thou wilt have to rise in the night, sweep out the house and light the fire before day break. Thou wilt have to leave thy bed every day before sunrise, take care, my child, not to disgrace us . . .[65]

The climax of the marriage ceremony consisted in knotting together the husband's blanket and the wife's frock and from then on they were acknowledged to be man and wife.

Now the *macehualli* had the full rights but also the duties of a member of a *calpulli*. He received from the *calpulli*'s reserve his own land and property and with the aid of the other members of the tribal community a house was built for him. Sometimes he and his family lived alone in this house. In other cases compounds were erected where several related families lived. Pedro Carrasco has examined significant data obtained by one of the earliest population censuses carried out in Mexico after the Spanish Conquest. He found that 253 out of 490 households in Tepoztlan were made up of two or more related couples.

The *macehualli* was now bound to take full part in the public works and tribute payments of the *calpulli*. These duties lasted until he was old and unable to work. Thereupon he was – if he had distinguished himself in battle – kept by the state. If this was not the case, this seems to have been the duty of his immediate family.

To what extent did the life of members of the *calpulli* change as a result of the great Aztec conquests? Is it possible to compare their situation in any way at all with that of the plebs in Rome? Very significant research carried out by Edward Calnek seems to imply that certain parallels could have existed. After studying the amount of land available for cultivation in Tenochtitlan he has come to the conclusion that only a minority of the population of the city had enough land at their disposal to make a living as peasants. Since the majority of the people were not craftsmen only two possibilities exist: either they had acquired lands outside Tenochtitlan (of which there is no proof) or the state was maintaining them and their families presumably in return for military service.

The other members of the *calpulli* were still peasants or fishermen. The great rise of Tenochtitlan had not left them untouched. The irrigation works had allowed the peasants to build larger and larger artificial islands – *chinampas* – and in this way to cultivate new soil.

One of the most important questions – whether the labour which the *macehualtin* owed to the state or to the nobility decreased as a result of the increasing flow of tribute – cannot unfortunately be answered.

It is possible that they benefited to a certain though diminishing extent from tribute money. At certain times of the year, when supplies were scarce, they were fed by the state. Feasts were arranged at which food was distributed to all present out of the state stores. The most important food of all was dedicated to the goddess Xilonen. Some chroniclers report that these festivities went on for eight days, during which meals were distributed from morning to night to all the poor, men, women and children.

A much more direct form of participation in the conquests was the booty and the presents received during the battle and immediately afterwards, which the peasants brought back to their homes. These gave them more spending power and also extended their productive capacity. The peasants were unable to buy land but they could – even if in a limited degree – lease public land or that of other *calpultin*. At the same time they had the opportunity of acquiring slaves. These were used not only on the peasant's own land, or on the land he leased, but also took his place in the execution of public works. Another result of the conquests which benefited even the lowest groups were the magnificent celebrations held in the capital city after every victorious campaign.

Above and beyond this the life of the peasants in the cities of the Triple Alliance and many other cities of the High Valley underwent further important changes. Urbanised peasants had developed from the inhabitants of villages, small communities and city states and now lived in huge cities. They were able to sell their products in the great market of Tlatelolco or in the specialised markets of other cities. The tens of thousands of boats which travelled daily on the Mexican network of lakes and carried goods from one part to another demonstrate the importance and extent of this commercial transport.

The members of the *calpulli* had to pay a considerable price both politically and socially for this material progress. From being a subject in politics they became an object. At the beginning of the fifteenth century the members of the *calpulli*, whether in the sphere of tribal elections or in the meetings of *calpulli* representatives, had a significant say in all the important decisions. Now these decisions depended on the will of the military aristocracy. It was they who took decisions regarding war and peace, the great city buildings and the distribution of booty and tribute.

It would nevertheless be wrong to say that the *macehualtin* had lost all their rights. At the end of the fifteenth century the possibilities of social improvement which were open to them, although still limited, were not out of the question. The *macehualtin* could not become either merchants or craftsmen, most official posts were barred to them because of their limited education – as has already been pointed out, reading and writing were not taught in the *telpochcalli*. There were however many possibilities open to the individual who had distinguished himself in battle or who showed a particular gift for priesthood.

Equally significant is the fact that the possibility of descending in society was also limited for the *macehualtin*. As previously the majority of land in the whole of the High Valley seems to have belonged to them. This was inalienable and could only be taken from them if they did not cultivate it, and even then only by their own *calpulli*. They could not lose their land but they could lose their freedom and in certain circumstances become slaves. This concerned a certain kind of slavery which in the majority of cases did not involve any loss of land, was not irreversible and always held the possibility of eventual freedom.

A considerable brake on the descent of the *macehualtin* was the fact that in many respects the *calpulli* law held good. Disputes were taken before the state courts in only the most important cases, and in theory at least there was a strict directive not to treat the *macehualtin* worse than members of other social groups. Whether these directives were observed is another question. There were however certain limitations on the arbitrary power of the magistracy such as the inalienability of the land belonging to the *macehualtin*, the limitation of slavery and the growing dependence of the nobility on the warlike activities of the members of the *calpultin* as the territory dominated by the Aztecs increased. At the end of the fifteenth century these limitations were still very much in evidence.

THE BONDSMEN

In describing the social order of Tenochtitlan so far as it concerns the nobility and those at the base of the social pyramid, a clearly marked slope is evident that becomes more pronounced as it reaches the base.

Indian historians of the post-Spanish period, who have left us a wealth of information about the history of their peoples, came from the nobility and had an understandable interest in emphasising the achievements, history and glory of their ancestors. In order to achieve their claims for recognition as nobles by the Spaniards, they had to equate as far as possible the lower groups of society with Spanish standards. Many Spanish chroniclers did the same for reasons which extended from ignorance and an inability to understand Indian institutions to the wish to make the lowest groups of Aztec society useful to the Spaniards. For these reasons European standards were often transposed to pre-Spanish Indian institutions. A slave was equated with a slave, although the Aztec *tlacotin* displayed very marked differences for example from the Roman slave.

In the case of the bondsmen, there was another reason. After the Spanish Conquest they were essentially in the service of the Indian nobility. Accordingly Spanish interest in them was limited. Before such an interest might have grown in the short space of a few decades after the Conquest the bondsmen together with the major part of the Indian nobility had ceased to exist.

For all these reasons it is extremely difficult to undertake any credible reconstruction of the lower groups of Aztec society.

One of the most important questions concerns the economic and social role of these groups. Were the slaves like those in ancient Rome or in classical Greece the backbone of the economy? Did the bondsmen, as in certain parts of medieval Europe, constitute the foundation of the social organisation? Statistical and numerical analyses of the time make it possible to answer this question at least in part. Only about five per cent of the Aztec population consisted of slaves.[66] Accordingly we know that this group was of secondary importance.

The bondsmen were in a different position. According to estimates, made over the last few years, they may have constituted thirty-three per cent of the population.[67] That is a percentage which deserves consideration. It is all the more regrettable that of all social classes, less is known about them than about any group. It is unlikely that the existence of bondsmen – called *mayeques* or *tlamaictes* – was a result of Aztec conquests, and they constituted an ancient institution in Mesoamerica the origin of which greatly varied from region to region. In the cities of the High Valley they were widespread over a long period. It has even been suggested that they were late immigrants who were not allocated their own land and were forced to cultivate the land belonging to existing city states. The bondsmen were tied to the land which they cultivated. They were compelled to give a considerable portion of the harvest to the owner and if the land changed ownership, the *mayeques* remained with the new owner. They were freed from tribute to the central authority, but in all probability not from military service, which they had to perform just like all the other inhabitants of the cities of the High Valley.

This is as far as the scanty and very hazy information goes concerning this group. All other questions about them can only be answered by hypotheses. Were the bondsmen organised into *calpultin*? There is no answer. Were the bondsmen subject to state law or to that of the landlord? If the latter, then surely Aztec society would show some feudal characteristics. This however does not seem to have been the case, and most sources, without necessarily referring to the bondsmen, repeatedly emphasise that all inhabitants of the cities of the Triple Alliance were subject to state laws. But here again an intermediate solution is possible. Perhaps landlords were often appointed to be state judges.

Probably the most significant and difficult question is whether the bondsmen constituted a closed or an open group. Were they the descendants of late immigrants or groups overthrown at an early date, or were their numbers continually increased by new members? Many other questions depend on the answer to this one, above all the problem of whether Aztec society developed into a feudalistic society.

However limited the interest of many chroniclers may have been in social questions, a number of the most important contingencies governing a change from one social class to another are indicated. We know how one could become a nobleman, a merchant or a craftsman, also how one could slip downwards to become a slave. No chronicle however contains a single word as to how one became a *mayeque*. This would indicate that it was only possible to become a *mayeque* by birth.

Another question arises in this connection. Bondsmen cannot live on air alone; there must be land to which they are tied. Since the land belonging to the members of the *calpultin* of the cities of the Triple Alliance could not in any circumstances be expropriated, such land could only become available from the conquered territories. Nevertheless the land which the Aztecs appropriated was not cultivated by *mayeques*. If it was assigned to the state the members of the *calpulli* it had previously belonged to had to cultivate it collectively. If it was assigned to an individual the same thing happened, only the members of the *calpulli* were now recognised as *tecallecs*, who had to pay a certain tribute to an Aztec noble. In contrast to the *mayeques*, these *tecallecs* were the acknowledged proprietors of their land and the right to their tribute labour was not, like that of the *mayeques*, automatically inherited; each case had to be endorsed by the Chief Speaker. It is not surprising that the Aztec state preferred this very limited form of ownership, which apart from being inalienable was constantly subject to the will of the Chief Speaker, to the much more complete form of ownership with bondsmen.

It has been widely presumed that members of the *calpulli* who did not possess land within the framework of their own tribe became *mayeques*. In this event free and uninhabited land would have been necessary. Since the Aztecs hardly ever drove anybody out of the territories they conquered, but made the inhabitants work for them, such land was rarely available. An exception might have existed among those territories where the entire population had been slaughtered by the Aztecs following a revolt. Even in these areas however it was not bondsmen but other groups that were settled. When localities on the borders of the other dominions were involved, colonists were sent there from the Triple Alliance. In other cases, tenants not in any way having the status of bondsmen were put in charge of those lands. Everything points to the fact that the bondsmen were not a developing group among the Aztecs, but a class taken over from before or in early Aztec times whose development was in no way increased by the conquests carried out by the cities of the Triple Alliance.

THE 'SLAVES'

One of the strangest institutions among the Aztecs was that of the *tlacotin*, called by the Europeans 'slaves'. In contrast to the bondsmen these slaves were neither an hereditary nor a closed social group. Anyone who thinks of slavery as the classical Greeks and Romans saw it must bring a completely new criterion to bear on Aztec slavery. This applies to the rights of slaves, to their economic significance and to the social status of their owners.

An Aztec could become a slave for many different reasons, and in many different ways.

One was by committing a crime. Anyone who had committed a theft could be condemned in certain circumstances to become the slave of the man from whom he had stolen; he could also be sold by that man and the proceeds used in compensation for the theft. The families of traitors and political offenders could also be sold into slavery, as well as anyone who did not repay his debts. The kinds of debts incurred could be very varied but the two most common types the chroniclers refer to were either debts incurred in times of famine, in order to survive, or quite a different kind of debt, such as gaming debts. Betting was widespread, specially at the ball game, and supporters of the losing team could pay with their own personal freedom for bad luck in the matches if they had placed large bets.

It was also possible to become a slave by selling oneself. In exchange for the commitment to become a *tlacoti* the future owner provided sufficient food and cocoa to last for a year or two and provide a livelihood. At the end of that time the recipient of these goods entered into slavery. Another widely practised method was by the sale of children, which usually took place in times of famine.

The rights of a slave were very extensive. His owner while disposing of his labour disposed of nothing else. Woe to him if he killed the slave or if he did him bodily harm. He was then sent before the court, and in certain circumstances could be executed. The family of a slave if it had not also sold itself was free. With the exception of the descendants of traitors, no child was born into slavery. The slave could possess his own land, indeed there are reports of cases where slaves disposed in turn of their own slaves. One of the most important rights a slave enjoyed was the chance of acquiring his freedom if he repaid to the owner the sum of money originally paid for him. It was not an illusory right for the *tlacoti* had the chance of earning the necessary sum, not necessarily by work on the side which his owner kindly allowed, as was the case in

Rome, but by means of war booty. The slaves were not excused from the great campaigns any more than were the other inhabitants of the cities of the Triple Alliance. The booty and presents that were received at this time provided the means with which to purchase freedom. This might explain why so many Aztecs – to the Spaniards' astonishment – sold themselves into slavery without being in very great need. Most of them probably regarded the money which they received for the sale of them-selves as a sort of loan, to be repaid to their master after a set term with booty won during the next campaign.

The fact that the owner could neither kill nor ill-treat his slave naturally weakened the power he had over him. There was only one threat able seriously to intimidate the slave and which could in fact endanger his life. His owner could sell him. If a slave was sold three times in succession he could be sacrificed in honour of the gods. Such a sale however was a double-edged weapon for the owner. In principle the slave was bound to agree to such a sale unless he had done some-thing wrong in which case this had to be proved in the presence of witnesses. If the owner got this far he was able to offer the slave for sale on the market but then he found himself in even greater danger. If the slave escaped from the market place and managed to reach the Chief Speaker's palace, he was then free. Anybody other than his owner who stood in his way would himself be made a slave. Understandably, no one could recognise in this sort of servitude any real similarities with the slavery of European antiquity.

The *tlacotin* worked mostly in transport and in the household. They were only to be found in very small numbers up to the end of the fifteenth century working in agriculture and in construction work, the two most important branches of Aztec economy. This is not at all sur-prising since there was little opportunity for them in these fields. Most of the *calpulli* peasantry could scarcely afford slaves of this kind, whom they would have had to feed and supervise, in view of the small patches of land at their disposal, and the members of the ruling class who pos-sessed private land did not require slaves for the cultivation of their land. This work was carried out much more cheaply by bondsmen, or the members of the *calpulli* in the form of tribute; they fed and main-tained themselves and did not require supervision. The same held good for state construction work, which was carried out by all tribute-paying peoples. On these grounds it is not difficult to understand why the Aztecs, even had they practised a different kind of religion, could never have used as slaves the enormous number of prisoners which they made.

Slavery as described here was an expensive undertaking for the slave owners. A slave who could buy his liberty at any time or fall in battle did not represent a very remunerative investment; even less so if he had the chance of escaping at the time of his sale. Slavery had to be made viable in other ways. By the end of the fifteenth century these other ways seem indeed to have been taken. One way consisted of bringing slaves from the conquered territories into the plateau. They were not prisoners of war but people who had been abducted or sold as slaves by their relatives. After their arrival in the cities of the Triple Alliance, they were naturally more defenceless than those slaves who had originated within the Triple Alliance, and whose families made sure that their rights were not infringed.

A second and even more evolved form of servitude existed which some chroniclers still call slavery, although this term is scarcely applicable. Generally in times of need a family agreed to pledge itself, in exchange for foodstuffs and other forms of economic aid, to supply in perpetuity one member of the family as a slave. This servant lived in his own house and worked only daily for his owner. He was kept by his own family who were free to exchange him at any time for another member of the family. A substitute also had to be found if the slave died or became ill. The family were only released from their duty if the relative died in his owner's house. Accordingly the owner was anxious to send his slave home as soon as work had stopped. There is no mention anywhere of any sort of ransom payable for setting these slaves free. This form of servitude did not contain the heavy risks which the old form of slavery imposed on the owners. If the slave died, he was replaced; he was unable to run away, and in any case he hardly represented an economic burden since he was kept by his own family. No wonder that this kind of servitude found more and more support.

The feature of slavery among the Aztecs which distinguished it from that in the Old World and gave it its own stamp was the character of the slave owner. This kind of slavery, especially the last form of servitude, can more or less be characterised as 'the slavery of the small man'. Slaves were not required most urgently by the nobility, who were able to count on the labour of tributary underlings and bondsmen. They were needed by those who had no access to the labour of subjugated peoples or bondsmen, that is by the richer members of the *calpulli* and the merchants. The first group used the slaves for carrying out their public works and if necessary for the cultivation of their leased plots of land. In view of the total absence of draught animals in Mesoamerica, porters were of vital importance to merchants.

So it is not surprising that slavery instead of being promoted in any way by the central administration, was on the contrary viewed with deep mistrust, all the more so since slavery was the only form of social change among the Aztecs that, apart from legal sentences condemning persons to slavery, was not subject to decisions of state and was not determined by the state. This was the particular feature of slavery in Tenochtitlan which occasioned the Chief Speaker at the beginning of the sixteenth century to take special measures that will be referred to again.

There were other slaves in the cities of the Triple Alliance and in the Mesoamerican plateau who had only the name *tlacotin* in common with these slaves. These were people sold on the slave markets with the sole object of immediate sacrifice to the gods. If a man had not taken any prisoners but wanted to earn the favour of the gods and to do his bit towards ensuring the continued existence of the sun, he bought such slaves on the market. They were for the most part people born beyond the frontiers of the Aztec dominions, often in the peninsula of Yucatan, where the Maya specialised in the selling of slaves. They were joined by the slaves who had already been sold three times. This kind of slave-buying for purposes of human sacrifice seems to have increased suddenly about the end of the fifteenth and the beginning of the sixteenth century. The fewer Aztecs who could participate in the campaigns of the Triple Alliance, the more they were at pains to substitute sacrifices which had been purchased in place of the prisoners of war who were lacking. In view of the rising prosperity in the cities of the Triple Alliance in Mesoamerica, the purchase money for this purpose was not too difficult to acquire.

THE 'UNDERWORLD'

As in every great city there were in Tenochtitlan, besides these social classes, marginal groups of society. Included in this group were ladies who practised the oldest trade in the world and who figured prominently throughout Tenochtitlan. Their vocabulary is even retained by chroniclers in impressive terms, especially when they expressed their contempt for all men who had not performed war service. While these ladies were tolerated as one of the marginal features of society in Tenochtitlan, the large numbers of thieves and murderers also present were ruthlessly pursued. It hardly seems possible however that the underworld in a city of thirty thousand could have been extinguished at all easily, especially where there was also a market that had room for eighty thousand people. This was all the more so as increasing numbers of people left the *calpultin* who had in a large measure provided for and guaranteed the security of their members. The undermining of the tribal order contributed everywhere to the increase of criminal life.

Anyone observing the enormously complicated and rapid development of Aztec society up to the end of the fifteenth century is impressed by one fact more than any other: the relative internal peace in which this development took place in the first few decades of the Aztec Empire. It was nevertheless a period of peace which was deceptive in character. The first slackening in Aztec expansion caused latent contradictions to come out into the open.

AZTEC LEARNING, TECHNOLOGY AND LITERATURE

The Aztecs seem to have reached a peak in the history of Mesoamerica in their public organisation and the extent of their sphere of influence.

In regard to Aztec art it is not easy to give a comprehensive judgement. A great deal has been destroyed, textiles of the Aztec period have not survived. The favourable conditions that existed in the deserts of Peru naturally did not exist in the damp climate of Mexico. Objects of gold and silver were for the most part melted down by the Spaniards and exported. The great buildings of Tenochtitlan were destroyed, together with most of the pictograms, and feather work was largely left to decay. A number of sculptures in stone survived and were mostly discovered years after the Conquest during construction work in Mexico City underneath churches and other Spanish buildings. The same goes for a few buildings which are however in a far worse condition than the buildings of earlier cultures such as Teotihuacan or Tula.

Those objects of feather work which did survive were sent by Cortés immediately after the Conquest to Europe. Perhaps the most celebrated among them is Moctezuma's jewelled ornamentation which is on view in the Museum of Ethnology in Vienna.

The absence of archaeological sources is partly compensated for by the existence of written evidence which has for example given us an accurate representation of the central lay-out of Tenochtitlan.

A close examination of Aztec art forces us to admit that, with the exception of feather handcraft, it by no means represented the peak of artistic development in Mesoamerica. The pottery of the Aztecs was much more standardised and less imaginative than that of their predecessors. And although Aztec architecture impresses by its range and monumentality one of the most important achievements of the peoples of Mesoamerica, namely the corbelled vault employed by the Maya, was never put into use by the Aztecs.

The reasons for this partial backwardness in the field of art are not easy to establish, for there is no doubt that there were more craftsmen in Aztec times than ever before, and more energy and materials were expended for purposes of artistic achievement than in most previous periods. The question why the powerful Roman Empire never achieved an artistic development comparable with that of the Greek cities also applies to the Aztecs. The bad taste of a class of *parvenus* who determined the direction of artistic development, powerful state intervention, mass production, the particularly narrow limits of Aztec religion with its extraordinarily pessimistic outlook on the world, could all have been contributing factors.

When all these allowances are made it may still be said that Aztec art deeply impressed all those who came into contact with it at the time of its fullest flowering. The perfection with which Indian craftsmen mastered feather handicraft was so great that the Spaniards who had nothing comparable ordered feather ornamentation for the Spanish churches.

Aztec sculpture, the most impressive work of which is the representation of the earth goddess Coatlicue, already mentioned earlier on, conveys a unique portrayal of the gloomy pantheon of the Aztecs. Coatlicue is more than just one figure among many in a whole pantheon. She represents the incarnation of a fundamental religious-philosophical concept, of a cosmic view of the world. Death precedes every birth. In this great Aztec work there is no analysis. None of the many legendary and horrifying activities of this deity are told. There is no history; there is no action. The goddess stands before the beholder in majestic repose, motionless and still – a fact and a certainty – a monument, a symbol, a concept. All the decorative and symbolic features, all the details, represented with clarity and precision, the reptilian mouth and the reptilian bodies, the human hearts and the severed hands, the zoomorphic claws: all these have only one aim in view, to emphasise and dramatise the tremendous power that the earth goddess represents so that the faithful believer, as he draws near to the figure, transmutes all this in his imagination into a living reality. As Stéphane Mallarmé once demanded: 'The reader should be allowed to create something new and that is what must happen here. The aim is not to limit the imagination, while bringing the work closer to reality, but to stimulate the imagination.'[68]

The Aztecs, with one notable exception, did not reach the zenith of Mesoamerican development in the fields of learning and technical science any more than they did in the field of art. This exception was their ability to master the network of lakes in Mexico. The Aztecs may not have discovered the *chinampa* system of agriculture, but they ensured its maximum development. The tremendous dams and dykes that were built in the lake were uniquely the work of the cities of the Triple Alliance. The erection of a huge city on an island in the middle of this network of lakes in Mexico, the building of three great causeways joining the island to the mainland were justifiably thought by the Spaniards to be a technical miracle.

In other fields of scholarship and technology however, the Aztecs remained far behind the rest of Mesoamerica, especially the Maya. The Aztec calendar did not contain the long count of the Maya. The Aztec graphology was much less of a genuine script than that of the Maya and was instead a mnemonic system. It appears to have contained far fewer phonetic elements than the Maya script.

Aztec pictograms were primarily written on paper, and the enormous quantities of paper contained in deliveries of tribute clearly indicate

the importance of written evidence amongst this people, though some
of the paper may have been used for religious purposes. A tremendous
archive with thousands of documents is said to have been discovered in
Tetzcoco. These documents are generally divided into six different
groups by the chroniclers:

1 Annals, in which daily events were recorded
2 Genealogies, recording the origin and deeds of the Chief Rulers
3 Maps, on which were marked individual villages, and above all
   the types of land tenure
4 Religious books, in which were laid down rites, laws and
   ceremonies
5 Books in which religious festivals were noted
6 Records of legal judgements and controversies

The weakness in the ideographic and phonetic components of the
script made it impossible to record exact texts. But it was enough for
recording great events. The representation of a burning temple with
the symbol signifying a locality was a sign that this place had been
overthrown. The drawing of a spear and a shield was synonymous with
war. By means of glyphs, partly phonetic in character, it was possible
to record the names of important people. The Aztec pictograms largely
served as mnemonics for texts that were memorised primarily in the
calmecac by the pupils. These texts, the majority of which were transposed
by the Aztecs into Latin script after the Spanish Conquest, give an
impressive picture of the variety and riches of Aztec literature.

From their classification it is possible to distinguish three types of
Aztec literature: religious literature, literature meant for the common
man and the beginnings of a court literature.

The religious poems, most of which have survived, are particularly
numerous. Aztec poetry is characterised by the accentuation of
particular syllables, since the poems were sung to the accompaniment
of flute and drum. They are also very rich in exceedingly florid
metaphor. These poems were partly traditional and of great antiquity.
At the same time new poems were constantly being written in honour
of the gods. The temples maintained professional poets for this purpose
who were fed and cared for and whose only duty consisted in composing
new prayers to the gods. These prayers, in so far as they were approved
by the temple hierarchy, were primarily taught in the *calmecac* and
presumably those meant for the common people, in the house of youth,
the *telpochalli*.

The term folk literature may be applied to long poems or long prose
descriptions which were recited either by individuals or in part by the
whole assembly on particularly festive occasions. These were mostly
songs of praise extolling warriors, and especially hymns of praise about
the rulers of the cities of the Triple Alliance.

Thus Moctezuma Xocoyotzin was greeted on his accession to office with the words:

> Oh mightiest Lord of this world! The clouds have lifted and the darkness in which we were enveloped has rolled back. The sun has risen, the light of day has returned after the darkness which the death of the King thy uncle called forth. But on that day the torch was again lighted which was to become the light of Mexico. We have received a mirror in which we can see ourselves. The great and mighty Lord has entrusted his Empire to thee, and with his finger has shown thee to thy place.

Metaphor and rhetoric, sometimes even poetic, language were not confined to great occasions only, but were also used inside the family circle at small celebrations. Some of the admonitions laid down, from speeches to a new-born baby to requests to the ruler, are written in a similarly poetic vein.

When a merchant returned from a long journey and gave a banquet to his fellow merchants at home, the following exchange took place: 'So – ye have come here', said the merchant to his guests.

> Yea – indeed I went off to take care of reputable porters, their walking sticks and their shoulders. I took every care of them. And see – nowhere did the Almighty Lord cause me to meet my death.
>
> Perchance, though I may somewhere have splashed somebody with water, or spattered him with mud? Ye must not just accept my stink and my rottenness, ye must not treat it jestingly.
>
> And despite all, I have now looked once more into your dear faces and upon your noble brows; I have, after all, returned to one or two who still live – my aunt, my niece and my other kith and kin by blood.
>
> Perchance the Almighty Lord will now cause me to meet my death here, will destroy me tomorrow or the next day. What is it that ye want to hear?[69]

The reply of the guests was no less rhetorical:

> Yea, here thou art and so we have eaten and drunk of that which is the reward of thy wanderings in hill, ravine and plain, also the reward of the sighs and tears which thou didst sigh and weep somewhere at some time to the Almighty omnipresent Lord.
>
> Yea, we are proud of the goodness which He in his mercy has shewn unto thee.
>
> But by giving us food and drink here, do ye mean thereby to seal our lips, that we might even fear thee so that there might be no more opportunity for us to educate and instruct thee?
>
> Whence didst thou get that which thou gavest us to eat and drink? Didst thou, perchance, make off with the pot and bowl of others?
>
> Hast thou perchance cheated at the ball game or at dice? Hast thou perchance outwitted someone who wears a loin-cloth or a woman's skirt? Perchance thou hast stolen somebody's property and possession? Perchance

it is no good and pure thing which thou givest us to eat and drink. Perchance it is dirty, perhaps dusty, perhaps filthy? Truly we cannot tell. But shouldst thou choose to plunge into a torrent or into an abyss, verily no ransom, no reward would be forthcoming for thee.

We give thee here what befits the education and instruction of a man: the thick smoking stick, the red hot stone, which penetrates thy body, which rages in one's bowels, which remains stuck in one's swollen throat, which eats out our heart, the cold water, the icy water and the stinging nettle birch-rod of the Lord, of the omnipresent Almighty. [70]

Even in the quarrels and invective which Sahagun recorded, the rhetorical speech full of metaphor was used. Thus, in a quarrel between two women:

Sit down. What hast thou, thou old whore, to say to me? Dost thou imagine that thou art my bedfellow? Why dost thou press upon me so grossly?

Shall I come to thee in thy cabin to stay or is thy life corroded because of me, doest thou seek here my livelihood? Dost thou perhaps provide me with nourishment?

Out upon that hussy with her head like a great straw shanty, with her rumpled hair. Stop it, thou with thy revolting over-painted mouth, thou utterly degenerate paragon of depravity.

She who loiters about in the shanties, destitute of everything, who has nothing to eat, who has no chile pepper, no salt, who is overpoweringly greedy, who is dying of hunger.

Fie upon thee, that thou mightest have wanted to practise deceit in front of everybody. What more dost thou want to bring forward before everyone: wilt thou up and away and jump into the water, wilt thou go up into the hills?

Depraved creature, that renders ill service to others, know what thou art. So that I do not have to chase thee away. It seems that thou doest not care, that thou art not ashamed of thyself. [71]

During the great and solemn ceremonies that took place in Tenochtitlan and the other cities of the Triple Alliance, not only were poems recited and sung together and epic sagas read out aloud, but poetic compositions were also spoken by several performers. The distinguished scholar of Aztec literature, Angel Maria Garibay, considers these were the beginnings of regular dramatic writing.

Besides these compositions which were meant for the great mass of the people, there also seems to have been cultivated in the cities of the Triple Alliance a sort of courtly poetry in connection with the tremendous development of the court of the Chief Speakers. These are poems that were presumably only read at court and which because of their rather complicated philosophical content were difficult to understand by those who had not studied in the *calmecac*. The authors of the poems meant for the people were usually professional poets who lived at court and could devote themselves chiefly to their poetry.

Courtly poetry on the other hand seems to have been the work of distinguished members of the nobility, including the Chief Speaker. The most beautiful poems of this kind were written either by Netzahualcoyotl or by his son Netzahualpilli. Characteristic is the song of a ruler in honour of his ancestors:

In tears of grief and offering flowers do I, the singer of this lay, dispose my words. I remember the Noble Ones, who linger in the realm of the dead, battered and broken. They had come to be lords and rulers on earth, these Lordly Ones, and now they lie there like drooping quetzal feathers, like precious stones that have been shattered. And so, in the light of the countenance of the gods, before their very eyes, in the knowledge of the Almighty and Universal God, they met their death on earth. Woe is me, as I begin my lay, when I think on these Noble Ones. Ah that I could but once more hold them in my embrace, woe is me that I should once more let them return to the realm of the dead. If but the Lordly Ones could rise again and live upon the earth, evermore to be honoured. What joy that would be for us. And Ipalmemoa could have loving joy of them. How doth it profit us, that we unworthy ones must feel such sadness. Thus my heart weeps and I, the singer, dispose my memories, these memories which return with tears and mourning.[72]

The regard enjoyed by poets and poetry among the Aztecs and their allies is evident in an episode taken from the history of Tetzcoco. The story goes that a nobleman had been accused of treason against Netzahualcoyotl. While waiting in prison before being led before the Chief Speaker, who was to pronounce the death sentence, he prepared a plea for mercy in flowery poetic language. After he had recited this to Netzahualcoyotl the latter was so inspired that he set the nobleman free and even generously rewarded him.

However rich the language of Aztec poetry was, its subject matter was ultimately very limited. It moved as Garibay has written,

in a small circle, war and sacrifice, which constantly recur in the most varied metaphors, and with constant, but in the long run wearisome intimations. Death, the unknown reasons for its occurrence, the horrifying memory which it leaves behind. The sweet conversation with friends who must part: for they have only 'come to earth on borrowed time', the irrevocable absence of the old princes who cannot return for a single moment . . . and nothing more.[73]

THE BEGINNING OF THE CRISIS IN THE DOMINION OF THE AZTECS

In 1502 Moctezuma Xocoyotzin, also called Moctezuma II by historians, was elected Chief Speaker of the Aztecs. In 1519 he was to experience the extensive conquest of his empire by the Spanish *conquistadores*, to whom he himself finally fell victim as well. But the unity of the High Valley, the union of the Triple Alliance, the coherence of the social classes in Tenochtitlan itself, in fact everything on which Aztec conquests had been based had long before begun to crumble under his rule.

Three factors were substantially responsible.

The Aztec conquests slowed down considerably in the beginning of the sixteenth century. Moctezuma nevertheless succeeded in making a number of important conquests, notably over the Mixtecs in the region now known as Oaxaca, although these were much less widely ranged than those which his predecessors had achieved. As a result the wealth that now flowed into Tenochtitlan diminished considerably. At the same time the number of 'unproductive' campaigns grew; expeditions had increasingly to be dispatched against rebellious localities and although they resulted in many prisoners of war there was relatively little booty.

Another factor which highlighted the internal weaknesses of the Aztecs was their inability to conquer the regions ruled over by the Tlaxcaltecs and the Tarascans, where the population was far below that of the Aztecs. The war against Tlaxcala had long ceased to be a Flower War as in the mid-fifteenth century. The days were past when after the fighting had ceased, the rulers of Tlaxcala came secretly to Tenochtitlan to be present at the sacrifice of their followers to Humming-bird on the Left. The war between Tlaxcala and the Aztecs was waged with increasing bitterness. The Aztecs had imposed an economic blockade on Tlaxcala, so that among other things, no salt had reached it for many years. Most of the inhabitants no longer even knew the taste of salt, as they informed the Spanish *conquistadores*. The hatred of the Aztecs against their much smaller adversary was probably due to the fact that it encouraged the city states overthrown by the Triple Alliance to revolt whenever possible. The rising of Cuetaxtlan already described was due to encouragement and promises given by Tlaxcala.

The military operations against the Tarascans were no more successful. Since the forces of Chief Speaker Axayacatl had been beaten in 1480 no Aztec army was able to make any headway. The constant battles and skirmishes on the borders of the region of the Tarascans were entirely without success.

These battles against Tlaxcala and the Tarascans, ever increasing in ferocity, raised war costs without bringing in anything in exchange except prisoners of war. The continued survival of those states marked the limits of Aztec power both for the cities of the Triple Alliance and for the peoples that they had overthrown.

A third quite different factor contributed even more than the first two towards undermining the foundations of Aztec society at the beginning of the sixteenth century. In 1505 a great famine broke out in the Valley of Mexico. It is reported that thousands of inhabitants of the cities of the Triple Alliance had to sell themselves into slavery in order to survive. It is probable that this famine was due to the termination of the irrigation system at the end of the fifteenth century and the virtual exhaustion of the ecological possibilities of the High Valley. The population of the High Valley, on the other hand, was in a state of constant expansion. If account is taken of the fact that since the famine of 1454 the efforts of the Aztecs and their allies had been bent on preventing famine, and that most probably towards this end millions of people were subjugated and huge public works undertaken, a deep-seated weakness among the Aztecs is revealed. They were no longer even in a position to afford protection to the privileged population of their own city. It is probable that this fact brought about a widespread crisis of confidence among large sections of the population. All these factors – growing war expenditure, smaller returns, an ever-increasing pressure of population and famine – led to radical changes in Tenochtitlan's relations with the dependent city states in the High Valley, with its own allies in the Triple Alliance and finally to growing tensions within the Aztec capital city itself.

First of all the Aztecs tried to extract from within the Valley what they could no longer get from outside it. Many small dependent city states, such as Chalco, had their tributes, which had been fixed for a considerable time, arbitrarily doubled.

The strongest partner of the Triple Alliance, Tetzcoco, was clearly put in its place. Moctezuma caused the son of the Hungry Coyote, Netzahualpilli, the Chief Speaker of this city state, to be informed '. . . that the times had changed, for where earlier the Empire had been governed by three rulers, now there was only one. He, Moctezuma, was the chief ruler of Heaven and of Earth and he desired that henceforward no one should any longer give him advice or directives'.[74] This autocratic manner was very soon translated into fact. When Netzahualpilli died Moctezuma forced on Tetzcoco a Chief Speaker of his own choice. In the ensuing revolt of a considerable part of the city against this measure the opponents of the ruler designated by Moctezuma were ferociously massacred. From now on an even greater share of the tribute that had originally been received by the other cities of the Triple Alliance flowed into Tenochtitlan.

Measures designed to curtail existing rights and to impose fresh burdens were not confined to regions lying outside Tenochtitlan. In the capital city itself those groups were hit who were regarded by the ruling military caste as a potential danger: that is the meritorious aristocracy and the merchants. In proportion as conquests receded and the number of official posts for disposal shrank, the search for such posts increased since the number of hereditary nobility constantly grew, no doubt as a result of polygamy, permitted to them only. No wonder that they exercised strong pressure on the Chief Speaker to put the meritorious aristocracy in its place in order to limit its chances of rising in the social scale. This measure was not at all easy to implement, since advancement through war service was deeply rooted in the customs and consciousness of the Aztecs.

It is not therefore surprising that such a step on the part of Moctezuma should have given rise to great consternation and presumably antagonism. Not long after he assumed office a chronicle composed in Spanish feudal style relates that Moctezuma had an old priest, whom he trusted, summoned to him:

Doubtless you know, my father, that I have decided that all those who wait upon me shall be knights, and sons of princes and lords, not only those who serve me in the running of my household, but all those who hold positions of importance in my kingdom. I am deeply perturbed by the thought that all the previous kings allowed men of humble birth to serve them in such matters. For this reason I have decided to deprive all those of low birth of whatever offices they hold, and to have my household and kingdom served only by people of good birth who have no common blood in their veins.[75]

However devoted the priest may have been, he nevertheless expressed his doubts to Moctezuma:

Great Lord, you are indeed wise and powerful and well able to do whatever you desire, but I do not believe that such an action on your part would be looked on very kindly. Some might say that you wish to abolish the laws of the previous kings, and you might so estrange the poor and humble *macehual* that he would scarcely dare to look on you or come to you.[76]

Moctezuma refused to be influenced by such objections. He not only dismissed all high officials who were not members of the nobility, but even had a considerable number of them executed. Another chronicle tells how deeply this measure affected the population and how strong the opposition was. 'And Moctezuma's arrogance was so great that he would not keep in his service some men because they were of plebeian stock who by reason of their services had become captains and warriors of courage and had risen to other honours. Some of them he had executed, others he banished from his court.'[77]

The meritorious aristocracy was not the only group sacrificed by Moctezuma's restrictive measures. The merchants also felt the hard hand of the Chief Speaker.

For [although] Moctezuma praised the merchants [another chronicle relates] they did not wish to be taken for rich men or to enter that profession. They were shy and humble: they very much feared fame and glory. For, as already indicated, the Ruler of Mexico held the merchants and slave dealers in great affection as though they were his own sons. If they shewed themselves to be proud and conceited by reason of their wealth and fame, the ruler grew sad and his affection for them vanished. He then sought untrue, even if apparently justifiable grounds to kill them and to kill them without reason because of his hatred of their pride and their presumptuousness.[78]

No wonder that the merchants did all they could to look like poor people and to conceal the mass of their wealth.

But no one really knew what possessions a man had [says another chronicle]; if possible the man hid them in a single boat, covering them all up . . . But the owner did not acknowledge his own property, did not call it his own, acted as though he had no claim to it and said to them to whom he entrusted it: 'Keep safely that which you have here. Do not go and say, that it is indeed the property belonging to such a man, who has entrusted it into your care, but say rather, I have been ordered to deliver the property of the directors of the body of merchants.'

Across whatever localities he may have carried his property, be it Tochtepec or Anaoac, Xoconocho or any other localities, he never admitted that it was his, acted as though it did not belong to him, as if it were not his own . . . Moreover he did not return to his own home, but more likely into any other house, perhaps into the house of his aunt or of his elder sister.[79]

The measures which the Chief Speaker of the Aztecs took were probably made possible by his success in very astutely playing off against each other the aspiring social groups, the meritorious aristocracy and the merchants against whom he turned, but primarily by bringing them into opposition against the free peasants. The expropriation of 'haughty' merchants was perhaps popular since part of their wealth was distributed to deserving old soldiers, some of whom belonged to the meritorious aristocracy.

Moctezuma's most astute measure in this direction was without doubt the abolition of slavery for debt which had grown to enormous proportions during the famine of 1505. With one stroke Moctezuma won enormous popularity among the peasants, secured the power of the state and simultaneously struck a heavy blow at the classes of aspiring merchants and rich *calpulli* peasants, who were the chief beneficiaries of slavery for debt.

As so often happens in times of increasing internal and external tension, the ruling class of Tenochtitlan tried to cover up the situation by reinforcing the power of the state and by the glorification, indeed the deification, of the persona of the ruler.

There is some evidence that in the time of the last Moctezuma a new system of organising the population in Tenochtitlan was carried out, which partly ran parallel with the *calpultin*. Twenty families were grouped together for purposes of labour and of tribute payments and placed under one official; five such groups making altogether a hundred families constituted a unit from a financial point of view. State officials kept scrupulous records of births and deaths.

New restrictions were imposed upon the merchants. An increasing number of them had to trade on behalf of the state and they were permitted to bring back only limited quantities of precious stones, cotton blankets and other high-value merchandise. From now on these had to be delivered in the form of tribute.

Craftsmen were compelled or induced to an ever-increasing degree to enter the service of the ruler.

The abolition of slavery for debt strengthened the power of the state over the free peasants, as we have seen.

Bondsmen who had always owed their master labour and tribute were no longer settled on lands which for some reason or another had become free, but became tenants pledged to the state.

The power and glorification of the ruler reached new heights. A Spanish chronicler pointed this out very strikingly: 'From all this it may be gathered that the ruler had no absolute power, and governed rather as a consul or a duke than as a king, although in later times . . . the power of the ruler grew, till it assumed tyrannical proportions, as was the case among the last rulers.'[80]

The concept of the God-King arose. He was surrounded by an ever more complicated ritual, which assumed an oriental stamp.

Whoever enters Moctezuma's palace [relates Cortés, the *conquistador*] must do so with bare feet. Whoever is summoned to him approaches with head and eyes lowered, in a humble posture. Even if anybody is addressed by him, he may not look straight at him. Respect and deference demand this. Many Mexican nobles have expressed surprise to me because my Spaniards stand up straight and look me in the eye when I speak with them, which appears to be insufficiently respectful and submissive.

When Lord Moctezuma goes out, which is seldom, all who accompany him remain in a very submissive posture. Anyone meeting him stands still and looks at the ground motionless until the ruler has passed by . . . The customs at the Mexican court are more varied, splendid and ceremonious than at the court of an oriental potentate.[81]

The Chief Speaker's deputy, the Snake Woman, became increasingly a second grade official whose power in no way even approximately equalled that of his predecessor, Tlacaellel. From a council of members enjoying equal rights the Supreme Council of the Four developed more and more into a submissive group of advisers. The way in which they consorted with the Chief Speaker in public already expressed this change. The *conquistador* Bernal Diaz describes the situation as follows:

Then the four women stood aside, and four great chieftains who were old men came and stood beside them, and with these Montezuma now and then conversed, and asked them questions, and as a great favour he would give to each of these elders a dish of what to him tasted best. They say that these elders were his near relations, and were his counsellors and judges of law suits, and the dishes and food which Montezuma gave them they ate standing up with much reverence and without looking at his face.[82]*

The story was circulated more and more that the whole territory of the Aztec domain was the property of the Chief Speaker, which he had always allowed his subjects to utilise. How effective were Moctezuma's measures? They undoubtedly contributed a great deal to increasing the power of the Chief Speaker and of the hereditary nobility both externally and internally. It had been possible to introduce a compliant ruler into Tetzcoco though it was not possible to exclude the sitting candidate fully. Moctezuma was forced to make a compromise that left the latter a great part of his power.

Moctezuma's power even inside Tenochtitlan and despite his God-Kingship was not absolute in all fields; however he was still forced before declaring war to summon a council of war to which the most courageous warriors belonged and in which the most animated discussions took place with regard to the occasion for war, possibilities of conquest, and so forth.

The measures for the complete subjugation of the merchants met with only limited success. Just as the *Pochteca* quickly succeeded, after the overthrow of Tlatelolco, in regaining their rights, so now they succeeded, substantially, in circumventing the restrictive measures of the Chief Speaker. The more they were restricted in trading in luxury goods the more they went over to slave trading. Increasing numbers of slaves were brought from the conquered territories to Tenochtitlan primarily for sacrifice. The slave traders rapidly became the richest and most esteemed merchants of the High Valley. The religious significance of their new business – were they not supplying the gods with food? – assured them additional protection.

The fiction that the Chief Speaker was the owner of the whole of the land was also hardly credible. The *calpulli* always felt themselves to be the owners and possessors of their land. On the whole however it may be said that the reinforcement of the Chief Speaker's power in fact succeeded, within the capital city of the Aztecs, in bridging over the social tensions that were beginning to appear. When the Spanish *conquistadores* arrived in Tenochtitlan they found no allies within the city right up to the time of the overthrow of Aztec power. The situation outside nevertheless was quite different, where the deification of Moctezuma and the oriental veneration of his person instead of reducing the growing bitterness against the Aztecs only added to it extraordinarily. This was to have a catastrophic effect on the Aztec state when the foreign *conquistadores* arrived.

* Maudesley's translation, II, pp. 62–3 (translator's note).

CHAPTER 11

THE POST-CLASSIC PERIOD IN THE ANDEAN REGION

HUARI-TIAHUANACO

The close of the classic period in the central Andean region was followed by a new era that displayed a large number of features of the previous period. The trends that crystallised during this development show, in general outline, striking similarities to those that developed in Mesoamerica: a stronger tendency towards secularism, which was most strikingly expressed in the application of an even greater proportion of the surplus product to temporal instead of religious purposes and in the development of states under secular leadership. Large cities and important states arose that on the eve of the Conquest in the Andean region virtually formed an empire. An unequivocal ascendancy of the highlands over the lowlands ensued.

If the main trends that developed in Mesoamerica were repeated in the Andean region, the stresses were quite different, as will be described later.

The scholar working in the Andean region encounters greater difficulties than his counterpart in the same period in Mesoamerica. While the first written sources occur at the beginning of the post-classic period in Mesoamerica they develop much later in the Andean region. For a knowledge of this period in the Andes archaeological evidence is all that is available. Even this is of limited significance by comparison with earlier periods – such as the time of the Mochica. The result is that there are greater obstacles to a historical reconstruction of the early post-classic period than was the case in Mesoamerica.

As in Mesoamerica, the beginning of this period is characterised by the predominance of a culture that impressed itself equally on the highlands and the lowlands. In most of the Andean region there suddenly appears, without transition, an art style displaying the closest connections with the culture of Tiahuanaco. Above all the art form of the Gate of the Sun and of the Puma and Condor bas-reliefs is universally and repeatedly conspicuous, whether in pottery or in

243

textiles. What did this diffusion of the Tiahuanaco style signify? There were for a long time two opposing theories. For some the diffusion of the Tiahuanaco style was the result of a religious movement, not a militaristic one. Tiahuanaco was regarded as a place of pilgrimage to which pilgrims thronged from the whole Andean region, even helping to construct it. The diffusion of the Tiahuanaco style was thought, in the first place, to have been the result of religious influences that were not necessarily bound up with any form of political expansion.

In the view of other scholars the diffusion of Tiahuanaco style was the result of a regular conquest, although the question of its extent or intensity is still disputed. Some scholars considered it was an empire on the lines of the later Inca Empire, others only saw in it the loose ascendancy of a nobility which despatched colonists and garrisons to various areas that had more or less been overthrown. Was Tiahuanaco in any case the real centre of the culture named after it?

Research carried out after the Second World War has helped to clarify some of these problems. When it was established incontrovertibly that Tiahuanaco had been largely erected before its style spread over the whole Andean region, scholars began to seek a new centre for Tiahuanaco culture.

These researches led to one result when at the beginning of the 1950s the remains of a large centre were found in Huari, far from Tiahuanaco in the highlands of Ayacucho. The buildings and the pottery of Huari bore unmistakable Tiahuanaco characteristics. Nevertheless these features were much more like the Tiahuanaco finds on the Peruvian coast than those of the Bolivian highlands. In contrast to Tiahuanaco, extensive remains of dwellings were found in Huari, so that most scholars believed that there had once existed a veritable city. They considered Huari rather than Tiahuanaco to have been the centre from which the Tiahuanaco style spread.

One of the most important problems remains unresolved: how did the Tiahuanaco style first spread from Tiahuanaco to Huari and later from Huari to the whole Andean region? Were the driving forces religious, commercial or military in character? A final answer is impossible in the present state of research. There exist however a number of plausible theories, of which those of the Peruvian archaeologist Lumbreras[1] are, in my opinion, the most credible. Lumbreras considers that Tiahuanaco was always the place of origin of Tiahuanaco style. An important commercial centre had existed here and merchants had wandered into many different parts of the Andean region with llamas and textiles. They arrived also in Huari where they encountered emigrants from the Valley of Nazca on the southern coast of Peru. In some way or another the two groups joined together and founded the city of Huari in a region where there had scarcely been any centres in earlier times. Lumbreras based this hypothesis, among other things, on the fact that in Huari there was a noticeable mingling of Nazca and Tiahuanaco styles, and furthermore that very few archaeological remains have been found in the region of Ayacucho for the period before the foundation of Huari. There then followed a militaristic expansion and Huari became the centre of an important dominion. Many archaeologists agree with these interpretations.

A number of fresh discoveries will probably result from exhaustive excavations both in Tiahuanaco and in Huari as well as in all other sites of Tiahuanaco culture, which still remain to be explored, and will confirm one or other of these hypotheses. These excavations are unlikely to produce any decisive conclusions regarding the history of the people who created Tiahuanaco culture or the type of state which they erected. Our knowledge is limited by the lack of written sources.

However there is one striking feature about Tiahuanaco culture. Whether the centre and the place of origin is considered to have been in Tiahuanaco itself or in Huari, all research carried out to date has proved conclusively that it lay in the highlands. Exactly as in the Chavin period and in the subsequent Inca period, all movements which extended over the whole Andean region always began in the highlands. This contradicts to a certain extent some of the results of archaeological research, which show a far greater degree of state integration and centralisation on the coast than in the highlands. Why did the highland peoples repeatedly succeed in overthrowing the lowlands or at least in influencing them more decisively than was conversely the case? An attempt will be made to examine this apparent contradiction in regard to the Empire of the Inca, which extended over the whole Andean region and for which there exists for the first time historical evidence.

Perhaps the most difficult problem when considering the culture of Tiahuanaco is the question of its effects. Was it temporarily superimposed so that when it vanished the old cultures reappeared almost unchanged? Or were there radical revolutions that put their stamp on all future cultures?

In the case of food production or technology there were, with one exception, no important innovations. There even appears to have occurred a certain retrogression in agriculture, at least on the coast. There is evidence that a number of irrigation works fell into disrepair and that the population of various coastal valleys grew smaller. Perhaps this retrogression in agriculture was counter-balanced by cultural contacts which involved transferring methods of cultivation from one area to another and spread cattle-breeding over wide areas. It appears that at this time llama breeding extended from the highlands of Lake Titicaca to the Huari area. The introduction of bronze, the only technical innovation in this period, had no decisive significance. Relatively few bronze objects have been found which could be from this era. There is no justification on the basis of research carried out to date for the hypothesis that bronze weapons made it possible for Tiahuanaco warriors to make far-reaching conquests in the Andean region.

It is in the social field rather than in the technical field where the decisive innovations in the Tiahuanaco period occur. Two of the most characteristic features of the post-Tiahuanaco period appear to have been introduced during the Tiahuanaco period.

The first trend to manifest itself was the termination of every form of government that could in any way be called theocratic. It has already been pointed out how problematical the concept of a 'theocracy' is when we have only archaeological evidence for its very existence. It can be clearly stated that in contrast to the cultures of the classical period an ever-increasing proportion of the labour force was applied to secular instead of religious construction. This development seems to have begun in Tiahuanaco. Closely connected with it is the second trend that became specially evident in this period, at least on the northern coast of Peru: the appearance of cities. The construction of large city centres, which reached its peak in the post-Tiahuanaco era, would appear in the opinion of Richard Schaedel[2] to have begun in the Tiahuanaco period. This trend is not yet expressed in the appearance of large cities, but in the appearance of small urban complexes. In Schaedel's view these combine, at least on the northern coast, dwellings, religious and administrative buildings for the first time. They are for the most part fortified walled cities that were built on the loftier parts of the coastal valleys, probably with defence in mind. Between these walls there are dwellings and spaces, large groups of houses which are termed palaces and pyramids. The big centres of this type are complete with parks, gardens and storage barns.

It is possible only to guess at the reasons why these centres appeared. Were they garrisons and administrative centres of a class of conquerors? Were they the dwelling place of a new secular nobility who, unlike the priests of the classical period scattered round the temples, needed to live together? Were these cities built as fortresses against possible attacks from outside? Were they the result of a trend towards the mass production of ceramics and textiles which required the concentration of large groups of craftsmen in one place? As yet no final answer to these questions is possible.

The rise of the carriers of the Tiahuanaco civilisation in the Andean region may in some respects be compared with the rise of the Toltecs in Mesoamerica. In both regions a conquering force appears to have overrun almost the whole of the area of culture. In neither case is it possible to say whether the conquerors formed a uniform imperium, which covered the whole area within their sphere of influence, or whether a number of different states developed. In both cases – and this seems to be the similarity which was decisive – the essentially theocratic culture was superseded by an essentially secular authority. This trend must not however be equated with the substitution of a peaceful culture by a warlike one. A period in which peaceful theocracies ruled certainly did not exist in the Andean region, and it is very doubtful whether such a thing ever existed in Mesoamerica.

However significant the similarity of the Toltec period was to that of Huari-Tiahuanaco, there were several important differences that cannot be overlooked. While the place of origin of Tiahuanaco culture was not culturally more retarded than the other areas of the Andean region, the position of the Toltecs appears to have been somewhat different. They came from the other side of Mesoamerica's cultural frontier, and had a markedly inferior standard of development both technically and artistically to the Mesoamerican cultures of the classic period. On the other hand the results of Toltec penetration went deeper than those of the Huari-Tiahuanaco period. Both among the Aztecs and the Maya the Toltecs were vividly remembered at the time of the Spanish Conquest. Against this Tiahuanaco culture appears to have been totally forgotten. Not a single historical testimony of any one of the multifarious peoples of the Andean region refers to the culture of Huari-Tiahuanaco. The ruined city of Tiahuanaco occurs only in the mythology of the Inca.

We can therefore do no more than erect very rough theories concerning the reasons for the disappearance of Huari-Tiahuanaco culture. As regards ceramics, textiles and sculpture it did vanish in about the thirteenth century over the whole of the Andean region, except in the highlands of Bolivia. Nor was it succeeded by any foreign incursion from beyond the cultural frontier as in Mesoamerica after the decline of the Toltec empire. In the Andean area there developed a regional differentiation and the impression we get is that the separate peoples which had been conquered once more raised their heads. It is only possible to guess what the political and economic conditions were which brought about this process. Did regional revolts take place against a centralised Huari-Tiahuanaco rule? The many fortresses which were erected precisely in the Huari-Tiahuanaco period on the coast of Peru indicate that the new nobility did not feel entirely secure. The decline of the irrigation installations could also have meant that they were unable to fulfil one of the most important functions of the ruling class on the coast, namely the maintenance of the irrigation system. This may well have led to rebellions and uprisings. These are however only conjectures. More detailed knowledge is lacking. It is just as possible that there existed a similar phenomenon in the Huari-Tiahuanaco period as among the Toltecs in Mesoamerica. Many Toltec groups of conquerors – particularly those which intruded into the region of the Maya – immediately became autonomous state entities which had practically no further connections with their original groups. In the course of a few centuries the Toltec nobility mingled to such an extent with the indigenous Maya groups that they were difficult to distinguish. It is possible that a similar process took place in the Andean region. There might be some evidence to this effect. Presumably we shall never know any more than this; for in contrast to the region of the Maya, there is no written evidence of any kind here which could one day be deciphered.

THE PRE-INCA STATES

The genuine historical era in the Andean region only begins after the decline of Huari-Tiahuanaco. Archaeological discoveries are for the first time supplemented by historical evidence. This is very varied in type. On the one hand it includes traditions, most of which – as in Mesoamerica – occur in the shape of legends or religious representations. They are however far fewer and much less easy to decipher than in Mesoamerica. This is due partly to the existence in the Mesoamerican region of pictographs which made it possible to record these traditions on paper, and partly to the fact that there was a different basic conception among the Inca as compared with the Aztecs. An account has already been given of the Aztecs' insistence on the value of promoting historiography and of their rigorous efforts to suppress all other but official representations. Nevertheless this presented great difficulties in the conquered territories where Aztec influence on religion and culture was limited. In addition the Aztecs, despite their misrepresentation of history, laid no claim themselves to having created every culture in Mesoamerica. They regarded themselves as the successors of the Toltecs and made efforts to maintain all Toltec traditions, even though they were at pains to misrepresent in some measure their connection with the Toltecs. It was quite different in the Andean region. The influence of the Inca on the peoples subjugated by them was far greater than had been the case among the Aztecs in Mesoamerica. Therefore the importance of the Inca and the Inca conception of history was intensively forced on the peoples subject to them. Although it was not possible to carry this through equally everywhere, it nevertheless contributed substantially towards extinguishing old traditions. Unlike the Aztecs the Inca did not regard themselves as the successors of another high culture, but as the creators of all existing cultures. According to their conception of history, before them only sheer barbarism had existed. It is therefore understandable that they should attempt to suppress or to remould all traditions that referred to a high culture preceding their own.

The second type of written evidence was of a different character. It consisted of the reports of Spanish missionaries and administrators in the period following the Conquest. The states overthrown by the Inca continued to exist even after their conquest, and the Spaniards reported on the government, structure and culture. However valuable this source may be, the problem recurs as to which of these institutions, customs and administrative patterns were pre-Inca and which had first been introduced by the Inca.

A third problem arises in connection with this type of written source available to the research worker: the discrepancy between written and archaeological sources. The most significant and important archaeo-logical sources at our disposal come from the Peruvian coast, where much has survived in very good condition, thanks to its aridity. The most important written evidence, on the other hand, originates in the highlands. This discrepancy makes the necessary co-ordination between archaeological and historical evidence very difficult. It is therefore easy to understand why the history of the last two hundred years before the Spanish Conquest gives rise to far greater controversies among scholars dealing with the Andean region than among Mesoamericanists.

Until about the thirteenth century, Mesoamerica and the Andean region displayed amazing similarities. A period of warlike troubles and a wave of conquest that engulfed the whole cultural region either in the Andes or in Mesoamerica followed a classical, essentially theocratic period. This centralised region dissolved almost as rapidly as it had arisen. After a renewed period of troubles and battles, in the fifteenth century there arose in both regions great state structures which, at least in one case, developed into an imperium. It would however be a mistake to ignore the great differences which simultaneously existed between the two regions. In Mesoamerica a process followed the dissolution of the Toltec Empire that might almost be termed atomisation. A great number of smaller and very small city states emerged. One of them succeeded in acquiring large areas of territory more rapidly than all the others, and thanks to the higher degree of centralisation finally overthrew important parts of the rest of Mesoamerica.

CHIMU

In the Andean region, on the other hand, the development seems to have progressed differently. The dissolution of Tiahuanaco culture was not followed by a process of atomisation, but by the appearance of powerful and extensive territorial states. It is only possible to guess at the reasons for this development but it would appear that the regions of the Peruvian coast, whose economy was based on irrigation, played a highly significant role in this process and may even have provided the initial impetus. As in the classical period the region of the Mochica on the northern coast of Peru – where irrigation played the most important role – appears to have had the most centralised state structure of that period, so one of the most centralised and powerful states of the Andean region arose in the same area. This was the state of Chimor. It appears, already in the fourteenth century, to have ruled over the greater part of the coastal valleys of north and central Peru. It extended for nine hundred kilometres along the Peruvian coast from Tumbez in the north to Paramonga in the south. It embraced only the coast and the whole basis of its existence was intensive irrigation. The system which in the time of the Mochica had only just begun now reached its zenith: tremendous irrigation installations were constructed which united as many as five valleys with one another. The maintenance of such installations required a unique degree of centralisation and state administration. That this was in fact the case is confirmed both by archaeological and by the few historical sources available to us. In the previous Mochica period, in spite of enforced state integration, there had still been a certain degree of decentralisation – the nobility lived scattered about in the vicinity of the hundreds of pyramids and holy places that sprang up in all the valleys. Now the situation was radically changed. Great cities arose on the northern coast of Peru, and in these the nobility of this state was concentrated.

The greatest but not the only one of these cities was Chan-Chan, in the Valley of Moche on the northern coast of Peru. The population of this city, still the centre of the region of Chimor at the time of the Spanish Conquest, though it was also under the domination of the Inca, is estimated to have been fifty to a hundred thousand. The city therefore attained about the same dimensions as Teotihuacan, but seems to have been smaller than the capital city of the Aztecs, Tenochtitlan. Its composition and structure hardly permit a comparison with the great cities of Mesoamerica. The differences are already evident in the building materials used. While in Mesoamerica stone was used, together with wood, this was hardly feasible in the coastal valleys of Peru, where both materials were scarce. The whole of Chan-Chan was therefore built of dried adobe bricks. The quality of these adobe bricks was such that the archaeologist Max Uhle reports that even in the twentieth century bricks from Chan-Chan fetch ten times the price of new clay bricks on the open market.

The differences in the structure of the city were even greater. All Mesoamerican cities showed a regular centre in which pyramids, temples, administrative buildings and a market place were concentrated. The dwelling-houses surrounded this centre. There is little to be seen of such a centre in Chan-Chan. It consisted of ten little walled cities. Each of these building complexes which are of varying size was surrounded by a clay-brick wall up to ten metres high. Within these walls there were palatial houses, simpler dwellings, pyramids and *canchones*. These were fields in which intensive agriculture was practised. The soil had been dug out in order to reach the ground-water. It is no exaggeration to say that each of these walled structures was a separate city with its own dwelling-houses, administrative and religious centres and cultivated land. Between the walled units there appear to have been graves. It is also presumed that dwelling-houses and shacks existed outside the walls of the smaller units of Chan-Chan. What these units signified is still not known to this day. Some presume that they were originally the dwellings of clans that kept on multiplying. Others believe that each walled structure embraced various classes and social groups. There is so far no evidence that only the ruling class lived in one of the structures and only their subjects in others.

Where did this enormous population come from? It has been possible to establish this archaeologically with some degree of certainty. In the not far distant Valley of Virú on the north coast of Peru, which belonged to the state of Chimor, the number of villages at this time suddenly diminished. Where in the Tiahuanaco period there had been almost a hundred villages in the Valley of Virú, their number decreased rather abruptly to forty. It is therefore presumed that a considerable proportion of the population of these coastal valleys was moved to Chan-Chan or to other cities.

These cities could be of varying character. Richard Schaedel has divided them up into two groups.[3] One he terms urban lay centres; these were small cities without great ceremonial or state buildings in which garrisons were quartered or where in the first place the common people congregated. In the other larger centres there were large state buildings which were secular and religious in function; he presumes that the nobility resided here. On the frontiers of the kingdom of Chimor, especially in the south, great fortresses were built like the one at Paramonga, designed to protect the kingdom against rival states both on the coast and in the highlands.

In contrast to all earlier states in this region archaeological data are for the first time borne out by historical evidence.

The inhabitants of the north coast of Peru belonged to quite different tribal groups from the inhabitants of the highlands. Their languages differed completely from the Quetchua and Aymara of the highlands. The most common language that was still spoken in some areas of the coast up to the end of the nineteenth century was Mochik. There also appear to have existed a number of other dialects or independent languages.

There are two legends concerning the origin of the peoples of the north coast, or their ruling dynasties, which create as many problems as they resolve. One tells of the settlement of the Valley of Lambayeque, which was not a constituent part of the kingdom of Chimor but was a late conquest:

The inhabitants of Lambayeque tell [says the legend and all the peoples in the vicinity of this valley agree with them] that once upon a time which is so long ago that they cannot tell when, a great fleet of *balsas* appeared from the northern parts of this area of Peru. Their leader was a man of great capacity and great courage called Naymlap. He brought with him a great many concubines, but his wife, so the legend says, was called Ceterni. Among those who accompanied him were many people, who followed him as their ruler and leader. A few of them who distinguished themselves by outstanding courage constituted his dignitaries, of whom there were forty . . . Naymlap himself arrived with this retinue and innumerable other high officials and distinguished men and also his house which was already decorated and furnished.

This prince Naymlap steered towards the coast with all his possessions and landed at the mouth of a river which today is called Fayuisllanga. Having left their *balsas* there they moved into the interior of the country, with the intention of founding a settlement. When they had covered half a league, they built certain palaces in their own style to which they gave the name of Chot and in this building and palace they worshipped with barbaric devotion an Idol which they had brought with them; it bore the features of their prince and was made of green stone. They called it Llampallec, which means 'Portrait and statue of Naymlap'.

After this people had lived for many years in peace and concord their prince and ruler, who in the meantime had acquired many descendants, knew that he had reached the point of death. In order that his subjects should not know that death had him in its power, his dignitaries buried him secretly and in the same room in which he had lived. They however spread the news all over the country that thanks to his magical powers he had given himself wings and had flown away. Those who had followed him on his arrival were so sorely grieved over his departure that although they now had many descendants and were greatly attached to their new and fertile country, they left everything behind and without a leader or any fixed plan, set out in all directions to seek him. Accordingly only those who had been born in the country remained behind – and that was a goodly number. The rest, on the other hand, scattered at random and without any sort of order in search of their prince, who, as they thought, had disappeared.

Now in the legend the descendants of Naymlap are counted to the very last member of this ruling race, Fempellec:

He was the last and also the most unfortunate member of this ruling house, for he conceived the idea of moving the Idol which as has been told, Naymlap had set up in the palace called Chot, to another place. He tried variously to carry out his intention but without success. There appeared to him the devil in the guise of a beautiful maiden. So great was the devil's art of temptation and so weak was Fempellec's self-control that he let himself be led astray, so they say. Hardly was this sinful union consummated than rain began to fall – an event which had never been witnessed before in these plains. The rains went on for 30 days; there followed a year of sterility and famine.

When it became known amongst the Idol's priests and the other nobility that their ruler had committed this serious offence, they realised that the people had been visited with famine, rain and misery as a punishment for his sin. In order to punish him, they seized his person while they quite forgot the fidelity towards the ruler owed to him by his subjects, and threw him, bound hand and foot, into the deep sea. With his death was extinguished the native ruling race in the valley of Llambayeque which was called after the Idol which Naymlap had brought with him and which was called Llampallec.

As a result of the death which his subjects meted out to Fempellec as he deserved, the government of Llambayeque and the surrounding territory was left without a ruler or a native prince. The populous community remained in this state for a long period, until a mighty despot called Chimu Capac drove in with an invincible army and took possession of these valleys, in order to plant garrisons.

In the valley of Llambayeque he installed a ruler and prince of his own choice, who was called Pong Massa and came from the land of the Chimu.[4]

Another legend tells of the settlement of the Valley of Moche, the real centre of the kingdom of Chimor. Similarly there came on rafts from the other side of the ocean a prince called Tancanaymo. He settled in a house in the Valley of Moche.

He remained in this house for the period of a year and carried out the necessary ceremonies and on the strength of the treaty which he had with the Indians whom he conquered, he learned their language and they obeyed him and gave him their daughters.

It is not known whence this conqueror came, other than that he gave them to understand that a great overlord who lived on the other side of the ocean had sent him to rule this country. The yellow powder which he used in his ceremonies, the cotton attire with which he clothed himself, are well known in this country, and rafts made of wood are used on the coast of Payta and Tumbez.[5]

It is not easy in these representations to sort out the core of historical truth from the legend. The Naymlap story is widely considered to be a legend of rather late origin. The fact is striking in both cases that conquerors are spoken of who came from the other side of the ocean. Is it possible that they were people of Asiatic origin? This is denied by

most archaeologists who, among other things, presume from archaeological similarities that the place of origin must have been in the
region of present-day Ecuador. Specially significant is the widely
accepted 'aristocratic' tradition. In contrast to the Andean highlands
where there are stories of power being exercised by primitive tribal
chieftains and tribal elders, all coastal representations tell of radical
social differences which developed rapidly, of godlike rulers and of an
extensive court nobility. As with all traditions of this nature, the more
contemporary they are the more exact they are likely to be.

The kingdom of Chimor, or as the Inca called it the 'kingdom of
Chimu', was founded in the first half of the fourteenth century. In 1370
the ruler Nancen Pinco created the basis for this kingdom when he
conquered the neighbouring valleys of Sana, Pacasmayo, Chicama,
Virú, Chao and Santa. The last great conqueror was at the same time
the last independent ruler of Chimor, Nimchcaman. He advanced
down to the Valley of Lima in the south where he was stopped by
another kingdom, that of the Chincha. His general Queruntumi carried
the attack through and was beaten back, whereupon he committed
suicide. The time of its greatest flowering was also the period of the close
of the kingdom of Chimor. It was defeated and conquered by the Inca
in the middle of the fifteenth century.

The kingdom of the Chimu was the only ancient American state
that depended on irrigation completely. What effect did this have
on its social organisation? Did it manifest as already described
the tendencies towards the ascendancy of a central administration so
often shown by such states?

It is very difficult to give a comprehensive picture of the social
organisation of the kingdom of the Chimu from the rather fragmentary
nature of historical representations and the limited archaeological
evidence. It is known however that the trend towards social development resembled that of regions where irrigation played a prominent
part in the economy. The power the state must have had in order to
mobilise the necessary labour for such undertakings is demonstrated by
the size of its capital city and of its public buildings. Historical sources
suggest that the ruler had great power and was worshipped as God,
while a deep gulf existed between the nobility and their subjects. This
gulf was found in the religious field too. 'The Indians of the coast
believed that man descended from four stars: two of these stars begat
the kings, caciques and nobility, the other two begat the common
people, the poor and the workers. The Archbishop of Lima, Don
Bartolomo Lobo Guerrero, attempted in vain to eradicate this heresy.'[6]

It is significant that in the legend of Naymlap already cited even the
ruler of one single valley on the coast was already worshipped as God.
However great the esteem in which the rulers were held, if they no

longer fulfilled their original function of ruling over nature in order to produce food, their divinity was no more use to them. It is certainly no accident that the only case recorded in the chronicles of the removal of a ruler by his subjects was when he was no longer able to guarantee the food supply. Presumably one of those tremendous rainstorms had fallen which only happened once in several decades on the Peruvian coast and brought in its train unimaginable disasters. If the God was unable to ward off this catastrophe he had presumably forfeited all claim to divinity.

Every valley had a royal governor, called Cie. It is unfortunately not possible to ascertain how far they exercised power in their own right, and to what degree they were subservient to the ruler.

There is considerable evidence that both trade and crafts were under state control. No independent merchants existed at the time of the Conquest in the coastal valleys of Peru nor in the rest of the Inca Empire. Trade would seem to have been entirely in the hands of the state. In one account it is said that 'the ruler had at his disposal six thousand Indians who had to supply him with gold, silver, *chaquiras* [small gold pearls] and copper from the highlands'. Less is known about the craftsmen. However the fact that they lived in the great cities, that they worked primarily for the nobility, that they were largely dependent on raw materials supplied to them by the state, indicates that they were under state control.

It is impossible to establish exactly what position religious institutions occupied and how great was their degree of independence. However the fact that the ruler was worshipped as God shows a very close connection between the state and religion.

Unfortunately there is less information about the life of the peasantry, who were presumably organised in clan-like groups. A considerable proportion of them appear however to have worked, in contrast to peasants in the Andean highlands, as bondsmen cultivating the lands belonging to the nobility.

Even though the reports of the chronicles are incomplete with regard to the relations of the social groups to each other and to the state, they do provide a great deal of information about daily life and the ordinary customs in the kingdom of the Chimu. Some aspects of their life might almost be adopted as targets by social groups today. Thus the admonitions which were given at a marriage:

In the presence of those who had brought the marriage about a new dish was placed between the man and woman about to be married filled with maize flour and llama suet, all this was burned in a big fire which the newly weds poked until the dish became red hot. Then the godfather said: 'Now ye are married to each other but take note, ye must love one another in such a way that the husband must work as much as his wife; for it was for this reason that ye poked the fire together. And one of you must not be idle while the other is working. Furthermore when the fire of love burns in one of you, the other must not be cold. Rather ye must not lag behind one another in love; for ye surely desire to be of equal rank.'[7]

These exhortations were not just empty words. Love-life played a far greater role among the Chimu than in any other part of the Andean region, and the puritanical Inca were horrified by the erotic habits of the coastal population.

Customs connected with the position of doctors would probably find fewer supporters:

The doctors in the coastal plains, who practised nature healing with the use of herbs, were highly esteemed. Besides the honorarium which they received from public moneys, they possessed honourable privileges. Any one of them, however, who lost a patient either through carelessness or ignorance was beaten and stoned to death. He was then bound with a rope on top of the corpse, which was buried, while the body of the doctor was left on top of the grave, so that the birds of prey might devour him.

The Spanish chronicler relating this adds sadly: 'Were this custom followed today there would not be so many lackeys of death nor so many deaths resulting from the appalling ignorance of doctors, who are paid the same irrespective of whether they kill or cure a patient.'[8] As with the Aztecs, punishments for offences among the Chimu were exceedingly severe.

A law was introduced against thieves which was as dreadful in itself as it was terrifying as a deterrent, for a man who had committed a robbery was suspended alive for so long that he was all but strangled as a result . . . The whole valley attended the execution of the sentence, which also fell on the parents and brothers, for the same punishment was meted out to anyone concealing an offence as to him who had committed it.

This was regarded among the Indians as an irreversible law, because they neither had houses which were protected nor doors to their dwellings. Furthermore, as we can see even today, their dwellings were built of fragile reeds without any tough binding of any kind and without clay walls. Here then fear and not the vine-dresser was the guardian of the vineyard. This all worked itself out in such a manner that they could be absent from their villages without having made their possessions secure and without having provided any particular protection for their houses.[9]

In contrast to the highland peoples, who worshipped the sun as god, the inhabitants on the coast regarded the moon as the supreme godhead.

This god [they believed] ruled over the elements, caused the fruits of the field to grow, called up the storm at sea, and also the thunder and the lightning. A *huaca* was its place of worship which was called Sian which in the language of the Yunka signifies 'House of the Moon'. The moon was regarded as mightier than the sun, because the latter does not shine by night whilst the moon was visible both by night and by day. Another reason was that the moon often eclipsed the sun, while the latter never eclipsed the moon. At eclipses of the sun there were therefore festivals held in honour of the moon, in which its victory over the sun was celebrated. During eclipses of the moon however, anguish was expressed in dances of lamentation. For the duration of the eclipse great distress was evinced and mourning was worn. The Indians of the coastal plains believed furthermore, if the moon did not appear for two days, that it had gone into the other world to punish thieves that had died.[10]

During eclipses of the moon, dogs were beaten so that they might howl and so call the moon back.

There were also human sacrifices made, though in lesser degree than in Mesoamerica. 'Children of five were sacrificed to the moon on dyed cotton-wool, together with chicha and fruits of the field.'[11]

Besides the moon, the sea and certain stones called Alec Pong were worshipped as godheads. 'These stones which were always worshipped by a certain group were regarded to be the earliest ancestors which the sun had turned to stone because of the death of the wife by whom he had had a son. When finally the sun's anger had abated, it instructed every family to worship the particular stone from which it had sprung.'[12] There seems in this way to have existed a kind of ancestor worship. It is not clear whether the tribal ancestors of individual great families or of larger units are in question.

The kingdom of Chimu attained the highest degree of state integration and state power which had ever existed on the Peruvian coast. Nevertheless no more than in the case of the Aztecs or in the case of the Inca was there any correlation between this development of power and the efflorescence of art. Like the Aztecs and the Inca, the Chimu were also inferior in matters of artistic achievement to their far less sophisticated predecessors in matters of state organisation.

This was especially evident in their ceramic ware. Pottery, for the most part black, or sometimes dyed red, does not display even a vestige of the artistic achievement, the imagination, the joy of life and the realism of the Mochica ceramics, which were unique. It has a plump appearance; there are only a few modelled or painted representations of people and of life. Only figures of little monkeys and birds reflect weakly past achievements. The predilection for eroticism remained, though the erotic scenes found in the pottery of the Mochica were now replaced by phallic symbols.

As among the Aztecs, the rise of the court and the development of a state bureaucracy appear to have produced a negative effect on art.

CHUCUITO

The kingdom of Chimor was probably the most powerful and most highly developed state of the pre-Inca era in the Andean region. It was however by no means the only state and in any case not typical of other state structures in this region.

The description of one of the many states, the state of Chucuito[13] in the highlands round about Lake Titicaca, demonstrates how pronounced were the differences in degree, content and type of state organisation on the eve of the Inca conquest.

The contrast between Chimor and Chucuito starts with their environment. The climate is hot and arid on the Peruvian coast and cold and damp round Lake Titicaca at a height of four thousand metres. Maize and cotton – basic for food and clothing on the coastal area – do not prosper here. Artificial irrigation, without which it is hardly possible to imagine agriculture on the coast and which exerted a decisive influence on the social organisation of the coastal peoples, was not viable. Like Chimor, though, the population here was dense. The basis of Chucuito's existence may be summed up in three words: potatoes, *quinoa* and llama.

In comparison with the maize cultivated on the coast, the potato, despite its great nutritive properties, had a decided drawback: it could only be stored for a relatively short period. The highland peoples nevertheless had found a solution. Most of the potato harvest, shortly after harvesting, was alternately dehydrated and frozen until a substance formed called *chuñu*. This *chuñu* could be stored for a long time – some say years – and retained most of the potato's nutritive properties. Besides potatoes, *quinoa*, often known as Andean rice, was cultivated.

The inhabitants of the southern highlands of Peru however regarded their greatest riches to be neither the potato nor the *quinoa*, but llama and alpaca which they kept in hundreds of thousands. This is not surprising in view of the extremely diversified usefulness of these creatures and the small amount of labour they required. Their grazing grounds were high up in the mountains, in the *puna*, which was quite unsuitable for agriculture. The animals fed exclusively on wild grass. Only a fraction of available labour was required for cattle breeding. Against these low costs there was balanced tremendous profit.

Llama and alpaca supplied the wool which constituted the main covering of the highland peoples. Alpaca wool was mostly used for clothing, while llama wool, which was much coarser, usually served other purposes. The finest wool came from the undomesticated type of Auchenia, the vicuña, which was found only rarely.

The skin of the llama was used for leather and the meat was a highly prized delicacy over the whole Andean region. Here too the highland peoples had discovered methods of preservation, which made it possible to keep meat dessicated as *charqui* for a long time. The llama droppings also fulfilled an important purpose. In the timber-starved highland areas the dung was an important source of fuel. In addition to providing wool, meat, leather and fuel, the llama served as a means of transport. Although it could never be ridden it was capable of carrying loads which were not very heavy. Above all in times of war it constituted the most easily transportable food reserves. It is therefore not surprising that in the highland areas it was regarded as the producer of wealth and many of the peoples inhabiting the region worshipped it as a god. They imagined the llama to be their ancestors, which nevertheless did not prevent them from making full use of these animals or from slaughtering them. There were no taboos. Llama were always sacrificed to the gods on festive occasions.

The states erected by these cultivators of potatoes and breeders of llama differed widely from the kingdom of the Chimu on the coast. The units were far smaller, and should be termed tribes rather than states.

The basis of Chucuito's social organisation was a clan-like organisation called *hatha*. To what degree it was in fact a clan will be more closely examined later in connection with the Inca *ayllu*.

The *hatha* was the owner of the land and allowed its members to use it. The individual areas of land appear to have been heritable. If a young man of the *hatha* married, he had a claim to land. He could receive it either from his father or, if there was not enough, from the clan itself which held land in reserve for such purposes. Thus far the *hatha* shows strong similarities to the *calpulli* in Mesoamerica. But there are also significant differences. In contrast to the Mesoamerican *calpulli*, whose members undertook the cultivation of the land privately and under their own management, cultivation here seems to have been carried out in common. Not only was the land of peasants who were present cultivated, but also the land of those who for various reasons were unable to take part in the work of cultivation: herdsmen who tended the cattle on the grazing lands, peasants who had been commandeered to work on public works, the sick, cripples, widows and orphans. Thus the *hatha* had an important effect in regulating matters concerning the lower classes of society and guaranteed every member a minimum livelihood which preserved him from hunger and want.

Did the *hatha* also have a regulating effect upwards, like similar organisations in many other parts of the Andean region? Was only a certain minimum of land granted to everybody and the excess again subdivided in favour of other members of the *hatha*? There is no evidence that this was so, and the constant references of the chronicles to their heritability of the land rather suggest the reverse.

Similar rules too also applied to the llama and alpaca which the highland peoples considered to be their real wealth. Here too there was a sort of regulation in favour of the lower social orders. Llama were herded in common, so that the animals belonging to those who were unable to work or were absent did not fare worse than the cattle of other members of the *hatha*. Anyone losing his cattle through disease or for any other reason was entitled to receive fresh beasts from the commune which possessed large herds in its own right. In times of famine, the communal cattle were either slaughtered or exchanged for the benefit of the members of the *hatha*. Just as we saw in the case of land, regulation downwards was not balanced by a regulation upwards. The differences in wealth however in relation to llama were greater than in relation to land. There were members of the *hatha* who possessed ten llama and others who owned more than several hundred beasts.

Did these differences in wealth result in any radical social stratification within the *hatha*? As far as it has been possible to ascertain, this was not so. The wealthier members of the clan were able to organise larger feasts and through 'liberality' were able to win esteem and power. They were not able however, thanks to the reserves under the control of the *hatha*, to plunge the poorer members into economic dependence.

Far more complicated and complex than the situation within these clans was their relation to each other. The complexity is immediately apparent in that substantial differences appear already to have existed in the status of individual *hatha*. Beside a great many *hatha* of cattle breeders and peasants there were clans which exclusively carried on fishing in Lake Titicaca whose members belonged to a different people, the Urus. These clans were looked down on as a lower social order by the cattle breeders. Conversely, other clans devoted in particular to handicraft – tribes of silversmiths and potters – appear to have occupied a higher status in society.

The complexity increases if the relationships between these clans are considered. All clans were grouped into seven rural provinces that were administered by seven villages. The apex of the whole organisation was situated in the village of Chucuito. At the same time there was another organisation. All villages were divided into two groups of clans: one group belonging to the upper and one to the lower moiety. This division, as will be described below in connection with the Inca, presumably had religious or kinship origins. At all events it was administratively decisive. In each of the seven villages there were two village headmen or chieftains. One led the clans of the lower moiety and the other led the clans of the upper moiety. Furthermore in Chucuito, the capital, there were two chieftains who, enjoying equal rights, generally speaking led both groups. Did this institution of the two moieties already exist before the Inca or was it first introduced by them in the highlands of

Lake Titicaca? This question cannot as yet be answered with certainty.

There was a governing class in Chucuito on three levels: the clan elders within the *hatha*, the village elders of the seven villages, composed respectively of two and in one village of three leaders of the moieties and the two head chieftains of Chucuito. These two were descended invariably and exclusively from two clans: from that of the Cari for the upper moiety and from that of the Cusi for the lower moiety. In each village they owned their own land and property and thousands of head of cattle. Their land was cultivated by the village communities who also placed members of the clan at their disposal for limited periods to herd the cattle or to perform household services. In addition individual clans designated certain members who had to serve the chieftains for the whole of their lives and for all practical purposes withdrew from the clan.

The functions of these chieftains were multifarious. They were the generals in war, they were the chief judges who settled quarrels between individual clans and villages. In times of hardship they were expected to donate part of their wealth for the benefit of the community. Finally they performed the extremely important function, as far as Chucuito was concerned, of trading with the coastal lowlands. At the time when this region was under Inca rule, and presumably in earlier times, the chieftains of Chucuito had sent a number of colonists into the coastal valleys to cultivate maize and coca there. These products were in tremendous demand in the highlands where they could not be cultivated. Chicha, a kind of maize beer primarily made from maize, was also used for religious purposes. Coca is a sort of narcotic, taken today by hundreds of thousands of Indians of the Andean region, but presumably at that time allowed only for religious purposes. Every year the chieftain sent heavily laden caravans to the coast, a few hundred kilometres distant, in order to receive the desired tropical products in return. The colonists living on the coast for their part received llama, wool, *chuñu* and other highland products. The function of the chieftain consisted in keeping free, by war or by negotiation, access to these areas which were separated from Chucuito by alien territories.

However exact our information may be on the incomes, wealth and functions of the chieftains we are still in the dark about their actual powers. We do not know what sort of relations existed between the two chieftains Cari and Cusi. Did they divide the work between them, did they mostly have equality of rights or was Cari, who disposed of a larger income, in the last resort effectively the head chieftain? Were they obliged to confer with the tribal elders or the headmen of the village or not? All these questions must remain open.

Were the leaders of Chucuito princes, like those in the coastal realm of Chimor, who were worshipped as gods? Did they live in oriental splendour, in palaces in the midst of great cities? Were they surrounded by a large bureaucracy, whose members served the community less and less and progressively served the ruler more and more, rather like dignitaries referred to in the legends and depicted accompanying the conqueror of the coastal valley of Lambayeque?

Archaeological evidence indicates that the relationship between conqueror and subject in the highlands of Chucuito was very different from that in the coastal realm of Chimor. There are no traces anywhere of great cities and splendid palaces. Chucuito was a village, inhabited for the most part by peasants. The most noteworthy constructions in the whole highland area in this period were built round Lake Titicaca where there were stone burial places, called *chullpas*. An extensive bureaucracy is not mentioned. A Spanish examining officer who visited Chucuito shortly after the conquest counted only forty important men in which he includes the fourteen headmen of the seven villages, in a population of a hundred thousand. The chieftains of Chucuito did not claim to be regarded as gods like the great Chimu and the princelings of the coastal valleys. Their relationship to their people was not that of a prince to his subjects, but was much more complex. The chieftains of Chucuito had to request every year that the various clans should cultivate their land and weave their textiles. Most probably this request was a mere formality which was always granted, but had to be renewed annually. Conversely a member of a clan whose llama had died could turn to the chieftain with the request for a new llama. It appears that this request was also complied with as a matter of course. For those members of the clan who had been commandeered to cultivate his soil and guard his llama, the chieftain kept coastal delicacies ready, as well as dishes of food and wool. If he did not do this, the peasants became angry, as the Indians in Chucuito informed a Spanish examining officer. None of this is characteristic of the rule of a despotic prince over his subjects. It rather reflects the relationship between tribal members and tribal elders translated onto the level of the clan.

This relationship has been appropriately designated by John Murra, when he described as follows the relationship between the chieftains of Chucuito, who were known as *mallku*, and the peasants who wove their textiles:

From the standpoint of anthropology we perceive that the 'influence' of the *mallku* was effective because compulsion and power constituted only one aspect of the relationship between master and weaver. A decisive component was the operation of an age old social custom in the Andean region, which forced the weaver and the *mallku* into an endless chain of lifelong 'obligations', the pattern of which constituted the mutual relationships at the level of the *hatha* or of the village.[14]

CHAPTER 12

THE INCA

THE BEGINNINGS

Chimor and Chucuito were far from being the only states which had developed in the Andean region, though they represented two extremes between which most of the greater states in the Andean region stood at that time.

Anyone travelling in the beginning of the fifteenth century from north to south in the region of present-day Peru encountered in some respects a noticeable decline. On the north coast there existed large and powerful states with imposing cities. The further south the traveller went, the more this characteristic diminished. On the south coast states and cities, if they existed at all, were much smaller. In the southern highlands cities almost entirely disappeared and the states resolved themselves into more or less firmly structured tribal units. While they were relatively large in the vicinity of Lake Titicaca, north-west of it in the neighbourhood of Cuzco there seem to have been a large number of village communities and small states that were constantly warring against each other. It was precisely this region however that was to become the starting point of the largest, most extensive and probably the most centralised state that ever existed in ancient America: the state of the Inca.

It is almost impossible to reconstruct the early history of this state. If a tribe or a people rise to become a world power their early history is usually rewritten. The revised account can over-emphasise the primitiveness, the backwardness and poverty of the early times, the better to represent the importance of the ascent. Alternatively the aspiration towards continuity can lead to the earliest clan being regarded as a pocket edition of the later state, with all its complicated social hierarchy. The Aztecs chose the first method, the Inca the second. The Inca historiographers were inclined to see the very earliest tribal chiefs as likenesses of the great imperial rulers who later governed the whole of the Andean region and to endow them with all

263

their attributes. If the fact is further taken into account that the Inca possess no script – their history consisting only of traditions orally transmitted – that the calendar and chronology were far less developed than in Mesoamerica and that the archaeological evidence of the region of Cuzco is extremely limited, it is possible to imagine the difficulties which have to be reckoned with in any reconstruction of the early history of the Inca.

Who were the Inca? Where did they come from? When did they settle in the Valley of Cuzco? The few myths and traditions about the early period of Inca history must be treated with particular reserve. If a tribe or a people accomplishes the ascent from mediocrity to the government of an empire, this is reflected in a great many different ways in its mythology. Traditional myths whose content is religious rather than historical are metamorphosed so as to be unrecognisable. A number of traditions, legends and historical representations belonging to conquered peoples, who were frequently more highly developed than their conquerors, are absorbed. An imperial mythology results from all this, that is meant to represent the ascent of the conqueror as being natural and legitimate. This is what happened amongst the Aztecs, and the many myths of the Inca exhibit similar trends. Like the Aztecs the Inca were convinced that they represented the peak of human development, while the period before their time had been characterised by constantly recurring setbacks. The Inca also believed, like the Aztecs, in four preceding periods of human history which had all closed with great catastrophes.

In the first period, the *Pacarimax Runa*, 'the aspiring people', lived. They were peace-loving peasants whose world was destroyed by wars and annihilating diseases. They left a few descendants who survived the catastrophe: their legitimate sons were the ancestors of the nobility, their bastards those of the common people.

The second period was that of the *Huari Runa*, the 'original peoples', who came out of caves. They were also peasants, but unlike their predecessors had learned the art of terracing and of an irrigation economy. They were peaceable, good people who nevertheless fell victims to a terrible catastrophe. The sun withdrew its light and its favour from mankind and appears finally to have burned them up.

The third period, the time of the 'savages', closed with catastrophic floods.

The fourth period was that of the warriors. Their end was not caused by a natural catastrophe. The peoples living at this time became progressively softer, devoted themselves to sodomy instead of to agriculture and to war, and were eventually superseded by the Inca.

This legend about the origins of the Inca differs in one very essential point from its Aztec counterpart in that the people and the nobility are represented as classes, that were predetermined since the creation. Such differences also appear in the later legends of migration. One tells that the Inca came from a number of caves in Paccari-Tambo, not far from Cuzco. From the middle cave there emerged four brothers, Ayar Manco, Ayar Cochi, Ayar Uchu and Ayar Auca, with their sisters who were also their wives. From the neighbouring caves there followed ten clans. Ayar Manco, who is known as Manco Capac, succeeded in ridding himself of his three brothers, who were dangerous rivals. One was imprisoned in a cave, and two others were turned into stone. Manco Capac, whom the legend calls the founder of the Inca dynasty, led his people as far as the Valley of Cuzco, where he planted in the earth a golden staff which he was carrying in his hand. Thus the sign was given that this was to be the dwelling place of the Inca as predetermined by the gods. Anyone remembering the Aztec legend about the founding of Tenochtitlan will recognise an almost staggering similarity. There is however a difference; the aristocratic tribal nobility is not present in Aztec traditions.

Another legend has a more imperial character. It relates that Manco Capac was a cultural hero created by the gods in the vicinity of Lake Titicaca. He was entrusted with the mission of bringing civilisation to the peoples who until then had been living in a most primitive state. Manco Capac reached the Valley of Cuzco and said to his wife and sister:

The sun, our father, wishes us to make a halt in this valley and to settle here. It is therefore necessary, my sister, my queen, that thou and I draw this people to us, that we gather them together in order to teach them so that we may show them all the good which our father, the sun, has taught us.

While our great Inca wandered about in order to populate the city, he instructed the Indians in a variety of things: how the soil should be cultivated, how maize and green vegetables should be grown, and he showed them the best and most tasty kinds . . . the queen was for her part not idle: she showed the Indian women the functions which are special to women, that is the weaving of cotton and wool and the making of clothes therefrom, for themselves, for their husbands and their children.[1]

He also taught the inhabitants of the Valley of Cuzco about irrigation, terracing and metallurgical skills.

There is not a great deal of historical evidence for either legend. All they do is show that the Inca migrated from somewhere into the Valley of Cuzco. When and from where remain open questions. Did they originate as the legends say from the neighbourhood of Cuzco, or did they, as others affirm, come from the highland region round Lake Titicaca? Were they originally an Aymara people? At all events at the time of the Conquest they spoke Quetchua and this language had become diffused over extensive areas of Peru. No less doubtful is the date of their arrival. While one chronicler, Montesinos, mentions forty Inca rulers and argues that they must have lived in the Valley of Cuzco for many thousands of years, most chroniclers speak of a total of eleven, from the settlement of the Inca in Cuzco until the Conquest of Peru by the Spaniards. John Rowe, one of the most distinguished authorities in the field of Inca culture, considers that the arrival of the Inca should be placed round the middle of the thirteenth century. Despite various contradictory opinions, most authorities adhere to this date – about 1250.

SOCIAL ORGANISATION

Fortunately there are some details available concerning the life of the Inca in this early period and their social organisation. In the same way as the Aztecs found the Valley of Mexico already populated, the Inca on their arrival in Cuzco found tribes already settled there. But in contrast to the highly organised states of the Valley of Mexico, there appear to have existed in Cuzco only small village communities and it was quite a simple matter to occupy their land, and to settle there as one village community among many. The Inca remained there in this way for hundreds of years. The Inca chroniclers tell of constant battles with the neighbouring peoples of Cuzco, without the Inca ever succeeding in overthrowing the neighbouring villages. Like the Aztec organisation at that time, the Inca society also consisted of a community of clans called *ayllu*. We have already seen how in Mesoamerica the clan was the foundation of all social structures, though its cohesiveness and significance were less than in Peru. Whereas the members of an Aztec *calpulli* felt themselves to be in some way or another akin, the members of the *ayllu* in Peru believed in their descent from one common ancestor. This could be either a human being, an animal or even a holy place. The land belonged, as in Mesoamerica, to the clan. But unlike the case in Mesoamerica where it was divided up only once and only a man who had no land applied to the clan, among the Inca the land was redistributed every two or more years according to the size of a man's family. Moreover the land was cultivated commonly by all members, who considered it their duty to care for those who were unable to cultivate their land by reason of age, youth or sickness. In contrast to Mesoamerica, the clan in Peru appears to have taken a part also in the choice of a marriage partner. The type of marriage arrangements, the existence of endogamous or exogamous clans is still debated. Inter-clan relations were very complicated. In Cuzco existed not only clans of the nobility and clans of the peoples, but all Inca clans fell into two 'moieties': *Hurin Saya* (upper Cuzco) and *Hanan Saya* (lower Cuzco). It has been impossible so far to determine the significance of this division. Both moieties rivalled each other at festivals and conducted separate religious ceremonies. Among some tribes of the Andean region, as in Chucuito, they even constituted separate political units with their own chieftains. At the apex of each 'society' among the Inca there was a common leader, the Sapay-Inca, who directed the destiny of the whole tribe. At the time the Spaniards conquered the Inca Empire, the Sapay-Inca was a God-King who ruled vast domains. Many chroniclers tend to ascribe these attributes to him from the beginning. But if we read between the lines, it is clear that there existed a council of *ayllu* elders, or warriors who made decisions – that there were Sapay-Inca who although they had to be descendants of one clan were not, as was later the case, chosen by their predecessors but were elected by an assembly. At this time the Sapay-Inca was probably one of many *Sinchis* – that is to say tribal or clan chieftains with very limited functions.

CONQUESTS

The transition of the Inca from one small tribe among man to the conquerors and rulers of a world empire took place in scarcely thirty years. They rapidly overthrew one area after another of the Andean region. Most historians regard the middle of the fifteenth century, in fact the year 1438, as the point of departure for the Conquest and the breakthrough to being a world power. In that year the Chancas, a federation of tribes north of the Valley of Cuzco, decided to overthrow the Inca. Apparently they surged down to the city's very gates. A number of chronicles which recorded the oral traditions of the Inca tell how the Inca Viracocha and the successor he had appointed, Urco, were seized with panic and were prepared to abandon the city of the Inca to the Chancas. They left the city in order to take refuge in a fortress a long way away from Cuzco.

In desperation the Inca nobility turned to another of Viracocha's sons, Inca Yupanqui, and entreated him 'to take over the conduct of the war for the benefit of all'.[2] 'One of the most respected of these men spoke for them all. Inca Yupanqui replied that when his father had desired to make him his successor they had not agreed, but had demanded that his cowardly brother should be accorded this honour instead. He himself had never aspired to kingly estate; now they must act in the right way to secure the public good, since they had perceived that Inca Urco was unfitted for the position which he occupied. The *orejones* (the Spaniards' name for the high Inca nobility whose members wore great ear-plugs) replied that they would take the necessary measures after the end of the war for the good of the government and of the kingdom. It is related that they sent messengers throughout the province and declared that all who would care to come to Cuzco could become citizens and receive lands and privileges in the valley. So people came from far and wide. After this had happened Inca Yupanqui came to the great plaza where the monolith stood and placed a tigerskin on his head as a sign that he wanted to be as strong as this animal.'[3]

Traditionally far fewer warriors came than Inca Yupanqui had expected. In his despair he summoned the stones to do battle, and these transformed themselves into warriors. Inca Yupanqui succeeded in driving the Chanca back from Cuzco and finally in defeating them roundly.

The chronicles relate that this victory brought little joy to his father Viracocha, who saw that his own position as Inca and that of his favourite son Urco as his successor was shaken. Urco therefore with his father's agreement tried to kill Inca Yupanqui. The attempt failed and Urco himself died in the ill-fated attack. Thereupon Inca Yupanqui forced his father, in a dramatic ceremony, to abdicate his position as Inca before the assembled people and had himself proclaimed Inca under the name of Pachacuti, 'he who transforms'.

Under the leadership of Pachacuti, there now began a tremendous campaign of conquest. First of all the smallest states round the Valley of Cuzco were overthrown. Then the Inca armies marched into the southern highlands of Lake Titicaca and allied themselves with Chucuito against the latter's rival, the highland state of Hatun Colla. Thereafter they overthrew their former allies, whom the smaller states of the highlands had followed.

Is this tradition correct? It is difficult to say and some historians consider that the role of Pachacuti is estimated too high and that of his predecessors too low. Whatever the case, this tradition is in many ways reminiscent of the Pact of Atzcapotzalco between the Aztec nobility and the common people. In so far as the nobility took part in the overthrow of Atzcapotzalco – an event responsible for the breakthrough of the Aztecs to become a great power – their power and their wealth were justified. The same thing applied, though not so obviously, to the Inca. By defeating the Chancas Pachacuti and his descendants earned the right to the dignity of Inca. The possession of their own land and property by a considerable part of the nobility was similarly legitimised by their courageous behaviour in the battle which smoothed the way of the Inca towards imperial power.

After the successful overthrow of the southern highlands the Inca armies penetrated into the northern highlands where they overthrew the state of Cajamarca before coming to the region of present-day Ecuador. By now the Inca armies, led by Pachacuti's son Topac Yupanqui, felt they were strong enough to proceed against their mightiest opponent in the Andean region, the state of Chimor. The Chimu had erected extensive and powerful fortifications like those of

Paramunga, the ruins of which are impressive even today, in order to protect themselves against the Inca. However the Inca did not approach from the south as had been expected but from the north where the fortifications were much weaker. They forced their way into the region of the Chimu and made very clever use of the defenders' ecological weakness. They occupied the sources of water supply and threatened to block the irrigation canals. Thereupon the great Chimu submitted to the Inca.

With the conquest of the 'kingdom' of Chimor, followed by the rapid overthrow of the remaining coastal regions, the Inca had subjugated almost all the areas of high culture except those in the north. While Topac Yupanqui and his successor Huayna Capac succeeded during their thrust northwards in overthrowing further areas of Ecuador and in penetrating as far as its present capital city of Quito, the advance of the Inca in other directions penetrated much poorer regions. In the south they went as far as the regions of present-day Argentina and Chile crossing inhospitable deserts on the way, and finally called a halt in the primeval forest region of the Araucanian Indians. In the east all thrusts into the primeval Amazonian forest region, which begins not far from Cuzco, were unsuccessful. The primeval forest and the presence of the nomadic tribes living there proved to be an insurmountable obstacle. The Inca even attempted to thrust westwards, across the ocean. There is a report that Topac Yupanqui equipped a fleet of balsa rafts, embarked his warriors on them and conquered a number of islands in the Pacific Ocean. There is no certainty, even today, which islands they were. Some historians believe that the island in question was La Plata, near the coast of Ecuador, others speak of the much more distant Galapagos islands. No archaeological evidence has so far been found.

On the eve of the Spanish Conquest the Inca ruled an Imperium which covered most of modern Ecuador, almost the whole of the region of present-day Peru, large areas of present-day Bolivia and smaller areas of Argentina and Chile. Estimates of population density in these regions differ widely. They extend from four to six million. The Inca – in contrast to the Aztecs in Mesoamerica – had overthrown almost all the regions of high culture that lay within their reach. The only exceptions were parts of Ecuador and in particular Colombia. Their Imperium was perhaps smaller in regard to population than that of the Aztecs in Mesoamerica, but it achieved a degree of integration which, as will be described, put in the shade everything else which existed in the American continent before the advent of the Europeans.

The Method of Conquest

Any attempt to understand the factors which in scarcely thirty years turned an insignificant highland tribe into a world power immediately forces difficult problems on one's attention. The complexity of this question stands out particularly clearly if the situation in the region of the Inca is compared with that in the Valley of Mexico, from where the second great wave of conquest on the American continent started.

A well-known anthropologist was quite right when he affirmed that 'whoever controls the Chinampas controls the Valley of Mexico, whoever controls the Valley of Mexico controls the plateau of Mexico and whoever rules the plateau of Mexico, rules ancient Mesoamerica.'[4]

In fact the Valley of Mexico offered all the necessary prerequisites to enable the Aztecs to conquer vast areas of Mesoamerica. It was the most densely populated region in ancient Mexico, from a strategic point of view it was most advantageously placed, and it was the first region to attain a high degree of centralisation. When the Aztecs set out to conquer Mesoamerica they encountered hardly a single state comparable in size and power or displaying as great a measure of centralisation as their own.

Apart from the strategic location these conditions did not exist for the Valley of Cuzco. In the first place it was not the most densely populated region of the Andes. In proportion to the total population of the Andean region the number of Inca was far less than the population of cities of the Triple Alliance in proportion to the population of Mesoamerica. When the Inca started out on their great campaigns of conquest in 1438 they were by no means the most centralised and powerful state in the Andean region. There were powerful states like the Chimu which far outstripped their own power. Yet the Inca erected an empire with a centralisation, power and integration substantially greater than that of the Aztecs.

The key to these questions may be found largely in the structure of the Aztec and Inca armies. The Mexican armies basically consisted of the inhabitants of the cities of the Triple Alliance, Tenochtitlan, Texcoco and Tlacopan, joined by a few peoples of the valley in subordinate positions. The Inca armies on the other hand were composed primarily of members of overthrown peoples, officered solely by the Inca. The Aztec conquests were the work of Aztecs and of the other inhabitants of the Valley of Mexico; the Inca conquests were for the most part carried out by the conquered peoples since the Inca were far too few in number to undertake this task by themselves. After every conquest one of the first duties that the Inca laid on the people they had overthrown consisted in providing soldiers for the next Inca campaign.

The control by a small Inca élite of an army consisting essentially of members of conquered and overthrown tribes required a great variety of measures both with regard to winning them over and to controlling and commanding them. The Inca therefore practised a policy which without exaggeration may be called a 'stick and carrot' policy. What did the carrot consist of? How was it possible to induce tribes who had just been overthrown to participate in campaigns of conquest on behalf of those who had robbed them of their independence?

The first of these expedients was success itself. In compensation for their own overthrow the subjugated peoples were offered participation in further conquests. The gifts which the Inca gave to victorious war-riors, the prestige they acquired by participation in victorious campaigns at least partially compensated them for their losses, as also no doubt did the opportunity of settling old scores. The Inca proceeded most cleverly in mobilising their armed forces and tended to use a tribe which they had conquered against another towards which it was already hostile. Nevertheless conciliating the overthrown tribes in this way required a special kind of dynamism and involved additional hazards. Constant campaigns had to be undertaken and they had to be both successful and rewarding. If this was not so, revolts could easily result. This was clearly demonstrated in the case of two small setbacks that the Inca suffered. When, having overthrown the Chanca, the Inca thrust forward to a further conquest, they successfully demanded that the Chanca provide a detachment of warriors for the proposed conquest. At the first encounter with the enemy it became evident that the Chanca had succeeded in annihilating them, while the Inca had only had limited success. Fearful that the Chanca would be regarded by the other peoples as the most successful conquerors and would therefore be able to attach the defeated peoples to themselves, the Inca ordered his allies to be secretly murdered. The Chanca, who discovered these plans in time, were only able to escape their fate by fleeing as fast as possible from the Inca encampment. A few years later when the Inca undertook an unsuccessful campaign into the jungle lowlands of the Amazon region, their allies abandoned them in the Colla region, returned home and started a serious revolt that the Inca were only able to put down with great difficulty and trouble. Such events however did not occur very often, for until the Spanish Conquest the Inca were almost always victorious.

As soon as all the territories in question had been conquered, there must still have been great problems. As we shall see, some of the con-flicts and confrontations that broke out in the Inca Imperium on the eve of the Spanish Conquest were certainly due to a reduction in the number of victorious campaigns.

What the Inca were able to offer the peoples they had conquered was not confined only to participation in further campaigns. One of the most significant achievements, as they constantly emphasised, that the Inca bestowed on their subject peoples was a *Pax Incaica*. Inca garrisons saw to it that attacks from outside were beaten off and that the quarrels between various tribes did not turn into wars. This represented some progress primarily for the smaller peoples, although the benefit was of course relative since the wars which they had previously waged among each other had now to be fought on behalf of the Inca. At all events these new campaigns were much more rewarding, and more important they did not endanger their own territory.

One of the chief results of Inca rule was that the conquered peoples were guaranteed regular and undisturbed access to the raw materials that they were unable to produce. This was managed *inter alia* on a basis of distribution. A certain amount of llama wool was given to all the inhabitants of the Inca Imperium, and herds of llama were sent to many districts which had previously had none. No less important were the resettlements carried out with the same aim in view. For example, in the coastal regions highlanders were settled who remained in the closest contact with their native territories and cultivated maize and coca for their benefit.

It is impossible to overestimate the importance of these measures. In the first place every small and medium-sized state with colonists living many hundreds of kilometres away and delivering the products that the state lacked had an interest in keeping access to these settlements free. To this end a strong central power such as the Inca represented was absolutely necessary.

Of equal importance, particularly for the many smaller states, was the fact that the Inca erected public works which they had until then, either through weakness or technical ignorance, not been able to build. They consisted primarily of irrigation canals and gigantic terraces on the mountain sides. Even though these constructions were primarily intended for the Inca themselves, they still benefited the conquered peoples to a certain extent.

The necessity of conciliating the conquered peoples led the Inca to take care, at least in theory, to avoid arbitrary methods, unlike the Aztecs. Anyone remembering the measures taken by the Aztecs, of slaughtering the inhabitants of a conquered region until its rulers declared their readiness to pay the tribute demanded of them, and anyone remembering that the Aztecs even then did not release their prisoners but sacrificed them, will notice the tremendous contrast between the two systems. Among the Inca prisoners of war were not sacrificed, but sent back to their native villages after their leaders had been executed.

The Inca proceeded on completely different lines in the fixing of tribute. After a region had been conquered, so a chronicler relates, the Inca sent

a trusted representative on whom he could rely, from one village to another, to discover the living conditions of the people, their capacity to pay, their lands, the number of their herds, what their metal production was and other things on which they set store. After these investigations had been completed, they made a report to their lord. He then summoned a general meeting of all the most important men of the realm, with the participation of the rulers of the provinces which had to pay the tribute and declared that in view of the fact that they were in the presence of the only lord and monarch of so many great provinces they should not consider it to be a burden to have to pay tribute, to which he, as ruler, had a claim. Care would be taken that tribute should not be too high so that they could easily pay it. After the leaders of the conquered province had agreed to all he wanted, they returned home accompanied by *orejones* who laid down what the tribute should be. In some parts of the country it was higher than that which is now paid to the Spaniards. But in view of the perfect system of the Inca these people did not regard these tributes as burdensome, since their well-being and their members were constantly increasing.[5]

It is extremely difficult to state whether the conquered peoples really had a say in determining how much was to be allotted to the Inca. One of the main factors that prevented Inca assessments from becoming too arbitrary was the census taken by Inca bureaucrats of the inhabitants and wealth of a given region.

The huge Inca armies had to be kept as far as possible from the villages while they were traversing a region since plundering was most strictly forbidden. It is however difficult to determine how far these theoretical intentions were a practical reality.

These measures towards conciliating tribes were reinforced by a purposeful propaganda that constantly emphasised the good deeds of the Inca rulers. This was clearly seen when a people, intimidated by the power of the Inca, submitted of their own free will. Their rulers were expected to regard subjugation as a special privilege and a particular benefit and constantly propagate such ideas. In one of the many traditional speeches that occur among the Inca, as described by Garcilaso de la Vega, this trend is very clearly seen. When the Inca Capac Inca Viracocha drew near to the state of the Tuema he was greeted as follows by members of the ruling class of this people:

Capac Inca Viracocha, in our land and much further afield we have heard of the wonderful deeds of the Inca who are thy ancestors, of thy wonderful honesty, of thy invariable justice, of the benevolence of thy laws, of the gentleness of thy rule, of the wonder of thy religion. Of thy steadfastness of belief, of thy consideration, thy friendly disposition and the great wonders which thy father the Sun has created on thy behalf. Not only we, but many other peoples have heard of these things. The Curacas of the entire Kingdom of Tuema are so much inspired by these rare qualities that they request thee to receive them into thy empire, so that they may be allowed to say to thy subjects that they have permission to share in thy benevolence. We therefore beg thee earnestly, Inca, to send us members of pure breed to abolish our

U

barbaric laws and customs, to lead us into the ways of the good religion and show us the ceremonies which we must fulfil. In gratitude for these favours we shall pray to you as the Son of the Sun in the name of our whole Kingdom, we will look upon you as our Lord and we offer you our persons and the good things which our country produces as a sign that we entirely belong to you.[6]

Such propaganda speeches had to be repeated by the conquered peoples at every celebration and on every solemn occasion. On the other hand such measures for conciliating and influencing the tribes were matched by extremely severe systems of control, intended to nip any revolt in the bud. All the inhabitants of an area and their wealth were minutely registered by Inca officials after every conquest. Then followed the introduction of garrisons and administrative officials, whose functions will be described later. Inspectors from the central administration regularly superintended the execution of the Inca's commands. The native chieftains and nobles 'remained in power' under the control of this Inca bureaucracy. They were obliged to send their sons to 'school', that is, as hostages to Cuzco. The conquered peoples were obliged to build a network of fortifications in which the Inca garrisons were stationed.

These measures of control were accompanied by direct efforts at integration. In contrast to the Aztecs, the Inca were at pains to diffuse their language, Quetchua, their religion and their ideology. A great number of measures were taken towards this end. One of the most important was to educate the sons of the nobility in Cuzco in the Inca spirit, in the Inca religion and in the Inca language. But this alone was by no means all that was required.

To spread the religion of the Inca, temples to the Sun and other Inca deities were erected in all the overthrown regions. The Inca religion claimed no exclusiveness for itself. As intended it was able to exist alongside the indigenous religions. In fact, the Inca, like the Aztecs, endeavoured to use the religion of the overthrown peoples positively for their own ends. The idols of these peoples were brought to Cuzco where they served, just like the sons of the conquered nobility, as hostages for their good faith.

The Inca were extraordinarily successful in making their language widespread. Even though the old languages still persisted, most of the inhabitants of the Inca Imperium understood Quetchua. How were languages taught in those remote times? This question, as far as the nobility is concerned, is easy to answer. It was taught by the priests either in Cuzco or, as far as we know, in the overthrown regions themselves. How the common people learned to speak Quetchua is not so easy to determine. Presumably religious ceremonies were carried on in Quetchua, but it was mainly constant contact with Quetchua-speaking people that contributed to the spread of the language. These contacts existed either with garrisons or colonists sent out by the central administration, or as a result of work that had to be done in foreign regions.

Resettlement

Deportation was the last expedient which the Inca used if a people or a tribe revolted despite all measures of control and conciliation. Large parts of conquered tribes were sent to a district which was usually some distance away to be among a different tribe that had been overthrown some time back and was known to be loyal to the Inca. Efforts were made to find a region with a similar climate. Under pain of the severest punishments these deportees were forbidden to return to their homes in any circumstances, even for visits. In their place inhabitants of territories loyal to the Inca were settled. Even if these people had not been particularly loyal to the Inca it was unlikely that they could reach an understanding with a foreign people whose land they had occupied, particularly since the members of the Inca-loyal people were given the prospect of a whole series of privileges, among them temporarily lower taxes, the right to receive aid from the peoples in the vicinity and so on, in order to render their resettlement attractive. It was a policy of 'divide and rule' that would have caused every colonialist of the nineteenth century to blanch with envy.

The resettlement of *mitimakuna* (as the colonists were called) also fulfilled cultural, political, religious and especially economic purposes as well as taking the Quetchua language and the Inca religion into the farthest corners of the Imperium. At the same time transplantation of colonists from one region to another was a means of introducing new economic methods into other territories. A few people introduced techniques of intensive agriculture and of irrigation to areas where they had not until then existed, while others domesticated the llama in territories where it was previously little known.

THE MILITARY ORGANISATION OF THE INCA

The political integration, the cohesiveness of the Inca Empire, the inducement of the overthrown peoples to perform military service enabled the Inca to build up a military machine that was unique in its effectiveness. This is best appreciated when compared with the military organisation of the Aztecs. Both Aztecs and Incas had very similar natural difficulties to overcome. They both existed in a highland region, and when starting out on campaigns of conquest they both had to overcome difficult mountain ranges. The regions that they invaded and conquered experienced the most extreme differences in climate; cold mountain valleys at a high altitude, tropical lowland, inhospitable deserts. The practice of arms of the two peoples did not differ a great deal. The most important weapons of the Inca were clubs studded with stone or copper points, two-edged swords, also mostly made of stone or copper and spear-throwers. Bows and arrows were only used by mercenaries from the tropical primeval forest regions. In addition to the weapons possessed by the Aztecs, the Inca had catapults and bolas. These were strings with a number of stones attached that were hurled at the enemy. In contrast to the Mesoamerican peoples the Inca used more copper and bronze in their arms. On the whole however the differences in the effectiveness of the weapons were not very marked.

Offensive tactics among the Inca did not differ greatly from those of the Aztecs. After the opposing forces had hurled spears, arrows, bolas and stones at each other they rushed towards each other and an organised battle took the place of isolated encounters. But in one respect the Inca armies behaved quite differently from the Aztecs. They were not concerned with taking prisoners, but with killing the enemy, so they had no inhibitions of any kind when they were fighting.

The Aztecs tried to overcome the natural difficulties of the terrain by sending into battle specially selected and hardened élite warriors, members of the military orders. The number had to be restricted since the villages through which they passed were only able to feed a small number of warriors. The Inca proceeded quite differently. The average quality of their soldiers probably did not equal that of the Aztec warriors since the Inca armies which carried out the great conquests did not consist of élite groups and professional soldiers. They were for the most part peasants, trained to war service. Only the members of Inca clans from whom the officers were drawn and a few of the élite units, the not very numerous garrison troops, the mercenaries from the forest tribes of the east and the members of the equatorial Cañari tribe, who constituted the life-guard of the Inca, could be described in the fullest sense of the word as professional soldiers.

The great advantage of the Inca as against the Aztecs was their organisation which guaranteed their power over the people they conquered. A considerable proportion of the troops mobilised for a campaign came from regions that were immediately contiguous with the region about to be conquered. As a result it was unnecessary to carry out any great troop movements in this gigantic empire. At the same time efforts were made to mobilise troops from areas which were ecologically, geographically and climatically similar to those about to be subjugated. It was thus possible to avoid for example sending troops from the cold highlands into the tropical lowlands where the heat could have severely limited their fighting capacity.

The system of conscripting the peasants of the Inca Empire was devised so that their mobilisation could in no way prejudice food production for the state or for their family. Enough men of age groups capable of work were left behind with the *ayllus* to undertake the tribute labour for the Inca and to cultivate the land belonging to the conscripts. This enabled the Inca armies to remain at war for a long time, although this did not often happen.

Probably the most decisive superiority of the Inca armies lay in the fact that their unique provisioning and mobility enabled them to send many more troops to distant regions than was ever possible for the Aztecs. Their superiority was based on the Inca road system which covered the whole empire. Two roads many thousands of kilometres in length ran lengthwise through the Inca Empire. One was built in the highlands and the other along the coast. A number of roads ran cross-wise linking these two roads to each other. The whole length of this Inca road has been estimated at sixteen thousand kilometres.

Only by taking into account the extraordinarily difficult climatic and geographical considerations of the Andean region – the mountains, deserts, boglands and so on, is it possible to appreciate the achievement which this road system represents. Rocks were hewn out of the mountains to make way for these roads, rivers were crossed, either by suspension bridges or by rafts. Every village was compelled to keep all roads in its vicinity in top condition. At regular intervals there were rest houses, called *tambos*, where food and clothing were stored. Officials, travelling by order of the Inca, were able to provision themselves here; huge stores supplied the many thousand troops passing through with clothing, food and weapons. The surrounding villages were responsible for the upkeep of these rest houses. The network of roads even today understandably excites the admiration of archaeologists, architects and historians, and it is not surprising that the Spaniards who came to Peru were deeply impressed by these roads.

For it appears to me [wrote a Spanish chronicler, who travelled about the Inca Imperium shortly after the conquest] that if the Emperor [he means the Spanish emperor] gave the command to build a similar royal road to this one, which runs from Quito to Cuzco, or the one leading from Cuzco to Chile I believe, that despite his power he would not be able to have this road built, I believe that there is nobody who could achieve such results, even if it were possible to rely on the *discipline* with which the commands of the Inca were executed . . .

Those who read this book and have been in Peru will recollect the roads, running from Lima to Xauxa through the mountains which are so difficult to cross from Huarochiri and over the snow-covered heights of Pariacaca. They will understand since they have seen more than I have described. Furthermore, they will know the road which leads to the river Apurimac and the road along the mountains of Paltas, Caxas and Ayancas and other parts of the kingdom, where it is more or less 15 feet in width. In the time of the kings they were kept clean, so that not a single stone was left lying about nor was a single blade of weed to be found; for the road was always maintained in the very best condition. In the inhabited areas near the cities there were large palaces and barracks for the soldiers. On the snow-covered heights and on the plains there were rest houses in which travellers could seek rest and protection from cold and rain. In many areas, such as Collao and other parts of the kingdom, there were milestones like those in Europe which also demarcate the boundaries, only in Peru they are wider and better made. They were called *topos* and the distance between each was 1½ Castilian leagues.[7]

Their road and provisioning systems made it possible for the Inca to send immense numbers of soldiery from one area of the empire to another very quickly; it was therefore comparatively easy to put down revolts at the outset and at the same time to send massive troop reinforcements to the frontiers of the empire.

Once the frontier had been crossed, the provisioning and road system ceased. But even here the Inca were still able to provision their troops, at least for a limited period. This was done with llama that accompanied every Inca army in their thousands. They served both as draught animals and as a source of food.

The military significance of the Inca roads was not confined to troop movements and the provisioning of the army. They also provided an extremely efficient system of conveying news. At regular intervals along the roads couriers were stationed at the ready. They ran carrying verbal messages and *quipus* to the next courier post. This reporting system functioned with such speed that the Inca in his capital city of Cuzco was able to receive reports from far distant Quito in an extraordinarily short time. In addition the Inca had a system of smoke signals, which made even speedier communication of messages possible.

The Zenith

At the beginning of the sixteenth century under the rule of the Inca Huayna Capac the Imperium reached the zenith of its expansion and power. This was reflected not only in Inca control over a vast territory reaching from present-day Ecuador to Chile and Argentina, but also in development of the capital city Cuzco.

The first task undertaken by Pachacuti after the beginning of the Inca conquests was the construction of the capital city, Cuzco. For many years between forty and sixty thousand tributary subjects were constantly employed on this project. When the Spaniards reached Peru and saw Cuzco for the first time they were greatly impressed by the size and character of the city. One eyewitness wrote: 'This is the best and largest city which I have seen in this country and in fact in the American continent, and we inform your Majesty that there are buildings which are so beautiful and well built that they would also be remarkable in Spain . . .'[8] Another *conquistador* wrote, 'Cuzco stood for something, it was an elegant city which must have been founded by important people.'[9] The almost exaggerated enthusiasm with which the conquerors of Mexico described Tenochtitlan and the neighbouring cities of the Valley of Mexico is not found among those who saw Cuzco in its glory.

Cuzco was the administrative, religious and spiritual centre of the Inca Imperium. Its population is estimated to have been about a hundred to three hundred thousand. Cuzco was the place where the Inca resided with his court and his many guards. The royal clans, the heads of the priesthood and a numerous bureaucracy consisting of officials of all ranks lived here. The rulers of the conquered territories also lived here from time to time and their sons were educated here together with the descendants of the Inca aristocracy. People from all parts of the Inca Empire were also gathered together in Cuzco to cultivate the land of the nobility and to serve them. These subject peoples varied a great deal in social and ethnic origin. They included the original inhabitants from the surrounding villages, who had been pressed into service for the Inca, but who with time had been elevated to the status of the Inca, and colonists from all parts of the empire whose status varied widely. They ranged from privileged gold and silver smiths from the 'kingdom' of Chimu who had been settled in Cuzco to rebellious llama herdsmen from the highlands of Lake Titicaca, who had been deported there for greater security. In addition there lived in the city many *yanaconas*, later called slaves by Spanish chroniclers, who had been brought there and also tributary labourers who had to enter upon their service in Cuzco. Some took part in the construction of the capital city, others possibly prepared for a campaign while a third category performed personal services for the nobility of Cuzco.

Because of the variety of its population Cuzco created a completely cosmopolitan impression. This was emphasised still more by the fact that all the inhabitants had to wear their national costume. The construction of the city reflected not only the complex social structure of its inhabitants but at the same time the whole social organisation of the Inca Empire. It was divided into four parts, like the empire, and as in all other cities of the empire there existed an upper and lower half of the city, *Hanan*-Cuzco and *Hurin*-Cuzco, a division corresponding to that of the clans.

The city had two great central points: the Sun Temple Coricancha and the huge central plaza, the Huacapata. The Coricancha was a complex of buildings which was without doubt one of the most impressive erected in the Inca Empire. The richness of these buildings was more evident inside than outside. Some of the buildings were specially remarkable by reason of the dark red stone used in their construction. The huge blocks of stone fitted so closely together that not even a razor blade could have been inserted between them. In contrast to these impressive and colossal blocks of stone masonry was the roof which like most others in the Inca Empire consisted of straw. The inside of the temple hid the real wealth; priceless tapestries hung on the walls and beside gigantic discs of gold and silver. The Coricancha was the place where important ceremonies took place and was at the same time the dwelling place of the many heads of the priesthood and of the virgins of the Sun of Cuzco.

The greatest ceremonies in the city took place in the Huacapata. Before the imperial expansion of the Inca there had been only bog-land at this site. Pachacuti ordered hordes of tributary peasants to come and dry out the bog and erect on this land the 'palaces' of the royal clans. These were low, generally one-storey buildings with rooms grouped round small courtyards. Among the dwellings themselves there were gardens and large storage barns that held the wealth of the clans. Round the outside a wall separated the 'palaces' from the outside world.

However, perhaps the most impressive construction which the Inca erected in the Valley of Cuzco was outside the capital city. This was the great fortress of Sacsahuaman. Since Cuzco itself was not fortified, Sacsahuaman was meant to serve as a fortress and refuge for the population. It was built on a small hill two hundred metres high. Three great walls running from the bottom to the top and a row of high towers constituted an almost impregnable obstacle for any attacker. The fortress was provided with all necessities for a long siege. As it was connected with sources of water at a great height by aqueducts and canals, a water supply was assured. With huge barns full of provisions, clothing and arms the fortress could presumably have withstood a very long siege. Even today the ruins tower up as impressive reminders of the time of the Inca in the Valley of Cuzco.

In stark contrast to the great buildings in the centre of Cuzco were the surrounding dwellings of the people constructed of dried adobe bricks, and in the highlands sometimes of stones. Hardly any vestiges are left of these small huts. Life inside them must have been more than spartan. They were always provided with a small entrance, but they had no windows and no vent for smoke. Almost the only furnishing was the blankets on which the inmates slept, but there were also niches in the wall in which some articles could be placed. Separate families lived in these huts, which they shared with a great number of the guinea pigs that were found in almost every peasant household.

The city of Cuzco certainly gave the impression of a great metropolis. Not only the imposing stone buildings contributed to this impression, but also the great ceremonies and celebrations that took place at regular intervals on the Huacapata, and the motley mixture of peoples from all parts of the empire.

However, Cuzco probably did not attain the splendour of Tenochtitlan with its character of a world city. Outwardly there was a striking contrast between the low stone frontages of Cuzco and the huge brightly coloured pyramids of Tenochtitlan. The contrast however went deeper than this. Both cities constituted the focal point of religious life and were the administrative centres of their empires, a function that was certainly more important in Cuzco by reason of the greater integration of the Inca Empire. Nevertheless two features were absent in the Inca capital city which gave Tenochtitlan the status of a world city. The Aztec capital was a unique commercial centre. According to the *conquistadores*, the great market of Tlatelolco attracted between sixty and a hundred thousand people daily. By contrast the lack of money and free trade in the empire of the Inca meant that Cuzco held a small market on a few days only, in which only a very limited amount of barter trade took place. Furthermore there was a very strict control of goods traffic at the entrances to the city. Guards saw to it that no more merchandise left Cuzco than came into it.

The second and no less significant contrast concerned the traffic between these cities and their environment. People were allowed to travel to and from Cuzco only if they were bound on state business or at least had state permission to do so. The number of travellers must always have been relatively large: officials travelling on various missions or tributary peasants returning to take up their labours, convoys laden with state tribute travelling to Cuzco, troops moving in and out and so forth. But this regimented traffic must have been very different from the Aztec arrangement which made it possible for thousands of people to cross in their boats from one great city to another over the network of Mexican lakes to buy and sell merchandise or to offer their services as craftsmen. Not without justification has Cuzco been called a city of bureaucrats. Such a designation could never have applied to Tenochtitlan.

However, unlike that of the Aztecs the urban building activity of the Inca was not confined to their capital city. Residences for Inca governors were built in the large centres among the conquered peoples, as well as temples for the Inca deities. The Inca bureaucracy had their own residential villages. Areas of land were sought for this purpose which were not suitable for agriculture but did occupy a commanding strategic position. One of the most striking examples of this kind is the city of Macchu Picchu in the Valley of Urubamba. The city, which contained some two to three hundred buildings, rises on the top of a hill dominating the whole valley. It is only accessible on one side, from the south, and great walls protect the entrances. On the other three sides it is hidden from the valley by deep ravines. Narrow, generally straight roads and low houses are characteristic of most of these small Inca administrative centres. Neither these nor the garrison centres can really be said to have had the character of a city.

THE SOCIAL ORGANISATION OF THE INCA

However much the building activities of the Inca may have impressed scholars, it was not this aspect of their culture that excited the greatest attention, but their social organisation.

Besides archaeologists, historians and ethnologists other scholars who have otherwise shown an only limited interest in the problems of archaeology and ethnology have been interested in the social organisation of the Inca. Utopians, social critics, social reformers, socialist theorists and their adversaries have always shown the liveliest interest in the Inca state. It was maintained recently that Thomas More's *Utopia* was based on the Inca state, in spite of the fact that More died in the same year that the Spaniards discovered the Inca state. Voltaire[10] was interested in the Inca, Alexander von Humboldt[11] dealt with this state in long essays, Marx and Engels[12] repeatedly referred to it and Rosa Luxemburg[13] devoted almost a whole chapter to the social organisation of the Inca in her *Introduction to a National Economy*.

This interest was based largely on descriptions which two chroniclers gave of the essential features of the social organisation of the Inca: these were Garcilaso de la Vega and Blas Valera, both sons of Spanish *conquistadores* and Inca mothers of noble birth. They are descriptions which in some respects correspond with those of other chroniclers although in essence they present a unique picture. Garcilaso de la Vega was descended from the family of the Inca Huascar. He and Blas Valera were received into Spanish society, one as a noble, the other as a Jesuit, though they were both always regarded as inferior because they were half-castes. It is not surprising that they were therefore anxious to extol the virtues of their Inca ancestors, in order to prove their equality with, even their superiority over the Spanish, and that they tended to idealise the Inca state. Moreover they recognised the ideal which the Inca rulers regarded as the mainspring of their state. The more time that elapsed after the fall of the Inca state, the more clearly did this ideal impress itself upon them. Nevertheless for many scholars and research workers the Inca origin of these chroniclers was taken as a proof of the credibility of the picture that they painted, above all because the dreams of the Inca Empire that they conjured up were truly fascinating. They desscribed a unique mixture of a centralised sovereign power and a welfare state, that was both attractive and repellent. For some thinkers of the eighteenth century the Inca were the prototype of a wise and enlightened despotism such as they hoped to achieve for their rulers. On the other hand scholars of the twentieth century saw in the same state an example of a despotic and omnipotent state in which the individual was forbidden all rights and all initiative. In fact both interpretations can be read into the representations of Garcilaso and Blas Valera.

Over the Inca Empire there reigned a God-King, the Sapay-Inca, who was the absolute lord of all. All land was his, all cattle and all the treasures of nature. He was of course infallible.

The Indians declare [writes Garcilaso] that an Inca of royal descent, was never, at least not publicly, punished if he had committed a serious offence. The reason is that the Inca, as their ancestors believed, were children of the Sun, who had come into the world to teach mankind and to do good . . . They added that the Inca were hardly ever able to make mistakes or commit faults like other people; they were not exposed to the same temptations and the love of woman, the urge to become rich and other emotions of the heart did not assail them.[14]

The ceremonial that surrounded the Inca was religious in character. All leftovers from an Inca's meals or the clothes he had discarded were carefully kept together and burned once a year at a great ceremony. Anyone received by the Inca had to approach him barefoot. Only on very rare occasions could a subject look the Inca in the face. He generally remained concealed by a wall. The clothing which the Inca gave away had an almost sacred value for those who received it. When the Inca died, his favourite wives and servants were made drunk at a great banquet and executed so that they might accompany him into the other world. His body however stayed here and was treated as though he were still alive. His palaces remained, and the members of his clan received the produce of the lands that had belonged to him in order to be able to continue to provide for him. The mummies of the dead Inca were brought with solemn ceremony to the main square of Cuzco. There they were given *chicha* beer, and servants surrounded them on all sides to keep flies away.

A ruling clan stood by the side of the Inca which, roughly speaking, consisted of three groups. The most important posts in the state or in the religious hierarchy, which we will examine later, were occupied by the descendants of the ten Inca, grouped always into ten *ayllus*. The new Inca alone withdrew from one such *ayllu* and formed his own.

One grade below were the members of the *ayllus* of Cuzco who were not royal, and a number of peoples in the districts surrounding the capital city, who were elevated to the rank of the Inca whenever the number of inhabitants in Cuzco became insufficient to carry out all the state functions of the Inca bureaucracy. The lowest grade consisted of the chieftains of the conquered peoples, the *curaquna*.

The nobility consisted essentially of a hereditary aristocracy, although it was possible in individual cases, by means of special war services or special technical and constructional achievements, to ascend into the ranks of the nobility. The meritorious aristocracy however always played a subsidiary role.

The nobility enjoyed extensive rights. Their position was recognised by outward symbols. Thus the members of the Inca nobility – not the *curaquna* – wore ear-plugs. The Spaniards accordingly named them *orejones*, the 'wearers of ear-plugs'. Only members of the nobility were allowed to wear certain materials of fine quality, which the Inca bought for them – *cumbi*, materials made of vicuña wool which was relatively rare and woven by the 'virgins of the sun' in special temples. Similarly only the nobility were entitled to wear gold and silver jewellery.

The nobility were educated, as in Mesoamerica, in their own schools by special teachers called *amauta*. The basic principle of these schools was that

only the nobility should receive education in knowledge but not the sons of inferior origin for fear that these skills might make them proud and this could do injury to the state. It was enough for them that each one learned the work of his father . . .

The *amauta* taught the Inca princes knowledge and scholarship, and also the princes of royal blood and the nobility of the Empire; they did not do this with the aid of letters, for they knew none, but by means of practical exercises and daily work. The task of these *amauta* consisted in teaching them the ceremonies, the foundations of religion; in teaching them the origins and bases of their laws by explaining them to them; in teaching them politics and warfare, in teaching them decorum, history and chronology by means of knots, by which they registered the years, in teaching them to express themselves elegantly, and to do everything to bring up their children and their families. These same *amauta*, who were much respected as philosophers and people of great learning, wanted to teach the little they knew of poetry, philosophy, music and astrology to the young.[15]

As was the case among the Aztecs the nobility enjoyed the right of polygamy; generally they were not permitted to choose their wives, but were given them by the Inca, who was himself obliged to practise inbreeding. He had to take his own sister to be his chief wife, the Coya. But in addition he could keep as many concubines as he wanted.

The nobility enjoyed extensive political, juridical and economic privileges. In the political field the most important posts in the Inca bureaucracy were reserved for them. In legal matters they had to appear before special courts and were less severely punished than the ordinary citizen was for the same offence. In the economic field members of the nobility were free from every kind of tribute labour. They were not required to cultivate the soil, but could live on extensive revenues which came from two main sources. The highest stratum of the successors of the Inca possessed their own estates, which were cultivated by a particular kind of bondsmen, *yanaconas*, that will be discussed later. The land was not in any case owned by individuals, but belonged to the whole *ayllus* and the yield was also divided among the members of the *ayllus*.

The members of the royal *ayllu* could count on two types of land ownership: firstly they had a share in the common land of the royal *ayllus*, which was cultivated for the deceased Inca; secondly many members of the Inca nobility had received their own land from the Inca. This land was inalienable and had to be left on their death to their children who cultivated it collectively as a clan.

The lower ranks of the nobility, the *curaquna*, possessed their own land only in a limited degree granted to them by the Inca. The basis of their existence was the access they had to the revenues of the Inca state. These were very extensive. After every conquest the land of the conquered people was divided into three parts. One part went to the Inca, the second to the religious hierarchy and the third to the peasants. By this act, to use the terminology of Garcilaso, the Inca left a portion of his own possessions to the peasants in token of his especial goodwill towards them. Garcilaso at any rate assures us that generally the expropriated land had not been cultivated till then, but was first brought into cultivation by the Inca state. A similar distribution of the herds of llama took place.

After this first expropriation the Inca demanded no more land or tribute in the form of individual production from his subjects but only labour. This work varied a great deal. All peasants were bound, before they worked their own land, to cultivate the land of the Inca and of the religious communities.

The Inca placed wool at the disposal of every peasant family to be manufactured for the state. This occupation fulfilled a double function. From an economic standpoint it was designed to place at the disposal of the Inca material which was regarded as the most valuable in the Andean region. At the same time because of a certain sacral character which the wool possessed, it created a special link between the Inca and the people.

Finally there were other forms of labour which every community, every *ayllu* had to perform: this was the *mita*. This meant in effect that a proportion of the *ayllu* inhabitants worked on public works. Work in the mines and military service in particular also counted towards the *mita*. During this time the land belonging to those who were absent was commonly cultivated by members of their *ayllu*.

A particular duty consisted of the delivery of *acclla* maidens. At regular intervals Inca officials came into the villages and sought out the most beautiful young maidens. These were then sent to special temples for education. Some became concubines of the Inca, or wives or secondary wives of members of the nobility. Others remained within the temples as so-called 'virgins of the sun' where they lived a vestal life and wove specially fine materials for the Inca.

All these services rendered by the subjects of the Inca Empire were very strictly controlled by an all-powerful bureaucracy. This bureaucracy had a very exact register, kept in the knotted script of the Inca, of all the inhabitants of the empire, of every head of cattle and area of land they owned.

The Inca Empire was divided into four provinces, which were subdivided into sub-provinces of ten thousand households. Each group of ten thousand consisted of smaller groups of a hundred each, which were again subdivided into groups of ten. At the head of the larger groups were members of the Inca bureaucracy, while the lower offices were filled by members of the indigenous nobility, the *curaquna*. The whole of the tributary population was divided into twelve age groups for the purpose of organising their labour service. The most important were the *hatun runa*, the married male heads of households aged between twenty-five and forty. The main burden of public works and activity in the Inca lands rested on their shoulders. Younger and older men could also be drawn in. Even small children had a duty to collect wild plants in the woods for the Inca, youths were occupied as shepherds of llama and older men performed supervisory duties.

The Inca bureaucracy had extensive juridical authority. It alone could pronounce the death sentence. This was only as a general rule exercised in the case of crimes against the Inca and against his state. In such cases the punishment could be horribly gruesome. The criminal was either stoned to death – the mildest form – or he was hurled into a subterranean cellar full of snakes and other wild animals.

The supervision of marriage was another important duty of the Inca bureaucracy. At regular intervals officials went into the villages and ordered couples of marriageable age to march up and stand opposite each other. The marriage took place without friction where the couples were in agreement. In other cases, when there might be two suitors for one girl, the official decided which suitor should have the preference and in cases where there were no suitors at all the Inca official often forced a marriage to take place. This concern to marry subjects is not surprising in view of the fact that only after marriage did full tribute become operative.

The Inca bureaucracy also exercised far-reaching political and administrative authority. Private journeys by Inca subordinates were forbidden without its permission. The nomination of local chieftains was strictly supervised by the bureaucracy, and after the death of a chieftain his successor had first to be confirmed by the Inca or by his deputy. In addition the Inca bureaucracy exercised the strictest economic controls, decided the allocation of tributes that had been brought in, and supervised crafts and trade. The craftsmen worked solely for the state or for the religious institutions. Trade was also a state monopoly in which it is impossible to speak of commerce in the true sense of the word. Merchandise, money dealings as carried out in Mesoamerica did not exist. Local barter only existed btween small groups. The exchange of products between one province and another, between one ecological region and another, was entirely the responsibility of the Inca, who distributed products from one area to another or gave them away to specially chosen groups.

Finally warfare and mobilisation were both the concern of the bureaucracy.

In return for their tremendous power and their far-reaching demands, the Inca concerned themselves, according to Garcilaso, with the welfare of every one of their subjects. This care took many forms. Every peasant had the right to a certain minimum of land, an area described as a *tupu*, which had to suffice for his own and his wife's needs. This area varied according to the fertility of the soil. When a child was born the family received another half *tupu* of land. Every young man on marriage was entitled equally to demand a *tupu* of land. To this end land was distributed among the peasants at regular intervals. If there was not enough of it, land was allocated to the peasants from land belonging to the Inca.

Land belonging to widows, orphans and any who were unable to work was by order of the Inca cultivated for them by the members of the *ayllu*. As a result these members and sometimes their groups too were provided for from the Inca's storehouses. In times of famine the same benevolent Inca took care of his people and gave them as much as they needed out of his own reserves.

Tributary labourers, actively employed on large projects or who rendered war service, were rewarded with special gifts and supplies of food. During campaigns or the erection of public works they thus acquired dried llama meat, *charqui*, which the peasants seldom ate. Finally raw materials, such as wool, were distributed to all inhabitants, even to those who had their own llama.

Garcilaso repeatedly emphasises that during conquests only infertile land was expropriated and points out that the great irrigation schemes and cultivation which the Inca introduced primarily benefited the people themselves.

INCA SOCIALISM?

It is not difficult to see from this description why critics of society and social reformers have concerned themselves in such detail with the state of the Inca and why this state has both attracted and repelled them.

Many were attracted by the social responsibility of the nobility, the right of the individual to be cared for by the state from the cradle to the grave, the proof that a great state could exist without money. Others were repelled by the despotic character of the Inca rule and the limits on individual initiative.

The former elements attracted most attention in the seventeenth and eighteenth centuries when many cherished the hope that an enlightened despotism could contribute to a renewal of the world. Were the Inca not an example? Was there not here an enlightened and socially orientated monarchy? Montaigne accordingly wrote that 'neither Greece nor Rome nor Egypt could show any comparison with the achievements of the Inca in their utility, difficulty or nobility'.[16] And another writer of the eighteenth century, Morell, calls the Inca Empire 'the most flourishing and the best organised that there has ever been'.[17] Disciples of Rousseau again saw in it the highest expression of the original goodness of man.

This idea of the Inca Empire nevertheless vehemently contradicted all concepts of individual freedom and the sanctity of private ownership which the citizens of the nineteenth century entertained. No wonder that admiration turned into aversion.

The Empire of the Inca [wrote Alexander von Humboldt] is like a great monastery, in which everyone is instructed what he must do for the common good. If we study these primitive Peruvians in their own terrain, with their spiritual concepts preserved through the centuries, we learn rightly to evaluate the Codex Manco Capac from every point of view, with all its effects on general development and on the public good. We find prosperity of the state but hardly of the private individual, more subjection to the ruler than love of the fatherland, passive obedience without courage towards individually audacious behaviour, severity, an all pervasive organisation of the details of private life, but no far-reaching ideas, no heights of character.

The most complicated political institution known to history stifled the germ of personal freedom and while the founders of the Empire of Cuzco flattered themselves that they had forced their subjects to be happy, they had really debased them into simple machines.[18]

It is not surprising that the social structure of the Inca aroused the liveliest interest among the theorists of socialism, though they never considered it to be a socialist society. Karl Marx called the state of the Inca a 'primitive community'.[19] Friedrich Engels placed the Inca in the middle stages of barbarism, in line with Morgan's formula. Karl Kautsky wrote that 'the communism of the Peruvians was nothing in particular, but corresponds essentially to the Germanic constitution of the Mark'.[20] Rosa Luxemburg who, as already mentioned, also concerned herself with the Inca, considered that they represented the clan which dominated other similar clans in a primitive communist system.[21]

All these writers who dealt with the social order of the Inca transposed it in one form or another into the concept of 'primitive communism'. Not one of them regarded it as socialism since for them socialism was indivisible from modern industry and bound up with a classless society. Even though they could not yet see any real ruling class emerging among the Inca, there seemed to be indications of this which, as they conceived it, were equally contrary to the essence of socialism.

The concept of Inca socialism was primarily preached by non-socialists. For them socialism could be reduced to a short formula – it signified omnipotence on the part of the state together with state care for the individual. Garcilaso's description seemed to indicate just that. There is a certain amount of evidence that the Jesuits, when they erected their own Indian state in Paraguay in the seventeenth and eighteenth centuries, were also influenced by the impression of the Inca state which Garcilaso had left. This state corresponded much more with the description that Garcilaso had given of the Inca than did the state of the Inca itself.

Heated confrontations went on for years among scholars who adhered to the one or the other of these interpretations. Recently a number of historians and ethnologists have taken up new paths. The facts painted by Garcilaso did not in their view reflect the reality of the Inca state, but a picture of the ideal situation which the Inca were aiming at, a representation of the official Inca ideology. They have accordingly questioned a considerable number of the facts which Garcilaso alleges.

In the first place they doubted the homogeneity of the Inca Empire, the omnipotent power and judgement of the Inca bureaucracy.

The states which the Inca had conquered differed substantially in size and manifested very different degrees of state integration. The Inca Empire contained states varying in size from the kingdom of the Chimu with its population of over a million, to states like Chucuito in the southern highlands of Peru with a population of about a hundred thousand, or small states like Huanuco with a population of less than ten thousand where, before the arrival of the Inca, the inhabitants themselves elected the successor to the dead ruler of the tribe. These states in no way ceased to exist as a result of the Inca conquest. Their rulers and their chieftains kept a considerable proportion of their rights, and above all they kept their wealth. For example the chieftains of Chucuito, Cari or Cusi, possessed their own lands in addition to so many llama and the right to so much labour from their subjects that their wealth was undoubtedly far greater than that of a considerable part of the bureaucracy ruling over them. These leaders of the conquered peoples also continued to carry out many of their former administrative juridical and economic functions.

The famous decimal system of the Inca, the division of families into groups of forty thousand, ten thousand, one thousand, one hundred, and ten, which more than anything else gives the impression of a powerful bureaucracy, does not seem to have existed throughout the whole empire. It existed primarily in the north but not in the south of the Inca Imperium, a fact that has led some scholars to assume that the Inca had taken over the system from the kingdom of the Chimu which they had overthrown. The significance of this decimal system is still not clear. Was it in fact a system into which were forced the various existing social groups, or was it only a numerical division for the purpose of calculating the labour required for carrying out public works?

When all these limitations have been considered regarding the power of the Inca bureaucracy, one must not go to the opposite extreme and take the view that the Inca Empire was more or less on the level of that of the Aztecs, in which the rulers of the conquered peoples retained their full powers apart from being obliged to supply their Aztec over-lords with tribute. At regular intervals Inca governors or inspectors visited the rulers of conquered territories in order to make sure that public works were progressing as planned and to examine death sentences. These were of particular interest to the Inca bureaucracy since the execution of even one man meant the reduction in the labour force available. Although the presence of Inca garrisons reduced the rebellious ideas, the strongest measure of control which most significantly reduced the power of the indigenous rulers was undoubtedly resettlement which the Inca undertook on a very large scale. Those who were compulsorily resettled no longer remained under their former overlord who consequently lost a good deal of influence. His position was further undermined by the fact that a new group, exclusively answerable to the central authority, established itself in the middle of his territory, spied for the Inca and forced his subordinates at any rate temporarily to provide labour for particular projects.

One of the most fascinating pictures sketched by Garcilaso, and which also left the deepest impression behind, was that the welfare and the well-being of the conquered peoples were the main concern of the Inca. It gave the impression that the Inca never expropriated the conquered peoples but only demanded uncultivated land labour services that were compensated by social assistance. Recent research however has shown that the Inca did not limit themselves, when it came to the expropriation, to virgin land. This may well have been the case in a number of highland areas, where small village communities were not yet in a position to build large irrigation works and much land may have remained virgin. But the principle did not apply to the coast and other regions where the possibilities of irrigation had already been fully exploited.[22] All reports of the coastal areas repeatedly mention far-reaching expropriations practised by the Inca of land that was already cultivated. In the highlands the inhabitants of Chucuito still recalled that after the Spanish Conquest very large herds of llama had been expropriated by the Inca from their owners.

The maintenance of the poor, widows, orphans and the needy was not at all the function of the Inca or of their bureaucracy, but of individual clans. Among the Lupaqa in Chucuito the poor were fed 'from cattle which belonged to the clan unit'.[23] In Huanuco Cochachi, Curak of Orondo 'gave' some portion of his llama to the poor.[24]

THE PECULIARITIES OF THE DEVELOPMENT OF THE INCA

If these qualifications are made, a different picture of the Inca state emerges from that of the 'socialistic welfare state' occasionally referred to. As John Murra describes, an additional fact which confused many writers was that the Inca transferred to the level of the state the same principle of mutual obligation as was the rule in the village community.

In this reciprocity it was envisaged that the peasants in a village should perform a number of services for the elders or the chieftain, who compensated them by reciprocal services. These largely consisted of his maintaining and rewarding those who worked for him. They extended into the realm of the religious and juridical life of the village and the protection of the village community's interests. Above all the chieftain or the elders were constantly asked for proofs of their 'lavish generosity'. At feasts he had to make gifts to the members of the community and in times of famine to distribute the reserves among them. The basis of this system was the allowance to individual peasant families of enough land on which to maintain themselves. Each family remained an autarchic community that placed only its surplus labour at the disposal of the village elders.

Whenever the Inca came across such a system – this was probably the case in most of the Andean region with the possible exception of the northern coast – they took over its outward form but gave it a completely new content. In the same way that the village elder had maintained and provided for all the peasants who had worked for him, the Inca state provided for and maintained all those who laboured for it. Since the assignment of labour planned for the village community was always looked upon as a joyful occasion, to be celebrated and introduced with festivities, the Inca state also instituted great celebrations at the beginning of each assignment of labour and rewarded and maintained all those who reported for work. Nevertheless the similarity of the forms could not conceal the radical differences that existed between limited labour voluntarily undertaken for a village elder and the organised labour for a state bureaucracy based on compulsion. Above all the similarity of form could not conceal the fact that in a village the work which the members carried out was at least paid back by the chieftains in the shape of benefits that were clear for all to see. In the Inca state a part of the enormous revenues were used for purposes that also benefited the village communities: aid in emergencies, the installation of large irrigation systems, religious ceremonies, various kinds of gifts. Nevertheless the greater part always went on the maintenance of the Inca, his court, his relatives, above all the enormous Inca bureaucracy, and for financing Inca wars. In addition, bureaucratic rigidity and ineptitude seem to have led to a considerable volume of produce which the state had acquired simply rotting because orders for its distribution were often not received from the central administration in Cuzco.

Since these contradictions, which might have led to rebellion, had to be concealed from the population of the Inca state, the Inca on the one hand introduced the centralised system of state organisation already described, and on the other propagated an official ideology, which justified the situation, and represented it as being advantageous for all. In order to emphasise more strongly the achievements of the Inca era, the pre-Inca period was pictured as a time of barbarism fraught with constant disorders and wars. Land was declared to belong not to the village communities but to the Inca, who generously made it available to them. The Inca state was represented as an all powerful and wise welfare state whose highest aim was to be fully responsible for the population in general.

The ideological attempt to transfer the conditions of traditional Andean reciprocity to the level of the state was at least partially successful: it convinced the European chroniclers and some modern students that the Inca crown controlled the country's whole economic life for what were essentially welfare purposes. In this process, the emphasis has been misplaced: we underrate the continuing self-sufficiency and reciprocity of peasant economic endeavour, even after the Inca conquest, and we misunderstand the nature and aims of the redistributive functions of the crown. After the crown had monopolised the compulsory labour of the peasantry and the productive effort of the retainers for the service of the state and had abolished trade, it had at its disposal great stores, of which only a fraction was used at the court. The greater part was distributed where it was thought to be of the most use. In this sense the Inca state functioned like a market: it absorbed the surplus production of a self-sufficient population and 'exchanged' it, while feeding the royalty, the army and the workers, and distributing a lot of it as grants and benefactions.[25]

How far these ideological efforts on the part of the Inca rulers convinced their subjects depended on various factors: the ratio between giving and taking on the one hand and the degree with which, even before the time of the Inca, the population of the Andean region had been forced into a rigid and powerful state organisation.

In parts of the southern and northern highlands these ratios were probably at their most propitious. There were still large reserves of land on the mountain slopes which could be brought into cultivation with the aid of new terracing techniques. In these areas the Inca had presumably not taken a great deal of land, but had instead created new sources of production. In addition they introduced llama into many parts of the highlands, especially northern Peru.

The ratio between giving and taking must have been very different on the coast. Here there was very little virgin land available for ex-propriation. For hundreds, if not thousands, of years the land had been used to the limit of its capacity. Accordingly Inca expropriations must have weighed very heavily on the people. On the other hand the popu-lation of this region had, over a long period, been accustomed to a rigid state organisation and presumably to exploitation by a closely knit nobility. Consequently the difficulties of the Inca in securing their rule in this region were not so very great.

The Inca encountered the greatest problems in places where they had least to give and in places where there was no regular rigid state organisation guaranteed by the nobility: this was the case in the southern highlands of Lake Titicaca. Here the Inca had taken from their owners most of the extensive herds of llama, and owing to climatic difficulties it was impossible to increase production through irrigation as in other areas of the Andean region. The degree of social stratification and state integration was far less than on the coast. It is not surprising therefore that it was precisely here that the most acute resistance to the Inca was found and that there were constant revolts.

If all the exaggeration and idealisation about the Inca state is discounted, there are still some particularities that no other state of this size and with similar technical and scientific attainments exhibits. For example there is no other state in pre-Spanish America, in the ancient East or in European antiquity in which trade was so uniquely controlled by the state that not a single general article of barter served as currency. There is also hardly a bureaucracy in history which had to solve such wide-ranging problems as the bureaucracy of the Inca with-out the aid of a genuine script: for the knot signs of the Inca which we will examine later cannot in any way be called a genuine script.

One thing must in any case be established. Even if the social mechanism guaranteeing every peasant enough land, and providing for the maintenance of the poor, widows and orphans was neither the creation nor the work of the Inca rulers and they had merely allowed this mechanism to continue, it is still strange that they should have retained it. Hardly any state of comparable size in antiquity, in the ancient East or in the American continent allowed the peasantry such far-reaching social rights as did the Inca state. This fact is mainly due to two circumstances. Firstly the Inca state continued to expand right up to the end of the fifteenth century. There was an outward expansion, as a result of new conquests, and an inward expansion deriving from the enlargement of cultivable areas by means of terracing and irrigation. The Inca nobility therefore had constant access to new sources of income, and there was no immediate necessity for it to encroach on the autarchy of Indian villages and their existing rights.

The second important point is this: in the ancient East and in the states of antiquity one of the most costly enterprises that contributed substantially to the exploitation of the people was the maintenance of a large professional army and the waging of tremendous and unproductive wars. Neither of these factors affected the Inca, at least not until the end of the fifteenth century. There were very few professional soldiers who had no other means of livelihood. Most Inca soldiers also engaged in a certain amount of productive activity. When not involved in campaigns they were peasants. Furthermore, since the campaigns were carefully arranged so that they did not take place in harvest time, these peasants were still able to contribute substantially to the work of agriculture. Accordingly the considerable public expenditure which the army incurred was very limited in comparison with the amount required to maintain a regular professional army. Again the wars up to the end of the fifteenth century were always productive. Not one was too costly and each one ended with great conquests that brought in much more than the war had cost.

THE BEGINNING OF THE CRISIS OF THE INCA EMPIRE

There is considerable evidence that at the beginning of the sixteenth century the special factors which had enabled the Inca state to leave the features of village organisation unaltered were in extreme jeopardy.

The undermining of village organisations had already begun with the expansion of the Inca Empire. In the vicinity of the capital city of Cuzco, the land belonging to nearby villages was taken and distributed among the Inca nobility, and instead of being worked by tributary working peasants who kept their own land, it was cultivated by a kind of bondsman who no longer possessed any land. These bondsmen, who were known as *yanacona*, seem to have had various origins. They were partly the descendants of tribes which had rebelled against the Inca, whose land had been taken away and whose members were now compelled to serve as bondsmen on Inca estates. The Spaniards had even called the *yanacona* 'slaves' since they were not free. The expression 'bondsmen' would probably be more apposite, for the *yanacona* were for the most part tied to the land they cultivated. Another kind of *yanacona* was provided by individual villages. The members left the village community and had to be fed by their masters. There is however evidence that one tie with the old tribal community remained. A family which had provided a *yanacona* could exchange him for another member of the family. The returning bondsman was taken back into the village community. These *yanas* fulfilled very different occupations. There were among them the bondsmen who cultivated the land and who represented the lowest order in the Inca Empire (as did the personal servants of the Inca) who could frequently ascend to high honours.

This initial undermining of the village organisation increased drastically at the beginning of the sixteenth century when the conquests became infrequent and agricultural production reached its limits. As a result fewer and fewer possibilities were available to the growing nobility. It is not surprising therefore that the Inca state sought new ways of expanding the wealth and possibilities of development of the nobility. One of the most important of these measures consisted in taking land and creating new bondsmen to cultivate it. It is not improbable as John Murra believes that it was chiefly the population of the most recently conquered territories who were affected.

The close of the conquests also brought about a crisis in the Inca nobility which perhaps had even more radical consequences for the state. As areas that could be conquered diminished, the rivalries within the nobility correspondingly increased. A highly significant symptom was the fact that one of the last Inca, Huayna Capac, created a professional life-guard for himself. Moreover this consisted not of members of royal *ayllus*, but of one of the most recently conquered peoples who had put up an extremely obstinate resistance, the Cañaris from the region of present-day Ecuador. Parallels occur with the emperors of the Roman Empire who no longer trusted their own citizens and relied on life-guards consisting of 'barbarians'.

Another symptom of these conflicts within the nobility was that one of the last Inca, Huascar, expropriated the property of the royal mummies, who, as has already been described, possessed palaces, lands and tributary labour.

The crisis that shook the Inca Empire at the beginning of the sixteenth century was most clearly expressed in the outbreak of regular civil war. The immediate occasion was the battle for the succession of the Inca Huayna Capac, who reigned from 1493 to 1525. Huayna Capac was the conqueror of Ecuador. For reasons that are not clear he had moved his habitation from Cuzco to the city of Tomebamba in Ecuador. While his 'official' son by his marriage with his sister, Huascar, who according to the Inca tradition was his successor, lived in Cuzco, the Inca kept his favourite son Atahuallpa, whose mother was a concubine, with him in Ecuador. It appears that Huayna Capac hoped to assist his natural son to the honourable estate of an Inca, even if it meant splitting the empire into a northern and southern half. But before he was able to achieve anything like this he died, in 1525. Huascar thereupon became Inca, but instead of submitting to this his half-brother Atahuallpa revolted, supported by the northern army and the northern provinces. The bitter conflicts that followed eventually led up to the battle of Riobamba in which Atahuallpa succeeded with the aid of two of his father's ablest generals, Quizquiz and Challcuchima, in inflicting a crushing defeat on Huascar's forces. Huascar retreated further and further and tried to take up the battle for the last time immediately before the capital city of Cuzco. His army was defeated and he himself taken prisoner by Atahuallpa. He had to witness the murder of his whole clan, women and children, and finally he too was executed. From his skull, which had been fashioned into a drinking goblet, Atahuallpa triumphantly drank maize beer.

Rivalries for the succession of an Inca had often occurred, though they did not take the form of a regular and bloody civil war until 1525. The most likely reason for this was that conquests had spectacularly receded in the beginning of the sixteenth century, armies were left with nothing to do and the desire for outward expansion which could no longer be satisfied was directed inwards. This confrontation was also partly a result of the conflict between the northern and southern regions, between Peru and Ecuador. The regions of present-day Ecuador were the last to be conquered. They had had to bear the heaviest burdens of the conquest, and had enjoyed the least advantages. They had not, like other peoples of the Inca Empire, been able to take part in further conquests. Extensive irrigation schemes like those on the west coast of Peru were only possible in a very limited degree in Ecuador. Here the Inca Empire appeared as a taker rather than as a giver more than in any other region. Consequently it is not surprising that the northern provinces were among the most rebellious of the Inca Empire and that they were glad to take part in a civil war so as to consolidate their position. This bloody civil war contributed a great deal towards weakening the Inca Imperium so that it fell to the Spanish *conquistadores* like a ripe fruit.

There were three men who led the Inca Empire in its flowering: Pachacuti, who reigned from 1438 to 1471, his son and successor Topa Inca Yupanqui who held the office of Sapay-Inca from 1471 to 1493 and finally his son and successor, Huayna Capac, who reigned from 1493 to 1525. These men's deeds, particularly those of the first two, are so intermingled with legends and religious representations that it is difficult to get at the real historical personality. In most of the Inca legends the creation of every culture and every social institution in the Andean region is attributed to Pachacuti. If exaggerations are sufficiently reduced and the pre-Inca elements borne in mind, there still remains a great deal of evidence. The very way by which he came to be Inca displays his unusual capabilities. He was the only Inca who attained this office neither by inheritance nor by appointment nor as the result of a plot, but by his prowess in the military field – he saved Cuzco from the Chanca – and in the political field by bringing the Inca nobility over to his side. Fundamental institutions of the Inca Empire could be traced back to his initiative. When he became Inca his people were only an unimportant village community. At his death they ruled over the mightiest empire of South America.

Pachacuti was an outstanding strategist as well as being a magnificent organiser and ideologist. He undoubtedly laid the foundation of those institutions which enabled the Inca to rule over their huge mixed empire. But it remains questionable whether all institutions may be traced back to him, or whether they came into being under his rule. There is much evidence that a number of features of the Inca system of government can be attributed to the inspiration of the 'kingdom' of the Chimu, which was only overthrown in the last years of Pachacuti's reign by his son Topa Inca Yupanqui. It is more than likely that these institutions were then only introduced under his successor.

The great urban achievements of the Inca – the rebuilding of Cuzco and erection of fortresses, terraces and canals – were also introduced under Pachacuti's reign. He was also an unusually clever ideologist, who had a masterly understanding of how to use propaganda and ideology to enhance his deeds, which were undoubtedly important. The story goes that after the victory over the Chanca he summoned all the historians of the Inca Empire and dictated to them an official history that was intended to supersede all older legends. Only the Inca himself, on ascending the throne, was to receive a sort of unofficial secret history that was clearly nearer the truth. It is probably this official ideology that makes it so difficult to extricate Pachacuti's genuine personality from the legendary hero figure. In all appreciations of his achievements the chronicles repeatedly mention that he was always capable of brutality and harshness. When his brother, Capac Yupanqui, successfully carried through the conquest of the state of Cajamarca against his orders, he returned to find, instead of the triumph he deserved, the hangman who killed him. Pachacuti feared, perhaps with good reason, that his brother might become a dangerous rival.

The almost inevitable process of emasculation which power and wealth bring for the successors of the first imperial conquerors did not appear in his son, Topa Inca Yupanqui, who followed in the footsteps of his father both as regards conquests and in the reorganisation of the state. This process however was already apparent in his grandson Huayna Capac who began to develop the characteristics of an oriental despot. It appears that under his reign, the God-Kingdom was introduced which placed the Inca above all that was earthly. While the first two Inca still exhibited very strongly the characteristics of the old tribal chieftains, Huayna Capac tended already to weaken this fidelity to the clan. He cut himself off from most of the members of the Inca *ayllus* who remained in Cuzco and erected a new capital city in Tomebamba, in the region of present-day Ecuador. The number of fresh conquests and new public works diminished. By contrast the exploitation of conquered peoples increased. The transformation of the nobility from a clan aristocracy into a regular nobility became recognisable under Huayna Capac.

THE RELIGION OF THE INCA

Religion among the Inca reflected, as it had among the Aztecs, the radical changes that had taken place at tumultuous speed in the second half of the fifteenth century, since the expansion of the Inca Imperium, and the incorporation of many new peoples and religions into the Inca Empire. At the same time it was imbued with the spirit of the very deep social differences that existed within the Imperium.

At least four different religions existed: the official religion of the Inca state, the religion of the educated people and the nobility of the Imperium, the religion of the conquered states and the religion of the *ayllus*, local groups and individuals.

The official religion of the Inca state exhibits a number of similarities to the Aztec religion. Here too it was an agrarian cult centred round the forces of nature.

The most important deity was the sun, Inti, usually represented as a circular golden disc with a human face, which shone in all directions. As already mentioned the largest temple in Cuzco, the Coricancha, the inner walls of which consisted mainly of decorations in gold, was dedicated to the sun. The Sapay-Inca was acknowledged as god of the sun and the Inca people regarded themselves – just as the Aztecs did – as special servants of this divinity who had given them a civilising mission. However the sun did not have the pronounced character of the god of war that it had in Tenochtitlan.

Besides the sun a large number of other personified forces of nature played an important role. The moon was looked on as the wife of the sun and as subordinate to him, although on the coast the moon always appears to have been the most important deity. Important roles were also played by the earth mother, the god of thunder and of rain, and deities representing various heavenly bodies.

Characteristic of the attempts at state integration made by the Inca Empire is the fact that the Inca cult of the sun was introduced into all the conquered territories. Temples of Inti with their own priests had to be built in every centre, and were maintained by the work of the subject peoples.

Among the members of the cities of the Triple Alliance in Mesoamerica and of the Inca, the official religion soon no longer sufficed for the élite and they looked for a more abstract god to serve who would be largely incomprehensible to the common people. Just as the greatest intellectual personality in the Valley of Mexico, Netzahualcoyotl of Tetzcoco, introduced in the cult of In Tloque Nahuaque the concept of an abstract and omnipresent god, the most important personality of the Inca Empire, Pachacuti, spread the cult of the god of creation, Viracocha. This god was acknowledged as the creator of all mankind and of all things, who was invisible and dwelt in heaven. Viracocha however was no new deity, but founded on a cult hero who had been worshipped for a very long time.

The idols of the conquered peoples were brought into their capital city by the Inca as evidence of their conquest, just as had been the practice among the Aztecs. In Cuzco they were placed in the sun temple, Coricancha, and were received into the Inca pantheon.

Typical of their deities was Pariacaca, a god of creation from the highland region of Huarochiri. Among his most important creations were the irrigation systems. In the myths belonging to the inhabitants of this region which the Spanish recorded it is said:

At this time a very beautiful woman lived in the village of which we are speaking; she was called Chuquisuso. One day she wept, while she watered her field of maize; she wept because the little water there was was not enough to water the dry land. Thereupon Pariacaca descended, and with his cloak stopped up the mouth of the little lake. The woman wept still more bitterly, when she saw that the little water she could count on had disappeared. So Pariacaca found her and asked: 'Sister, what is troubling you?' And she replied, 'My field of maize is perishing with thirst.' 'You must not suffer on this account,' said Pariacaca. 'I will see to it that much water shall come from the lake; which you have up in the heights. But you must agree beforehand to sleep with me.' 'Let the waters appear first. When the field of maize has been watered, then will I sleep with you,' she answered. 'Good,' said Pariacaca and caused much water to appear. The happy woman watered not only her own field, but many another as well. After she had watered the fields, Pariacaca said, 'Now we will go and sleep.' 'Not today, but the day after tomorrow,' said she. Since Pariacaca loved her very much, he promised her everything that she desired, for he wished to sleep with her. 'I will transform these fields into watered meadows with water out of the river,' he said. 'First complete this work, then I will sleep with you,' she said. 'Agreed,' said Pariacaca and accepted.

Pariacaca then built a wide irrigation canal which carried much water and let this flow as far as the fields of the men of Huracubara. Pariacaca succeeded in winning all animals to help him. Pumas, foxes, snakes and birds of great variety helped in the building and in the maintenance of the canal.

When the canal was finished Pariacaca said to the woman: 'Let us now go and sleep together.' But she replied: 'Let us go to the lofty crags. There we shall sleep together.' And so it was. They slept together beside a precipice which was called Yanaccacca. And after they had slept together the woman said to Pariacaca: 'Let us go to another place.' 'Let us go,' he replied. And he brought the woman to the mouth of the canal of Cocochalla. When they reached this spot, the woman Chuquisuso said: 'I will stay by this canal.' And immediately she was turned to stone.[26]

It is characteristic of the creation myths concerning agriculture in the Andean region that unlike Mesoamerica, the creation of irrigation schemes counted as the most important gift god had brought to man.

The *huaca* cult was on a somewhat different level although it still contained strong animistic elements. *Huaca* means a holy place, and the most varied sites counted as such: they could be large temples or small stone cairns. It was believed that spirits dwelt in these *huacas* which had to be propitiated to show mercy by prayer, worship and sacrifice. The *huacas* round Cuzco were organised along the *ceque* system. The *ceques* were imaginary lines which bound the various *huacas* to the centre of Cuzco. These lines traversed almost symmetrically the four quarters of the capital city. In three of these quarters there were nine *ceques* in each, which were again divided into three, while in the fourth fourteen of these lines ran through. R.T.Zuidema has defined these *ceques* as having two meanings. On the one hand they represented a calendrical system. He presumes that there was a holy place for every day of the calendar. At the same time these lines and their subdivisions symbolised the exceedingly complicated social organisation of the Inca capital city. Every *ayllu* had to maintain a group of holy places which were arranged within the framework of the *ceques* system. The *ayllu* hierarchy and their relationship amongst each other were reflected, Zuidema believes, in this complicated system of *ceques*.[27]

The lowest rank in the divine hierarchy was occupied by the gods of individual clans of the *ayllus*, as well as by a sort of personal tutelary genius, the *conopas*. The *ayllu* worshipped mythical ancestors who could be people, animals or objects such as stones. The belief in the descent from an animal or a plant did not – as among many peoples of north America – prevent the members of the *ayllu* from killing and eating them.

The Sapay-Inca, the Inca in chief, who presumably was worshipped as god, as the sun's son, did not play an important role within this pantheon until the end of the fifteenth century. The ceremonial surrounding the Inca had, as we have seen, certain religious features.

The official religion of the Inca did not have the sombre pessimism of the Aztecs. On the contrary, the world was seen in a rosy light. It had reached the zenith of its development under the Inca and the fact that the infallible Inca in chief was a son of the sun guaranteed that it would follow its pre-ordained course into eternity.

It is interesting to note that here, as among the cities of the Triple Alliance in Mesoamerica, the members of the élite had some doubts about this simple view of the world. In Mesoamerica the religion of the élite was more optimistic than the official cult. Netzahualcoyotl and his disciples apparently believed that the unknown god might be able to prevent the end of the world. The idea of the world of the élite in the Inca Empire on the other hand contradicted the rosy, optimistic idea of the official cult. The god of creation, Viracocha, was far more remote from mankind, and was less amenable to influence by them than the sun, which after all was the father of the Sapay-Inca.

How could mankind influence the gods? The first way lay in sacrifice. However Inca sacrifices were very different in Peru from those among the Aztecs. They were not meant to feed the gods and to protect the world from extinction, but only to win their goodwill. Human sacrifices existed among the Inca but on a much smaller scale than in Mesoamerica. Such sacrifices were made only on special occasions, for instance at the coronation of an Inca. Children of about ten years, young girls, were usually chosen for the purpose and perhaps a few prominent prisoners of war. As in Mesoamerica, their hearts were torn out of their breasts. Nevertheless these sacrifices only represented a fraction of the number carried out in Mexico. Instead animals and valuable objects were sacrificed: llama were slaughtered in honour of the god, white llama in honour of the sun and brown llama in honour of the thunder. In addition finely woven clothing was brought which was regarded as being particularly valuable. The gods also accepted *chicha* beer.

Sacrifices were not the only means of propitiating the gods. In one particular respect the religion of the Inca had a certain resemblance to Christianity, that greatly facilitated the work of the missionaries in Peru later on. Both religions believed in atonement. This was not just possible once as in Mesoamerica, but was much more like the Catholic concept. Anyone who had committed an offence or a crime could by atonement receive absolution from the priests who laid down a number of punishments and actions to be performed. But in two respects at least, this form of atonement differed from that of the Catholics. In the first place the priest did everything he could to discover whether the atonement had in fact been carried out; if not, then absolution was valueless. In order to establish this, the priest could even resort to force. Secondly the coveted absolution had for some crimes not only a spiritual but also a temporal significance and was able to protect the penitent from punishment.

In yet another aspect the religion of the Inca bore greater resemblances to the Christian than to the Aztec religion and contained more elements of an imperial religion than the latter. This concerned the conception of life after death. It was not the manner of death, as among the Aztecs, which was decisive in respect of life after death, but the manner in which a man's life had been led. Whoever had led a good life went to heaven, which was beside the sun, and an abundant and eternal life awaited him beyond the grave. But whoever had led a sinful life was banished into hell, which was at the centre point of the earth. There was however a significant exception which revealed the deep social gulf in the Inca Empire. Members of the nobility, irrespective of whether they had sinned or not, always went to heaven.

The complicated character of the Inca religion corresponded to a no less complicated hierarchy among the priesthood. This was organised in three very different stages. The first contained the members of the official Inca cult, the second that of the cults of the conquered peoples and the third the priests of the *ayllus*. Within the two first of these groups there was a complex hierarchy. In the official Inca cult, it extended from the Chief Priest, who was related to the Inca and ruled over the whole religious hierarchy with a council of nine other priests down to the lowest priestly candidate in a small temple to the sun. The structure of the religious hierarchy of the conquered regions was most likely different and was probably dependent on the size and the extent of state integration in these regions in pre-Inca times. Both these religious hierarchies had at their disposal extensive estates, which were cultivated compulsorily by the peasants of the conquered regions. The villages owed labour service both to the religious hierarchy and to the Inca. There were however whole villages which exclusively served the temples. In addition certain religious institutions also disposed of bondsmen.

There was yet another category appertaining to the priesthood beside the actual priests and their servants: the *mamacunas*, the 'virgins of the sun'. Some of the girls were chosen by the Inca inspectors in various villages when they were about ten years old, and were placed in the service of the religious hierarchy. They served both the sun and other deities. Since however most of them worked for the sun, the Spaniards called them virgins of the sun. They represented a unique economic gain both for the Inca and for the religious hierarchy. The materials which they wove were considered to be among the finest and most valuable in the whole realm of the Inca. These virgins of the sun were strictly forbidden to have sexual relations with men, and, with one exception, on the discovery of such relations both the maiden and the intruder were stoned to death. The only exception was the Inca. One chronicler relates that if the Inca had spent the night with a virgin of the sun, a temple watchman went up to him and said softly, 'Ye have spent this night with a virgin of the sun.' Whereupon the Inca said, 'Yea, I have sinned' and the disagreeable matter was settled.[28]

The duties of the priesthood were wide, varying. Naturally, encouraging plants to grow was one of the most important. With the aid of stone pillars they marked the seasons and introduced ceremonies for seed-time and harvest.

The great feast of purification in September was typical of these kinds of ceremonies. The whole population cut down eating to one meal a day which could not contain either meat or fish. At night special cakes of maize flour mixed with child's blood were prepared which people rubbed into themselves the following day to drive out diseases.

After sunrise the people prayed and thus ended their fast. Then a richly attired Inca of royal blood appeared from the fortress of Sacsahuaman holding a spear, and joined four other Inca of royal blood who were waiting for him.

After this messenger had arrived, he touched with his own lance the lances of the four Inca and said to them that the sun commanded them as its messengers to drive out of the city and its surroundings all diseases, all that was bad which they might discover. The Inca then simultaneously took to the four great highways which led to the city, highways which they believed led to the Four Quarters, Tahuantinsuyu. When the inhabitants, men and women, young and old saw these four messengers passing by they came to the doors of their houses, clapped and rejoiced, shook out their clothes as though to get rid of the dust, then placed their hands on their heads, touched their faces, their arms and legs which they rubbed as though wanting to wash these parts of their bodies; they believed that in this way they were banishing all that was bad from their houses, and the messengers of the sun would bear all that was evil out of the city.[29]

The messengers went as far as the city boundaries, where they planted their lances to announce that the evil spirits had been exorcised up to that point.

Ritual races usually leading on to a mountain, such as the mountain of Pariacaca which was reputed to be the incarnation of the god of the same name, were ceremonies of special importance. At these ceremonies prayers, of which a few have survived, were addressed to the gods.

Among the priests' most important duties was their prophesying as soothsayers. They made use of a variety of different things. Llama entrails were thought to be particularly favourable for the making of oracles. After they had been taken out of the sacrificed animals, they were inflated and the future foretold from their appearance. The temple of Pachacamac which has often been compared with that of Delphi in ancient Greece was especially famous for its oracles. Whether the art of clairvoyance was as far advanced among the priesthood of Pachacamac as in Delphi is however questionable. Pilgrims and suppliants thronged to this place from the whole Inca Empire.

The temple enclosure is very large [writes Hernando Pizarro, one of the *conquistadores*] and contains great buildings and patios. On the outside there is a large space bounded by a rampart with a gateway, leading to the temple. In this space are the houses of the women, who are, as they say, the wives of the devil. Here also are the store rooms in which the gold was kept. Apart from these women, there is no one living in this plaza. Their sanctuaries are the same as those of the sun, which I have already described. Before anyone was allowed to enter the first court of the temple, he had to fast for 20 days; and before he could ascend to the upper court, he had to fast for a year. When the messengers of the chieftains, who had fasted for a year, ascended to ask this god to grant them a good harvest, they found the priest sitting with his head shrouded. There are still other Indians called the 'servants of the sun'. If the chieftains' messengers delivered their reports to the priests, the servants of the devil went into a room in which they stated that he would speak with them there, and that the devil had said that he was angry with the chieftains concerning the sacrifices they were compelled to bring him and also concerning the gifts which they desired to bring to him. I do not think that they were speaking with the devil, but that the servants were deceiving the chieftain. For I took great pains to go into the matter and an old servant, one of the most respected and trusted of their god, told a chieftain who repeated it to me, that their devil had said they should not be afraid of the horses, since they could do no harm. I caused this servant to be tortured, but he was so obstinate in his evil faith, that I could get nothing else out of him, other than that they really take their devil for a god. This temple is so much feared by all Indians, that they believe if one of these priests of the devil asked them for anything, and they should refuse, they would have to die on the spot.[30]

The priesthood in the Inca Empire, like the Aztecs' priesthood, was also responsible for the education of the nobility and of the bureaucracy. The *amauta* who undertook this education came from their ranks. The priests of individual *ayllus* were quite distinct from the official priesthood. They were completely independent of the state and church hierarchy; they were mostly older men freed from most of the labour services. The clan sometimes saw to it that they did not have to work at all, though sometimes this was not possible. They were naturally closely connected with the peasants, and it is no accident that after the conquest of Peru by the Spaniards it was precisely this group which survived the longest and lived for many years after the state and church hierarchy had long since been extinguished.

The religious hierarchy represented a tremendous force in the Inca Empire. It is nevertheless not clear to what extent this was clearly integrated. How were the large revenues distributed between the Inca temples and the local cults? How far did the control of the high priest extend over the religious hierarchy of the overthrown peoples? To what extent did the Inca in fact succeed in forcing their religion on the peoples they had conquered? It is not possible yet to answer these questions.

The relations between state and church were not without friction, although the Sapay-Inca was regarded as God and one of his kin was Chief Priest. The chronicles report constant conflicts and confrontations between the state and the various church groups. This is quite understandable. These conflicts reflected the constant disputes within the nobility of the Inca Empire and the problems posed by the religious integration of so vast an empire must have been overwhelming.

TECHNOLOGY, SCIENCE AND ART

In considering technology and science at the time of the Inca, it may be said – perhaps with one or two exceptions – that there were no new achievements to record. On the other hand intensive cultivation and terracing which had existed long before the Inca reached new dimensions during the period of the Inca. Large cities had already existed before the Inca, but their number and the extent of urbanisation in general had never been so great. Roads and highways had also existed earlier, but the network of roads constructed by the Inca reached dimensions which eclipsed all those which had previously existed. So although new discoveries were not made, expansion took place on a vast scale.

The intellectual attainments of the Inca were pre-eminently of a practical nature. Besides building and intensive cultivation the Inca concentrated largely on medicine and achieved amazing results in this field. They performed trepanning operations and were already acquainted with forms of anæsthetisation. At an operation a patient was first given *chicha* to drink, which intoxicated him; then he was given coca to chew to reduce his sensitivity to pain.

The most famous doctors of the time of the Inca were descended from the Callahouaya tribe who dwelt in the valley to the east of Lake Titicaca. They not only performed operations but experimented in using animals for medicinal purposes. A snake mixture was alleged to cure nervous diseases and sexual impotence, and a mixture of spider's web and tree bark to heal wounds. Bee stings were used to combat rheumatism.

There is a formidable difference between the achievements of the Inca in the practical and technical sphere and those in a rather more abstract sphere. This difference is very clear in relation to writing. The Inca Empire was presumably the only state of comparable size in history that did not possess a script. The detailed records of the entire population, the supervision of the extensive State revenues, the control of the labour service performed by each individual, the communication of instructions by the Inca to his numerous officials, the complicated juridical system that applied to all ranks from the highest to the lowest – all these matters proceeded without the aid of a genuine script. A substitute for it was the *quipus*, wrongly labelled as a 'knot-script'. There was no question here of a genuine script, for it was merely a mnemonic system. There were two sorts of *quipu*: the first was statistical and was used to record merchandise, population figures or labour services; the second recorded historical facts, traditions and instructions. The principle was the same. About a hundred cords were suspended from one cord, differing in size and colour. The knots made in these cords differed in their significance, in accordance with their size and nature, and were therefore worthless without the memory of specially trained professionals, known as *quipu-camayoc*. These officials presumably underwent memory-training for years. Spaniards who spoke with them after the collapse of the Inca Empire were constantly surprised and impressed by their feats of memory. A discovery made in recent times could force us to revise certain concepts about the Inca. At the Congress of Americanists in Lima in 1970 Thomas Barthel, a German anthropologist, stated that designs found on Inca textiles were pictographic writings. The texts for which he has furnished interpretations up to now were religious in nature.

The absence of a genuine script explains why our historical knowledge of the Inca past is so much less than our knowledge of the Mesoamerican peoples and why it is so much more difficult to obtain any exact information about the intellectual achievements of the Inca. The great intellectual achievements in Mesoamerica – script, the calendar and mathematics – were doubtless the work of the priests. When eventually political power fell into secular hands, such achievements were simplified and became more practical. But in Peru there is no evidence, at least in relation to the beginnings of a script and of mathematics, that they were of similar origin. It is possible that the priesthood was the first to discover them, but they could equally have had a secular origin.

Inca mathematics, with which we are less well acquainted than with that of the Mesoamerican peoples, again, because they left no written evidence, seems to have been simpler. It was also more akin to European ideas in that the Inca inclined towards a decimal system. Attainments in astronomy were certainly the result of observations made by the priesthood. They knew of the solar and lunar years and of the revolution of Venus. It was presumed for a long time that they only knew the lunar year and calculated the twelve months in accordance with the lunar calendar. The missing days were eventually made good by a supplementary number, the function of which was never very clear. Recently Zuidema has put forward a new hypothesis, which indicates that the Inca had always recognised the solar year and divided up their calendar accordingly. There was no complicated liturgical calendar – as in Mesoamerica, with its cycles of fifty-two years that enabled the exact fixing of every day within this cycle. The Inca calendar was much more practical and far more dependent on the cycle of the seasons, on harvests and seed-time.

If a lesson is to be drawn from artistic development in the Andean region, it is that rigid State regimentation does not necessarily contribute to the advancement of art. In comparison with the earlier periods in the history of the Andean region, especially with the classical period on the coast, Inca art appears in general to have been very poor. Sculpture hardly existed and what there was did not in the remotest degree approach either that of the Chavin period, which even today evokes surprise and admiration, or that of Tiahuanaco. In pottery there is no sign of the variety of ornament that made the Mochica potters world famous. It is mostly made in *aryballus* form and has only abstract geometrical designs. Only in textile production and in weaving is the decline less pronounced.

What Inca art forfeited in taste, in comparison for instance with that of Paracas and other areas on the south coast of Peru, it made up in technical perfection. This is hardly surprising when it is considered that an *acclla* weaver sometimes worked for months on a single woollen shirt.

Inca Literature

Because of the absence of any script only very limited portions of Inca literature have survived, and as their language and culture persisted into colonial times it is not certain whether or not many poems and drama stemmed from the pre-Spanish epoch.

The Inca, like the Aztecs, had a sort of official epic poetry that sang of the glorious deeds of the Inca in long, effusive hymns of praise. The authors usually belonged to the category of the *amauta*, the educators of the young, while the Inca themselves – in contrast to the Chief Speaker of the Aztecs – do not appear to have composed any poems or to have set much store by being regarded as poets. Besides the epic poetry there is a large collection of religious poetry, containing a number of hymns that are addressed primarily to the god of creation, Viracocha.

> O Viracocha, Lord of the Universe,
> Whether male or female, Thou that createst and makest all things,
> I pray humbly before Thee.
> Where art Thou hidden from me?
> Am I perchance not Thy son?
> In the heights, in the depths,
> Upon thy judgement seat,
> Hear me.
> Creator of the world, Creator of man,
> Lord Almighty,
> My eyes fail me
> Though I long to see Thee.
> We seek Thee in the vast spaces
> In which Thou dwellest,
> In the depths of the ocean where Thou doest abide.
> Could I but know Thee,
> I would look upon Thee,
> And then would I Thee comprehend.
> I should also be seen by Thee
> And Thou wouldest me protect.[31]

In Inca poems the features that are so characteristic of Aztec literature – the philosophical meditations and also the tones of destruction and of deep depression – are absent. Instead there are many love poems and hymns to nature.

> Where is my little swallow, the one
> I seek for day and night?
> Perchance thou art weeping, lost somewhere far away,
> Without knowing how thou canst return home.
> I ask of everyone.
> Perchance I shall discover her face so that I may seek her.
> Where art thou, swallow mine, thou whom I seek year in year out?[32]

Other poems glorify an irrigation canal:

> Great channel, that leadest the waters on to our fields,
> Let us tread, let us tread with might and main, let us tread,
> Let us tread again with all our strength,
> Let us tread.
> Through thee will our plants receive their blossoms
> Tread them in.
> Through thee will our plants receive their blossoms
> Tread, through thee will the finest fruits be borne,
> Tread! Let us tread with might and main,
> Let us tread again. Tread![33]

The Inca, in contrast to the Aztecs, seem to have been acquainted with regular dramas. The most celebrated is the *Ollantay*, which first became known in the eighteenth century; its origin has been much disputed among scholars.

The drama is made up of fifteen scenes and takes place in the time of the Inca Pachacuti. One of his most famous generals, Ollanta, of humble origins, is in love with the Inca's daughter, the maiden Cusi-Coyllur. He meets her in secret but may not marry her since he is not of royal Inca stock. When he nevertheless addresses the Inca Pachacuti with the request that he should give him his daughter, the Inca refuses and says to him: 'Remember, thou art a simple vassal; everyone should keep his place.'[34] And he had Cusi-Coyllur taken to a convent of virgins of the sun, where she was delivered of a child a few months later. Ollanta then decides to rebel against the Inca. He marches to the city of Ollantaytambo, and his army defeats the Inca's troops, who were under the command of General Ruminahui. In order to cancel out his defeat Ruminahui goes to Ollanta and states that he is afraid that the Inca will punish him for his defeat, asking Ollanta for his protection. Ollanta takes him with him and a few days later, while the rebel general and his army are asleep, Ruminahui opens the fortress gates to the Inca armies, who take the rebels prisoner. Ollanta must face the death penalty, but the play nevertheless has a happy ending. Pachacuti has in the meantime died, and his successor, Tupac Yupanqui, restores to Ollanta not only his life but also the woman he loves.

This play written in Quetchua and its happy ending has caused some scholars to regard it as primarily of Spanish inspiration. Others strongly contest this and believe that it is definitely an Inca play of pre-Colombian origin, containing perhaps a few small alterations dating from the colonial period. A final judgement is made very difficult, both because of the extraordinary vitality of the Quetchua language, which is still spoken by millions of people and in which new poems and plays are constantly being written, and because of the vitality of Inca traditions, which even today exercise a very strong influence and inspire poems and other creative literature.

CHAPTER 13

RETROSPECT AND COMPARISON

The various American high cultures have quite rightly been compared with those of the Old World. It is equally illuminating to compare the two high cultures of ancient America, Mesoamerica and the Andean region. In this way far-reaching discoveries can be made about their growth. Development in many respects ran parallel, both in the forms it took and to a large extent from the chronological point of view. Within these forms, however, radical differences naturally emerged.

In both regions many thousands of years were to elapse from the moment when man discovered agriculture to the point when this substantially altered his life. Only after this did agricultural products become the chief source of nourishment for the populations of both these regions, and a similar lapse of time was necessary before one of the most important potentials of agriculture, the liberation of a considerable proportion of the population from direct food production, was realised.

The first people in both regions to be set free in this way were the priests, and the earliest large buildings to be erected were temples. In both Mesoamerica and Peru these very soon developed into ceremonial centres. The most important of these early centres – those of the Olmecs in Mesoamerica and of Chavin in the Andean region – appear suddenly and without transition. Is this a sign that they came from outside or merely an expression of the fact that changes do not always take place at snail's pace but can sometimes happen in the form of sudden mutations and explosions? This question remains today one of the most controversial in the history of ancient America. No less controversial is the problem of whether links ever existed between these two high cultures, each of which exercised so enduring an influence.

A development that can properly be called explosive followed the first high cultures. The most important material discovery was that of intensive agriculture, with the potential contained in irrigation. In parts of Mesoamerica and of the Andean region important irrigation works came into being that laid the foundation for a rapid increase of population and for new developments, for building towns and for creating the State. Did the discovery of intensive agriculture constitute the basis of the high cultures that followed? This was certainly so in parts of Mesoamerica and of the Andean region. In the southern highlands of Lake Titicaca and presumably of the Maya region intensive agriculture played either no part at all or only a very limited one. Did the regions where intensive agriculture was practised act as a catalyst for the development of others? Possibly, although there is no evidence of this, the less so in that in a whole series of developments (script and the calendar among the Maya, sculpture in the region of Lake Titicaca) the culture of these other regions was in some respects superior to that of regions where irrigation was practised.

The appearance of the first ceremonial centres, both in Mesoamerica and in the Andean region, followed a period of almost a thousand years, usually referred to as theocratic by historians and ethnologists. Many scholars presumed for a long time that it was an age characterised by two essential features: peaceful development and the hegemony of a priestly nobility. The first assumption is increasingly suspect today. The very many traces of war in classical Peruvian times have made such an idea seem rather improbable. However with regard to Mesoamerica there is also increasing doubt concerning the peaceful character of this period, even though evidence of war, for reasons that have already been given, is less. Did power rest in the hands of the priestly nobility in classical times? Can we really speak of theocracies? A number of scholars have drawn attention to the fact that when the Europeans arrived not a single society of this nature existed in ancient America, so that no one had ever actually discovered a theocracy. On the other hand many archaeologists point out that never in the history of American high cultures had so great a proportion of the surplus product been applied to religious purposes as in that period. Accordingly most of them stick to the idea of a theocracy.

Apart from this controversy most historians are agreed on two characteristics of this period: it is the longest and most stable period in the history of American cultures, and it is the period of the greatest intellectual and artistic achievements – the script, the calendar, Maya mathematics, the great pyramids and temples of Teotihuacan, the ceramics of the Mochica, the sculpture of Tiahuanaco.

Social development in both regions differs. In the Andean region a good many state structures developed that had few cities or even none at all. However important these states were, not one of them proved itself capable of overruling the others. In Mesoamerica large cities did develop, of which the most important, Teotihuacan, appears to have exercised a hegemony over a long period of time.

In the second half of the first millennium AD all these magnificent classical cultures come to an untimely end: the cities of the Maya were abandoned, Teotihuacan was overrun and the north coast of Peru and the greater part of the Andean highlands were occupied by foreign conquerors. The disappearance of these cultures constitutes one of the least resolved, most discussed and most complex problems raised by the ancient American cultures. Is there after all a common denominator?

The causes of the decline are not all the same. In Mesoamerica there is a certain amount of evidence that during this period the discrepancy that manifested itself so clearly in the historical period made itself felt; I refer to the discrepancy between the constantly growing population and the increasing requirements of the nobility and the far less rapid growth of agricultural production, manufacture and trade. If it is further appreciated that the nobility consisted of priests, it is not unlikely that the revolts assumed the character of religious schisms, which increasingly rejected the greater material demands of the official State church. Then when foreign invaders arrived these schisms and internal quarrels must have smoothed their path.

The Andean region escaped the first cause. The huge irrigation installations and the vast herds of llama may have prevented the serious discrepancy existing between the increase of population and the food available for them. The signs of internal tension are much less evident here even though there is a certain amount of evidence of the beginnings of conflict between the nobility of the priesthood and the secular nobility. Here the advance by a people living in a particularly favourable strategic situation within the region of the high culture played a decisive role. What is common to both regions is that in the post-classic period a far greater part of the wealth of society was devoted to secular purposes than ever before. The nobility was by now predominantly secular.

In the time of the great conquests that followed the classic cultures in the period of Huari-Tiahuanaco in the Andean region and of the Toltecs in Mesoamerica, metallurgy developed further in the Andean region (bronze) and metal made a sudden appearance in Mesoamerica. This was nevertheless only of limited significance in both cases and failed to produce the same revolutionary results as in the Old World.

In the important field of increasing food production the conquerors achieved little. In the time of Huari-Tiahuanaco a number of irrigation works on the Peruvian coast even seem to have fallen into ruin; and in Mesoamerica the Toltecs did very little about increasing food production. This may have contributed to the short life of these empires.

After their end further developments ensued that differed in character in the Andean region and in Mesoamerica. The Toltec Empire was literally reduced to atoms and replaced by innumerable small and middle-sized cities and city states. In Peru, on the other hand, mighty and large states developed and flourished, now containing, in contrast to the classical period, extensive cities.

On this different foundation there began in both regions in the middle of the fifteenth century a steep ascent towards an *Empire*.

The similarities existing in the construction of the Aztec and Inca Empires cannot be overlooked.

In the first half of the fifteenth century – for the Aztec and Inca chronology generally coincides with a difference of only ten years – insignificant and until then obscure peoples still living in tribally organised communities began campaigns of conquest that within a few decades raised them to the status of world powers. They built up the largest empires that had so far existed on the American continent.

The personalities of the conquerors are also alike. Pachacuti of Cuzco, and Netzahualcoyotl of Tetzcoco and Tlacaellel of Tenochtitlan all belong to the ruling groups although they were in some respects outsiders. They owed their power not to inheritance, but to their own extraordinary capabilities. Pachacuti only became Inca after he had defeated the Chanca against his royal father's will. Netzahualcoyotl returned from exile to liberate his city while leading a rebellion against the domination of Atzcapotzalco. Tlacaellel, originally a deputy in the official hierarchy, was able by force of personality to reach a pre-eminence that was never equalled.

Both the Aztec and Inca Empires raised food production to a higher level than ever before. The most important irrigation installations and water control schemes in the whole American continent developed in these empires. The existing tribal organisation was largely undermined both among the Inca and among the Aztecs. Immediately after the first conquests important land expropriations were undertaken in favour of the members of the upper class. It developed into a nobility or a ruling bureaucracy. At the lower end of the social scale bondsmen and slave-like conditions of dependence began to appear.

In both cases there was a substantial revision of history to correspond with these sweeping changes. It is characteristic that one of the first acts of the ruler whether Inca or Aztec, after a successful conquest, was to dictate to the 'historians' a new version of history. Under threat of the most rigid punishment previous historiography and traditions were consigned to oblivion.

At the beginning of the sixteenth century a crisis began to develop among the peoples of the Triple Alliance in Mexico and among the Inca. The rate of conquests declined, the increase of food production that had resulted from the construction of irrigation works slowed down. Serious differences appeared between the allied cities of Tenochtitlan and Tetzcoco and tensions developed within Tenochtitlan between the hereditary and the meritorious aristocracy. In the Inca Empire there was even a civil war between Huascar and Atahuallpa, the rival claimants to the Inca throne.

The crisis in both empires was also reflected in the personality of their rulers, Moctezuma and Atahuallpa are only weak reflections of the founding fathers of the empires. They attempted to make up for their personal weakness and the increasing crisis in their empires either by declaring or by reinforcing the concept of the divine rulers. These tensions must have played a significant role in paving the way for the Spanish *conquistadores*.

Despite these striking similarities the tremendous differences between the two empires cannot be ignored. They were very marked in various fields: in the degree of integration, in the social organisation of the conquering peoples, in the strength and weakness of the clan organisation, in the capability of the imperial leadership to solve the food problem and last but not least in the role played by trade.

The differences between the two empires in respect of state integration were radical. While the Inca set up a rigid system of administration throughout their empire, carried out gigantic movements of population, encouraged public works, threw up a network of roads and introduced an integration of religion and language, among the Aztecs there was hardly a sign of any of this in their conquered territories. There was no state administration, but only collectors of tribute. In most of the territories overthrown hardly any great buildings or roads were constructed, and there was no religious or language integration or registration of the entire population as among the Inca.

Only in the Valley of Mexico were there the beginnings of an integration similar to that of the Inca: the division of a large part of the population into groups of tributary workers, a centralised juridical administration, the carrying out of large projects all increased the food production and facilitated communications. This diversity was the result as much of the varying degrees of strength existing between the conquerors and the conquered as of the variety in ecological conditions.

On the eve of their conquests the Inca were a smaller and less powerful group than the cities of the Triple Alliance in the Valley of Mexico. They were confronted by much more powerful and integrated states, such as the great 'kingdom' of the Chimu. This difference between state integration in Mesoamerica and in the Andean region was most likely due to the great irrigation works which were more widespread in the Andean region than in Mesoamerica and required a considerable degree of state control. To secure their conquests the Inca necessarily had to pursue an extensive policy of integration. They had to apply rigid control over the conquered territories, appearing not only as takers but also as givers: by proclaiming the *Pax Incaica*, by instituting or maintaining great irrigation schemes, by redistributing raw materials among the various ecological areas of the Andean regions.

The situation in Mesoamerica was quite different. As far as state integration, numerical strength and strategic position were concerned, the peoples of the Mexico Valley were incomparably stronger than all the other peoples of Mesoamerica. The cities of the Triple Alliance usually encountered either village communities, relatively loosely knit individual tribes and occasionally state communities which were nevertheless much weaker than they were themselves. A policy of integration like the Inca one was not necessary *vis à vis* these communities, at least not outside the Valley of Mexico. Once the Aztecs controlled the valley, they were convinced that the rest of Mesoamerica also belonged to them. Integration measures were therefore limited to the Valley of Mexico proper.

Outside their territory the Aztecs almost invariably appeared as takers not givers. It would have been difficult for them had they wished to emulate the Inca functions of 'givers' to carry out even in a limited degree beyond the Valley of Mexico great irrigation works like those that the Inca either built or administered in Peru. The redistribution of raw materials, a typical Inca practice, was also difficult to carry out in the Mexican lowlands. The Inca had the advantage of controlling a region in which highland and lowland products were equally balanced, particularly raw materials. The coastal inhabitants could receive wool and the highlanders maize and coca. Even had they wanted to do so, what highland products could the Aztecs have given to the lowland inhabitants? They had nothing to equal the cotton, the coca, and the feathers from the tropical regions. This was made even more difficult by the comparatively inadequate transport facilities among the Aztecs. In Peru the llama enabled merchandise to be given a much wider distribution than was possible on men's backs.

The fact that the Aztecs neither wanted to nor were able to carry out a large-scale integration of their Imperium had lasting consequences. If the overthrown peoples could not be won over naked terror had to be used. In this respect the human sacrifices fulfilled a purely political purpose. Nor is it surprising that the Aztec Empire employed much stronger arbitrary measures than the Inca Empire. The Inca armies were kept at a distance from villages and provisioned from state reserves. Aztec troops swept through all the villages and could plunder them at the discretion of the army. The services which the conquered peoples of the Inca Empire had to provide were established after their wealth and resources had been examined. They were not subject to modification. The tribute laid down by the Aztecs was arbitrarily calculated and could be increased at any time. The fact that the Inca only demanded labour services, while the Aztecs demanded real tribute meant that in times of hardship the demands on the conquered peoples in Mesoamerica were much more severe than in the Andean region.

In theory at least the inhabitants of the Inca Empire could complain to the central authority about the Inca administration. Complaints about the many excesses of the Aztec tribute collectors were unknown in Mesoamerica. The prisoners of war captured by the Inca, with the exception of a few leaders who were executed, were liberated and returned to their villages. Prisoners of war taken by the Aztecs faced the inevitable sacrificial death.

In these comparisons between the Inca and the Aztecs the pendulum must not be allowed to swing too far against Mesoamerica. Massive deportations and the extensive requisitioning of women practised by the Inca never took place among the Aztecs.

The difference in the degree of integration in the Aztec and Inca empires had very paradoxical consequences. To a certain extent it was expressed in the magnificent development of Tenochtitlan, which received most of the wealth which flowed in from the conquered territories while Inca revenues were destined for all parts of their empire. It is therefore not surprising that its buildings far surpassed those of Cuzco and that the features of a great city that characterised the Aztec metropolis were much more prominent than those of the capital city of the Inca.

The differences in the degree of integration between the two empires nevertheless involved unique military disadvantages for the Aztecs. The great road system that straddled the Inca Empire, the depots installed everywhere, above all the use of conquered peoples for war service resulted in a great increase in the striking power of the Inca Empire after every new conquest. The reverse was the case among the Aztecs. Since the wars always originated in the Valley of Mexico the striking power of the army, in view of the fact that no roads or depots had been provided, decreased the further they went from the Valley of Mexico. The larger the Imperium became, the less accessible the neighbouring regions were. This contrast explains how it was that the Inca controlled the whole of the region of high culture in the Andean area, whereas the Aztecs were unable to conquer distant territories such as that of the Tarascans even though they often had a far smaller population than the territory under their own domination. There was also another side to this. Since the Aztecs had to fight their battles themselves, the need for élite warriors was substantially greater than among the Inca and they could put only a limited number of soldiers into the field. From a military standpoint the individual warrior's experience of battle was presumably more significant than it was among the ordinary Inca soldiers, who were in the first place peasants. These contrasts became very clear as we shall see in the battles that the Spaniards fought against the Aztecs and against the Inca.

It has already been said that the old egalitarian tribal order was undermined, that a privileged nobility provided with private ownership of land emerged among both the Inca and the Aztecs, and that at the foot of the social pyramid bondsmen and slaves appeared. The form, content and extent of these developments differ widely in the Valley of Mexico and the Andean region.

The Inca nobility in principle represented a state bureaucracy. Almost every one of its members had some kind of role in the extensive administrative machinery of the Inca Empire. Among the Aztecs this was true only of a part of the nobility, while a great number of its members had the sole function of carrying on war.

Consequently the political dependence of the Inca nobility on the state was far greater than that of the Aztec nobility. The same goes for the economic sphere. The Aztec nobleman could to some extent alienate his land; he could sell his products and acquire slaves in the market. Things were different in the Inca Empire. Land was inalienable and the sale of its produce hardly possible. Slaves could not be bought and could only be awarded by the state. The Inca nobility was on the other hand a much more privileged and closed group than that of the Aztecs. Both in Mexico and in Cuzco a noble who had committed an offence was taken before a special court. However judgements differed. In Cuzco punishments were not particularly harsh and frequently consisted only of pillorying in public; in Mexico punishment was much more severe. While the ordinary man had to reckon with a reprimand, a noble could be executed for the same offence. New admissions into the nobility as a reward for services rendered were far easier to obtain in the cities of the Triple Alliance until the end of the fifteenth century than in the Andean region. Among the Aztecs a few outstanding deeds in battle, the taking of a few enemy prisoners were sufficient for elevation to the nobility. Among the Inca only exceptionally difficult services achieved this purpose.

Social differences seem to have been more crude in some respects. It is therefore the more surprising to discover that the traditions of the communal order among the Inca nobility were much more strongly developed than among the Aztecs. Every Inca noble who received his own land continued to belong to his clan. The members of his family collectively looked after his land. It was quite the reverse among the Aztecs where the member of the nobility withdrew from the clan organisation. For him the effective organisation was the military society which displayed no kinship characteristics.

317

What could explain these radical differences? Perhaps the most compelling reason for them was the numerically different proportion of the Inca and of the cities of the Triple Alliance to the total population of their empires. After the Inca conquests the whole population of Cuzco down to the last man was elevated into the nobility. Indeed, because this population was too small to meet the demand for state officials other tribes in the vicinity were given a similar status. This would explain the sharp limits imposed on the downward social stratification among the Inca. It was otherwise among the inhabitants of the cities of the Triple Alliance in Mexico. They were far too numerous, the Empire far too little organised and integrated to enable all to ascend into the nobility. Only the old nobility and the meritorious aristocracy succeeded in moving upwards. The remaining population benefited from the conquests in only a very limited degree. It is not surprising that the Inca aristocracy in no uncertain terms made their privileges and power openly felt by their subordinates who were after all subjugated members of alien peoples. The Aztec nobility had to tread more carefully, for an important section of their subordinates were primarily members of their own people.

The collective elevation of the Inca population to the nobility probably explains the survival of the kinship order among the nobility since the whole *ayllu* was elevated at once. Among the Aztecs, on the other hand, it was always individuals who then had to retire from the *calpulli*.

However great the differences among the nobility were, they were still greater lower down the social scale.

The Inca clan was egalitarian. There were no marked differences between rich and poor within the peasant *ayllu*. If they occurred they were largely eliminated by the periodical fresh distribution of land. Agriculture was carried out collectively, and the clan cared for the poor, the sick and orphans and those incapable of work. The Aztec clan was quite different. There was no fresh redistribution of land, poor and rich were members of the same *calpulli*, and conditions of slavery and bondsmanship were even possible within it. The only limitation consisted in the inalienability of the land of the *calpulli* members. There is scarcely any reference as far as the Mexican *calpulli* is concerned to communal work or social care of the poor and injured. Lower down the differences were even more marked: the number of bondsmen in the southern Andean highlands is estimated at one per cent. Among the Aztecs the figure was thirty per cent, to which it is necessary to add five per cent for the number of slaves. This is a tremendous difference which gives a completely different stamp to the two societies.

One of the most striking differences – when considering both empires – is the position of the craftsmen and the role played by trade. In Mesoamerica a large proportion of craftsmen were independent. They offered their services in the largest markets. In the Inca Empire they were generally dependent on the state, on local *curacas* or on the church and operated in their service. In Mesoamerica there were tremendous markets and large, powerful merchant guilds that played a decisive role in trade. In the Inca Empire there were only small local markets and only a limited form of barter. There are no references to merchants. Even should a few new hypotheses be confirmed as to the existence of small groups of such merchants, it is probably correct to say that they played no conspicuous role in the Inca Empire.

The exchange of merchandise was largely in the hands of the state. While in Mesoamerica a genuine currency existed in the form of cocoa beans, there is no mention of such a thing in the Inca Empire. An easy all-embracing explanation of these great differences is not available. Ecological differences, which always encourage trade, existed in both regions. In the Inca Empire these differences were perhaps even more pronounced; for maize was cultivated in the whole of Mesoamerica, but there were parts of the Andean highlands where this sought-after product could not be cultivated.

Was there a greater division of labour between craftsmen and peasants in Mesoamerica than in the Andean region? In both regions the village was in principle autarchic. The peasants produced what they needed and most craft-work was directed towards luxury goods. In so far as craft-work was also utilitarian and directed towards practical necessities, this was more evident in the Andean region than in Mesoamerica. In the Andean region bronze already existed and metallurgy played a far greater role in handicraft and in war than in Mesoamerica.

Were communications in Mesoamerica easier than in the Andean region? This was not the case. Access from the highlands to the lowlands was much easier in the Andean region. In Mesoamerica there was nothing to compare with the great highways that the Inca had layed out. Furthermore in Mesoamerica draught animals were lacking whereas in Peru they existed in pre-Spanish days in the form of the llama. This was the only region of the continent where this was so. Based on these criteria it could be assumed that a flourishing trade existed in the Andean region which far surpassed that of Mesoamerica. The contrary however was the case.

The reason for this phenomenon may have lain largely in the extent of conquest. The Inca had conquered the greatest variety and the most important raw material producing areas of their region. Whether llama or metals, maize, cocoa or cotton, all these were produced within the empire. The situation was different in Mesoamerica where important raw material producing areas were outside Aztec control. In order to obtain its raw materials the state was forced *nolens volens* into trading.

Equally important was the fact that the Inca Empire was much more closely integrated than that of the Aztecs. The Inca were able to make full use of the excess products of individual provinces. This was much more difficult for the Aztecs because of the varying degrees of control and integration in their empire. It must also be remembered that the Inca were substantially interested in a 'redistribution' of raw materials to the population, whilst the Aztecs neither desired nor could they implement such a policy.

Does this finally exhaust the enquiry? Were these differences only a product of the Inca period, or did they already exist in the pre-Inca period? Only hypotheses may be put forward in reply, and not very concrete ones at that. It is not known whether there perhaps existed great merchant guilds before the arrival of the Inca; in the few reports that exist concerning the larger states overthrown by the Inca, there is no mention of merchants. Did they vanish or was their existence in the pre-Inca period not very marked? No one can tell.

Two factors however could explain why long before the formation of great empires on the American continent trade developed so much more strongly in Mesoamerica than in the Andean region. One was without doubt the poverty in raw materials of the Mesoamerican plateau in comparison with the lowlands. A second possible factor was the practice in the Andean region of sending colonists to distant areas, separated from the 'motherland' by other states, to cultivate raw materials that only flourished in different climatic conditions. Not only great states, such as Chucuito, supported colonists in the tropics, far away from their regions, but much smaller and less powerful states, such as Huanaco with hardly ten thousand inhabitants. In the Inca period, access to these territories was guaranteed by the *Pax Incaica* and through the long arm of Inca bureaucracy. What was it like however in the pre-Inca period, when there was no central power to guarantee security of access? This sort of colonisation appears to have existed long before the Inca arrived, and reciprocity probably played an important role. The inhabitants of the highlands were able to send colonists into the tropical lowlands to cultivate maize or coca, while the inhabitants of the tropics sent other colonists into the highlands where they cultivated types of potato which only flourished at fairly high altitudes, or bred llama. These colonisation and resettlement activities in the pre-Inca period might show the measures of colonisation and deportation practised by the Inca in a different light. They were not nearly so novel as many historians have thought, but appear to have been based on an existing tradition in the Andean region.

This sort of system in which not merchandise but annexed land was exchanged led to a certain autarchy on the part of each state and reduced trade to a minimum. Such a system never existed in Mesoamerica, and is scarcely conceivable there. The decisive prerequisite, the reciprocal incentive, was lacking. In the lowlands there were a great many raw materials which attracted the dwellers on the plateau; the converse was not true on the plateau.

As it was not possible in Mesoamerica to obtain the desired tropical products through colonists or land exchange as in the Andean region, there were only two methods left open: one was to conquer the tropical regions. It is not surprising that repeatedly, far earlier than in the Andean region, armies from the plateau regions penetrated into the Mexican lowlands. The second method consisted of trade, which played a decisive role from the beginning of the first high culture in Mesoamerica.

It should not be assumed however that there was no trade in pre-Inca Peru for there undoubtedly was. Nevertheless it operated on a much smaller scale than in Mesoamerica, and its much simpler form enabled the state authorities to intervene much more than in Mesoamerica. In the 'kingdom' of Chimu in Peru, the ruler could simply gather maize or cotton into his barns and order his underlings to sell these products in a neighbouring highland region in exchange for other products. In the plateau of Mexico trade was much more complicated. It was not simply a matter of collecting raw materials to sell, as hardly any existed. Merchandise such as ceramics, produced in the cities by craftsmen, was necessary to obtain raw materials from more distant regions that were then manufactured in the cities according to the taste of future buyers. Very often these products had then to be taken back through enemy territories to find customers. Many of the traditions of the people of Mesoamerica tell of the adventurous journeys made by merchants in disguise who made their way through a great number of enemy territories. During such commercial journeys the initiative of the merchants played a special role. Even if to begin with they traded by order of the state, they soon reached an ever increasing degree of autonomy and claimed a corresponding place in society.

The influence of the merchants in Mesoamerica in comparison with the Andean region was further strengthened by the fact that in the case of the Aztecs, on the eve of development into an Imperium, the city state predominated whereas the regular and extensive state has still to be found in many parts of the Andes. In a city state the influence of the ruler was less and that of urban social groups greater. One only has to think of the city of Tlatelolco in the plateau of Mexico where, until its conquest by the Aztecs, the real power was wielded not by the Chief Speaker but by the merchants, who took all the decisions. The well-being and prosperity of Tlatelolco depended on those who brought the largest revenues into the city. A similar situation must have existed in a number of Mesoamerican regions.

There remains one last decisive difference between the Aztec and Inca Empires. Perhaps the most vital problem for the people of these regions had been solved by the Inca but not by the Aztecs. This was the problem of famine. In Peruvian traditions great famines are rarely mentioned. It is constantly emphasised that among the Inca this problem had been solved and that in times of natural catastrophe the local or central authorities came to the rescue. It was quite otherwise in the Valley of Mexico, where at the peak of the Aztec Imperium in 1505, one of the most devastating famines in the history of Mesoamerica broke out. It is not difficult to explain this. The extensive irrigation works installed throughout the Andean region, the important terracing and drainage works which the Inca undertook in all the conquered regions would be a sufficient explanation. If account is taken of the existence of the llama, which served equally as food in times of famine and as means of transport, as well as the important measures of colonisation which undoubtedly made for a certain balance between ecology and population, it is possible to get some idea of the difference that existed between the two regions.

If all this is to be reduced to a common denominator it is necessary to establish one factor above all others: the Inca appeared in all overthrown territories both as takers and as givers. The ratio undoubtedly varied in different periods and was not always the same in the various provinces. There was more taking than giving in the provinces in Ecuador and in the highlands of Lake Titicaca. It was however always a fundamentally different ratio than among the Aztecs. They appeared almost exclusively as takers, except in the Valley of Mexico, and only in a very limited degree as givers. It is not surprising therefore that the reactions to the Spanish Conquest of the conquered peoples of the Andean region and those of Mesoamerica were so entirely different.

When examining the ancient American civilisations the question naturally arises whether there was a correlation between the degree of state integration and the development of Imperia on the one hand, and the unfolding of technology, science and art on the other. Undoubtedly there were very close relations between imperial development and the technology of food production. Among both the Inca and the Aztecs, food production reached unprecedented levels.

There also existed an unmistakable correlation between imperial development, state integration and the appearance of great irrigation installations. Whether these were the cause or the effect of state integration is still a matter of contention even today. Finally, the organisation of labour with regional specialisation in the provinces was achieved in both empires of ancient America to an extent never known before.

But these facts do not do away with the fact that in other spheres there was no sort of correlation between state and intellectual development. The most advanced system of mathematics was achieved in the region where it had the least practical significance. It was not the Inca, with their records of all wealth in the country and of the entire population, who achieved wonders in the sphere of mathematics, but the Maya city states, which were hardly integrated at all and had small numbers of inhabitants.

As regards art, Inca and Aztec achievements bear no comparison with those of classical times. These great works of art of the classic period mostly developed before empires were built, before huge, consolidated, powerful states were in a position to free thousands of craftsmen from food production. The buildings of Tiahuanaco which are so much admired rose before the carriers of that culture spread over the whole Andean region.

It was not in the highly centralised state of Chimu but in the far less developed state structure of the Mochica that a ceramic art developed that is admired throughout the world even today. The great works of art of the Maya were created at a period of relatively limited state integration. Only in Teotihuacan does art seem for a time to have developed while the state was itself expanding. But here too the period of greatest political and economic power was also the period in which art showed clear signs of decadence.

The reasons for this development are difficult to assess; was it mass production, ever-growing state intervention in artistic production or the bad taste of *parvenus* who constituted the main portion of the great imperial courts? This problem requires more detailed study.

CHAPTER 14

THE END

At the moment of their ending the similarities and the radical differences between the state of the Aztecs in Mesoamerica and the empire of the Inca in the Andean region were very clear to see.

THE END OF AZTEC RULE

In the year 1517 Moctezuma Xocoyotzin discovered the existence of the Spaniards for the first time. In that year a reconnaissance expedition under the leadership of Juan de Grijalva appeared in the region of the modern city of Veracruz, which at that time belonged to the dominion of the Aztecs.

Moctezuma received reports of 'a number of mountains floating in the middle of the water moving about hither and thither without ever coming to shore'.[1] Messengers despatched by Moctezuma described how they had observed the foreigners fishing from a distance: 'Some were holding rods, others were casting nets. They fished till it grew late. Then they went back to their two great towers and climbed in . . . They have very light skins, much lighter than ours. They all wear long beards but their hair only reaches to their ears.'[2] 'When Moctezuma had listened to this report, he was cast down and spoke never a word.'[3] The Aztecs were reassured and optimistic when the Spanish expedition left their empire without attempting to penetrate more closely.

But Moctezuma's hopes were to prove deceptive.

On 21 April 1519 five hundred Spaniards landed under the command of Hernan Cortés, in the region of modern Veracruz, firmly determined to conquer the Aztec Empire the first reports of which had just trickled through to them. The year in which they appeared was the one in which, according to ancient prophecies, the god Quetzalcoatl was to return to his earthly kingdom. 'News was immediately brought to Moctezuma,' an Indian chronicle reports, 'and he forthwith despatched messengers, for he thought: "Now is our Lord Quetzalcoatl returned." He felt in his heart: "He has appeared, he has returned.

Now he will again occupy my throne, as he promised before he left us."[4] He said to his messengers: "Draw nearer, my Jaguar warriors, draw nearer! It appears that our Lord has returned to his country. Go hence to receive him worthily. Hearken to his message: give heed exactly to his words and remember them well!" Then Moctezuma said to his messengers: "Come hither, now take what you are going to give to our Lord. This is Quetzalcoatl's treasure which belongs to him." '[5]

The messengers were solemnly received by Cortés, who accepted their gifts and very cunningly impressed them with his power. 'Thereupon the Captain ordered them to be bound, and chains slung round their ankles and round their necks. That being done, the great cannon was fired. The messengers lost consciousness, they fell to the ground and lay there unconscious. But the strangers restored them to consciousness. They lifted them up, gave them wine to drink and offered them food.'[6]

The report that the messengers gave to Moctezuma was dictated by fear and the conviction that the strangers were in fact supernatural beings:

A thing like a ball of stone flies out of their bellies and flashes sparks and rains fire. The smoke smells of sulphur or foul mire. It takes away your senses, for it penetrates right into the brain. If the ball hits a tree, it blows away in splinters, as though a magician had blown it away from inside.

. . . Their battle dress and their arms are all made of iron. They attire themselves in iron from head to foot, they wear iron helmets, their spears are made of iron, also their bows, their shields and sabres. They are carried on the backs of stags wherever they like to go; Lord, they are as high as roofs on the backs of these stags.

Their bodies are completely hidden, only their faces are not covered. Their skin is white, as though made of chalk. Their hair is yellow, though some have black hair. They also have long yellow beards and their whiskers are also yellow. Their hair is curly falling in shining locks.

Their food is bounteous like that of the nobility. It is plentiful, it is white and light, like chaff, like the cobs of maize. It tastes of ground maize cobs like the marrow of the maize cob, sweet, as though mixed with honey.

Their dogs are great monsters with flat ears and long tongues which hang out. They have fiery yellow eyes, sparks fly and flash. Their bellies are flat as spoons, their flanks long and narrow. They are wild and indefatigable, they jump about hither and thither, are always panting with their tongues hanging out. They are spotted like the jaguar.

When Moctezuma heard this report, he was seized with fright. His heart grew weak to the point of faintness, it shrank within him. And despair overcame him . . .[7] His people were as confused as he, they talked over and discussed the reports. People came out into the streets, collected together in groups, rumours spread fear. People wept and lamented. The populace was beaten down, they crept about with bowed heads, they greeted each other in tears.[8]

Moctezuma decided to send human sacrifices to these gods, to feed them, to silence them and perhaps to cause them to withdraw. The result was however quite different from what he had expected and hoped: 'The prisoners were sacrificed in the presence of the foreigners, though when the white people saw it they trembled with horror and disgust. They spat on the ground, wiped tears away, shudderingly closed their eyes, and turned away with dismay.' This is related in an Indian chronicle. 'They did not want the dishes of food sprinkled with precious blood. They saw them steaming, which made them sick and they were revolted by the savour of blood.'⁹

Moctezuma had no idea that the foreign 'gods' were facing difficult problems, the danger of the dispersal and collapse of their military forces.

Hernan Cortés, who was in command of the expedition, had at first acted on the orders of the Governor of Cuba, Diego Velasquez. After his arrival in Veracruz he renounced his employer and declared that he was directly representing the Spanish Crown. Thereby he had courted the opposition of a considerable number of the Cuban governor's followers, who were joined by those of his followers who regarded an expedition to overthrow an empire like that of the Aztecs, of whose power they were hearing more and more, with only a few hundred men as both mad and doomed to failure. Cortés succeeded in discovering and defeating a plot by his adversaries to kill him and then return to Cuba. In order to put a stop to such an attempt once and for all he decided to take a drastic step: he had his ships set alight, so that the only way for the Spaniards to go was forwards. To penetrate into the empire of the Aztecs in this manner nevertheless seemed to have little hope of success. Moctezuma had provided the foreigners for a long time with all they required, but now he partly overcame his fear and decided to block their access to foodstuffs in order to force them to retreat. Cortés's position seemed to be getting more and more hopeless, when he made a discovery that influenced the whole of the remainder of the campaign of conquest.

The leader of the Totonac state of Cempoala, one of the states overthrown by the Aztecs, invited Cortés to visit him and complained bitterly against the gruesome and despotic rule of the Aztecs. In that moment Cortés, who was undoubtedly the cleverest of the *conquistadores* to come to America from Spain, realised the tremendous potential of a group of dissatisfied conquered peoples within the Aztec Empire. When Aztec tribute-collectors came to Cempoala and threatened the inhabitants because they had received the Spaniards, Cortés induced the Totonacs to capture them and thus put themselves on his side without possibility of retreat. But in order not to provoke a head-on collision with Moctezuma, he secretly liberated the Aztec tribute-collectors and told them that it was the Totonacs who had caused them to be captured, not himself.

Cortés's aim was now to win over as allies the inhabitants of Tlaxcala, of whose resistance to the Aztecs the Totonacs had told him. Accompanied by Totonac warriors the Spaniards set out into the plateau of Mexico. Still convinced that they were dealing with gods, and also perhaps misled by constant expressions of friendship made to him by Cortés, Moctezuma did not dare to act against the foreigners. He may also have hoped that they would meet their end when attacking Tlaxcala.

Despite all the expressions of friendship on the part of the Spaniards, the inhabitants of Tlaxcala mistrusted the foreigners, the more so when they discovered the close relations that existed between them and Moctezuma. They accordingly joined battle with the Spaniards, together with their allies, the Otomi.

The Otomi [an Indian chronicle relates] had ranged themselves in battle order, they hailed the foreigners with their shields and began to do battle against them.

The foreigners however, were victorious against the Otomi from Tecoac, they rode them down, they split their ranks, fired cannon against them and attacked them with sabre and cross-bow. Not only some, but all were destroyed in this battle. Tecoac perished utterly.[10]

Further defensive action by the Tlaxcaltecas was defeated by the Spaniards, who repeatedly reassured their victims that they wanted only their friendship and their alliance.

The chieftains and captains of the warriors therefore met together and conferred about this happening. They said 'What shall we do? Should we receive them as friends? The Otomi is a great and courageous warrior, and yet he was helpless and they treated him with contumely. They felled the poor *mecchual* with a single glance, they extinguished him with the flashes of their eyes. We should not provoke them, we should receive them as friends and become their allies, otherwise they would destroy us.'

Therefore the nobles of Tlaxcala went forward to meet them as friends. They thereupon conducted the foreigners into the city, allowed them to enter the palace and did them the greatest honours. They complied with all their wishes, became their allies and even gave them their daughters.[11]

In company with thousands of allied Tlaxcala warriors the Spaniards marched in the direction of Tenochtitlan. Moctezuma, who had learnt of the defeat of the Tlaxcaltecas, was more than ever afraid of confronting the foreigners and sent a message that he would receive them in his capital city.

Before the Spaniards reached Tenochtitlan they made a bloody massacre in the city of Cholollan, which was subject to the Aztecs and which lay in their path.

When they arrived [an Indian chronicle relates] the Tlaxcaltecas and the Cholultecas exchanged shouts and greetings. In the court of the Temple a large gathering was held, though when everyone had arrived, the nobles, the leaders, the chieftains and the people, the approaches were sealed so that nobody could escape.

And then the massacre began: stabbing with knives, slashing with sabres, death. The people of Cholula had come without suspicion, the warriors were without their arms. They confronted the Spaniards having no swords and without shields.[12]

The reasons for this massacre are still disputed. The Spaniards later declared that there was an Aztec conspiracy against them: warriors disguised as harmless citizens were alleged to be going to offer them help, only to cut them down in an unguarded moment. Indian sources give a different version. Some state that the Tlaxcaltecas, who were allied to the Spaniards, wanted to seize the opportunity to take revenge against the city of Chollollan, which had been their enemy for a long time. That was why they told the Spaniards of a plot against them. Other Indian sources consider it to have been a conscious attempt on the part of Cortés to intimidate Moctezuma, even before his arrival in Tenochtitlan. Whether it was intentional or not, this purpose was achieved.

Shortly before the arrival of the Spaniards in the capital city of the Aztecs a stormy meeting of the war council of Tenochtitlan was held. Moctezuma's brother Cuitlahuac warned him urgently: 'I pray to our gods that Thou wilt not allow the foreigners to enter Thy house. They will throw Thee out and will destroy Thy rule, and if Thou shouldest attempt to regain that which Thou hast lost, it will be too late.'[13] But Moctezuma refused to follow this advice. Unopposed and unhindered the Spaniards reached the lake shore of Mexico, where they gazed on the magnificent spectacle which awaited them, filled with wonder and amazement. At the city boundary of Tenochtitlan, they were solemnly greeted by Moctezuma, who received them as though they were gods. 'My Lord, Thou art weary,' he said to Cortés, 'the journey has exhausted Thee, but now Thou art arrived upon the earth. Thou art come to thy city of Mexico. Thou art come hither to sit upon Thy throne, to sit under the canopy of Thy throne. The Kings, who have already gone hence, Thy deputies, have protected and kept it against Thy return.'[14]

A palace was assigned to Cortés and his soldiers, and Moctezuma commanded that they should be given all they needed. 'The Chieftains' a chronicle relates, 'who received these orders were angry with the King. They did not obey him and paid no more heed to him. Nevertheless the Spaniards were provided with all that was necessary, they received food, drink and water for their horses.'[15]

Resistance to the Spaniards in Tenochtitlan was growing. The fear that the foreigners might indeed be gods and the power exercised by Moctezuma, who was unwilling to oppose them in any way, sufficed at first to delay armed resistance.

Cortés was well aware of the threatening situation in which he found himself in the middle of the huge capital city of the Aztecs. Their guests were turning out more and more clearly to be intruders, and an increase in Aztec resistance had to be reckoned with. Cortés therefore resorted to a radical expedient. On some pretext or other he took Moctezuma prisoner and kept him in his palace as a hostage. He even succeeded in ruling for a few months, acting as an *eminence grise* behind the throne. Moctezuma had gold and silver brought to Tenochtitlan from all parts of the empire, in the hope that the foreigners would finally leave his capital.

The recurrent rivalries among the *conquistadores* themselves did at least constitute a breathing-space for the peoples who had been attacked by the Spaniards though it did not release them. There is hardly a campaign of conquest on the American continent that is not characterised by bloody fights between rival Spanish bands. These fights were probably encouraged by the fact that the *conquistadores*, although acting by order of and with the permission of the Spanish state, nevertheless enjoyed a far-reaching feudal autonomy and were not an integral part of a Spanish army.

A few months after his entry into Tenochtitlan Cortés received the news that a Spanish striking force far exceeding his own troops in number and equipment had landed in Mexico by order of the Governor of Cuba. These new invaders declared Cortés to be a traitor and called for his destruction. With most of his troops Cortés went to the camp of the new arrivals. By a skilful mixture of blackmail, persuasion and surprise attack he succeeded in winning over the majority of these Spaniards to his side. With his power greatly strengthened he now turned back in the direction of Tenochtitlan.

In the meantime events had taken place there that made a continuation of the previous form of Spanish domination impossible. Thousands of Aztecs had assembled in the great Temple to celebrate the feast of Toxcatl.

The hymns had scarcely begun when the Christians left the palace and entered the court of the Temple. They stationed four sentries at each entrance. Then they massacred the young Cuatlazol, the Chieftain, who was leading the dances.

Some of the Spanish struck the idol in the face, others murdered the three drummers. And then the great massacre began, till the corpses heaped up in the Temple court. A priest from the patio of the reeds called with a loud voice: 'Mexicans, who said that we should not wage war against them? Who said that we could trust them?'

The Mexicans were only able to defend themselves with wooden staves, they were cut to pieces by the swords.[16]

Why Pedro de Alvarado, whom Cortés had left behind as his deputy in Tenochtitlan, should have carried out this massacre is still a matter of dispute. Did he fear an Aztec rising? Did he want to intimidate the Aztecs so strongly that they would never again attempt anything against the Spaniards? Did he simply lose his nerve? At any rate, the results were disastrous for the Spaniards. The Aztecs rose against the foreigners, cut off their food supplies and besieged them in their palace. The attacks did not cease until the Spaniards had forced Moctezuma to command the Aztecs to stop. But even Moctezuma's authority no longer sufficed to persuade his subjects to allow food supplies to reach the Spaniards.

When Cortés entered Tenochtitlan again, with his army reinforced, the streets were completely empty, the markets closed. Cortés then freed Moctezuma's brother Cuitlahuac, whom he had held prisoner, in the hope that he would restore the former conditions. The opposite occurred. Cuitlahuac placed himself at the head of the resistance against the *conquistadores*, who in consequence were even more hard-pressed. When Cortés attempted to push Moctezuma once more into the forefront, he was stoned to death by his own people.

The situation thus became so hopeless for the Spaniards that they decided to flee the city with their allies. This flight was to become the greatest defeat in the course of their campaign. They stole out of the city during the night. To reach the mainland they had to cross the causeway that led across the lake from Tenochtitlan, where the bridges had been removed by the Aztecs.

They crossed the first three canals undetected [writes the Aztec chronicle] and passed over the Teopantzingo, the Tzapotlan and the Atenchicalco unhindered. But when they reached the fourth, the Mixcoatechialtitlan, their withdrawal was discovered.

A woman drawing water from this canal saw them and called out: 'Mexicans, hasten hither, your enemies are fleeing, they are fleeing secretly over the canal.' Then a priest of Huitzilopochtli called. From high up on the Temple pyramid he called men to arms. His voice rang out far over the city: 'Chieftains, warriors, Mexicans! Our enemies are in flight! Pursue them in your war-boats!' Angry shouting answered this call. The warriors leapt into their boats, followed the enemy with strong strokes of their oars . . .

When the Spaniards reached Tlaltecayohuacan and the Toltec canal, they plunged head first into the water, jumping as though off a cliff. The Tlaxcaltecas, the Tliliuhquitepec allies, the Spanish infantry, the cavalry, the few women accompanying the army, they all reached the steep sides and jumped off. Soon the canal was stuffed full of the bodies of men and of horses; the drowned stopped up the gaps in the causeway with their bodies. And those who followed after them stepped over their bodies to the other shore.[17]

During the night, known in history books as *Noche Triste*, the 'Fateful Night', Cortés lost most of his army. With those who remained he went to Tlaxcala, constantly pursued and attacked by the Aztecs.

While the Spaniards were in Tlaxcala, where the population received them in a friendly way, recovering and forging fresh plans of attack against Tenochtitlan, the Aztecs were not idle. The Fateful Night had finally destroyed the myth of the divinity and immortality of the Spaniards. Furthermore Moctezuma's brother Cuitlahuac, who was his successor as Chief Speaker of the Aztecs, was made of sterner stuff. Even before the Spaniards entered the capital city of the Aztecs he had called for battle against them. Now he was determined to drive them out of Anahuac. But to this end – and Cuitlahuac was aware of this all along – the invaders had to be isolated from their allies and an alliance of all the peoples of Mesoamerica formed against them. Messengers from Cuitlahuac went to enemies, to the conquered peoples and to friends. Peace was offered to the Tarascans, while Tlaxcala was offered an alliance and a lifting of the blockade. Thus all the peoples belonging to the dominion of the Aztecs were summoned to make common cause with them against the invaders.

The success of these Aztec efforts was very limited, both among their enemies and among the members of the Aztec Empire. The Tarascans replied to the Aztec offer of peace in the negative. There was a similar result in Tlaxcala, although there the final decision was preceded by bitter confrontations among the leaders of the state. Xicotencatl, who had waged the short battle of the Tlaxcaltecas against the Spaniards, called for an alliance with the Aztecs against the foreigners. But he was outvoted. The Tlaxcaltecas' hatred of their old rival Tenochtitlan and their mistrust of the Aztecs were too strong for them to resist the opportunity of putting an end to the power of their old enemy.

The effect of the Aztecs' gruesome methods of government now manifested itself to the conquered peoples and almost everywhere they appeared as takers and not as givers. Most of the peoples conquered by the Aztecs, apart from the Valley of Mexico, refused to come to the help of their former overlords. This refusal was encouraged by the fact that Cortés knew how to take advantage of their opposition to the Aztecs. 'He sent messengers to those cities and informed them that he had come to free them from the tyranny of Mexico City, that they would now gain their freedom and be liberated from the domination of Mexico.'[18] Only in the Valley of Mexico did most of the allied and conquered cities remain faithful to the Aztecs.

When Cortés's troops again appeared on the shores of the Mexican lakes in May 1521 and began besieging Tenochtitlan, the position of the Aztecs was more than difficult and very soon became desperate.

Cortés succeeded in kindling a sort of social revolution against his adversaries and more Indians fought on his side than on that of the Aztecs. The technical superiority of the Europeans became more evident every day. In some respects the great ships that they brought into the lake of Mexico were even more dangerous for the Aztecs than firearms and horses for they obstructed the boat traffic between Tenochtitlan and the mainland, which was so essential for the provisioning of the city.

As if this were not enough, an epidemic of smallpox brought in by the foreigners broke out in Tenochtitlan.

In the thirteenth month the great plague broke out here in Tenochtitlan. It spread very rapidly and raged for seventy days. It attacked people, beat them down all over the city and killed enormous numbers. Swellings broke out on our faces, on our breasts, on our bodies, and we were encrusted from head to foot with festering sores. The disease was so terrible that no one could any longer stand up or walk. Those afflicted lay about helpless, like corpses on their beds, they were unable to move their limbs or lift their heads. They could not turn on their beds, could not turn onto their sides, they could not lie face downwards. If they tried to move they cried out with pain.[19]

Despite all this the Aztecs resisted and stood their ground for three months, which provoked astonishment and even admiration in their Spanish adversaries.

The battle was first fought under the leadership of Cuitlahuac. After he had died of smallpox, his nephew Cuauhtémoc took over the leadership of the Aztecs and carried on the fight just as bitterly. Not until 13 August 1521, when most of Tenochtitlan and Tlatelolco had been destroyed and the majority of the population killed so that further resistance seemed pointless, did the Aztecs decide to capitulate.

The Aztec nobles gathered together in Tolmayecan and considered what more could now be done. Cuauhtémoc and the other nobles wished to decide what tribute they should offer and how they could surrender most worthily to the foreigners.

Then the nobles required Cuauhtémoc to enter a war-boat. Only three men accompanied him, the Chieftain Teputztitóloc, the body guard Iaztachímal and the rower Cenyáutl. When the people saw their last King setting off, they wept. 'Our youngest ruler is leaving us! He will surrender to the Spaniards! He is submitting to the gods!'

The Spaniards went to meet Cuauhtémoc. They took hold of him. They seized his hands and conducted him on to the roof, before Captain Cortés. The captain stared at him for a long time. Then he nodded his head to him. He pointed to a comfortable chair, and they both sat down.

The Spaniards fired their guns, but they did not aim any more. They just loaded and fired and the cannon balls flew away over the heads of the people. Later they carried one of the guns into a boat and took it to Coyohuehuetzin's house where they pulled it right up on to the roof.

Once more the Spaniards began their massacring and many Aztecs died. The flight from the city began. The war was now at an end. The people cried, 'We have suffered enough. Let us depart hence out of our city, wretched herbs must now be our portion.'

Many fled across the lake, others across the great causeways, and there, too, many were killed . . .[20] On the day 'One Serpent' under the sign of the year 'Three Houses' we laid down our shields and were beaten.[21]

With the capture of Tenochtitlan came the end of the Aztec Empire, both as a political unit and as a psychological and historical reality. The hopes of some Aztecs for a successful rising against the Spanish *conquistadores* ended once and for all with the execution of Cuauhtémoc by Cortés a short time later.

THE END OF THE INCA EMPIRE

The men who landed in Tumbez, on the north coast of the Inca Empire, twelve years after the conquest of the Aztec Empire by Cortés, knew exactly what had taken place in Mexico. They had drawn a number of conclusions from Cortés's experiences. First of all the ruler of the region about to be conquered had to be propitiated and reassured that only a short-term visit to his country was planned. Once they had arrived in his city the ruler had to be taken prisoner in a surprise attack, and the élite of his empire destroyed, which would inevitably lead to the terrorisation and disorganisation of his apparatus of government. Finally it was necessary to make use of every type of social or political opposition within the territory to be conquered, and to gain followers from the classes of society hitherto oppressed and overthrown by the ruler.

Francisco Pizarro used these tactics in Peru, and they resulted in the same amazing successes as in Mexico.

After their landing in Tumbez the Spaniards assured the Inca Atahuallpa of their friendship and informed him that they would only be paying him a short visit in order to admire his empire and to be of service to him. Atahuallpa did not attempt, as Moctezuma had done in Mexico, to obstruct the Spaniards, but allowed them to advance unhindered as far as his military encampment in Cajamarca. The reasons for his behaviour are not clear. The Indian sources in Peru are less eloquent and credible on this question than those of Mexico. Nevertheless it appears that it was less fear of the supernatural powers of the Spaniards than an underestimation of their strength that caused Atahuallpa to behave as he did. Surrounded by his troops he felt himself strong and secure enough to receive the foreigners and he may even have hoped that they might serve him in his fight with those followers of his half-brother Huascar who were still alive.

In their march through the difficult terrain of the Andes the Inca road and provisioning system served the Spaniards well. They marched along the great roads, lived and were cared for in the *tambos* reserved for the armies of the Inca. When the 150 Spanish soldiers, or thereabouts, under Francisco Pizarro reached Cajamarca in November 1532 and saw the tremendous armies of the Inca drawn up before them they came to the conclusion that only an immediate and brutal attack could enable them to gain the upper hand. No one has given a clearer description of the events that took place on 16 November 1532, during the visit of Atahuallpa to the Spanish encampment in Cajamarca, than one of the *conquistadores*, Hernando Pizarro, the brother of the Spanish leader.

He [Atahuallpa] arrived in a litter, preceded by three or four hundred liveried Indians, who swept the dirt off the road and sang. Then came Atahuallpa, surrounded by his leaders and chieftains, the most important of whom were carried on the shoulders of underlings. When they came to the open plaza, twelve or fifteen Indians went to the small fortress standing there and occupied it . . . When Atahuallpa reached the middle of the plaza, he remained standing and a Dominican monk, sent by the governor, went up to him to inform him that the Governor [Francisco Pizarro] awaited him in his apartment . . . The monk then told Atahuallpa that he himself was a priest and that he had been sent to teach the Christian religion. He showed Atahuallpa a book which he was carrying and said that it contained the Word of God. Atahuallpa asked for the book, threw it on the ground and said; 'I shall not leave this place until you have given me back all that you have taken from my country. I know who you are and what you want,' . . . The monk returned to the Governor, reported to him and said that no time must be lost. [Another description relates that the monk said to Pizarro, 'Can you not see what is happening: why do you parley so amicably with this arrogant dog? The fields are full of Indians. Throw yourselves upon them forthwith. I give you all absolution.'] [22] The Governor called after me; I had already settled matters with the commander of artillery to the effect that at a given signal he should give the order to shoot. Thereupon all the troops were to surge forward together. This happened. Since the Indians were unarmed they were beaten without danger to a single Christian. The bearers of the litters and the chieftains surrounding Atahuallpa were all killed and their corpses lay round about him. The Governor emerged, took Atahuallpa prisoner and as he was trying to protect him he was wounded in the hand by a Christian. [23]

It is estimated that between five and six thousand members of Atahuallpa's army and retinue were cut down by the Spaniards on that November day in Cajamarca.

The Spaniards wanted to make a tool of Atahuallpa by which they might rule his empire. They were not entirely unsuccessful. Atahuallpa, when a prisoner in Peru, could no more resolve to summon his people to fight against the *conquistadores* than Moctezuma could have done in Mexico. Like the Aztec ruler he harboured the illusion that he could induce the Spaniards to leave by passiveness, obedience and gifts. He offered much more ransom to the Spaniards than Moctezuma had done. Pizarro accepted his offer and Atahuallpa had a great hall filled with precious metal, which had been gathered together from all the corners of his empire, for the Spaniards. When the booty was complete the Spaniards decided to execute Atahuallpa all the same. They feared that despite all his assurances to the contrary he would summon his people to war against them.

Atahuallpa was accused of a hotch-potch of offences, including his paganism, the murder of his brother Huascar and a planned rising against the Spaniards. The court assembled by the Spaniards condemned him to death.

They brought Atahuallpa to the execution [one of the Spanish *conquistadores* describes] and when he was brought into the plaza he declared that he wished to become a Christian. The Governor was informed and commanded that he should be baptised. The ceremony was performed by the holy Father Valverde. The Governor then commanded that Atahuallpa should not be burned but bound to a stake and strangled. [This was presumably the chief attraction in Atahuallpa's last-minute conversion. As long as he was not burned, he could believe in life after death.] This was done, and the body was left lying until the morning of the next day, when the monks, the Governor and the other Spaniards took the body with great ceremony to the church, where it was buried with all possible honours.[24]

The execution of Atahuallpa and the unique mixture of horror and hypocrisy accompanying it did not, as Moctezuma's death in Mexico had done, immediately favour the instigation of a great rising against the invaders. There did not exist in Peru, as there did among the Aztecs, the remains of an ancient democratic tribal organisation, in which decisions could be taken without the ruler or even against his will.

The quarrel between Atahuallpa and his half-brother proved extraordinarily advantageous to the Spaniards. Atahuallpa's armies were disorganised and his generals helpless. They did not feel strong enough to wage an effective battle both against the Spaniards and against Huascar's followers, who began to rely on the Spaniards and hoped through them to reach power in the Inca state.

With Atahuallpa's death a vacuum was created for the Spaniards. They had to discover another Inca who would be their willing tool and at the same time possess sufficient authority in the empire. Their first choice was a follower of Atahuallpa, Toparca. He was crowned Sapay-Inca with full ceremony, and marched with the Spaniards in the direction of Cuzco. However he died on the way and it is more than doubtful whether he would have possessed the authority to maintain his position effectively in the empire.

The Spaniards were all the more pleasantly surprised when a solution offered itself. Manco Inca, the last heir to the throne of Huascar's clan, sought out Pizarro and asked him to support his claim. The latter was more than delighted at this opportunity of allying himself with one of the rival parties in the Inca Empire. Manco aided the Spaniards from time to time in suppressing resistance movements by followers of Atahuallpa as they occurred and was solemnly crowned Sapay-Inca in Cuzco. All the same it did not occur to the Spaniards to let him have any real authority. They did not even respect the position he was supposed to occupy, so that when he was drawn against his will into fights among rival Spanish groups, Pizarro had him imprisoned. In prison he was humiliated in every possible way: his wives were raped before his very eyes, and he himself was spat upon by Spanish warders and smeared with their excrement. This was too much even for a man who had so long been a willing collaborator with the *conquistadores*. Yet the Spaniards had so low an opinion of his will to resist that when he promised to bring them a gold statue of one of his ancestors they released him temporarily from prison.

After he had gained his freedom Manco held a colloquy with those members of the Inca nobility who were still alive. As one chronicle relates they abjured him

not to trust the promises of the foreigners, and commanded that the greatest possible number of warriors should be mobilised with all haste and as much equipment mustered as possible. We must not let the opportunity pass by, they declared, which has been given to us of the Spaniards having split into so many groups. In this way it will be easier to kill them than had they all remained together.[25]

Wholly unexpectedly tens of thousands of Inca warriors appeared in February 1536 at the gates of Cuzco. Their number has been estimated as high as two hundred thousand. 'In the evening their camp fires were so numerous', writes one of the *conquistadores*, 'that they give the impression of a calm sky full of stars.'[26] Manco's call to battle was obeyed throughout the empire. This occasion clearly demonstrated the marked differences between the Aztecs and the Inca, with their much greater vitality and national unity. Cuitlahuac and Cuauhtémoc had called in vain for the unity of all Mesoamerican peoples against the foreigners, whereas in the Andean region Manco had achieved an all but complete unity of all Indians against the Spaniards. In the face of the enemy all differences disappeared between the followers of Atahuallpa and Huascar. Only the Cañaris, who came from the area of modern Ecuador and were now in Cuzco, and some Yanaconas joined the Spaniards, but there were only a few of them.

The comparatively limited military success of the Inca warriors is all the more surprising. The Aztecs had defeated and annihilated a thousand Spaniards and ten thousand of their Indian allies in Tenochtitlan. They had held out for months against a numerical superiority of Spaniards and their Indian followers. Yet the tens of thousands of Inca warriors besieging Cuzco did not succeed in driving out of the capital city of the Inca two hundred Spaniards or so and a few hundred of their Indian allies. The exact reasons for their failure must be more closely studied. Certainly the fact that the Inca armies consisted mainly of peasants, and had only a small number of the élite warriors who were so predominant in the Aztec armies, played a decisive role. The élite warriors of the Inca had largely been decimated in the civil wars between Atahuallpa and Huascar and in the Spanish massacres. The Spaniards' firearms and horses were a particular asset in their defensive strategy of Cuzco.

Manco set his hopes on a long siege, which would cut off all the Spaniards' food supplies and would finally defeat them through famine. His own army however was unable to sustain this long siege. The great advantage held by every Inca army, provisioning from the important food depots, became largely inoperative for the civil war armies of Atahuallpa and Huascar and finally the Spaniards themselves had used up too large a proportion of the supplies. When harvest time came the Inca armies began to break up and the peasants returned to their villages. Manco found himself obliged to call off the siege of Cuzco and to retreat.

THE ROLE OF THE AZTECS AND THE INCA IN LATER HISTORY

At the moment of defeat and afterwards the deeper roots and vitality of the Inca Empire, compared to that of the Aztecs, became evident. After the capture of Tenochtitlan all resistance by the Aztecs ceased and the memory of the Aztec Empire played no more part, from the political point of view, in the life of Mexico. During the Spanish colonial period and in 1810 and 1910 there were important revolutionary movements in Mexico, in which the Indians of the country played an important part. But only among a few intellectuals, never among the Indian peasants, did the memory of the glory and might of Tenochtitlan have any motive power. Social and political changes were fought for, but not under the banner of a restoration of the past glories of the Aztec Imperium.

Development in the Andean region was in a completely different direction. The defeat of Cuzco was not in any way the end of the Inca Empire. Manco withdrew with his warriors into the highlands of Vilcabamba and in this virtually inaccessible region the Inca Empire continued for another forty years, until it was conquered by Spanish troops in the year 1572. Even after that the memory of the Inca past remained a living and effective political reality in the Andean region. When the biggest Indian rising in the history of Peru broke out in 1780, it did so under the leadership of a descendant of the Inca, who adopted the name of the last of the Inca rulers, Tupac Amaru. One of the first measures taken by the Spanish authorities after the suppression of the rising was to prohibit the work of Garcilaso de la Vega, which had idealised the Inca Empire.

The tradition of the Inca Empire was so alive and so deeply rooted among the peoples of the Andean region that one of the nineteenth-century liberators of South America, San Martin, conceived a plan of declaring a descendant of the Inca to be the ruler of an American Imperium that was to be created.

Even today the memory of the Inca Empire that once extended over the Andean region plays a role there in decisive social and political movements that should not be underestimated.

NOTES

Chapter 1

1 Robert McC.Adams, *The Evolution of Urban Society. Early Mesopotamia: Prehispanic Mexico* (Chicago 1965) p. 31.
2 Adams, *Evolution.*
3 Francisco López de Gomara, *Historia General de las Indias* (Madrid 1749); Gonzalo Férnandez de Oviedo y Valdés, *Historia General y Natural de las Indias* (Madrid 1851–5).
4 Hérnan Cortés, *Briefe an Karl V* (Leipzig 1918); Bernal Díaz del Castillo, *Historia Verdadera de la Conquista de la Nueva España* (Mexico 1967).
5 Pedro Pizarro, *Relación del Descubrimiento y Conquista del Perú* (Paris 1938).
6 Diaz, *Historia.*
7 Bernardino de Sahagún, *Historia General de las Cosas de la Nueva España* (Mexico 1956).
8 See *inter alia* Diego de Landa, *Relación de las Cosas de Yucatan* (Mexico 1938).
9 Pedro Cieza de León, *Del Señorío de los Incas* (Madrid 1880); *La Cronica del Perú* (Buenos Aires 1945).
10 Pedro Sarmiento de Gamboa, *Historia de los Incas* (Buenos Aires 1947).
11 Alonso de Zurita, *Breve y Sumaria Relación de los Señores de la Nueva España* (Mexico 1941).
12 *Visita hecha a la provincia de Chucuito por Garci Diez de San Miguel en 1567.* This contains a very important essay, 'Apreciación de la visita' by John V.Murra.
13 Woodrow Borah and Sherburne F.Cook, *The Aboriginal Population of Central Mexico on the Eve of the Spanish Conquest* (Berkeley and Los Angeles 1963).
14 Fernando de Alva Ixtlilxóchitl, *Obras Históricas* (Mexico 1891–2).
15 Fernando Alvarado Tezozomec, *Histoire Mexicaine* (Paris 1838–53).

16 Garcilaso de la Vega, *Comentarios reales de los Incas* (Madrid 1723).
17 The best-known of them are those of Chilam Balam de Chumayel. See Alfredo Barrera Vazquez, *El Libro de los Libros de Chilam Balam* (Mexico 1948).
18 See Borah and Cook, *The Aboriginal Population*.
19 Charles Gibson, *The Aztecs under Spanish Rule* (Stanford 1964).
20 John V. Murra, 'The Economic Organisation of the Inca State', PhD thesis (University of Chicago 1956); regrettably unpublished.

Chapter 2

1 See Robert Wauchope, *Lost Tribes and Sunken Continents* (Chicago 1962). For European ideas held between the sixteenth and eighteenth centuries about the origin of American Indians, see Lee Eldridge Huddleston, *Origins of the American Indians, European Concepts 1492–1729* (Austin and London 1967).
2 Elliot Smith, *Elephants and Ethnologists* (London 1924) and *Human History* (New York 1929).
3 W.S. Blacket, *Researches into the Lost Histories of America*, (London 1883); Augustus Le Plongeon, *Archaeological Communication on Yucatán* (Worcester 1879) and *Queen Moo and the Egyptian Sphinx* (New York 1900).
4 James Churchward, *The Lost Continent of Mu* (New York 1932); W.S. Cerve, *Lemuria – The Lost Continent of the Pacific* (San José).
5 Edward King, Lord Kingsborough, *Antiquities of Mexico* (London 1831–48).
6 See Wauchope, *Lost Tribes*, pp. 51–2.
7 Wauchope, *Lost Tribes*, p. 177.
8 Florentino Amenghino, 'De l'Homme Tertiaire en Amérique', Congrès International des Américanistes, (1879) and *La Antiguedad del Hombre en el Plata*, (Paris, Buenos Aires 1880–1).
9 Ales Hrdlicka, *Early Man in South America* (Washington 1912) and *Early Man in America: What have the Bones to Say?* (Philadelphia 1937).
10 See also Alex D. Krieger, 'Early Man in the New World', in *Prehistoric Man in the New World*, ed. Jesse D. Jennings, Edward Norbeck (Chicago 1964); Pedro Bosch Gimpera, *L'Amérique avant Christophe Colombe* (Paris 1967).
11 Krieger, in *Prehistoric Man*.
12 Bosch Gimpera, *L'Amérique avant Colombe*.
13 Morris Swadesh, 'Linguistic Overview' in *Prehistoric Man*.
14 See Swadesh, in *Prehistoric Man*.
15 Robert Heine-Geldern, 'Das Problem vorkolumbischer Beziehungen

zwischen Alter und Neuer Welt und seine Bedeutung für die Allgemeine Kulturgeschichte', off-print from the *Anzeiger der phil. hist. Klasse der oesterreichischen Akademie der Wissenschaften*, 24 (1954), (Vienna 1955).

16 Robert Heine-Geldern, 'The Problem of Trans-pacific Influences in Mesoamerica', in *Handbook of Middle-American Indians*, (Austin 1964) IV; and 'Theoretical Considerations Concerning the Problem of Pre-Columbian Contacts between the Old World and the New', reprinted from *Selected Papers of the Fifth International Congress of Anthropological and Ethnological Sciences* (Philadelphia September 1956).

17 Paul Kirchhoff, 'The Diffusion of a Great Religious System from India to Mexico', *Proceedings, Int. Cong. of Americanists, 1962* (1964), I, pp. 73–100.

18 See Alfred Kidder II, 'South American High Cultures', in *Prehistoric Man.*

19 Robert Heine-Geldern, 'Kulturpflanzengeographie und das Problem vorkolumbischer Kulturbeziehungen zwischen Alter und Neuer Welt', in *Internationale Zeitschrift für Völker und Sprachenkunde*, offprint, 53 (Fribourg 1958).

20 Robert Heine-Geldern, 'Traces of Indian and South-East Asiatic Hindu-Buddhist Influences in Mesoamerica', in *Proceedings, Int. Cong. of Americanists, 1962* (1964), I, pp. 47–54.

21 See also Alfonso Caso, 'Relations between the Old and the New Worlds; a note on Methodology', in *Proceedings, Int. Cong. of Americanists, 1962*, I, pp. 55–72; Philip Philips, 'The Role of Transpacific Contacts in the Development of New-World Pre-Columbian Civilisation', in *Handbook of Middle American Indians*, IV.

22 Caso, in *Proceedings, Int. Cong. of Americanists.*

23 Gordon F. Ekholm, 'Transpacific Contacts', in *Prehistoric Man.*

24 Julian Steward, Louis C. Faron, *Native Peoples of South America* (New York 1959), p. 43.

25 Robert McC. Adams, *The Evolution of Urban Society* (Chicago 1965).

26 Adams, *Evolution of Urban Society*, p. 174–5.

27 Thor Heyerdahl, *Kon-Tiki* (London 1950).

28 Hermann Trimborn, *Das Alte Amerika* (Stuttgart 1959).

Chapter 3

1 See also Krieger, in *Prehistoric Man*; Gordon R. Willey, *An Introduction to American Archaeology*, I; *North and Middle America* (New Jersey 1966); José Alcina Franch, *Manual de Arqueología Americana* (Madrid 1965), pp. 80 *et seq.*

2 Franch, *Manual*.

3 Gordon Childe, *What happened in History?* (London 1950).

4 These ideas are presented and discussed in R.S.MacNeish, 'The Origins of American Agriculture', in *Antiquity*, 154, (June 1965); R.S.MacNeish, 'The Origins of New World Civilisation', in *Scientific American* (November 1964).

5 MacNeish, 'Origins'.

6 MacNeish, 'Origins'.

7 MacNeish, 'Origins'.

8 MacNeish, 'Origins'.

9 MacNeish, 'Origins'.

10 MacNeish, 'Origins'.

11 Henry F.Dobyns, 'Estimating American Population. I. An Appraisal of Techniques with a New Hemispheric Estimate', *Current Anthropology*, VII (1966), pp. 395–460.

12 Jacques Soustelle, *Mexique*, (Geneva, Paris 1967).

Chapter 4

1 Childe, *What Happened in History?*

2 Paul Kirchhoff, 'Mesoamerica, sus Limites Geográficos, Composición Etnica y Caracteres Culturales', supplement to *Revista Tlatoani* (Mexico 1960).

3 The most detailed ecological description of Mesoamerica is contained in vol. I of the *Handbook of Middle American Indians*.

4 These details are based primarily on the ecological description and analysis of the Andean region in John V.Murra's unpublished thesis, 'The Economic Organisation of the Inca State' (Chicago 1956); and on Paul Kosok's *Life, Land and Water in Ancient Peru* (New York 1965).

5 Murra, 'The Economic Organisation', chapter I.

6 See also Angel Palerm, 'La Base Agrícola de la Civilización Urbana en Mesoamérica', in *Revista Interamericana de Ciencias Sociales*, I, 1 (1961).

7 William T.Sanders, 'Cultural Ecology of Nuclear Mesoamerica', in *Man in Adaptation, the Biosocial Background*, ed. Yehudi A.Cohen (Chicago 1968).

8 Sanders, in *Man in Adaptation*.

9 John V.Murra, 'Rite and Crop in the Inca State', in *Culture in History, Essays in honor of Paul Radin* (New York 1960).

10 The concept of the influence of hydraulic works and other public works that can be undertaken only by a strictly organised society on the development of states and social organisation goes back to Karl Marx. He formulated the idea of the 'Asiatic method of

production', in which he attributed the inherent development of many Asiatic countries, such as India and China, partly to the influence of irrigation works and to the necessity of erecting public works. Marx never, however, expanded his idea in detail. Today there are widely differing views on this problem. Karl A. Wittfogel, in his *Oriental Despotism, A Comparative Study of Total Power* (New Haven 1964) regards as primary the influence of irrigation on the development and building up of states, in the economic structure of which hydraulic works are important. But Marxists today differ widely from this view in their approach to this problem. At any event there is no agreement among them on this matter, and the significance of irrigation and other public works on the development and structure of states has given rise to much discussion on an international level among historians, anthropologists and economists. The debate is still in full swing. In this connection see Jean Chesneaux, 'Le Mode de Production Asiatique', *La Pensée*, 114 (1964); F.Tokei, *Sur le Mode de Production Asiatique* (Paris 1963); Roger Garaudy, *Le Problème Chinois* (Paris 1967).

11 See also Pedro Armillas, 'Cronología y periodificación de la Historia de la América Precolombina', *Journal of World History*, 3: 2 (1956), pp. 463–503.

Chapter 5

1 Jacques Soustelle, *Mexique*, chapters 1 and 2.
2 Soustelle, *Mexique*.
3 Soustelle, *Mexique*.
4 Soustelle, *Mexique*.
5 Soustelle, *Mexique*.
6 See Georges C.Vaillant, *Aztecs of Mexico* (New York 1962), chapter 2.
7 R.S.MacNeish, 'The Origins of American Agriculture', *Antiquity*, 154 (1965).
8 MacNeish, 'Origins'.
9 MacNeish, 'Origins'.
10 See also, *inter alia*, Michael D.Coe, *The Jaguars' Children, Preclassic Central Mexico* (New York 1965); Ignacio Bernal, *El Mundo Olmeca* (Mexico 1968).
11 For the history of research into Olmec culture see Bernal, *El Mundo Olmeca*, pp. 38 *et seq.*
12 Bernal, *El Mundo*.
13 Bernal, *El Mundo*.
14 Robert Heine-Geldern, 'The Problem of Transpacific Influences in Mesoamerica', in *Handbook of Middle American Indians*, IV.

15 Heine-Geldern, 'Transpacific Influences'.

16 William T.Sanders, 'Cultural Ecology'.

17 Sanders, in *Man in Adaptation*. See also William T.Sanders, critique by Michael D.Coe, 'Mexico', *American Anthropologist*, 65.

18 Michael D.Coe, *Mexico* (London 1962), chapters IV and V.

19 Coe, *Jaguars' Children*, pp. 122 *et seq.*

20 Coe, *Jaguars' Children*.

21 Angel Palerm, 'Sistemas de Regadío en Teotihuacán y en el Pedregal', *La Agricultura y el Desarrollo de la Civilizacion de Mesoamerica, Revista Interamericana de Ciencias Sociales*, I, 2 (1961).

22 For the history of the first excavations carried out in Teotihuacan, see *inter alia* Jacques Soustelle, *Mexique*, chapters 1 and 2; Pedro Armillas, 'Exploraciones Recientes en Teotihuacán', *Cuadernos Americanos* (Mexico, July-August 1944); and 'Teotihuacán, Tula y los Toltecas: Las Culturas Postarcaicas y Preaztecas de México, Excavaciones y Estudios, 1922–50', *Runa*, 3 (1950).

23 William T.Sanders, *The Cultural Ecology of the Teotihuacan Valley. A Preliminary Report of the Teotihuacan Valley Project*, (University of Pennsylvania 1965).

24 René Millon, 'The Teotihuacan Mapping Project', *American Antiquity*, 29 (1964).

25 The following interpretations are based substantially on the work of Pedro Armillas and William T.Sanders, to which reference has already been made, and on contributions made by René Millon and a number of his colleagues at a round-table discussion held by the Mexican Anthropological Society on 9 and 10 August 1966; the following contributions were kindly placed at the author's disposal by the Museum of Anthropology: René Millon, 'Extensión y Población de la Ciudad de Teotihuacán en sus diferentes Periodos: Un Calculo Provisional' and 'El Problema de Integración en la Sociedad Teotihuanaca'; Michael W.Spence, 'Los Talleres de Obsidiana de Teotihuacán'; Bruce Drewitt, 'Planeación en la Antigua Ciudad de Teotihuacán'.

26 Matthew Wallrath, 'The Calle de los Muertos Complex: a possible Macro-complex of Structures near the Center of Teotihuacan', paper presented at the same round-table conference on 9 August 1966.

27 Georges C.Vaillant, *Aztecs of Mexico*, p. 46.

28 Paul Westheim, *Die Kunst Alt-Mexicos* (Cologne 1966).

29 Pedro Armillas, in *Runa*, 3 (1950) and 'Northern Mesoamerica', *Prehistoric Man*.

30 William T.Sanders, *Cultural Ecology*.

31 Robert Heine-Geldern, 'Das Problem vorkolumbischer Beziehungen zwischen Alter und Neuer Welt und seine Bedeutung für die

Allgemeine Kulturgeschichte', offprint from the *Anzeiger der phil. hist. Klasse der oesterreichischen Akademie der Wissenschaften,* 24 (1954), (Vienna 1955).

32 Adams, *Evolution of Urban Society,* pp. 120 *et seq.*

33 John Lloyd Stephens, *Incidents of Travel in Central America, Chiapas and Yucatan,* 2 vols (London 1844), pp. 82 *et seq.*

34 So many books have been written about the Maya that it is not possible to refer to them in detail here. The reader will find detailed bibliographies and also an outline of Maya culture in the following: S.J.Morley and G.W.Brainerd, *The Ancient Maya* (Stanford 1956); J.Eric S.Thompson, *The Rise and Fall of the Maya Civilisation* (University of Oklahoma Press 1956); Michael D.Coe, *The Maya* (London 1966).

35 See Thompson, *Rise and Fall,* pp. 17 *et seq.*

36 Angel Palerm, *Aspectos Agrícolas del Desarrollo de la Civilización* (1961).

37 Michael D.Coe, *The Maya,* pp. 63 *et seq.*

38 Coe, *The Maya,* pp. 60 *et seq.*

39 Eric R.Wolf, *Sons of the Shaking Earth* (Chicago 1959).

40 de Landa, *Relación de las Cosas de Yucatán.*

41 The problem of deciphering Maya script is considered in the books mentioned above by Morley, Thompson and Coe. See also Thomas A.Barthel, 'Die gegenwärtige Situation in der Erforschung der Maya Schrift', *Journal de la Société des Américanistes,* 45 (1956); Yuri Knorosov, 'Principios para Descifrar los Escritos Mayas', *Estudios de Cultura Maya,* 3 (1965).

42 Tatiana Proskuriakov, 'The Lords of the Mya Realm', in John A.Grahame, *Ancient Mesoamerican Selected Readings* (Palo Alto 1966).

43 Morley and Brainerd, *The Ancient Maya.*

44 Michael D.Coe, *The Maya,* pp. 60 *et seq.*

45 Sanders, *Cultural Ecology.*

46 Robert Heine-Geldern, 'The Problem of Transpacific Influences in Mesoamerica', *Handbook of Middle American Indians,* IV.

47 Sanders, *Cultural Ecology.*

48 Coe, *The Maya.*

49 Angel Palerm and Eric Wolf, 'Potencial Ecológico y Desarrollo Cultural de Mesoamérica', in *La Agricultura y el Desarrollo.*

50 Bennett Bronson, 'Roots and Subsistence among the Ancient Maya', *Southwestern Journal of Anthropology,* 22, 3 (autumn 1966).

51 Gordon Willey, 'The Structure of Ancient Maya Society, Evidence from the Southern Lowlands', in *Ancient Mesoamerica,* ed. Grahame.

52 Egon Z.Vogt, 'Some Implications of Zinancantan Social Structure for the Study of the Ancient Maya', in *Ancient Mesoamerica,* ed. Grahame.

53 Coe, *The Maya.*

54 The cultures of Oaxaca are described in detail in a series of essays in volume 2 of the *Handbook of Middle American Indians*. See also John Paddock (ed.), *Ancient Oaxaca, Discoveries in Mexican Archaeology and History* (Stanford 1966).

55 Michael D. Coe, *Mexico* (London 1962), p. 95.

56 Coe, *Mexico*, p. 98.

57 Ronald Spores, 'The Zapotec and Miztec at Spanish Contact', *Handbook of Middle American Indians*, 3, pp. 362 *et seq.*

Chapter 6

1 A very large number of books dealing with the decline of the classical cultures of Mesoamerica in their entirety is available. The following provide a summary of the most important theories and also a guide to the bibliography: Wolf, *Sons of the Shaking Earth*; Gordon Willey, *An Introduction to American Archaeology, I: North and Middle America* (New Jersey 1966); William T. Sanders, *Mesoamerica, The Evolution of a Culture* (New York 1963); Pedro Armillas, 'Mesoamerica', in *Prehistoric Man*.

2 Adams, *The Evolution*, chapter IV.

3 Pedro Armillas, 'Condiciones Ambientales y Movimientos de Pueblos en la Frontera Septentrional de Mesoamérica', in *Homenaje a Fernando Marqués-Miranda* (Madrid 1964).

4 J. E. Thompson, *Rise and Fall*.

5 Gordon Willey, 'The Structure of Ancient Maya Society: Evidence from the Southern Lowlands', in *Ancient America*, ed. Grahame; and 'Problems Concerning Prehistoric Settlement Patterns in the Maya Lowlands', in *Prehistoric Settlement Patterns in the New World* (New York 1956).

6 William Bullard, 'Settlement Patterns and Social Structure in the South Maya Lowlands during the Classic Period', *Readings in Mesoamerica*, ed. Grahame.

7 George L. Cowgill, 'The End of Classic Maya Culture. A Review of Recent Evidence', in *Readings in Mesoamerica*, ed. Grahame.

8 Sherburne F. Cook, 'Human Sacrifice and Warfare, as Factor in the Demography of Precolumbian Mexico', in *Mesoamerica*, ed. Grahame.

9 Morley and Brainerd, *The Ancient Maya*.

Chapter 7

1 Frédérick Engel, 'Sites et Établissements sans Céramique de la Côte Péruvienne', *Journal de la Société des Américanistes*, Nouvelle Série, XLVI (1957).

2 Edward P.Lanning, *Peru before the Incas* (New Jersey 1967), chapter IV.

3 John H.Rowe, *Urban Settlements in Ancient Peru. Nawpa Pacha*, II (Berkeley 1963).

4 Julio C.Tello, *Chavin, Cultura Matriz de la Civilización Andina*, primera parte, Publicación Antropológica del Archivo Julio C. Tello, II (Lima 1956).

5 Michael D.Coe, 'An Olmec Design on an Early Peruvian Vessel', *American Antiquity*, 27 (1962) and 'Olmec and Chavin, Rejoinder to Lanning', *American Antiquity*, 27 (1962).

6 Robert Heine-Geldern, *Das Problem*.

7 Paul Kosok, *Life, Land and Water in Ancient Peru* (New York 1965).

8 John H.Rowe, *Urban Settlements*.

9 See chapter IV, note 10.

10 Gerdt Kutscher, *Chimu, eine altamerikanische Hochkultur* (Berlin 1950).

11 Kosok, *Life*.

12 Arthur Poznansky, *Tiahuanaco – the Cradle of American Man*, 1 and 2 (New York 1945).

13 John V.Murra, 'An Aymara Kingdom in 1567', *Ethnohistory*, 15, 2 (1968).

Chapter 9

1 Sahagún, *Historia General*, I, pp. 278–9.

2 Sahagún, *Historia General*, I, pp. 278–9.

3 Walter Lehmann (ed. and trans.), *Die Geschichte der Königreiche von Culhuacán und Mexico* (Stuttgart 1938), pp. 78–9.

4 Sahagún, *Historia General*, I, p. 280.

5 Sahagún, *Historia General*, I, p. 282.

6 Paul Kirchhoff, 'Das Toltekenreich und sein Untergang', *Saeculum*, XII, 3.

7 Wigberto Jiménez Moreno, José Miranda, María Teresa Fernández, *Historia de Mexico* (Mexico 1967), chapter 6, pp. 99 *et seq.*

8 Paul Kirchhoff, 'Quetzalcoatl, Huemac y el Fin de Tula', in *Cuadernos Americanos* (Mexico 1955); and *Das Toltekenreich*.

9 Kirchhoff, *Das Toltekenreich*.

10 Paul Kirchhoff, 'Civilising the Chichimecs', in *The Cultural History of Ancient Mexico. Some educational and anthropological aspects of Latin America* (Austin 1948), pp. 80–5.

Chapter 10

1 Moreno and others, *Historia de México*, pp. 115 *et seq.*

2 Paul Kirchhoff, *Dos Tipos de Relaciónes entre Pueblos en el México*

Antiguo, A Bosch Gimpera en el Septuagésimo Aniversario de su Nacimiento (Mexico 1963).

3 Diego Durán, *Historia de los Indios de nueva España* (Mexico 1867–80), I, p. 74.

4 F.Alvarado Tezozómoc, *Crónica Mexicáyotl* (Mexico 1949).

5 Paul Kirchhoff, 'The Principles of Clanship in Human Society', *Davidson Journal of Anthropology*, I (1957).

6 Durán, *Historia*, I, pp. 317–19.

7 Sahagún, *Historia General*.

8 Durán, *Historia*, I, p. 75.

9 Durán, *Historia*, I, p. 97.

10 Quoted in Miguel Leon-Portilla, *La Filosofía Nahuatl estudiada en sus fuentes* (Mexico 1959), p. 245.

11 Leonhard Schultze Jena, 'Gliederung des alt-aztekischen Volks in Familie, Stand und Beruf', from the original Aztec text of Bernardino de Sahagún', in *Quellenwerke zur alten Geschichte Amerikas*, V, (Stuttgart 1952).

12 Durán, *Historia*, I, p. 192.

13 Durán, *Historia*, I, p. 172.

14 Durán, *Historia*, I, p. 172.

15 Durán, *Historia*, I, p. 332.

16 Pedro Dávila, quoted in Eric R.Wolf and Angel Palerm, 'Irrigation in the Old Acolhua Domain, Mexico', *Southwestern Journal oj Anthropology*, II, 3 (1955), p. 271.

17 Sahagún, *Historia General*, II, p. 260.

18 Alfonso Caso, *El Pueblo del Sol* (Mexico 1953), p. 73.

19 Sahagún, *Historia General*, II, p. 259.

20 Quoted in Leon-Portilla, *La Filosofía*, p. 201.

21 Leon-Portilla, *La Filosofía*, p. 212.

22 Leon-Portilla, *La Filosofía*, p. 213.

23 Sahagún, *Historia General*, II, pp. 76–81.

24 Durán, *Historia*, I, p. 95.

25 Díaz, *Historia*.

26 An unknown *conquistador*, 'Das Reich Mexico und seine Haupstadt Temixtitan' (Report by an Officer of Hernán Cortés's army, trans. Arthur Schurig), contained in Hernán Cortés, *Briefe* (Leipzig 1918).

27 Durán, *Historia*, I, p. 242.

28 Díaz, *Historia*.

29 Cook, 'Human Sacrifice'.

30 Miguel Leon Portilla, *Trece Poetas del Mundo Azteca* (Mexico 1967), pp. 49 *et seq.*

31 Durán, *Historia*, I, p. 326.

32 Durán, *Historia*, I, pp. 202 *et seq.*

33 Portilla, *Trece Poetas*, pp. 151–3.
34 Portilla, *Trece Poetas*, p. 107.
35 Díaz, *Historia*.
36 Cortés, *Briefe*, pp. 143–4.
37 Díaz, *Historia*.
38 Cortés, *Briefe*, p. 145.
39 Cortés, *Briefe*, pp. 141–2.
40 Díaz, *Historia*, p. 159.
41 Angel Rosenblat, *La Población Indígena y el Mestizaje en América* (Buenos Aires 1954).
42 Dobyns, 'Estimating American Population'.
43 Woodrow Borah and Sherburne F.Cook, 'The Aboriginal Population of Central Mexico on the Eve of the Spanish Conquest', *Ibero-Americana*, 45 (1963).
44 William T.Sanders, review of the book referred to in note 43, Grahame, *Readings*.
45 Durán, *Historia*, I, p. 241.
46 Durán, *Historia*, I, pp. 202 *et seq.*
47 Durán, *Historia*, I, pp. 202 *et seq.*
48 Alfredo López Austin, *La Constitución real de México Tenochtitlan* (Mexico 1961), p. 105.
49 Sahagún, *Historia General*, I, pp. 305 *et seq.*
50 Díaz, *Historia*, I, p. 155.
51 Cortés, *Briefe*, p. 147.
52 Ixtlilxóchitl, *Obras Históricas*, II, p. 266.
53 Durán, *Historia*, I, pp. 317–19.
54 Tezozómoc, *Histoire Mexicaine*, I, pp. 202 *et seq.*
55 Durán, *Historia*, I pp. 368 *et seq.*
56 Peter Martyr, *De Orbo Novo*, quoted in William H.Prescott, *The Conquest of Mexico and the Conquest of Peru* (New York 1945), p. 84.
57 Durán, *Historia*, II, pp. 125 *et seq.*
58 Tezozómoc, I, pp. 244–5.
59 Durán, *Historia*, I, p. 164.
60 See Anne C.Chapman, 'Ports of Trade Enclaves in Aztec and Maya Civilisations', in K.Polanyi *et al.* (eds), *Trade and Markets in the Early Empires* (Glencoe 1957), pp. 114–53.
61 Durán, *Historia*, II, pp. 124–6.
62 Tezozómoc, II, p. 1.
63 Sahagún, *Historia General*, II, p. 186.
64 Sahagún, *Historia General*, II, pp. 152 *et seq.*
65 Sahagún, *Historia General*, II, pp. 152 *et seq.*
66 Sherburne F.Cook and Woodrow Borah, 'Quelle fut la stratification du centre du Mexique durant la première moitié du XVIe

siècle?', *Annales, Economies, Sociétés, Civilisations* XVIII, (1963), pp. 226–58.

67 Cook and Borah, 'Quelle fut la stratification ...?'.

68 Westheim, p. 208.

69 Leonhard Schultze-Jena (ed. and trans.), *Bernardino de Sahagún, Gliederung des Altaztekischen Volks in Familie, Stand und Beruf* (Stuttgart 1952), p. 201.

70 Schultze-Jena, *Gliederung*, p. 201.

71 Schultze-Jena, *Gliederung*, p. 67.

72 Schultze-Jena, *Gliederung*, p. 19.

73 Angel María Garibay K., *Historia de la Literatura Náhuatl*, (Mexico 1953–4), I, p. 99.

74 López Austin, *La Constitución*, p. 51.

75 Paul Radin, *The Sources and Authenticity of the History of the Ancient Mexicans* (Berkeley 1920), p. 120.

76 Radin, *Sources*.

77 Ixtlilxóchitl, II, p. 310.

78 Sahagún, *Historia General*, II, p. 363.

79 Schultze-Jena, *Gliederung*, p. 205.

80 José de Acosta, *Historia Natural y Moral de las Indias* (Madrid 1792), VI, p. 441.

81 Cortés, *Briefe*, pp. 148 *et seq.*

82 Díaz, *Historia*.

Chapter 11

1 Luis G.Lumbreras, 'Espacio y Cultura en los Andes', *Revista del Museo Nacional*, 29 (1960); Lumbreras and David B.Smith, 'Cultural Development in the Central Andes – Peru and Bolivia', in *Aboriginal Cultural Development in Latin America, an Interpretative View*, eds. Betty Meggers and Clifford Evans, (Washington 1963).

2 Richard P.Schaedel, 'Incipient Urbanization and Secularization in Tiahuanaco Peru', *American Antiquity*, 31, 3, part I (January 1966).

3 Schaedel, 'Major Ceremonial and Population Centers in Northern Peru', in *Civilisations of Ancient America, Selected Papers, 29th International Congress of Americanists* (Chicago 1951), pp. 232–43.

4 Kutscher, *Chimu*, p. 92.

5 John H.Rowe, 'The Kingdom of Chimor', *Acta Americana*, 6 (1948), pp. 25–59.

6 Kutscher, *Chimu*, p. 97.

7 Kutscher, *Chimu*, p. 97.

8 Kutscher, *Chimu*, p. 97.

9 Kutscher, *Chimu*, p. 100.

10 Kutscher, *Chimu*, p. 89.

11 Kutscher, *Chimu*, p. 90.
12 Kutscher, *Chimu*, p. 96.
13 See *Visita hecha a la Provincia de Chucuito por Garci Diez de San Miguel en el ano 1567* (Lima 1964); and Murra, *Apreciación*.
14 Murra, *Apreciación*, p. 438.

Chapter 12

1 Garcilaso, *Comentarios*, I, p. 93.
2 de Léon, *Del Señorio de los Incas*, p. 171.
3 de Léon, *Del Señorio de los Incas*, p. 171.
4 William T.Sanders, *The Anthropo-geography of Central Veracruz in Huastecos Totonacos y sus vecinos* (Mexico 1952), p. 77.
5 de Léon, *Del Señorio de los Incas*, pp. 65–6.
6 Garcilaso, *Comentarios*, I, p. 390.
7 de Léon, *Del Señorio de los Incas*, pp. 51 *et seq.*
8 Quoted in Jorge E.Hardey, *Ciudades Precolombinas* (Buenos Aires 1964), p. 435.
9 Hardoy, *Ciudades*, p. 435.
10 Quoted in Alfred Métraux, *Les Incas* (Paris 1961).
11 Alexander von Humboldt, *Vues des Cordillères et Monuments des Peuples Indigènes de l'Amérique* (Paris 1816).
12 See Karl Marx, *Zur Kritik der politischen Oekonomie*, in *Karl Marx und Friedrich Engels: Gesammelte Werke*.
13 Rosa Luxemburg, *Ausgewählte Reden und Schriften* (Berlin 1951).
14 Garcilaso, *Comentarios*.
15 Garcilaso, *Comentarios*.
16 Quoted in Métraux, *Les Incas*, p. 12.
17 Métraux, *Les Incas*.
18 von Humboldt, *Vues des Cordillères*, I, pp. 41–2.
19 *Karl Marx und Friedrich Engels: Gesammelte Werke*, 23, p. 102.
20 Karl Kautsky to Friedrich Engels, 5 April 1891.
21 Luxemburg, *Ausgewählte Reden*.
22 See Murra, *Economic Organization*.
23 Diez de San Miguel, *Visita hecha*.
24 Inigo Ortiz de Zúniga, *Visita de la Provincia de Léon de Huánaco en 1562* (Huánaco, Peru 1967).
25 Murra, *Economic Organisation*, p. 204.
26 José María Arguedas, *Dioses y hombres de Huarochiri* (Lima 1967), p. 51.
27 R.T.Zuidema, *The Ceque System of Cuzco: The Social Organisation of the Capital of the Inca* (Leiden 1964).
28 Bernabé Cobo, *Historia del Nuevo Mundo*, quoted in Mason, *Ancient Civilisations*, p. 209.

29 Garcilaso, *Comentarios*.
30 Quoted in Ferdinand Anton, *Alt Peru und seine Kunst* (Leipzig 1962).
31 Abraham Arias-Larreta, *Literaturas aborigenes* (Los Angeles 1951).
32 Arias-Larreta, *Literaturas*.
33 Arias-Larreta, *Literaturas*.
34 Arias-Larreta, *Literaturas*.

Chapter 14

1 Alvarado Tezozómoc, *Crónica Mexicana*, quoted in *Visión de los Vencidos* eds. Miguel Leon-Portilla and Renate Heuer (Mexico 1959), p. 17.
2 *Visión*, p. 18.
3 *Visión*.
4 *Codex Florentino*, Book XII, chapter 3, quoted in *Visión*, p. 25.
5 *Visión*, p. 25.
6 *Visión*, p. 25.
7 *Visión*, pp. 35–6.
8 *Visión*, p. 41.
9 *Visión*, p. 38.
10 *Codex Florentino*, Book XII, chapters 10 and 11, *Visión*, pp. 46–7.
11 *Visión*, p. 47.
12 *Visión*, p. 49.
13 *Codex Ramirez*, Fragments 3 and 4, *Visión*, p. 75.
14 *Codex Florentino*, Book XII, chapters 16, 17 and 18, *Visión*, p. 79.
15 *Visión*, pp. 82–3.
16 *Codex Aubin*, *Visión*, p. 104.
17 *Codex Florentino*, Book XII, chapters 23 and 24, *Visión*, pp. 107–10.
18 Díaz, *Historia*.
19 *Codex Florentino*, Book XII, chapters 28–32, *Visión*, pp. 117–18.
20 *Codex Florentino*, Book XII, chapters 39, 40 and 41, *Visión*, pp. 149–50.
21 *Visión*, p. 101.
22 *Relación del Primer Descubrimiento de la Costa y Mar del Sur*, quoted in William H. Prescott, *History of the Conquest*, p. 940.
23 Hernando Pizarro, *Carta de los oidores de la audiencia de Santo Domingo*, Buenos Aires 1953.
24 Pedro Pizarro, quoted by J.M.Coher (ed.), *The Conquest and discovery of Peru* (Harmondsworth 1968).
25 Garcilaso, *Comentarios*, II, p. 176.
26 Pedro Pizarro, quoted by William H. Prescott, *History of the Conquest*, p. 1021.

BIBLIOGRAPHY

Thousands of books and articles have been written about the cultures of ancient America. This bibliography cannot aim at giving a comprehensive survey of these works, but the reader will find such a survey in a number of bibliographies such as:

Bernal, Ignacio, *Bibliografía de Arqueología y Etnografía* (Mexico 1962).
Horkheimer, Hans, *Breve bibliografía sobre el Perú prehispánico* (Lima 1947).
Martinez, Hector, Cameo, Miguel, and Ramirez, Jesus, *Bibliografía Indigena Andina* (Lima 1968).

The most important books, articles and essays are listed in the *Handbook of Latin American Studies* (Gainesville), which appears at regular intervals and prints reviews of such works. Comprehensive bibliographies are also contained in many of the books listed below.

This bibliography is restricted essentially to suggestions to the reader for supplementary study. At the same time it indicates some (though by no means all) of the most important works on which this book has been based.

A: *Comprehensive studies of ancient America*

Stewart, Julian, *Handbook of South American Indians*, Smithsonian Institution, Bureau of American Ethnology (Washington 1946).
Wauchope, Robert, and Steward, T. Dale (eds.), *The Handbook of Middle American Indians* (Austin 1964, etc.).

Both these works contain extensive bibliographies. The former, however, has been partly superseded since its publication twenty-two years ago, though it is still compulsory reading for anyone wishing to study the ancient cultures of South America in greater detail. So far only part I has appeared of the second symposium, and it has not yet dealt with the whole complex of Middle American culture.

An equally important survey is another symposium:
Jenning, Jesse D., and Norbeck, Edward (eds.), *Prehistoric Man in the New World* (Chicago 1964).

This contains a number of essays by various authors and a survey for the academic year 1964 regarding the archaeology of the whole of America.

B: *Surveys by individual authors*

Armillas, Pedro, *Programa de Historia de América Periodo Indigena* (Mexico 1962).
Bosch-Gimpera, Pedro, *L'Amérique avant Christophe Colombe* (Paris 1967).
Disselhoff, H.D., *Geschichte der altamerikanischen Kulturen* (Munich 1953).
Franch, José Alcina, *Manual de Arqueología Americana* (Madrid 1965).
Lehmann, Henry, *Les Civilisations Précolombiennes* (Paris 1965).
Trimborn, Hermann, *Das alte Amerika* (Stuttgart 1959).
Willey, Gordon R., *An Introduction to American Archaeology, I: North and Middle America* (Englewood Cliffs, New Jersey 1966).

C: *Complete surveys of the art of ancient America*

Bushnell, G.H.S., *Ancient Arts of the Americas* (New York 1965).
Kubler, George, *Art and Architecture of Ancient America* (Harmondsworth and Baltimore 1962).

D: *Surveys of the art of Mesoamerica*

Anton, Ferdinand, *Alt Mexico und seine Kunst* (Leipzig 1965).
Hardoy, Jorge Enrique, *Ciudades Precolombinas* (Buenos Aires 1964).
Westheim, Paul, *The Art of Ancient America* (New York 1965).

E: *Archaeological sources for the cultures of Mesoamerica and the Andean region*

Bernal, Ignacio, *Mexico before Cortés* (New York 1963).
Chan, Román Piña, *Una visión del México Prehispánico* (Mexico 1967).
Coe, Michael D., *Mexico* (London and New York 1962).
Krickeberg, Walter, *Altmexikanische Kulturen* (Berlin 1956).
Sanders, William T., and Price, J.B., *Mesoamerica: The Evolution of a Culture* (New York 1963).
Soustelle, Jacques, *Archeologia Mundi, Mexique* (Paris and Geneva 1967).
Wolf, Eric R., *Sons of the Shaking Earth* (Chicago 1959).

F: *The archaeology of the Andean region*

Bennett, Wendell C., and Bird, Junius B., *Andean Culture History* (New York 1964).

Bushnell, G.H.S., *Peru* (London and New York 1963).

Lanning, Edward P., *Peru Before the Incas* (Englewood Cliffs, New Jersey 1967).

G: *Cultures as known from written sources*

Mason, J. Alden, *The Ancient Civilizations of Peru* (Harmondsworth and Gloucester, Massachusetts 1957).

CHAPTER I ANCIENT AMERICA: THE SOURCES

A critical evaluation of archaeological and historical sources for the history of Ancient America is mostly to be found in the works already referred to. The history of the archaeological excavations in Mesoamerica is contained for the most part in the work of Jacques Soustelle. The most recent survey of archaeological research carried out in Peru is provided by Edward P.Lanning.

Katz, Friedrich, '*Die sozialökonomischen Verhältnisse bei den Azteken im 15 und 16 Jahrhundert*', *Ethnographisch-Archäologische Forschungen*, 3, 2 (Berlin 1956).

Murra, John V., 'The Economic Organization of the Inca State', Ph.D. Thesis, University of Chicago (1956) (regrettably so far unpublished).

Radin, Paul, *The Sources and Authenticity of the History of the Ancient Mexicans* (Berkeley 1920).

Rowe, John H., 'Inca Culture at the Time of the Spanish Conquest', in *Handbook of South American Indians*, ed. Stewart, Julian (Washington 1946).

CHAPTER 2 THE ORIGINS OF THE NATIVE POPULATION OF AMERICA AND THE AMERICAN CULTURES

The following deal with the problem of the origin of man in America and his immigration from Asia:

Bosch-Gimpera, Pedro, *L'Amérique avant Christophe Colombe* (Paris 1967).

Krieger, Alex D., 'Early Man in the New World', in *Prehistoric Man* (ed. Jennings and Norbeck).

European notions of the origins of the inhabitants of America from the sixteenth to the seventeenth centuries are discussed in:

Huddleston, Lee Eldridge, *Origins of the American Indians, European Concepts 1492–1729* (Austin and London 1967).

The following deals in an entertaining but realistic fashion with the fantasies that have been thrown up in the course of history, about the origin of man in America and American cultures:

Wauchope, Robert, *Lost Tribes and Sunken Continents* (Chicago 1962).

The most important works relating to diffusionist concepts are the following:

Ekholm, Gordon F., 'Transpacific Contacts', in *Prehistoric Man* (ed. Jennings and Norbeck).

Heine-Geldern, Robert, 'The Problem of Transpacific Influences in Mesoamerica', in *Handbook of Middle American Indians* (ed. Wauchope), IV.

Heine-Geldern, Robert, 'Das Problem vorkolumbischer Beziehungen zwischen Alter und Neuer Welt und seine Bedeutung für die Allegemeine Kulturgeschichte', in *Anzeiger der Phil. hist. Klasse der österreichischen Akademie der Wissenschaften*, 1954, Nr. 24 (Vienna 1955).

The anti-diffusionist theories are contained in the following:

Caso, Alfonso, 'Relations between the Old and New Worlds: A Note on Methodology', in *Actas, Int. Cong. of Americanists 1962* (Mexico 1964).

Philips, Philip, 'The Role of Transpacific Contacts in the Development of New-World Pre-Columbian Civilisation', in *Handbook of Middle American Indians* (ed. Wauchope).

Rowe, John H., 'Diffusionism and Archaeology', in *American Antiquity*, 31 No. 3 (January 1966).

My own ideas on this subject as expressed in this book largely coincide with those of the following authors:

Adams, Robert McC., *The Evolution of Urban Society, Early Mesopotamia and Prehispanic Mexico* (Chicago 1965), Chapters 1 and 5.

Steward, Julian, and Faron, Louis C., *Native Peoples of South America* (New York 1959), p. 43.

CHAPTER 3 THE BIRTH OF AGRICULTURE IN AMERICA

The most detailed examination in regard to Mesoamerica is contained in the following:

MacNeish, Robert S., 'The Origins of American Agriculture', *Antiquity*, 154 (June 1965).

MacNeish, Robert S., 'The Origins of New World Civilization', *Scientific American* (November 1964).

The same problem in regard to the Andean region is dealt with in:

Lanning, Edward P., 'Early Man in Peru', *Scientific American*, 4 (1965), pp. 68–76.

Lanning, Edward P., *Peru Before the Incas* (Englewood Cliffs, New Jersey 1967), chapters 4 and 5.

CHAPTER 4 THE GEOGRAPHICAL SETTING OF THE ANCIENT AMERICAN CULTURES

Ecological studies of Mesoamerica and the Andean region were made mainly in the period immediately following the Second World War. Of particular relevance for Mesoamerica are the following:

Armillas, Pedro, '*Notas relativas a sistemas de cultivo en Meso-América*', in *Anales del Instituto Nacional de Antropolgia e Historia* (Mexico 1949).

Palerm, Angel, '*La Base agrícola de la Civilizacion Urbana en Mesoamérica*', *Revista Interamericana de Ciencias Sociales*, I, No. 1 (1961).

Sanders, William T., 'Cultural Ecology of Nuclear Mesoamerica', in *Man in Adaptation: The Biosocial Background* (ed. Cohen, Yehudi A.) (Chicago 1968).

Wolf, Eric R., *Sons of the Shaking Earth* (Chicago 1959).

In describing the ecology of the Andean region I have relied especially on the following:

Kosok, Paul, *Life, Land and Water in Ancient Peru* (New York, 1965).

Murra, John V., 'The Economic Organisation of the Inca State', (Chicago 1956), unpublished thesis.

CHAPTER 5 THE ADVANCED CIVILISATIONS OF MESOAMERICA

The precursors of Mesoamerican high culture are exhaustively examined in the books by Gimpera and Soustelle that have already been referred to. The most exhaustive and most recent descriptions of the Olmec problem are contained in:

Bernal, Ignacio, *El Mundo Olmeca* (Mexico 1968).

Caso, Alfonso, 'Hubo un imperio olmeca?', in *Memorias del Colegio Nacional* (1965).

Coe, Michael D., *The Jaguar's Children: Pre-Classic Central Mexico* (New York 1965).

Recent research has revolutionised our knowledge and ideas concerning Teotihuacan. Further research is still in full swing. In describing the development of Teotihuacan I have relied specially on the following:

Millon, René, 'The Teotihuacan Mapping Project', in *American Antiquity*, 29 (1964).

Millon, René, '*Extensión y población de la Ciudad de Teotihuacán en sus diferentes periodos: Un Cálculo provisional'* (*Ponencia presentada en la XI Mesa Redonda de la Sociedad Mexicana de Antropología, sobre el tema: El Valle de Teotihuacán y su Contorno,* 9 August 1966).

Millon, René, '*El Problema de integración en la sociedad Teotihuacana*' (*Ponencia presentada en la XI Mesa Redonda, etc.,* 9 August 1966).

Sanders, William T., *The Cultural Ecology of the Teotihuacan Valley,* a preliminary report of the Teotihuacan Valley Project (Philadelphia 1965).

There is hardly a culture of ancient America about which so much has been written as the Maya. Three books give the best survey of Maya culture:

Brainerd, G.W., and S.J. Morley, *The Ancient Maya* (Stanford 1956).

Thompson, J. Eric, *The Rise and Fall of Maya Civilisation* (Norman, Oklahoma 1956).

One further book surveys research up to 1966:

Coe, Michael D., *The Maya* (London and New York) 1966.

Volume II of the *Handbook of Middle American Indians* (ed. Wauchope) gives a detailed summary of our state of knowledge with regard to the Maya in 1964. The various ideas regarding the social organisation of the Maya are contained especially in the following essays:

Lhuillier, Alberto Ruz, 'Aristocracia o democracia entre los antiguos Mayas', *Anales de Antropología,* I (Mexico 1964).

Vogt, Egon Z., 'Some Implications of Zinancantan Social Structure for the Study of the Ancient Maya', in Grahame, John A., *Ancient Mesoamerica, Selected Readings* (Palo Alto 1966).

The problem of deciphering the Maya script created vehement controversies. This complex problem is dealt with in detail in the general works already referred to on the culture of the Maya. The following papers convey additional information about the many viewpoints with regard to this problem:

Barthel, Thomas, 'Die gegenwartige Situation in der Erforschung der Maya schrift', *Journal de la Société des Américanistes,* No. 45 (Paris 1956).

Thompson, J. Eric, *Maya Hieroglyphic Writing: An Introduction* (Norman, Oklahoma 1960).

Knorozov, Yuri, 'Principios para descifrar los escritos Mayas', *Estudios de Cultura Maya,* 3 (Mexico 1965).

Proskuriakov, Tatiana, 'The Lords of the Maya Realm', in John A. Grahame, *Ancient Mesoamerica, Selected Readings* (Palo Alto 1966).

Cordan, Wolfgang, *Introducción a los glifos mayas* (Mérida 1963).

CHAPTER 7 THE CIVILISATIONS OF THE MIDDLE ANDES

Lanning, Edward P., *Peru before the Incas* (a synopsis of the many archaeological researches carried out in recent years which have revolutionised the views previously held concerning the antiquity and development of Andean cultures.)

Rowe, John H., *Chavín Art, an Inquiry into its Form and Meaning* (New York 1962) (a radical analysis of this subject).

The best known amongst the cultures of the Classic Period in the Andean region is that on the north coast of Peru. Nowhere else in the Andean region have such exhaustive and extensive excavations been undertaken as those in the Viru valley, since 1946. The most important account of them is contained in:

Willey, Gordon R., 'Prehistoric Settlement Patterns in the Viru Valley, Peru', *Bulletin 155 of Bureau of American Ethnology* (Smithsonian Institution, Washington 1953).

The important irrigation work of this region is described in:

Kosok, Paul, *Life, Land and Water in Ancient Peru* (New York 1965).

In the following book, conclusions are drawn from the decoration and modelling of their pottery for the social organisation, religion and daily life of the Mochica:

Kutscher, Gerdt, *Chimu, eine altindianische Hochkultur* (Berlin 1950).

Edward Lanning provides the best synopsis of the most recent results of research carried out on the central and southern coast of Peru and in the southern highlands of the Andean region in his *Peru Before the Incas.*

The problem of the origin of cities in the Andean region are analysed in the following, though the conclusions reached do not agree in every detail:

Hardoy, Jorge E., *Ciudades Precolombinas.*

Rowe, John H., *Urban Settlements in Ancient Peru. Nawpa Pacha II* (Berkeley 1963).

Schaedel, Richard, 'Major Ceremonial and Population Centers in Northern Peru', in *The Civilizations of Ancient America, Sol Tax,* ed. Schaedel (Chicago 1959).

Schaedel, Richard, 'On the Definition of Civilisation, Urban, City and Town in Pre-Hispanic America', *Actas y memorias,* XXXVII Congresso de Americanistas (Buenos Aires 1968).

CHAPTER 9 THE FIRST POST-CLASSIC CULTURES OF MESOAMERICA

The rise and fall of the Toltec Empire are dealt with in the following:

Kirchhoff, Paul, 'La Ruta de los Tolteca-Chichimeca entre Tulay Cholula', in *Miscelanea Paul Rivet* (Mexico 1958).

Kirchhoff, Paul, 'Quetzalcoatl, Huemac y el fin de Tula', in *Cuadernos Americanos* (Mexico 1955).

Kirchhoff, Paul, 'Das Toltekenreich und sein Untergang', *Saeculum*, XII, 3.

Moreno, Wigberto Jiménez, 'Síntesis de la Historia Precolonial del Valle de México', in *Revista Méxicana de Estudios Antropológicos* 14 (1956), pp. 219-36.

Moreno, Wigberto Jiménez, Miranda, José, and Fernández, María Teresa, *Historia de México* (Mexico 1967).

The most detailed analysis of the religion and mythical ideas of the Toltecs is contained in Walter Krickeberg's *Altmexikanische Kulturen.*

The same authors have dealt in the greatest detail with the Chichimec immigration into Mesoamerica, and also with the early history of the Aztecs. But see especially Moreno's *Historia de México* and the following:

Kirchhoff, Paul, *Civilizing the Chichimecs.* A chapter in *The Cultural History of Ancient Mexico* (Austin 1948).

Kirchhoff, Paul, 'Dos Tipos de Relaciones entre Pueblos en el México Antiguo', in *A Pedro Bosch Gimpera en el septuagesimo aniversario de su nacimiento* (Mexico 1963).

In describing the social organisation of the Aztecs I have relied on my own research, recorded in the following:

Katz, Friedrich, 'El Papel del Comercio en el Imperio Azteca', in *Actas del XXXVI Congreso Internacional de Americanistas* (Seville 1966).

Katz, Friedrich, 'Die Sozialökonomischen Verhältnisse bei den Azteken im 15. und 16. Jahrhundert', in *Ethnographisch-Archäologische Forschungen*, Part 3, No. 2 (Berlin 1956).

This subject has been particularly widely discussed in the nineteenth and twentieth centuries.

William H. Prescott, in his *The Conquest of Mexico* (New York 1845), suggested that a state with marked class distinctions existed among the Aztecs. This idea was vehemently contested in the following book:

Morgan, Lewis H., *Ancient Society* (London 1877), and by one of Morgan's students:

Bandelier, Adolf F., 'On the Distribution and Tenure of Lands and the Customs with Respect to Inheritance among the Ancient Mexicans', in *Eleventh Annual Report of the Peabody Museum of American Archaeology and Ethnology* (Cambridge 1878).

Bandelier, Adolf F., 'On the Social Organization and Mode of Government of the Ancient Mexicans', in *Twelfth Annual Report of the Peabody Museum of American Archaeology and Ethnology* (Cambridge 1880).

The social organisation of the Aztecs was regarded by these authors as being essentially a tribal community, with far-reaching similarities to those of the North-American Iroquoi. These views were contested by an ever increasing number of writers from 1930 onwards. They took the view that the Aztecs had a fully developed state with marked social and class differentiation. Among these writers we may mention the following:

Austin, Alfredo Lopez, *La constitución real de México-Tenochtitlán* (Mexico 1961).

Carrasco, Pedro, 'The Civil-religious Hierarchy in Mesoamerican Communities; pre-Spanish background and colonial development', *American Anthropologist* 63, No. 3.

Caso, Alfonso, 'Instituciones Indígenas Precortesianas', in *Memorias del Instituto Nacional Indigenista* (Mexico 1954), VI.

Caso, Alfonso, 'Land Tenure among the Ancient Mexicans', *American Anthropologist*, 65, No. 4 (1963).

Kirchhoff, Paul, 'Land Tenure in Ancient Mexico. A preliminary Sketch', *Revista Mexicana de Estudios Antropológicos*, XIV (1954–7).

Moreno, Manuel, *La Organización Política y Social de los Aztekas* (Mexico 1931).

Soustelle, Jacques, *La Vie quotidienne des Aztèques à la veille de la conquête espagnole* (Paris 1955).

The following authors have dealt in particular with the Aztec *calpulli* and its relations with tribes or clans:

Kirchhoff, Paul, 'The Principles of Clanship in Human Society', *Davidson Journal of Anthropology*, I (1957).

Monzón, Arturo, *El calpulli en la organización social de los tenochca* (Mexico 1949).

A very important study which has forced the author of this book to change a number of ideas previously held is:

Calnek, Edward R., 'Settlement Patterns and Chinampa Agriculture at Tenochtitlan,' *American Antiquity* (1971).

The most exhaustive examination of the expansion of the Aztec Empire has been undertaken in:

Barlow, Robert H., *The Extent of the Empire of the Cultura Mexica* (Berkeley and Los Angeles 1949).

Highly contradictory views regarding population figures for Mesoamerica and in particular for the Aztec Empire on the eve of the Spanish Conquest are expressed in the following:

Rosenblat, Angel, *La Población Indígena y el Mestizaje en América* (Buenos Aires 1954).

Woodrow Borah, and Cook, Sherburne F., 'The Aboriginal Population of Central Mexico on the Eve of the Spanish Conquest', in *Ibero-americana*, 45 (Berkeley and Los Angeles 1963).

The findings of Borah and Cook are supported by:

Dobyns, Henry F., 'Estimating American Population', *Current Anthropology* (October 1966).

Very thorough studies of Aztec religion were undertaken by:

Caso, Alfonso, *El Pueblo del Sol* (Mexico 1953).
Krickeberg, Walter, *Die Religionen des alten Amerika* (Stuttgart 1961).

The following authors have been particularly concerned with the literature and thought of the Aztecs:

Garibay K., Angel Maria, *Historia de la literatura náhuatl* (Mexico 1953-4).
Leon-Portilla, Miguel, *Filosofia náhuatl, estudiada en sus fuentes* (Mexico 1966).
Leon-Portilla, Miguel, *Trece poetas del mundo azteca* (Mexico 1967).

A comprehensive survey of the development of science among the Aztecs is given in the first part of:

Gortari, Eli de, *Historia de la ciencia en México* (Mexico 1964).

The following book is compulsory reading for anyone wishing to concern himself more closely with the Aztecs. It deals primarily with the fate of the Aztecs in the colonial period, but decisive conclusions may be drawn from it retrospectively for the pre-Spanish period:

Gibson, Charles, *The Aztecs Under Spanish Rule* (Stanford 1964).

CHAPTER 11 THE POST-CLASSIC PERIOD IN THE ANDEAN REGION

The description of the culture of Tiahuanaco has given rise to a number of fantastic notions. These were, and still are, fostered by the limited nature of the excavations so far carried out in Tiahuanaco. The most important works of scholarship on Tiahuanaco culture are the surveys already mentioned: Bennett and Bird, *Andean Culture History*; Mason, *The Ancient Civilisations of Peru*; and Lanning, *Peru Before the Incas*. My own work is also based on the following:

Lumbreras, Luis G., 'La cultura de Wari, Ayacucho', in *Etnología y Arqueología*, I, No. 1 (1960), pp. 130–227.

Lumbreras, Luis G., *'Espacio y Cultura en los Andes'*, in *Revista del Museo Nacional*, 29 (Lima 1960).

Lumbreras, Luis G., and Smith, David B., 'Cultural Development in the Central Andes-Peru and Bolivia', in *Aboriginal Cultural Development in Latin America: An Interpretative View*, ed. Meggers, Betty, and Evans, Clifford (Washington 1963).

The historical sources for Chimu culture are analysed exhaustively in:

Rowe, John H., 'The Kingdom of Chimor', in *Acta Americana*, VI, Nos. 1–2 (1947), pp. 26–59.

In my description of the culture of Chucuito I have relied primarily on:

Murra, John V., *Una apreciación etnológica de la visita* (Lima 1967).

San Miguel, Garci Diez de, *Visita hecha a la provincia de Chucuito en el ano 1567*, ed. Murra, John V. (Lima 1967).

Chimu art and culture have been described in particular in Kutscher's *Chimu, eine altindianische Hochkultur,* which has already been mentioned.

The impressive irrigation work of this Kingdom has been described by Kosok in his *Life, Land and Water in Ancient Peru.* The social organisation and history of the Inca Empire attracted the attention of many writers in the sixteenth, seventeenth and eighteenth centuries. Most of them, however, relied for their description of the empire on the work of Garcilaso de la Vega, taking no note of other sources. A radical and scholarly evaluation of the Inca began in 1896 with the publication of:

Cunow, Heinrich, *Die soziale Verfassung des Inkareiches* (Stuttgart 1896).

This was followed by:

Trimborn, Hermann, 'Der Kollektivismus der Inkas in Peru', in *Anthropos*, XVIII (1923–4).

Trimborn, Hermann, 'Die Gliederung der Stände im Inkareich', in *Journal de la Société des Américanistes* (1927).

The whole field of knowledge with regard to the Inca as it stood in 1946 was summarised in Rowe's 'Inca Culture at the Time of the Spanish Conquest', to which we have already referred.

The most controversial ideas about the nature of the Inca Empire are contained in the following, which regards the Inca Empire as a 'socialist state':

Baudin, Louis, *L'Empire socialiste des Inka* (Paris 1928).

The following reject Baudin's ideas:

Métraux, Alfred, *Les Incas* (Paris 1961).

Moore, Sally Falk, *Power and Property in Inca Perú* (New York 1958).

My description of the socio-economic organisation of the Inca relies primarily on the pioneering but alas unpublished dissertation already referred to by John V. Murra ('The Economic Organisation of the Inca State') and on a series of essays by the same author:

Murra, John V., 'Rite and Crop in the Inca State', in *Culture in History: Essays in Honor of Paul Radin* (New York 1960).

Murra, John V., 'El tejido en varios contextos sociales en el estado inca' in *Actas, Segundo Congreso de la Historia del Perú* (1958) (Lima 1962), II.

Murra, John V., 'Grupos serviles en la organización social del Tawantinsuyu', in *Actas, XXXVI Congreso Internacional de Americanistas, Barcelona, Madrid, Sevilla.*

The most thorough description and analysis of the religion of the Inca is contained in John H. Rowe's 'Inca Culture at the Time of the Spanish Conquest' and in Hermann Trimborn' scontribution to the symposium of Walter Krickeberg and others: *Die Religionen des alten Amerika.*

An account of Inca literature is given in:

Arias-Larreta, Abraham, *Literaturas aborigenas Azteca Incaica Maya-Quiche* (Los Angeles 1951).

One of the most interesting myths of the pre-Spanish inhabitants of Peru, the legends of Huarochiri, are translated from Quechua into German in:

Trimborn, Hermann, *Quellen zur Kulturgeschichte des präkolumbischen Amerika* (Stuttgart 1936).

They are translated into Spanish by one of the most important Peruvian poets:

Arguedas, José María, *Dioses y hombres de Huarochiri* (Lima 1967).

CHAPTER 13 RETROSPECT AND COMPARISON

A comparative examination of the history, social organisation and culture of the Inca and Aztecs has so far scarcely been attempted. An exception is:

Gorenstein, Shirley, 'The differential development of military and political organisation', unpublished thesis (Columbia University 1963).

The comparisons in this book of the Incas and the Aztecs rely mainly on my own research, first recorded in:

Katz, Friedrich, 'Einige Vergleichsmomente zwischen der sozialen Organisation der Inca und Azteken', in *Estudios de cultura Náhuatl* (Mexico 1960), II.

Many of the final conclusions of this first essay are, however, enlarged and supplemented in the present book, and have also in part been amended.

CHAPTER 14 THE END

The best descriptions of the conquest of Mexico and Peru by the Spaniards remain, despite the lapse of a hundred years:

Prescott, William H., *History of the Conquest of Mexico* (1845).
Prescott, William H., *History of the Conquest of Peru* (1847).

Although Prescott used unpublished manuscripts in Spanish archives to an astonishing extent, he had only a few of the Indian descriptions of the conquest of Mexico at his disposal. The most important of them have recently been collected together in:

Leon-Portilla, Miguel (ed.), *Rückkehr der Götter. Die Aufzeichnungen der Azteken über den Untergang ihres Reiches* (Leipzig 1964).

GLOSSARY

Aautli	Lake flies regarded as dainties by the Aztecs.
Aclla maidens	Beautiful maidens chosen from the Inca population to be brought up as concubines for the nobility or as 'Sun Maidens' for service in the temples.
Achcacauhtin	Aztec executioner.
Akapana	The largest construction among the ruined sites of Tiahuanaco.
Alec pong	Stones, embodying deities and worshipped in the coastal valleys of Peru.
Amantecas	Aztec feather-workers.
Amaranth	Plant cultivated as a vegetable or as bread fruit (such as millet).
Amauta	Educators of Inca youth.
Atl Atl	Wooden spear-thrower among the Meso-american peoples.
Ayllu	Form of clan-organisation in the Inca Empire.
Aymara	Highland language in the Andean region.
Bactun	A period of twenty *Katun* (or 144,000 days) in the Maya calendar.
Balsas	Spanish name for rafts used in pre-Columbian times on the coast of Peru.
Batab	A sort of village noble amongst the Maya, immediately subordinate to the *Halach Uinic*.
Bolas	Stone-throwers used by Inca warriors.
Calabtun	A period of twenty *Pictun* (or 57,000,000 days) in the Maya calendar.
Callahouaya	Tribe settled east of Lake Titicaca from which specially able Inca doctors originated.
Calmecac	School conducted by priests in Tenochtitlan;

367

virtually only the children of the nobility were educated here.

Calpixque	Aztec tribute collectors.
Calpullec	The head of a *calpulli*, a hereditary office within the family.
Calpulli	'Big House': a form of communal living in central Mexico, particularly among the Aztecs, a community of owners of house and land; later it was also a religious and military unit under one head, the *Calpullec*.
Canari	An Ecuadorian tribe conquered by the Inca; from it were drawn the Inca life-guards.
Canchones	Fields in Chan-Chan in which intensive agriculture was practised.
Cari	Chieftains' clan of the 'upper moiety' in Chucuito.
Ceibo-tree	A fibrous plant; a species of tall tree yielding kapok, indigenous today in America, Africa and the East Indies.
Cenotes	Subterranean water-holes in the peninsula of Yucatan, used for irrigation.
Ceques	Imaginary lines connecting the various *Huacas* (Holy Places) in the Inca capital city of Cuzco with the centre of the city.
Chac Mool	'Reclining god' of Toltec origin; the rain god of the Maya.
Chalchihuites	Aztec name for a green semi-precious stone, presumably jadeite.
Chaquiras	Small gold 'pearls' used in the coastal valleys of Peru.
Charqui	Inca name for dried llama meat.
Chicha	A sort of maize-beer which was drunk through-out the Inca Empire and made from chewed maize grains.
Chimalman	'Prostrate Shield', wife of the Toltec ruler Mixcoatl.
Chinampa system	A process for the construction of artificial islands involving ramming in piles, planting trees and building rafts; employed by the Aztecs in expanding their capital city of Tenochtitlan.
Chot	Palaces and buildings in the Naymlap legend.
Chullpas	Stone burial-places in the highlands round Lake Titicaca.

Chuñu	Substance made from dried and frozen potatoes in the southern Andean highlands.
Cie	Royal governors in the coastal valleys of Peru.
Cihuacoatl	'Snake Woman'; an important office, presumably embodying the female principle among the Aztecs, immediately subordinate to the Chief Speaker.
Cinteotl	Aztec god of maize.
Coa	Aztec digging-stick.
Coatlicue	'Serpent skirt'; Aztec earth goddess, mother of the tribal god Huitzilopochtli.
Coca	Stimulant or narcotic that is chewed; it comes from the leaves of the *Coca* – a shrub cultivated in Peru.
Cochenille	Red dye made from the cochineal beetle.
Cocijo	The highest deity and rain god of the Zapotecs.
Conopas	A sort of personal guardian-spirit among the Inca.
Corichanca	The Sun Temple of the Inca in Cuzco.
Coya	The chief wife of the Inca.
Cuachic	Military order in Tenochtitlan, composed, as were other military orders, of élite warriors.
Cumbi	Fine textiles woven of vicuña wool and reserved for the highest nobility, the 'wearers of earplugs' among the Inca.
Curaquna	A lower Inca nobility, chieftains of conquered tribes.
Cusi	Chieftains' clan of the 'lower moiety' in Chucuito.
Danzantes	'Dancers'; early reliefs in Monte Alban, depicting people who are apparently dancing but are presumably about to be sacrificed or executed.
Guano	Sea-birds' droppings used as fertiliser.
Halach Uinic	Secular rulers of Maya cities at the time of the Conquest; the office of ruler was hereditary.
Hanan-Saya	One of the two moieties of Inca clans (the 'lower moiety').
Hatha	A clan-like organism in Chucuito.
Hatun Runa	Married male representatives of Inca households, between the ages of twenty-five and forty.
Huaca	Places of devotion (in the Quetcha language).

Huacapata	The central 'plaza' in the Inca capital city of Cuzco.
Huaca Sian	Place of devotion among the Chimu, meaning 'house of the Moon'.
Huari Runa	The 'original peoples', peasants who emerged from caves in the second period of the Inca Empire.
Huehueteotl	God of fire and light, the most identifiable god in Mexico.
Huemac	Secular ruler of the Toltecs at the time of Ce Acatl Topiltzin (= Quetzalcoatl).
Huey Calpixque	The chief tribute-collector among the Aztecs.
Huey Tlatoani	The 'Chief Speaker' of the Aztecs, an office first filled in 1376 and representing a transitional rank between a tribal chieftain and a state ruler.
Huitzilihuitl	An Aztec leader.
Huitzilopochtli	Tribal god of the Aztecs, who in time rose to be the Sun God.
Hurin Saya	One of the 'two moieties' of the Inca clans (the 'upper moiety').
Ikat	A textile technique whereby the threads are tied round several times consecutively before being woven and dipped so that the threads are only partly dyed and form patterns when woven.
Inti	The Inca Sun God.
In Tloque Nahuaque	The Almighty Being, worshipped in Tetzcoco by the Chief Speaker Netzahualcoyotl and his disciples.
Itzamna	Cult hero of the Maya.
Kalasasaya	Modern name of a large building in Tiahuanaco that is 135 metres long by 130 metres wide; it encloses a courtyard, at the entrance of which is the famous monolithic 'Gateway of the Sun'.
Katun	A period of twenty *Tun* (or 7,200 days) in the Maya calendar.
Llampallec	A statue of Naymlap carved out of green stone.
Legua	A Spanish linear measurement.
Lomas	Small oases, green for only part of the year, on the desert-like plains of north Peru.

Maccahuitl	Sticks with obsidian points used by the Aztecs as weapons.
Macehualli	Members of the *Macehualtin*.
Macehualtin	Aztec freemen (as distinct from bondsmen).
Maguey	Type of agave, the juice of which is fermented to make an alcoholic drink called *pulque*.
Mallku	Name for the chieftains of Chucuito.
Mamaconas	'Sun Maidens' who served the Inca religious hierarchy.
Mayeques	Aztec bondsmen; one of the three groups of 'common people'.
Mictlan	The Aztec Realm of the Dead.
Mictlantecuhtli	The Aztec god of death.
Mita	Labour performed by the members of the *ayllu* apart from tilling the soil.
Mitimakuna	Colonists in the Inca Empire.
Mixcoatl	'Cloud Serpent'; Toltec ninth- or tenth-century ruler and conqueror of central Mexico.
Mochica	Tribe in the north-west of Peru, creators of the first state structure in the Andean region; transmitted the Mochica culture in about the third century AD, which is distinguished by its highly realistic sculpture and painting.
Mochik	The most widely diffused language spoken in the coastal regions of the Andean region until the end of the nineteenth century.
Nahua	Mesoamerican linguistic family to which the Aztec language Nahuatl also belonged.
Nanauatzin	A poor Aztec god.
Nauhcampa	The 'four directions' of the Aztec winds.
Naymlap	Legendary ruler in the Valley of Lambayeque on the north coast of Peru.
Netzahualcoyotl	The 'Hungry Coyote'; ruler of Tetzcoco who allied with the Aztecs and helped to overthrow Atzcapotzalco during the period 1429 to 1433; the most important poet of ancient Mexico.
Ollantay	An Inca drama consisting of fifteen scenes.
Omecihuatl	The 'Wife of Duality'; female principle of creation in the Aztec religion.
Ometecutli	The 'Ruler of Duality'; male principle of creation in the Aztec religion.

Orejones	'Wearers of ear-plugs'; Spanish name for members of the Inca nobility who wore ear-plugs as marks of their membership of the upper class.
Pacarimac Runa	The 'Aspiring People', peaceful peasants belonging to the first period of the Inca Empire.
Pariacaca	God of creation of the highland region of Huarochiri.
Pictun	A period of twenty *Bactun* (or 2,880,000 days) in the Maya calendar.
Pipiltin	One of the groups of the Aztec upper class. It included the sons, descendants and relatives of all Chief Speakers who had ruled up to date.
Pitao Cozobi	Maize god of the Zapotecs.
Pochteca	Aztec merchants.
Pumapunku	Modern name of one of the pyramidal constructions among the ruins of the site of Tiahuanaco.
Puna	Upland steppes, highly suitable for breeding cattle.
Quetchua	Highland language of the Inca in the Andean region.
Quetzalcoatl	The 'Feathered Serpent'; the god of nature in Teotihuacan, then the god of wind, of the heavens and of the earth among the Toltecs and the Aztecs; the Toltec hero Ce Acatl Topiltzin, son of Mixcoatl, later adopted his name.
Quetzal	A bird indigenous to Guatemala and Chiapas; has spectacularly coloured plumage that is used for head-dresses and for decorating cult apparel.
Quinoa	(Latin: *Chenipodium quinoa*) a type of grain that thrives only in the highlands; also known as Andean rice.
Quipu	A mnemonic system of the Inca, erroneously labelled 'knot script', in which figures and facts were registered by the use of knots and colours.
Quipu-Camayoc	Experts and officials of the *Quipu*.
Sacsahuaman	An Inca fortress in the Valley of Cuzco.

Sapay-Inca	Originally the common leader of the two moieties of the Inca clans *Hurin-Saya* and *Hanan-Saya*; later, since the fifteenth century, the God King and Chief Ruler of the empire.
Sinchis	Clan or tribal chieftain in the Valley of Cuzco.
Tambos	Rest-houses on the Inca highways.
Tamemes	Aztec porters.
Tamoanchan	Aztec paradise of the Gods.
Tawantinsuyu	'Realm of the Four Quarters'; the Inca name for their empire.
Teccallec	Tributary peasants of the Aztec nobility.
Tecpantlalli	Lands belonging to the palace of the Chief Speaker of the Aztecs.
Tecuciztecatl	Rich Aztec god.
Telpochcalli	House of Youth and School for the members of the *Calpulli* in which agriculture and the arts of war were chiefly taught.
Telpochlato	Aztec teacher and head of the *Telpochcalli*.
Teocalli	Religious centre of Tenochtitlan; a complex of buildings consisting of temples and pyramids surrounded by a high wall.
Tequitlato	Aztec legal officer.
Tezcatlipoca	The 'Smoking Mirror'; Aztec god of night and darkness, also god of war.
Tezozomec	Ruler of the kingdom of the Tepanecs of Atzcapotzalco allegedly reigned for sixty-three years and died in 1426.
Tianguez	Aztec word for 'market'.
Tlacxitlan	Higher Aztec Court.
Tlaloc	Rain god of the Aztecs and Toltecs; already found in the culture of Teotihuacan.
Tlamaictes	Aztec bondsmen, also called *mayeques*.
Tlapixcatzin	State censor of the Aztecs; any new teaching matter for the *Calmecac* required his approval.
Tlaquimilotecnuhtli	Official of the Aztec priesthood whose function was roughly that of treasurer.
Tlatelolco	Northern part of Tenochtitlan, the capital city of the Aztecs; the city's market and economic centre.
Tlatlacotin	Aztec 'slave', one of the three groups of common people.
Tlatltecutli	Aztec deity embodying the sun and the earth.

Tonanzin	Aztec mother of the gods, presumably a manifestation of the earth goddess Coatlicue.
Topilli	A sort of constable or legal official among the Aztecs.
Topos	Milestones on Inca highways.
Toxcatl	Aztec festival.
Tun	A period of eighteen *uinales* (or 360 days) in the Maya calendar.
Tupu	The minimum of land – its dimensions are disputed – needed by an Inca couple.
Uinal	A period of twenty days in the Maya calendar.
Viracocha	Inca God of Creation.
Yanacona, also *Yana*	Inca bondsmen of diverse origin.
Yoalli Ehecatl	Another name for the Aztec god of darkness and of war, Tezcatlipoca.
Xilonen	Aztec goddess of maize.
Xipe Totec	Aztec god of Spring.
Xochipilli	Aztec god of love, of sport and of Summer.
Xochiquetzal	Aztec goddess of beauty, of love, of flowers, of the household and 'patron saint' of women of easy virtue.
Zapotes	Species of American tropical tree bearing delicious fruit.

MAPS

Map 1   Ancient civilisations of South America

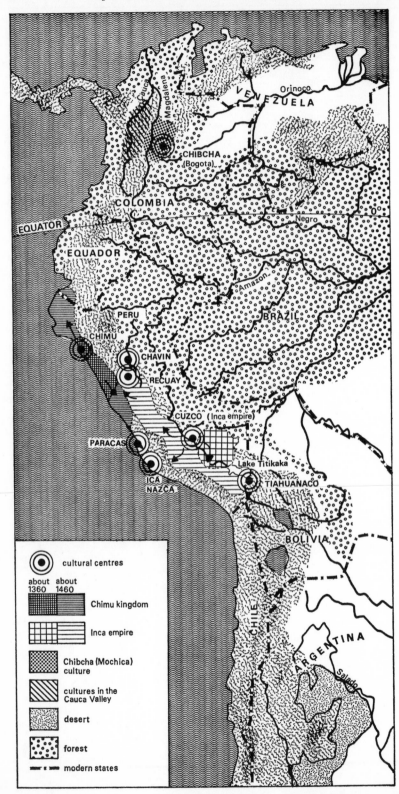

Map 2   The Inca Empire 1460–1532

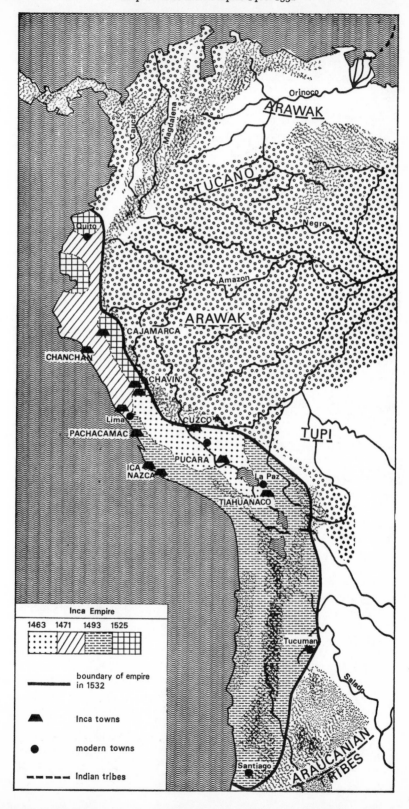

Inca Empire

1463	1471	1493	1525

boundary of empire
in 1532

Inca towns

modern towns

Indian tribes

ARAWAK

Orinoco

TUCANO

Negro

Amazon

Quito

CAJAMARCA

CHANCHAN

CHAVIN

Lima

CUZCO

PACHACAMAC

PUCARA

ICA
NAZCA

La Paz

TIAHUANACO

TUPI

Tucuman

Salado

Santiago

ARAUCANIAN TRIBES

Cauca

Magdalena

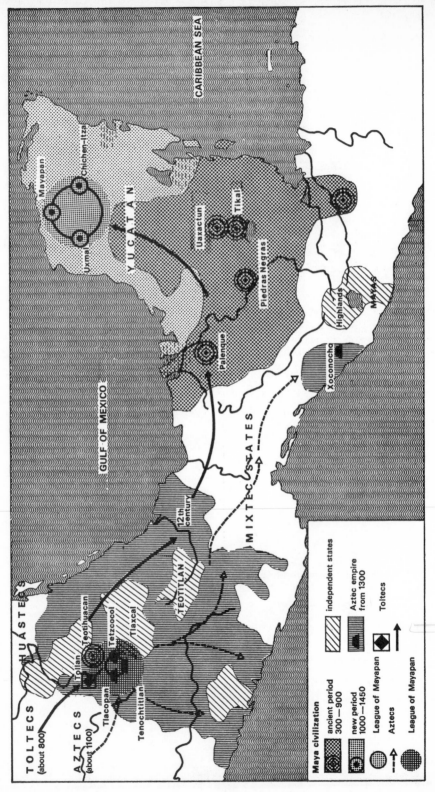

Map 3   Middle American civilisations up to 1520

Maya civilization
- ancient period 300 — 900
- new period 1000 — 1450
- League of Mayapan
- Aztecs
- League of Mayapan

- independent states
- Aztec empire from 1300
- Toltecs

CARIBBEAN SEA

TOLTECS (about 800)

AZTECS (about 1100)

HUASTECS

Tollan
Teotihuacan
Tetzcoco
Tlaxcal
TEOTITLAN
Tlacopan
Tenochtitlan

12th century

GULF OF MEXICO

MIXTEC STATES

Palenque

Piedras Negras

Uaxactun
Tikal

YUCATAN

Mayapan
Chichen-Itza
Uxmal

Xoconocha

Highlands

MAYAS

INDEX

Acamapichtli, Aztec Chief Speaker, 141, 173
Acari Valley, 97, 105
Acolhua people, 141
Acolman, 211
Adams, Robert McC., 17–18, 54
Africa, 39
agriculture, 12, 17; in Andes region, 83–4, 85–6, 89–91, 94, 95–7, 104, 245, 251, 275; *chinampa* system, *see* main entry; as cultural basis, 23, 24, 40, 44, 50–1, 94; development of, 19–22, 33–5; fertilisers, 21, 27, 97; intensive, 22, 24, 25, 29, 40, 44, 50–1, 67, 68, 72, 74, 85, 103 310–11, *see also* Andes region, Mexico; irrigation systems, *see* main entry; in Mexico, 20–1, 25, 85–6, 114, 128, 129–30, 145, 184, 185, *see also chinampa* system; plants, 12, 15, 20–1, 34–5, 58, *see also* cocoa, cotton, maize, potatoes; and rainfall, *see* rainfall; slash and burn type, 22, 40, 42, 58, 67, 81, 129; surpluses, 17, 29–30
Ahuitzotl, Aztec Chief Speaker, 167, 173, 177–8, 187, 207
alpaca, 27, 84–5, 108, 258, 259–60
Amazon basin, 26, 67, 269, 271
Amenghino, Fernando, 11
Andes region, 20, 23–4; agriculture, *see* main entry; beginnings of culture, 88–92; classic cultures, 94–7, *see also* Chavin, Mochica, Nazca Valley, Tiahuanaco; end of classic cultures, 112–15, 312; geographical and ecological conditions, 26–7, 28–31, 83–5, 107; post-classic cultures, 116–18, *see also* Chimu, Chucuito, Inca
Annam, 15
Araucanian Indians, 26, 269
arch, true, 15, 16
archaeological excavations and findings, 1–3, 11–12, 20–1, 117; in Andes region, 87–8, 94, 107, 111, 243, 249; in Meso-america, 32, 36–9, 42, 45–6, 56, 57, 71–2, 73, 120, 124
archaeological 'pirates', 3, 36
archaeological sources, 1–3, 87
architecture, in Andes region, 92, 100–1, 108–9, 279–80; in Mesoamerica, 46–8, 60–1, 73, 74, 75, 124, 180–1, 231

Argentina, 23, 26, 269
Armillas, Pedro, 47, 50, 54, 79
arrowheads, *see* weapons
Asia, cultural links with, 13–18, 90; migration from, 11–13, 15; as Olmec origin, 39–40; South-East, 13, 15, 40, 66
Atahuallpa, Inca King, 296, 314, 333–5, 337
Atetelco, 135
Atlantic Ocean, 24
Atlantis, 9–10, 13, 110
Atzcapotzalco, 53, 77, 79, 131, 136, 137–8, 150, 211; conquest of, 145–6, 148, 151, 173, 174; pact of, 146, 268
Axayacatl, Chief Speaker, 173, 176–7, 186, 237
Ayacucho, 244–5
Aymara language, 251; people, 265
Aztec Empire, 53, 188–96; administration, 190–1; colonisation, 191; comparison with Incas, 313–23; end of, 324–33; integration, 189–90, 193, 314–17, 320, 322; *Pax Azteca*, 193–5; revolts, 191–3, 196, 237–8; tribute, *see* main entry; *see also* Aztecs, Triple Alliance
Aztecs, 4–5, 28, 134–242; agriculture, *see* agriculture, Mexico, and *chinampa* system; army, 197–8; art and architecture, 231–2; betting, 227; bureaucracy, 142, 143, 144, 172, 196–7, 198–200, 207, 238–9; *calmecac*, 180, 204–5, 208, 209, 217, 233, 235; *calpixque*, 189, 198–200, *see also* tribute; *calpullec*, 139–40, 205; *calpulli*, 138–141, 142–7 *passim*, 200, 201, 219–20, 229, 259, 318; decline of power, 147, 197, 205, 223, 240; rights and duties, 142, 203, 222–3, 226; censorship, 147, 204, 210; Chief Speaker, 141–3, 147–8, 172–3, 188, 189, 190, 195, 196–7, 199–200, 202, 205–7, 208, 209, 216, 236; *chinampa* system, *see* main entry; craftsmen, 143, 149, 159, 174, 189, 212, 214, 215, 217–19, 231–2, 241, 319; crime, 230; deification of ruler, 172–3, 196, 240–1, 242; early history, 134–8; education, *see calmecac, telpochcalli*; Empire, *see* Aztec Empire; espionage, 151, 216; garrisons, 53, 190, 191, 195, 198, 217; human sacrifice, *see* main entry; land tenure, 6, 138–9,

379

Inca Empire, 26, 28, 67, 83, 85, 109, 263–309, 313–23; *acclla* maidens, 285–6, 307; administration, 286–7; *amauta*, 284, 304, 307; army, 270–1, 273, 275–8, 294, 336–7; art, 307; *ayllu* system, 90, 266, 277, 283, 285, 287, 295, 298, 300, 304, 318; building activities, 281; bureaucracy, 273–4, 281, 286–7, 289–90, 292, 293, 317; *ceque* systems, 300; civil war, 295–6, 314; colonisation, 272, 275, 320; comparison with Aztecs, 313–23; conscription, 276–7; conquests, 267–71; couriers, 278; the Coya, 284; craftsmen, 287, 319; *curaquna* (chieftains), 283, 285, 286, 291; deportation, 275, 290, 320; distribution of raw materials, 272; early history, 263–6; education, 274, 284; end of, 333–8; expropriation, 290–1, 293, 295; festivals, 303; garrisons, 271–2, 274, 290; historic conceptions, 248–9; integration, 274, 289, 314–17, 320, 322; journeys, 281, 286; land tenure, 284–5, 287, 294–5; literature, 307–9; marriage, 266, 286; mathematics and astronomy, 306–7; medicine, 305–6; *mita* labour, 285; nobility 283–4, 294, 295, 298; *Pax Incaica*, 271, 315, 320; peasants, *see* main entry; priesthood, 185, 301, 302–5, 306; punishments 286; *quipus*, 103, 117, 278, 306; rafts, 18; reciprocity, 291–3, 320–1, 322; religion, 274, 298–302; revenues, 285, 292; revolts, 271, 275, 278, 293; roads, 114, 277–8, 305, 316; rulers, *see* Sapay-Inca; sacrifices, 257, 301; Sapay-Inca, Inca god-king, 267, 283, 298, 305, 336; services, 285–6, 291–2, 302; socialism, 287–91, 293–4; social organisation, 282–7; soothsaying, 304; state trading, 287, 292, 293, 319; tribute, *see* main entry; village communities, 291–2, 294; virgins of the sun, (*mamacunas*), 286, 302–3; *yanaconas* (or *yanas*), 279, 284, 294–5; *see also* Cuzco

India, 13
Indonesia, 15, 52–3
Inti, Inca sun god, 298–9
In Tloque Nahuaque, Texcocau god, 172, 178, 299
irrigation systems, 26–7, 29–30, 113–15, 116–17, 310–11, 313–15 *passim*; in Andes region, 84, 94, 95–7, 98, 99, 103, 105, 107, 245, 247, 250; Aztec, 129–31, 141, 148, 153–5, 158, 174, 186, 194, 195, 238; Inca, 272, 275, 287, 290, 296, 305, 322; in Mesoamerica, 40, 50–1, 74, 75, 128
Israel, 10
Itzamna, 65
Itzcoatl, Aztec Chief Speaker, 147, 173, 176, 208, 210
Itztapalapa, 179
Ixtlilzochitl, 145
Izapa, 42, 43, 59, 66

jade, 36–7, 41, 57
jaguar cult and symbols, 41, 54, 59 60 75, 93, 124
jaguar order, 144

Japan, 15, 90
Jesuits, 5, 289
Jimenez Moreno, Wigberto, 124, 131, 134

Kaminaljuyu, 52, 59
Khmer, Kingdom of, 15
Kingsborough, Lord, 10
kinship organisation, 99; *see also* Aztecs, *calpulli* and Inca, *ayllu*
Kirchhoff, Paul, 13, 124, 134, 139, 141
Kosok, Paul, 96, 106
Kotosh, 91
Kutscher, Gerdt, 100

labour, organisation of, 30, 38–9, 55, 59, 68, 98–9, 154, 291–2, 322; as tribute, 189, 222, 228, 279, 285, 287
lakes, 129–30; *see also* Titicaca
Lambayeque, Valley of, 96, 252
land tenure, *see under* Aztecs, Inca
languages, Indian, 5, 7, 13, 18; *see also* Aymara, Nahua, Quetchua
Lanning, Edward P., 89, 91, 111
La Quemada, 125
Las Aldas, 91
Lauricocha, Cave of, 88–9
La Venta, 36–9, 41–2, 119
legends and myths, Andean, 248, 252–4, 264–5, 299–300; Mesoamerican, 120–3, 132, 136, 137, 156
Lemuria, 10
Le Plongeon, Augustus, 10
Lima, Valley of, 254
limestone, 58
linguistic studies, 2, 13
llama, 27, 84–5, 108, 111, 113, 245, 258–60, 272, 275, 278, 285, 293, 301, 322
Lobo Guerrero, Don Bartolomo, 254
lomas (oases), 89
lotus blossom motif, 13
Lumbreras, Luis Guillermo, 244–5
Luxemburg, Rosa, 282, 288

Macchu Picchu, 281; *63–6*
macehualtin, see Aztecs
McNeish, R.S., 20–1, 33–5, 73
maize, 27, 29–30; in Andes region, 84, 89, 91, 94, 95, 107, 112, 272, 319; gods of, 157, 158, 159; in Mesoamerica, 33, 34–5, 58, 68, 121, 123, 319
mammoth, 32, 34, 45
Manco Inca, 336–8
Mantaro, 84
Marx, Karl, 282, 288
mathematics, 75, 117, 126, 323; *see also* Inca, Maya
mattock, 29
Maya culture, 13, 25, 55–72, 73, 192, 232, 311; achievements, 30, 56, 65–6, 71, 95, 103; agriculture, *see* agriculture, slash and burn type; architecture, 60–1; astronomy, 62–4; calendar, 38, 43, 56, 61, 62–4, 163; centres, 57, 60, 70, 188; classic period, 60; decline, 76–7, 80–2; dress and ornaments, 69; ecological bases, 67; geographical locations, 57–8;

382